The Writer's Reader

The Writer's Reader

Vocation, Preparation, Creation

Edited by
Robert Cohen and Jay Parini

Bloomsbury Academic
An imprint of Bloomsbury Publishing Inc

BLOOMSBURY
NEW YORK · LONDON · OXFORD · NEW DELHI · SYDNEY

Bloomsbury Academic

An imprint of Bloomsbury Publishing Inc

1385 Broadway	50 Bedford Square
New York	London
NY 10018	WC1B 3DP
USA	UK

www.bloomsbury.com

BLOOMSBURY and the Diana logo are trademarks of Bloomsbury Publishing Plc

First published 2017

Library of Congress Cataloging-in-Publication Data
Names: Cohen, Robert, 1957- editor. | Parini, Jay, editor.
Title: The writer's reader: vocation, preparation, creation / edited by
Robert Cohen and Jay Parini.
Description: New York: Bloomsbury Academic, 2017.
Identifiers: LCCN 2015033746 | ISBN 9781628925388 (hardback) |
ISBN 9781628925371 (paperback)
Subjects: LCSH: Authorship. | Authorship–Vocational guidance. |
BISAC: LITERARY CRITICISM / General. | LANGUAGE ARTS & DISCIPLINES /
Composition & Creative Writing.
Classification: LCC PN151 .W75 2017 | DDC 808.02/023–dc23 LC record available at
https://lccn.loc.gov/2015033746

ISBN: HB: 978-1-6289-2538-8
PB: 978-1-6289-2537-1
ePub: 978-1-6289-2539-5
ePDF: 978-1-6289-2540-1

Cover design: Alice Marwick

Typeset by Deanta Global Publishing Services, Chennai, India
Printed and bound in the United States of America

Contents

Part Three Creation 215

Introduction

"When I sit down to write I feel at ease," writes Natalia Ginsberg in her essay, "My Vocation," "and I move in an element which, it seems to me, I know very well."

This sense of fluency and ease, of sustained immersion in the element of language, is the dream of everyone who sets out to write in a serious way. But how to achieve it? There is of course no simple answer. But if all writers, as Saul Bellow once observed, are only readers moved to emulation, then perhaps a complicated answer—or rather a whole series of complicated answers—may be approached the same way writers approach every other seemingly insoluble problem: not by writing alone, but by browsing through the bookshelves, consulting favorite writers, discovering new ones, quarrying for treasure in mines already dug, finding inspiration and solace in the words of others, who found inspiration and solace in the words of still others, and so on. It's something of a daisy chain, in short, this demanding, peculiar, and often singularly lonely vocation. But you're never in it entirely by or for yourself, even if it often feels that way. It's often felt that way to others too. How can it not? And yet as they all—as *we* all—go about making fictions from the stuff of life (and vice versa), the commonalities among us begin to seem greater by far than the differences.

Hence the idea of a Writer's Reader, a portable bookshelf to consult in times of loneliness and self-doubt. By no means do we claim that these extraordinary essays—classic and contemporary, familiar and less familiar, foreign and domestic—are in any sense definitive. But they all share, in our view, a certain quality of rigorous self-reflection about the writerly vocation that is keenly felt and eloquently, often thrillingly expressed. In them we see sensibilities being forged from confusion, talents honed, languages located and put to use.

We see the processes of the artist under development: the preparation, the creation, the revision, the additional revision, the revision that comes after the additional revision, and the revision that comes after that. God knows it can be a long and difficult apprenticeship. One has to feel one's way forward, often proceeding from what Donald Barthelme, in "Not Knowing", calls only "a slender intuition, not much more than an itch." Then of course, problems and obstacles begin to multiply: what point of view to take, how to manage the tone, what is the plot and how much do I need, what "levels of reality," as Italo Calvino puts it, can be achieved, or should one even *attempt* to achieve, and so on. Ultimately, no matter what we attempt there is a sense of bumping up against our limits, again and again. As Zadie Smith and others here remind us, failure is not so much an option as a *requirement*, an integral part of what may well turn out to be what some call "success."

Readers will find a broad range of voices in this book, authors from different decades, different cultures, different countries, all of them engaged in a heartfelt, demanding process of putting into words that which is felt or found, however tentative, however transient. It's our hope that writers at any stage of development—young or old, inside classrooms and workshops or "out in the cold" (in Ted Solotaroff's phrase) as one of "those who dare" (in Bolaño's)—will find in them a source of interest, solace, and encouragement as they work alone-but-not-alone at their desks, turning sentences around, and brooding over the results.

Part One

Vocation

My Vocation

Natalia Ginzburg

My vocation is to write and I have known this for a long time. I hope I won't be misunderstood; I know nothing about the value of the things I am able to write. I know that writing is my vocation. When I sit down to write I feel extraordinarily at ease, and I move in an element which, it seems to me, I know extraordinarily well; I use tools that are familiar to me and they fit snugly in my hands. If I do something else, if I study a foreign language or try to learn history or geography or shorthand or if I try and speak in public or take up knitting or go on a journey, I suffer and constantly ask myself how others do these things: it always seems to me that there must be some correct way of doing these things which others know about and I don't. And it seems to me that I am deaf and blind and I feel a sort of sickness in the pit of my stomach. But when I write I never imagine that there is perhaps a better way of writing which other writers follow. I am not interested in what other writers do. But here I had better make it plain that I can only write stories. If I try to write a critical essay or an article that has been commissioned for a newspaper I don't do it very well. I have to search laboriously, as it were outside myself, for what I am writing now. I can do it a little better than I can learn a foreign language or speak in public, but only a little better. And I always feel that I am cheating the reader with words that I have borrowed or filched from various places. I suffer and feel that I am in exile. But when I write stories I am like someone who is in her own country, walking along streets that she has known since she was a child, between walls and trees that are hers. My vocation is to write stories — invented things or things which I can remember from my own life, but in any case stories, things that are concerned only with memory and imagination and have nothing to do with erudition. This is my vocation and I shall work at it till I die. I am very happy with my vocation and I would not change it for anything in the world. I realized that it was my vocation a long time ago. Between the ages of five and ten I was still unsure, and sometimes I imagined that I would be a painter, sometimes that I would ride out on horseback and conquer countries, sometimes that I would invent new machines that would be very important. But I have known since I was ten, and I worked as hard as I could at poems and novels. I still have those poems. The first poems are clumsy and they have errors of versification in them, but they are quite pleasant; and then, little by little, as time passed I wrote poems that became less and less clumsy but more and more boring and silly. However I didn't know this and I was ashamed of the clumsy poems, while those that were silly and not so clumsy seemed to me to be very beautiful, and I used to think that one day some famous poet would discover them and have them published and write long articles about me; I imagined the words and phrases of those articles and I composed them, from beginning to end, in my head. I imagined that I would win the Fracchia prize. I had heard that there was such a prize for writers. As I was unable to publish my poems in a book, since I didn't know any famous poets, I copied them neatly into an exercise book and drew a little flower on the title page and made an index and everything. It became very easy for me to write poems. I wrote about one a day. I realized that if I didn't want to write it was enough for me to read some poems by Pascoli or Gozzano or Corazzini and then I immediately wanted to. My poems came out as imitation Pascoli or imitation Gozzano or imitation Corazzini and then finally very imitation D'Annunzio when I found out that he also existed. However I never thought that I would write poetry all my life. I wanted to write novels sooner or later. I wrote three or four during those years. There was one called *Marion or the Gipsy Girl,* another called *Molly and Dolly* (a humorous detective story) and another called *A Woman* (*à la* D'Annunzio; in the second person; the story of a woman abandoned by her husband; I remember that there was also a cook who was a negress) and then one that was very long and complicated with terrible stories of kidnapped girls and carriages so that I was too afraid to write it when I was alone in the house: I can remember nothing about it except that there was one phrase which pleased me very much and that tears came into my eyes as I wrote it, 'He said: ah! Isabella is leaving'. The chapter finished with this phrase which was very important because it was said by the man who loved Isabella although he did not know this as he had not yet confessed it to himself. I don't remember anything about this man (I think he had a reddish beard), Isabella had long black hair with blue highlights in it, I don't know anything else about her; I know that for a long time I would feel a shiver of joy whenever I said 'Ah! Isabella is leaving' to myself. I also often used to repeat a phrase which I had found in a serialized novel in *Stampa* which went like this, 'Murderer of Gilonne, where have you put my child?' But I was not as sure about my novels as I was about the poems. When I reread them I always discovered a weakness somewhere or other, something wrong which spoiled everything and which was impossible to change. I always used to muddle up the past and the present, I was unable to fix the story in a particular time; parts of it were convents and carriages and a general feeling of the French Revolution, and parts of it were policemen with truncheons; and then all of a sudden there would be a little grey housewife with a sewing-machine and cats as in Carola Prosperi's novels, and this didn't go very well with the carriages and convents. I wavered between Carola Prosperi and Victor Hugo and Nick Carter's stories; I didn't really know what I wanted to do. I was also very keen on Annie Vivanti. There is a phrase in *The Devourers* when she is writing to a stranger and says to him, 'I dress in brown'. This was another phrase which, for a long time, I repeated to myself. During the day I used to murmur to myself these phrases which gave me so much pleasure: 'Murderer of Gilonne', 'Isabella is leaving', 'I dress in brown', and I felt immensely happy.

Writing poetry was easy. I was very pleased with my poems, to me they seemed almost perfect. I could not see what difference there was between them and real, published poems by real poets. I could not see why when I gave them to my brothers to read they laughed and said I would have done better to study Greek. I thought that perhaps my brothers didn't know much about poetry. Meanwhile I had to go to school and study Greek, Latin, mathematics, history — and I suffered a good deal and felt I was in exile. I spent my days in writing poems and copying them out in exercise books; I did not study for my lessons so I used to set the alarm for five in the morning. The alarm went off but I went on sleeping. I woke at seven, when there was no longer any time to study and I had to dress to go to school. I was not happy, I was always extremely afraid and filled with feelings of guilt and confusion. When I got to school I studied history during the Latin lesson, Greek during the history lesson, and so on, and I learnt nothing. For quite a while I thought it was all worth it because my poems were so beautiful, but at a certain moment I began to think that perhaps they were not so beautiful and it became tedious for me to write them and take the trouble to find subjects; it seemed to me that I had already dealt with every possible subject, and used all the possible words and rhymes — *speranza, lontananza; pensiero, mistero; vento, argento; fragranza, speranza* (hope, distance; thought, mystery; wind, silver; fragrance, hope). I couldn't find anything else to say. Then a very nasty period began for me, and I spent the afternoons playing about with words that no longer gave me any pleasure while at the same time I felt guilty and ashamed about school. It never entered my head that I had mistaken my vocation — I wanted to write as much as ever, it was just that I could not understand why my days had suddenly become so barren and empty of words.

The first serious piece I wrote was a story. A short story of five or six pages; it came from me like a miracle in a single evening, and when afterwards I went to bed I was tired, bewildered, worn out. I had the feeling that it was a serious piece, the first that I had ever written: the poems and the novels about girls and carriages suddenly seemed very far away from me, they were the naïve and ridiculous creatures of another age and they belonged to a time that had disappeared for good. There were characters in this new story. Isabella and the man with the reddish beard were not characters; I didn't know anything about them beyond the words and phrases with which I described them — they appeared as if at random and not by my design. I had chosen the words and phrases I used for them by chance; it was as if I had a sack and had indiscriminately pulled out of it now a beard and now a cook who was a negress or some other usable item. But this time it was not a game. This time I had invented characters with names that I could not possibly have changed; I could not have changed any part of them and I knew a great deal about them — I knew how their lives had been up to the day of my story even though I did not talk about this in the story as it was not necessary. And I knew all about the house, the bridge, the moon and the river. I was seventeen and I had failed in Latin, Greek and mathematics. I had cried a lot when I found out. But now that I had written the story I felt a little less ashamed. It was summer, a summer night. A window that gave on to the garden was open and dark moths fluttered about the lamp. I had written my story on squared paper and I had felt happy as never before in my life; I felt I had a wealth of thoughts and words within me. The man was called Maurizio, the woman was called Anna and the child was called Villi, and the bridge, the moon and the river were also there. These things existed in me. And the man and the woman were neither good nor evil, but funny and a little sad and it seemed to me that I had discovered how people in books should be — funny and at the same time sad. Whichever way I looked at this story it seemed beautiful to me: there were no mistakes in it; everything happened as it should, at the right time. At that moment it seemed to me that I could write millions of stories.

And in fact I wrote quite a few, at intervals of a month or two — some were quite good and some not so good. Now I discovered that it is tiring to write something seriously. It is a bad sign if it doesn't make you tired. You cannot hope to write something serious frivolously flitting hither and thither, as it were with one hand tied behind your back. You cannot get off so lightly. When someone writes something seriously he is lost in it, he is sucked down into it up to his eyebrows; and if there is a very strong emotion that is preoccupying him, if he is very happy or very unhappy for some let us say mundane reason which has nothing to do with the piece he is writing, then if what he is writing is real and deserves to live all those other feelings will become dormant in him. He cannot hope to keep his dear happiness or dear unhappiness whole and fresh before him; everything goes off into the distance and vanishes and he is left alone with his page; no happiness or unhappiness that is not strictly relevant to that page can exist in him, he cannot possess or belong to anything else — and if it does not happen like this, well that is a sign that the page is worthless.

And so for a certain period — which lasted about six years — I wrote short stories. Since I had discovered that characters existed it seemed to me that to *have* a character was enough to make a story. So I was always hunting for characters, I looked at the people in the tram and on the street and when I found a face that seemed suitable for a story I wove some moral details and a little anecdote around it. I also went hunting for details of dress and people's appearance, and how their houses looked inside; if I went into a new room I tried to describe it silently to myself, and I tried to find some small detail which would fit well in a story. I kept a notebook in which I wrote down some of the details I had discovered, or little similes, or episodes which I promised myself I would use in stories. For example I would write in my notebook 'She came out of the bathroom trailing the cord of her dressing-gown behind her like a long tail', 'How the lavatory stinks in this house — the child said to him — When I go, I hold my breath — he added sadly', 'His curls like bunches of grapes', 'Red and black blankets on an unmade bed', 'A pale face like a peeled potato'. But I discovered how difficult it was to use these phrases when. I was writing a story. The notebook became a kind of museum of phrases that were crystallized and embalmed and very difficult to use. I tried endlessly to slip the red and black blankets or the curls like bunches of grapes into a story but I never managed to. So the notebook was no help to me. I realized that in this vocation there is no such thing as 'savings'. If someone thinks 'that's a fine detail and I don't want to waste it in the story I'm writing at the moment, I've plenty of good material here, I'll keep it in reserve for another story I'm going to write', that detail will crystallize inside him and he won't be able to use it. When someone writes a story he should throw the best of everything into it, the best of whatever he possesses and has seen, all the best things that he has accumulated throughout his life. If you carry details around inside yourself for a long time without making use of them, they wear out and waste away. Not only details but everything, all your ideas and clever notions. At the time when I was writing short stories made up of characters I had chanced on, and minute descriptive details, at that time I once saw a hand-cart being pushed through the street and on it was a huge mirror in a gilded frame. The greenish evening sky was reflected in it and as I stopped to watch while it went past I was feeling extremely happy, and I had the impression that something important had happened. I had been feeling very happy even before I saw the mirror, and it suddenly seemed to me that in the greenish resplendent mirror with its gilded frame the image of my own happiness was passing by me. For a long time I thought that I would put this in a story, for a long time simply remembering that hand-cart with the mirror on top of it made me want to write. But I was never able to include it anywhere and finally I realised that the image had died in me. Nevertheless it was very important. Because at the time when I was writing my short stories I always concentrated on grey, squalid people and things, I sought out a contemptible kind of reality lacking in glory. There was a certain malignancy in the taste I had at that time for finding minute details, an avid, mean desire for little things — little as fleas are little; I was engaged on an obstinate, scandal-mongering hunt for fleas. The mirror on the hand-cart seemed to offer me new possibilities, perhaps the ability to look at a more glorious and splendid kind of reality which did not require minute descriptions and cleverly noticed details but which could be conveyed in one resplendent, felicitous image.

In the last analysis I despised the characters in the short stories I was writing at that time. Since I had discovered that it works well if a character is sad and comic I made characters who, because of their comic and pitiable qualities, were so contemptible and lacking in glory that I myself could not love them. My characters always had some nervous tic or obsession or physical deformity, or some rather ridiculous bad habit — they had a broken arm in a black sling, or they had sties in their eyes, or they stuttered, or they scratched their buttocks as they talked, or they limped a little. I always had to characterize them in some such way. For me this was a method of running away from my fear that they would turn out too vague, a way of capturing their humanity (which, subconsciously, I did not believe in). Because at that time I did not realize — though when I saw the mirror on the hand-cart I began, confusedly, to realize it — that I was no longer dealing with characters but with puppets, quite well painted and resembling men, but puppets. When I invented them I immediately characterized them, I marked them with some grotesque detail, and there was something nasty in this; I had a kind of malign resentment against reality. It was not a resentment based on anything real, because at that time I was a happy girl, but it appeared as a kind of reaction against naïvety; it was that special resentment with which a naïve person who always thinks she is being made a fool of defends herself — the resentment of a peasant who finds himself in a city for a while and sees thieves everywhere. At first I was bold, because this seemed to me to be a great ironic triumph over the naïvely pathetic effusions which were all too apparent in my poems. Irony and nastiness seemed to be very important weapons in my hands; I thought they would help me write like a man, because at that time I wanted terribly to write like a man and I had a horror of anyone realizing from what I wrote that I was a woman. I almost always invented male characters because they would be the furthest and most separate from myself.

I became reasonably good at blocking out a story, at getting rid of superfluous material and introducing details and conversations at the appropriate moments. I wrote dry, clear stories that contained no blunders or mistakes of tone and that came to a convincing conclusion. But after a while I had had enough of this. The faces of people in the street no longer said anything interesting to me. Someone had a sty and someone had his cap on back to front and someone was wearing a scarf instead of a shirt, but these things no longer mattered to me. I was fed up with looking at things and people and describing them to myself. The world became silent for me. I could no longer find words to describe it, I no longer had any words capable of giving me pleasure. I didn't have anything anymore. I tried to remember the mirror, but even that had died in me. I carried a burden of embalmed objects around inside of me — silent faces and ashen words, places and voices and gestures that were a dead weight on my heart, that had no flicker of life in them. And then my children were born and when they were very little I could not understand how anyone could sit herself down to write if she had children. I did not see how I could separate myself from them in order to follow someone or other's fortunes in a story. I began to feel contempt for my vocation. Now and again I longed for it desperately and felt that I was in exile, but I tried to despise it and make fun of it and occupy myself solely with the children. I believed I had to do this. I spent my time on creamed rice and creamed barley and wondering whether there was sun or not or wind or not so that I could take the children out for a walk. The children seemed extremely important to me because they were a way of leaving my stupid stories and stupid embalmed characters behind. But I felt a ferocious longing within me and sometimes at night I almost wept when I remembered how beautiful my vocation was. I thought that I would recover it some day or other but I did not know when: I thought that I would have to wait till my children grew up and left me. Because the feeling I then had for my children was one that I had not yet learnt to control. But then little by little I learnt, and it did not even take that long. I still made tomato sauce and semolina, but simultaneously I thought about what I could be writing. At that time we were living in very beautiful countryside, in the south. I remembered my own city's streets and hills, and those streets and hills mingled with the streets and hills and meadows of the place where we were, and a new nature, something that I was once again able to love, appeared. I felt homesick for my city and in retrospect I loved it very much, I loved and understood it in a way that I had never done when I lived there, and I also loved the place where we were then living — a countryside that was white and dusty in the southern sunlight; wide meadows of scorched, bristling grass stretched away from my windows, and a memory of the avenues and plane-trees and high houses of my city assailed me; all this slowly took fire in me and I had a very strong desire to write. I wrote a long story, the longest I had ever written. I started writing again like someone who has never written, because it was a long time since I had written anything, and the words seemed rinsed and fresh, everything was new and as it were untouched, and full of taste and fragrance. I wrote in the afternoons while a local girl took my children out for a walk, and I wrote greedily and joyfully; it was a beautiful autumn and I felt very happy every day. I put a few invented people into my story and a few real people from the countryside where we were living; and some of the words that came to me as I was writing were idioms and imprecations local to that area, and which I had not known before, and these new expressions were like a yeast that fermented and gave life to all the old words. The main character was a woman, but very different from myself. Now I no longer wanted to write like a man, because I had had children and I thought I knew a great many things about tomato sauce and even if I didn't put them into my story it helped my vocation that I knew them; in a strange, remote way these things also helped my vocation. It seemed to me that women knew things about their children that a man could never know. I wrote my story very quickly, as if I were afraid that it would run away. I called it a novel, but perhaps it was not a novel. But up till then I had always written very quickly, and always very short things, and at a certain moment I thought I realized why. Because I had brothers who were much older than me and when I was small if I talked at table they always told me to be quiet. And so I was used to speaking very fast, in a headlong fashion with the smallest possible number of words, and always afraid that the others would start talking among themselves again and stop listening to me. Perhaps this seems a rather stupid explanation; nevertheless that is how it was.

I said that the time when I was writing what I called a novel was a very happy time for me. Nothing serious had ever happened in my life, I knew nothing about sickness or betrayal or loneliness or death. Nothing in my life had ever fallen to pieces, except futile things, nothing dear to my heart had ever been snatched away from me. I had only suffered from the listless melancholy of adolescence and the pain of not knowing how to write. And so I was happy in a fulfilled, calm way, without fear or anxiety, and with a complete faith in the stability and durability of earthly happiness. When we are happy we feel that we are cooler, clearer, more separate from reality. When we are happy we tend to create characters who are very different from ourselves; we see them in a cold, clear light as things separate from us. While our imagination and inventive energy work assertively within us we avert our eyes from our own happy, contented state and pitilessly — with a free, cruel, ironic, proud gaze — fix them on other beings. It is easy for us to invent characters, many characters, who are fundamentally different from us, and it is easy for us to construct our stories solidly — they are as it were well-drained and stand in a cold, clear light. What we then lack, when we are happy in this special way that has no tears or anxiety or fear in it, what we then lack is any tender, intimate sympathy with our characters and with the places and things we write about. What we lack is compassion. Superficially we are much more generous in the sense that we always find the strength to be interested in others and devote our time to them — we are not that preoccupied with ourselves because we don't need anything. But this interest of ours in others, which is so lacking in tenderness, can only get at a few relatively external aspects of their characters. The world has only one dimension for us and lacks secrets and shadows; we are able to guess at and create the sadness we have not experienced by virtue of the imaginative strength within us, but we always see it in a sterile, frozen light as something that does not concern us and that has no roots within us.

Our personal happiness or unhappiness, our *terrestrial* condition, has a great importance for the things we write. I said before that at the moment someone is writing he is miraculously driven to forget the immediate circumstances of his own life. This is certainly true. But whether we are happy or unhappy leads us to write in one way or another. When we are happy our imagination is stronger; when we are unhappy our memory works with greater vitality. Suffering makes the imagination weak and lazy; it moves, but unwillingly and heavily, with the weak movements of someone who is ill, with the weariness and caution of sick, feverish limbs; it is difficult for us to turn our eyes away from our own life and our own state, from the thirst and restlessness that pervade us. And so memories of our own past constantly crop up in the things we write, our own voice constantly echoes there and we are unable to silence it. A particular sympathy grows up between us and the characters that we invent — that our debilitated imagination is still just able to invent — a sympathy that is tender and almost maternal, warm and damp with tears, intimately physical and stifling. We are deeply, painfully rooted in every being and thing in the world, the world which has become filled with echoes and trembling and shadows, to which we are bound by a devout and passionate pity. Then we risk foundering on a dark lake of stagnant, dead water, and dragging our mind's creations down with us, so that they are left to perish among dead rats and rotting flowers in a dark, warm whirlpool. As far as the things we write are concerned there is a danger in grief just as there is a danger in happiness. Because poetic beauty is a mixture of ruthlessness, pride, irony, physical tenderness, of imagination and memory, of clarity and obscurity — and if we cannot gather all these things together we are left with something meagre, unreliable and hardly alive.

And you have to realize that you cannot hope to console yourself for your grief by writing. You cannot deceive yourself by hoping for caresses and lullabies from your vocation. In my life there have been interminable, desolate empty Sundays in which I desperately wanted to write something that would console me for my loneliness and boredom, so that I could be calmed and soothed by phrases and words. But I could not write a single line. My vocation has always rejected me, it does not want to know about me. Because this vocation is never a consolation or a way of passing the time. It is not a companion. This vocation is a master who is able to beat us till the blood flows, a master who reviles and condemns us. We must swallow our saliva and our tears and grit our teeth and dry the blood from our wounds and serve him. Serve him when he asks. Then he will help us up on to our feet, fix our feet firmly on the ground; he will help us overcome madness and delirium, fever and despair. But he has to be the one who gives the orders and he always refuses to pay attention to us when we need him.

After the time when I lived in the South I got to know grief very well — a real, irremediable and incurable grief that shattered my life, and when I tried to put it together again I realized that I and my life had become something irreconcilable with what had gone before. Only my vocation remained unchanged, but it is profoundly misleading to say that even that was unchanged — the tools were still the same but the way I used them had altered. At first I hated it, it disgusted me, but I knew very well that I would end up returning to it, and that it would save me. Sometimes I would think that I had not been so unfortunate in my life and that I was unjust when I accused destiny of never having shown me any kindness, because it had given me my three children and my vocation. Besides, I could not imagine my life without my vocation. It was always there, it had never left me for a moment, and when I believed that it slept its vigilant, shining eyes were still watching me.

Such is my vocation. It does not produce much money and it is always necessary to follow some other vocation simultaneously in order to live. Though sometimes it produces a little, and it is very satisfying to have money because of it — it is like receiving money and presents from the hands of someone you love. Such is my vocation. I do not, I repeat, know much about the value of the results it has given me or could give me: or it would be better to say that I know the relative though certainly not the absolute value of the results I have already obtained. When I write something I usually think it is very important and that I am a very fine writer. I think this happens to everyone. But there is one corner of my mind in which I know very well what I am, which is a small, a very small writer. I swear I know it. But that doesn't matter much to me. Only, I don't want to think about names: I can see that if I am asked 'a small writer like who?' it would sadden me to think of the names of other small writers. I prefer to think that no one has ever been like me, however small, however much a mosquito or a flea of a writer I may be. The important thing is to be convinced that this really is your vocation, your profession, something you will do all your life. But as a vocation it is no joke. There are innumerable dangers besides those I have mentioned. We are constantly threatened with grave dangers whenever we write a page. There is the danger of suddenly starting to be flirtatious and of singing. I always have a crazy desire to sing and I have to be very careful that I don't. And there is the danger of cheating with words that do not really exist within us, that we have picked up by chance from outside of ourselves and which we skilfully slip in because we have become a bit dishonest. There is the danger of cheating and being dishonest. As you see, it is quite a difficult vocation, but it is the finest one in the world. The days and houses of our life, the days and houses of the people with whom we are involved, books and images and thoughts and conversations — all these things feed it, and it grows within us. It is a vocation which also feeds on terrible things, it swallows the best and the worst in our lives and our evil feelings flow in its blood just as much as our benevolent feelings. It feeds itself, and grows within us.

Silences

Tillie Olsen

Literary history and the present are dark with silences: some the silences for years by our acknowledged great; some silences hidden; some the ceasing to publish after one work appears; some the never coming to book form at all.

What is it that happens with the creator, to the creative process, in that time? What *are* creation's needs for full functioning? Without intention of or pretension to literary scholarship, I have had special need to learn all I could of this over the years, myself so nearly remaining mute and having to let writing die over and over again in me.

These are not *natural* silences—what Keats called *agonie ennuyeuse* (the tedious agony)—that necessary time for renewal, lying fallow, gestation, in the natural cycle of creation. The silences I speak of here are unnatural: the unnatural thwarting of what struggles to come into being, but cannot. In the old, the obvious parallels: when the seed strikes stone; the soil will not sustain; the spring is false; the time is drought or blight or infestation; the frost comes premature.

The great in achievement have known such silences—Thomas Hardy, Melville, Rimbaud, Gerard Manley Hopkins. They tell us little as to why or how the creative working atrophied and died in them—if ever it did.

"Less and less shrink the visions then vast in me," writes Thomas Hardy in his thirty-year ceasing from novels after the Victorian vileness to his *Jude the Obscure*. ("So ended his prose contributions to literature, his experiences having killed all his interest in this form"—the official explanation.) But the great poetry he wrote to the end of his life was not sufficient to hold, to develop the vast visions which for twenty-five years had had expression in novel after novel. People, situations, interrelationships, landscape—they cry for this larger life in poem after poem.

It was not visions shrinking with Hopkins, but a different torment. For seven years he kept his religious vow to refrain from writing poetry, but the poet's eye he could not shut, nor win "elected silence to beat upon [his] whorled ear." "I had long had haunting my ear the echo of a poem which now I realised on paper," he writes of the first poem permitted to end the seven years' silence. But poetry ("to hoard unheard; be heard, unheeded") could be only the least and last of his heavy priestly responsibilities. Nineteen poems were all he could produce in his last nine years—fullness to us, but torment pitched past grief to him, who felt himself "time's eunuch, never to beget."

Silence surrounds Rimbaud's silence. Was there torment of the unwritten; haunting of rhythm, of visions; anguish at dying powers, the seventeen years after he abandoned the unendurable literary world? We know only that the need to write continued into his first years of vagabondage; that he wrote:

> Had I not once a youth pleasant, heroic, fabulous enough to write on leaves of gold: too much luck. Through what crime, what error, have I earned my present weakness? You who maintain that some animals sob sorrowfully, that the dead have dreams, try to tell the story of my downfall and my slumber. I no longer know how to speak.

That on his deathbed, he spoke again like a poet-visionary.

Melville's stages to his thirty-year prose silence are clearest. The presage is in his famous letter to Hawthorne, as he had to hurry *Moby Dick* to an end:

> I am so pulled hither and thither by circumstances. The calm, the coolness, the silent grass-growing mood in which a man ought always to compose,— that, I fear, can seldom be mine. Dollars damn me. . . . What I feel most moved to write, that is banned,—it will not pay. Yet, altogether, write the *other* way I cannot. So the product is a final hash . . .

Reiterated in *Pierre,* writing "that book whose unfathomable cravings drink his blood . . . when at last the idea obtruded that the wiser and profounder he should grow, the more and the more he lessened his chances for bread."

To be possessed; to have to try final hash; to have one's work met by "drear ignoring"; to be damned by dollars into a Customs House job; to have only weary evenings and Sundays left for writing—

> How bitterly did unreplying Pierre feel in his heart that to most of the great works of humanity, their authors had given not weeks and months, not years and years, but their wholly surrendered and dedicated lives.

Is it not understandable why Melville began to burn work, then ceased to write it, "immolating [it] . . . sealing in a fate subdued"? And turned to occasional poetry, manageable in a time sense, "to nurse through night the ethereal spark." A thirty-year night. He was nearly seventy before he could quit the customs dock and again have full time for writing, start back to prose. "Age, dull tranquilizer," and devastation of "arid years that filed before" to work through. Three years of tryings before he felt capable of beginning *Billy Budd* (the kernel waiting half a century); three years more to his last days (he who had been so fluent), the slow, painful, never satisfied writing and re-writing of it.

Kin to these years-long silences are the *hidden* silences; work aborted, deferred, denied—hidden by the work which does come to fruition. Hopkins rightfully belongs here; almost certainly William Blake; Jane Austen, Olive Schreiner, Theodore Dreiser, Willa Cather, Franz Kafka; Katherine Anne Porter, many other contemporary writers.

Censorship silences. Deletions, omissions, abandonment of the medium (as with Hardy); paralyzing of capacity (as Dreiser's ten-year stasis on *Jennie Gerhardt* after the storm against *Sister Carrie*). Publishers' censorship, refusing subject matter or treatment as "not suitable" or "no market for." Self-censorship. Religious, political censorship—sometimes spurring inventiveness—most often (read Dostoyevsky's letters) a wearing attrition.

The extreme of this: those writers physically silenced by governments. Isaac Babel, the years of imprisonment, what took place in him with what wanted to be written? Or in Oscar Wilde, who was not permitted even a pencil until the last months of his imprisonment?

Other silences. The truly memorable poem, story, or book, then the writer ceasing to be published. Was one work all the writers had in them (life too thin for pressure of material, renewal) and the respect for literature too great to repeat themselves? Was it "the knife of the perfectionist attitude in art and life" at their throat? Were the conditions not present for establishing the habits of creativity (a young Colette who lacked a Willy to lock her in her room each day)? or—as instanced over and over—other claims, other responsibilities so writing could not be first? (The writer of a class, sex, color still marginal in literature, and whose coming to written voice at all against complex odds is exhausting achievement.) It is an eloquent commentary that this one-book silence has been true of most black writers; only eleven in the hundred years since 1850 have published novels more than twice.

There is a prevalent silence I pass by quickly, the absence of creativity where it once had been; the ceasing to create literature, though the books may keep coming out year after year. That suicide of the creative process Hemingway describes so accurately in "The Snows of Kilimanjaro":

> He had destroyed his talent himself—by not using it, by betrayals of himself and what he believed in, by drinking so much that he blunted the edge of his perceptions, by laziness, by sloth, by snobbery, by hook and by crook; selling vitality, trading it for security, for comfort.

No, not Scott Fitzgerald. His not a death of creativity, not silence, but what happens when (his words) there is "the sacrifice of talent, in pieces, to preserve its essential value."

Almost unnoted are the foreground silences, *before* the achievement. (Remember when Emerson hailed Whitman's genius, he guessed correctly: "which yet must have had a long *foreground* for such a start.") George Eliot, Joseph Conrad, Isak Dinesen, Sherwood Anderson, Dorothy Richardson, Elizabeth Madox Roberts, A.E. Coppard, Angus Wilson, Joyce Cary—all close to, or in their forties before they became published writers; Lampedusa, Maria Dermout *(The Ten Thousand Things)*, Laura Ingalls Wilder, the "children's writer," in their sixties. Their capacities evident early in the "being one on whom nothing is lost"; in other writers' qualities. Not all struggling and anguished, like Anderson, the foreground years; some needing the immobilization of long illness or loss, or the sudden lifting of responsibility to make writing necessary, make writing possible; others waiting circumstances and encouragement

(George Eliot, her Henry Lewes; Laura Wilder, a writer-daughter's insistence that she transmute her storytelling gift onto paper).

Very close to this last grouping are the silences where the lives never came to writing. Among these, the mute inglorious Miltons: those whose waking hours are all struggle for existence; the barely educated; the illiterate; women. Their silence the silence of centuries as to how life was, is, for most of humanity. Traces of their making, of course, in folk song, lullaby, tales, language itself, jokes, maxims, superstitions—but we know nothing of the creators or how it was with them. In the fantasy of Shakespeare born in deepest Africa (as at least one Shakespeare must have been), was the ritual, the oral storytelling a fulfillment? Or was there restlessness, indefinable yearning, a sense of restriction? Was it as Virginia Woolf in *A Room of One's Own* guesses—about women?

> Genius of a sort must have existed among them, as it existed among the working classes, but certainly it never got itself onto paper. When, however, one reads of a woman possessed by the devils, of a wise woman selling herbs, or even a remarkable man who had a remarkable mother, then I think we are on the track of a lost novelist, a suppressed poet, or some Emily Brontë who dashed her brains out on the moor, crazed with the torture her gift had put her to.

Rebecca Harding Davis whose work sleeps in the forgotten (herself as a woman of a century ago so close to remaining mute), also guessed about the silent in that time of the twelve-hour-a-day, six-day work week. She writes of the illiterate ironworker in *Life in the Iron Mills* who sculptured great shapes in the slag: "his fierce thirst for beauty, to know it, to create it, to *be* something other than he is—a passion of pain"; Margret Howth in the textile mill:

> There were things in the world, that like herself, were marred, did not understand, were hungry to know. . . . Her eyes quicker to see than ours, delicate or grand lines in the homeliest things. . . . Everything she saw or touched, nearer, more human than to you or me. These sights and sounds did not come to her common; she never got used to living as other people do.

She never got used to living as other people do. Was that one of the ways it was?

So some of the silences, incomplete listing of the incomplete, where the need and capacity to create were of a high order.

Now, what *is* the work of creation and the circumstances it demands for full functioning—as told in the journals, letters, notes, of the practitioners themselves: Henry James, Katherine Mansfield, André Gide, Virginia Woolf; the letters of Flaubert, Rilke, Joseph Conrad; Thomas Wolfe's *Story of a Novel,* Valéry's *Course in Poetics*. What do they explain of the silences?

"Constant toil is the law of art, as it is of life," says (and demonstrated) Balzac:

> To pass from conception to execution, to produce, to bring the idea to birth, to raise the child laboriously from infancy, to put it nightly to sleep surfeited, to kiss it in the mornings with the hungry heart of a mother, to clean it, to clothe it fifty times over in new garments which it tears and casts away, and yet not revolt against the trials of this agitated life—this unwearying maternal love, this habit of creation—this is execution and its toils.

"Without duties, almost without external communication," Rilke specifies, "unconfined solitude which takes every day like a life, a spaciousness which puts no limit to vision and in the midst of which infinities surround."

Unconfined solitude as Joseph Conrad experienced it:

> For twenty months I wrestled with the Lord for my creation . . . mind and will and conscience engaged to the full, hour after hour, day after day . . . a lonely struggle in a great isolation from the world. I suppose I slept and ate the food put before me and talked connectedly on suitable occasions, but I was never aware of the even flow of daily life, made easy and noiseless for me by a silent, watchful, tireless affection.

So there is a homely underpinning for it all, the even flow of daily life made easy and noiseless.

"The terrible law of the artist"—says Henry James—"the law of fructification, of fertilization. The old, old lesson of the art of meditation. To woo combinations and inspirations into being by a depth and continuity of attention and meditation."

"That load, that weight, that gnawing conscience," writes Thomas Mann—

That sea which to drink up, that frightful task . . . The will, the discipline and self-control to shape a sentence or follow out a hard train of thought. From the first rhythmical urge of the inward creative force towards the material, towards casting in shape and form, from that to the thought, the image, the word, the line, what a struggle, what Gethsemane.

Does it become very clear what Melville's Pierre so bitterly remarked on, and what literary history bears out—why most of the great works of humanity have come from lives (able to be) wholly surrendered and dedicated? How else sustain the constant toil, the frightful task, the terrible law, the continuity? Full self: this means full time as and when needed for the work. (That time for which Emily Dickinson withdrew from the world.)

But what if there is not that fullness of time, let alone totality of self? What if the writers, as in some of these silences, must work regularly at something besides their own work—as do nearly all in the arts in the United States today.

I know the theory (kin to "starving in the garret makes great art") that it is this very circumstance which feeds creativity. I know, too, that for the beginning young, for some who have such need, the job can be valuable access to life they would not otherwise know. A few (I think of the doctors, the incomparables: Chekhov and William Carlos Williams) for special reasons sometimes manage both. But the actuality testifies: substantial creative work demands time, and with rare exceptions only full-time workers have achieved it. Where the claims of creation cannot be primary, the results are atrophy; unfinished work; minor effort and accomplishment; silences. (Desperation which accounts for the mountains of applications to the foundations for grants—undivided time—in the strange bread-line system we have worked out for our artists.)

Twenty years went by on the writing of *Ship of Fools,* while Katherine Anne Porter, who needed only two, was "trying to get to that table, to that typewriter, away from my jobs of teaching and trooping this country and of keeping house." "Your subconscious needed that time to grow the layers of pearl," she was told. Perhaps, perhaps, but I doubt it. Subterranean forces can make you wait, but they are very finicky about the kind of waiting it has to be.

Before they will feed the creator back, they must be fed, passionately fed, what needs to be worked on. "We hold up our desire as one places a magnet over a composite dust from which the particle of iron will suddenly jump up," says Paul Valéry. A receptive waiting, that means, not demands which prevent "an undistracted center of being." And when the response comes, availability to work must be immediate. If not used at once, all may vanish as a dream; worse, future creation be endangered —for only the removal and development of the material frees the forces for further work.

There is a life in which all this is documented: Franz Kafka's. For every one entry from his diaries here, there are fifty others that testify as unbearably to the driven stratagems for time, the work lost (to us), the damage to the creative powers (and the body) of having to deny, interrupt, postpone, put aside, let work die.

"I cannot devote myself completely to my writing," Kafka explains (in 1911). "I could not live by literature if only, to begin with, because of the slow maturing of my work and its special character." So he worked as an official in a state insurance agency, and wrote when he could.

> These two can never be reconciled. . . . If I have written something one evening, I am afire the next day in the office and can bring nothing to completion. Outwardly I fulfill my office duties satisfactorily, not my inner duties however, and every unfulfilled inner duty becomes a misfortune that never leaves. What strength it will necessarily drain me of.

1911

> No matter how little the time or how badly I write, I feel approaching the imminent possibility of great moments which could make me capable of anything. But my being does not have sufficient strength to hold this to the next writing time. During the day the visible world helps me; during the night it cuts me to pieces unhindered. . . . In the evening and in the morning, my consciousness of the creative abilities in me then I can encompass. I feel shaken to the core of my being. Calling forth such powers which are then not permitted to function.

. . . which are then not permitted to function . . .

1911

I finish nothing, because I have no time, and it presses so within me.

1912

When I begin to write after such a long interval, I draw the words as if out of the empty air. If I capture one, then I have just this one alone, and all the toil must begin anew.

1914

Yesterday for the first time in months, an indisputable ability to do good work. And yet wrote only the first page. Again I realize that everything written down bit by bit rather than all at once in the course of the larger part is inferior, and that the circumstances of my life condemn me to this inferiority.

1915

My constant attempt by sleeping before dinner to make it possible to continue working [writing] late into the night, senseless. Then at one o'clock can no longer fall asleep at all, the next day at work insupportable, and so I destroy myself.

1917

Distractedness, weak memory, stupidity. Days passed in futility, powers wasted away in waiting. . . . Always this one principal anguish—if I had gone away in 1911 in full possession of all my powers. Not eaten by the strain of keeping down living forces.

Eaten into tuberculosis. By the time he won through to himself and time for writing, his body could live no more. He was forty-one.

I think of Rilke who said, "If I have any responsibility, I mean and desire it to be responsibility for the deepest and innermost essence of the loved reality [writing] to which I am inseparably bound"; and who also said, "Anything alive that makes demands, arouses in me an infinite capacity to give it its due, the consequences of which completely use me up." These were true with Kafka, too, yet how different their lives. When Rilke wrote that about responsibility, he is explaining why he will not take a job to support his wife and baby, nor live with them (years later will not come to his daughter's wedding nor permit a two-hour honeymoon visit lest it break his solitude where he awaits poetry). The "infinite capacity" is his explanation as to why he cannot even bear to have a dog. Extreme—and justified. He protected his creative powers.

Kafka's, Rilke's "infinite capacity," and all else that has been said here of the needs of creation, illuminate women's silence of centuries. I will not repeat what is in Virginia Woolf's *A Room of One's Own,* but talk of this last century and a half in which women have begun to have voice in literature. (It has been less than that time in Eastern Europe, and not yet, in many parts of the world.)

In the last century, of the women whose achievements endure for us in one way or another, nearly all never married (Jane Austen, Emily Brontë, Christina Rossetti, Emily Dickinson, Louisa May Alcott, Sarah Orne Jewett) or married late in their thirties (George Eliot, Elizabeth Barrett Browning, Charlotte Brontë, Olive Schreiner). I can think of only four (George Sand, Harriet Beecher Stowe, Helen Hunt Jackson, and Elizabeth Gaskell) who married and had children as young women. All had servants.

In our century, until very recently, it has not been so different. Most did not marry (Selma Lagerlof, Willa Cather, Ellen Glasgow, Gertrude Stein, Gabriela Mistral, Elizabeth Madox Roberts, Charlotte Mew, Eudora Welty, Marianne Moore) or, if married, have been childless (Edith Wharton, Virginia Woolf, Katherine Mansfield, Dorothy Richardson, H.H. Richardson, Elizabeth Bowen, Isak Dinesen, Katherine Anne Porter, Lillian Hellman, Dorothy Parker). Colette had one child (when she was forty). If I include Sigrid Undset, Kay Boyle, Pearl Buck, Dorothy Canfield Fisher, that will make a small group who had more than one child. All had household help or other special circumstances.

Am I resaying the moldy theory that women have no need, some say no capacity, to create art, because they can "create" babies? And the additional proof is precisely that the few women who have created it are nearly all childless? No.

The power and the need to create, over and beyond reproduction, is native in both women and men. Where the gifted among women *(and men)* have remained mute, or have never attained full capacity, it is because of circumstances, inner or outer, which oppose the needs of creation.

Wholly surrendered and dedicated lives; time as needed for the work; totality of self. But women are traditionally trained to place others' needs first, to feel these needs as their own (the "infinite capacity"); their sphere, their satisfaction to be in making it possible for others to use their abilities. This is what Virginia Woolf meant when, already a writer of achievement, she wrote in her diary:

> Father's birthday. He would have been 96, 96, yes, today; and could have been 96, like other people one has known; but mercifully was not. His life would have entirely ended mine. What would have happened? No writing, no books;—inconceivable.

It took family deaths to free more than one woman writer into her own development. Emily Dickinson freed herself, denying all the duties expected of a woman of her social position except the closest family ones, and she was fortunate to have a sister, and servants, to share those. How much is revealed of the differing circumstances and fate of their own as-great capacities, in the diaries (and lives) of those female bloodkin of great writers: Dorothy Wordsworth, Alice James, Aunt Mary Moody Emerson.

And where there is no servant or relation to assume the responsibilities of daily living? Listen to Katherine Mansfield in the early days of her relationship with John Middleton Murry, when they both dreamed of becoming great writers:

> The house seems to take up so much time. . . . I mean when I have to clean up twice over or wash up extra unnecessary things, I get frightfully impatient and want to be working [writing]. So often this week you and Gordon have been talking while I washed dishes. Well someone's got to wash dishes and get food. Otherwise "there's nothing in the house but eggs to eat." And after you have gone I walk about with a mind full of ghosts of saucepans and primus stoves and "will there be enough to go around?" And you calling, whatever I am doing, writing, "Tig, isn't there going to be tea? It's five o'clock."

I loathe myself today. This woman who superintends you and rushes about slamming doors and slopping water and shouts "You might at least empty the pail and wash out the tea leaves." . . . O Jack, I wish that you would take me in your arms and kiss my hands and my face and every bit of me and say, "It's all right, you darling thing, I understand."

A long way from Conrad's favorable circumstances for creation: the flow of daily life made easy and noiseless.

And, if in addition to the infinite capacity, to the daily responsibilities, there are children?

Balzac, you remember, described creation in terms of motherhood. Yes, in intelligent passionate motherhood there are similarities, and in more than the toil and patience. The calling upon total capacities; the reliving and new using of the past; the comprehensions; the fascination, absorption, intensity. All almost certain death to creation—(so far).

Not because the capacities to create no longer exist, or the need (though for a while, as in any fullness of life, the need may be obscured), but because the circumstances for sustained creation have been almost impossible. The need cannot be first. It can have at best, only part self, part time. (Unless someone else does the nurturing. Read Dorothy Fisher's "Babushka Farnham" in *Fables for Parents*.) More than in any other human relationship, overwhelmingly more, motherhood means being instantly interruptable, responsive, responsible. Children need one *now* (and remember, in our society, the family must often try to be the center for love and health the outside world is not). The very fact that these are real needs, that one feels them as one's own (love, not duty); *that there is no one else responsible for these needs*, gives them primacy. It is distraction, not meditation, that becomes habitual; interruption, not continuity; spasmodic, not constant toil. The rest has been said here. Work interrupted, deferred, relinquished, makes blockage—at best, lesser accomplishment. Unused capacities atrophy, cease to be.

When H. H. Richardson, who wrote the Australian classic *Ultima Thule*, was asked why she—whose children, like all her people, were so profoundly written—did not herself have children, she answered: "There are enough women to do the child-bearing and childrearing. I know of none who can write my books." I remember thinking rebelliously, yes, and I know of none who can bear and rear my children either. But literary history is on her side. Almost no mothers—as almost no part-time, part-self persons—have created enduring literature . . . so far.

If I talk now quickly of my own silences—almost presumptuous after what has been told here—it is that the individual experience may add.

In the twenty years I bore and reared my children, usually had to work on a paid job as well, the simplest circumstances for creation did not exist. Nevertheless writing, the hope of it, was "the air I breathed, so long as I shall breathe at all." In that hope, there was conscious storing, snatched reading, beginnings of writing, and always "the secret rootlets of reconnaissance."

When the youngest of our four was in school, the beginnings struggled toward endings. This was a time, in Kafka's words, "like a squirrel in a cage: bliss of movement, desperation about constriction, craziness of endurance."

Bliss of movement. A full extended family life; the world of my job (transcriber in a dairy-equipment company); and the writing, which I was somehow able to carry around within me through work, through home. Time on the bus, even when I had to stand, was enough; the stolen moments at work, enough; the deep night hours for as long as I could stay awake, after the kids were in bed, after the household tasks were done, sometimes during. It is no accident that the first work I considered publishable began: "I stand here ironing, and what you asked me moves tormented back and forth with the iron."

In such snatches of time I wrote what I did in those years, but there came a time when this triple life was no longer possible. The fifteen hours of daily realities became too much distraction for the writing. I lost craziness of endurance. What might have been, I don't know; but I applied for, and was given, eight months' writing time. There was still full family life, all the household responsibilities, but I did not have to hold an eight-hour job. I had continuity, three full days, sometimes more—and it was in those months I made the mysterious turn and became a writing writer.

Then had to return to the world of work, someone else's work, nine hours, five days a week.

This was the time of festering and congestion. For a few months I was able to shield the writing with which I was so full, against the demands of jobs on which I had to be competent, through the joys and responsibilities and trials of family. For a few months. Always roused by the writing, always denied. "I could not go to write it down. It convulsed and died in me. I will pay."

My work died. What demanded to be written, did not. It seethed, bubbled, clamored, peopled me. At last moved into the hours meant for sleeping. I worked now full time on temporary jobs, a Kelly, a Western Agency girl (girl!), wandering from office to office, always hoping to manage two, three writing months ahead. Eventually there was time.

I had said: always roused by the writing, always denied. Now, like a woman made frigid, I had to learn response, to trust this possibility for fruition that had not been before. Any interruption dazed and silenced me. It took a long while of surrendering to what I was trying to write, of invoking Henry James's "passion, piety, patience," before I was able to re-establish work.

When again I had to leave the writing, I lost consciousness. A time of anesthesia. There was still an automatic noting that did not stop, but it was as if writing had never been. No fever, no congestion, no festering. I ceased being peopled, slept well and dreamlessly, took a "permanent" job. The few pieces that had been published seemed to have vanished like the not-yet-written. I wrote someone, unsent: "So long they fed each other—my life, the writing—; —the writing or hope of it, my life—; but now they begin to destroy." I knew, but did not feel the destruction.

A Ford grant in literature, awarded me on nomination by others, came almost too late. Time granted does not necessarily coincide with time that can be most fully used, as the congested time of fullness would have been. Still, it was two years.

Drowning is not so pitiful as the attempt to rise, says Emily Dickinson. I do not agree, but I know whereof she speaks. For a long time I was that emaciated survivor trembling on the beach, unable to rise and walk. Said differently, I could manage only the feeblest, shallowest growth on that devastated soil. Weeds, to be burned like weeds, or used as compost. When the habits of creation were at last rewon, one book went to the publisher, and I dared to begin my present work. It became my center, engraved on it: "Evil is whatever distracts." (By now had begun a cost to our family life, to my own participation in life as a human being.) I shall not tell the "rest, residue, and remainder" of what I was "leased, demised, and let unto" when once again I had to leave work at the flood to return to the Time-Master, to business-ese and legalese. This most harmful of all my silences has ended, but I am not yet recovered; may still be a one-book silence.

However that will be, we are in a time of more and more hidden and foreground silences, women *and* men. Denied full writing life, more may try to "nurse through night" (that part-time, part-self night) "the ethereal spark," but it seems to me there would almost have had to be "flame on flame" first; and time as needed, afterwards; and enough of the self, the capacities, undamaged for the rebeginnings on the frightful task. I would like to believe this for what has not yet been written into literature. But it cannot reconcile for what is lost by unnatural silences.

Letter to a Young Gentleman who Proposes to Embrace the Career of Art

Robert Louis Stevenson

With the agreeable frankness of youth, you address me on a point of some practical importance to yourself and (it is even conceivable) of some gravity to the world: Should you or should you not become an artist? It is one which you must decide entirely for yourself; all that I can do is to bring under your notice some of the materials of that decision; and I will begin, as I shall probably conclude also, by assuring you that all depends on the vocation.

To know what you like is the beginning of wisdom and of old age. Youth is wholly experimental. The essence and charm of that unquiet and delightful epoch is ignorance of self as well as ignorance of life. These two unknowns the young man brings together again and again, now in the airiest touch, now with a bitter hug; now with exquisite pleasure, now with cutting pain; but never with indifference, to which he is a total stranger, and never with that near kinsman of indifference, contentment. If he be a youth of dainty senses or a brain easily heated, the interest of this series of experiments grows upon him out of all proportion to the pleasure he receives. It is not beauty that he loves, nor pleasure that he seeks, though he may think so; his design and his sufficient reward is to verify his own existence and taste the variety of human fate. To him, before the razor-edge of curiosity is dulled, all that is not actual living and the hot chase of experience wears a face of a disgusting dryness difficult to recall in later days; or if there be any exception - and here destiny steps in - it is in those moments when, wearied or surfeited of the primary activity of the senses, he calls up before memory the image of transacted pains and pleasures. Thus it is that such an one shies from all cut-and-dry professions, and inclines insensibly toward that career of art which consists only in the tasting and recording of experience.

This, which is not so much a vocation for art as an impatience of all other honest trades, frequently exists alone; and so existing, it will pass gently away in the course of years. Emphatically, it is not to be regarded; it is not a vocation, but a temptation; and when your father the other day so fiercely and (in my view) so properly discouraged your ambition, he was recalling not improbably some similar passage in his own experience. For the temptation is perhaps nearly as common as the vocation is rare. But again we have vocations which are imperfect; we have men whose minds are bound up, not so much in any art, as in the general ARS ARTIUM and common base of all creative work; who will now dip into painting, and now study counterpoint, and anon will be inditing a sonnet: all these with equal interest, all often with genuine knowledge. And of this temper, when it stands alone, I find it difficult to speak; but I should counsel such an one to take to letters, for in literature (which drags with so wide a net) all his information may be found some day useful, and if he should go on as he has begun, and turn at last into the critic, he will have learned to use the necessary tools. Lastly we come to those vocations which are at once decisive and precise; to the men who are born with the love of pigments, the passion of drawing, the gift of music, or the impulse to create with words, just as other and perhaps the same men are born with the love of hunting, or the sea, or horses, or the turning-lathe. These are predestined; if a man love the labour of any trade, apart from any question of success or fame, the gods have called him. He may have the general vocation too: he may have a taste for all the arts, and I think he often has; but the mark of his calling is this laborious partiality for one, this inextinguishable zest in its technical successes, and (perhaps above all) a certain candour of mind to take his very trifling enterprise with a gravity that would befit the cares of empire, and to think the smallest improvement worth accomplishing at any expense of time and industry. The book, the statue, the sonata, must be gone upon with the unreasoning good faith and the unflagging spirit of children at their play. IS IT WORTH DOING? - when it shall have occurred to any artist to ask himself that question, it is implicitly answered in the negative. It does not occur to the child as he plays at being a pirate on the dining-room sofa, nor to the hunter as he pursues his quarry; and the candour of the one and the ardour of the other should be united in the bosom of the artist.

If you recognise in yourself some such decisive taste, there is no room for hesitation: follow your bent. And observe (lest I should too much discourage you) that the disposition does not usually burn so brightly at the first, or rather not so constantly. Habit and practice sharpen gifts; the necessity of toil grows less disgusting, grows even welcome, in the course of years; a small taste (if it be only genuine) waxes with indulgence into an exclusive passion. Enough, just now, if you can look back over a fair interval, and see that your chosen art has a little more than held its own among the thronging interests of youth. Time will do the rest, if devotion help it; and soon your every thought will be engrossed in that beloved occupation.

But even with devotion, you may remind me, even with unfaltering and delighted industry, many thousand artists spend their lives, if the result be regarded, utterly in vain: a thousand artists, and never one work of art. But the vast mass of mankind are incapable of doing anything reasonably well, art among the rest. The worthless artist would not improbably have been a quite incompetent baker. And the artist, even if he does not amuse the public, amuses himself; so that there will always be one man the happier for his vigils. This is the practical side of art: its inexpugnable fortress for the true practitioner. The direct returns - the wages of the trade are small, but the indirect - the wages of the life - are incalculably great. No other business offers a man his daily bread upon such joyful terms. The soldier and the explorer have moments of a worthier excitement, but they are purchased by cruel hardships and periods of tedium that beggar language. In the life of the artist there need be no hour without its pleasure. I take the author, with whose career I am best acquainted; and it is true he works in a rebellious material, and that the act of writing is cramped and trying both to the eyes and the temper; but remark him in his study, when matter crowds upon him and words are not wanting - in what a continual series of small successes time flows by; with what a sense of power as of one moving mountains, he marshals his petty characters; with what pleasures, both of the ear and eye, he sees his airy structure growing on the page; and how he labours in a craft to which the whole material of his life is tributary, and which opens a door to all his tastes, his loves, his hatreds, and his convictions, so that what he writes is only what he longed to utter. He may have enjoyed many things in this big, tragic playground of the world; but what shall he have enjoyed more fully than a morning of successful work? Suppose it ill paid: the wonder is it should be paid at all. Other men pay, and pay dearly, for pleasures less desirable.

Nor will the practice of art afford you pleasure only; it affords besides an admirable training. For the artist works entirely upon honour. The public knows little or nothing of those merits in the quest of which you are condemned to spend the bulk of your endeavours. Merits of design, the merit of first-hand energy, the merit of a certain cheap accomplishment which a man of the artistic temper easily acquires - these they can recognise, and these they value. But to those more exquisite refinements of proficiency and finish, which the artist so ardently desires and so keenly feels, for which (in the vigorous words of Balzac) he must toil "like a miner buried in a landslip," for which, day after day, he recasts and revises and rejects - the gross mass of the public must be ever blind. To those lost pains, suppose you attain the highest pitch of merit, posterity may possibly do justice; suppose, as is so probable, you fall by even a hair's breadth of the highest, rest certain they shall never be observed. Under the shadow of this cold thought, alone in his studio, the artist must preserve from day to day his constancy to the ideal. It is this which makes his life noble; it is by this that the practice of his craft strengthens and matures his character; it is for this that even the serious countenance of the great emperor was turned approvingly (if only for a moment) on the followers of Apollo, and that sternly gentle voice bade the artist cherish his art.

And here there fall two warnings to be made. First, if you are to continue to be a law to yourself, you must beware of the first signs of laziness. This idealism in honesty can only be supported by perpetual effort; the standard is easily lowered, the artist who says "IT WILL DO," is on the downward path; three or four pot- boilers are enough at times (above all at wrong times) to falsify a talent, and by the practice of journalism a man runs the risk of becoming wedded to cheap finish. This is the danger on the one side; there is not less upon the other. The consciousness of how much the artist is (and must be) a law to himself, debauches the small heads. Perceiving recondite merits very hard to attain, making or swallowing artistic formulae, or perhaps falling in love with some particular proficiency of his own, many artists forget the end of all art: to please. It is doubtless tempting to exclaim against the ignorant bourgeois; yet it should not be forgotten, it is he who is to pay us, and that (surely on the face of it) for services that he shall desire to have performed. Here also, if properly considered, there is a question of transcendental honesty. To give the public what they do not want, and yet expect to be supported: we have there a strange pretension, and yet not uncommon, above all with painters. The first duty in this world is for a man to pay his way; when that is quite accomplished, he may plunge into what eccentricity he likes; but emphatically not till then. Till then, he must pay assiduous court to the bourgeois who carries the purse. And if in the course of these capitulations he shall falsify his talent, it can never have been a strong one, and he will have preserved a better thing than talent - character. Or if he be of a mind so independent that he cannot stoop to this necessity, one course is yet open: he can desist from art, and follow some more manly way of life.

I speak of a more manly way of life, it is a point on which I must be frank. To live by a pleasure is not a high calling; it involves patronage, however veiled; it numbers the artist, however ambitious, along with dancing girls and billiard markers. The French have a romantic evasion for one employment, and call its practitioners the Daughters of Joy. The artist is of the same family, he is of the Sons of Joy, chose his trade to please himself, gains his livelihood by pleasing others, and has parted with something of the sterner dignity of man. Journals but a little while ago declaimed against the Tennyson peerage; and this Son of Joy was blamed for condescension when he followed the example of Lord Lawrence and Lord Cairns and Lord Clyde. The poet was more happily inspired; with a better modesty he accepted the honour; and anonymous journalists have not yet (if I am to believe them) recovered the vicarious disgrace to their profession. When it comes to their turn, these gentlemen can do themselves more justice; and I shall be glad to think of it; for to my barbarian eyesight, even Lord Tennyson looks somewhat out of place in that assembly. There should be no honours for the artist; he has already, in the practice of his art, more than his share of the rewards of life; the honours are pre-empted for other trades, less agreeable and perhaps more useful.

But the devil in these trades of pleasing is to fail to please. In ordinary occupations, a man offers to do a certain thing or to produce a certain article with a merely conventional accomplishment, a design in which (we may almost say) it is difficult to fail. But the artist steps forth out of the crowd and proposes to delight: an impudent design, in which it is impossible to fail without odious circumstances. The poor Daughter of Joy, carrying her smiles and finery quite unregarded through the crowd, makes a figure which it is impossible to recall without a wounding pity. She is the type of the unsuccessful artist. The actor, the dancer, and the singer must appear like her in person, and drain publicly the cup of failure. But though the rest of us escape this crowning bitterness of the pillory, we all court in essence the same humiliation. We all profess to be able to delight. And how few of us are! We all pledge ourselves to be able to continue to delight. And the day will come to each, and even to the most admired, when the ardour shall have declined and the cunning shall be lost, and he shall sit by his deserted booth ashamed. Then shall he see himself condemned to do work for which he blushes to take payment. Then (as if his lot were not already cruel) he must lie exposed to the gibes of the wreckers of the press, who earn a little bitter bread by the condemnation of trash which they have not read, and the praise of excellence which they cannot understand.

And observe that this seems almost the necessary end at least of writers. LES BLANCS ET LES BLEUS (for instance) is of an order of merit very different from LE VICOMTE DE BRAGLONNE; and if any gentleman can bear to spy upon the nakedness of CASTLE DANGEROUS, his name I think is Ham: let it be enough for the rest of us to read of it (not without tears) in the pages of Lockhart. Thus in old age, when occupation and comfort are most needful, the writer must lay aside at once his pastime and his breadwinner. The painter indeed, if he succeed at all in engaging the attention of the public, gains great sums and can stand to his easel until a great age without dishonourable failure.

The writer has the double misfortune to be ill-paid while he can work, and to be incapable of working when he is old. It is thus a way of life which conducts directly to a false position.

For the writer (in spite of notorious examples to the contrary) must look to be ill-paid. Tennyson and Montepin make handsome livelihoods; but we cannot all hope to be Tennyson, and we do not all perhaps desire to be Montepin. If you adopt an art to be your trade, weed your mind at the outset of all desire of money. What you may decently expect, if you have some talent and much industry, is such an income as a clerk will earn with a tenth or perhaps a twentieth of your nervous output. Nor have you the right to look for more; in the wages of the life, not in the wages of the trade, lies your reward; the work is here the wages. It will be seen I have little sympathy with the common lamentations of the artist class. Perhaps they do not remember the hire of the field labourer; or do they think no parallel will lie? Perhaps they have never observed what is the retiring allowance of a field officer; or do they suppose their contributions to the arts of pleasing more important than the services of a colonel? Perhaps they forget on how little Millet was content to live; or do they think, because they have less genius, they stand excused from the display of equal virtues? But upon one point there should be no dubiety: if a man be not frugal, he has no business in the arts. If he be not frugal, he steers directly for that last tragic scene of LE VIEUX SALTIMBANQUE; if he be not frugal, he will find it hard to continue to be honest. Some day, when the butcher is knocking at the door, he may be tempted, he may be obliged, to turn out and sell a slovenly piece of work. If the obligation shall have arisen through no wantonness of his own, he is even to be commanded; for words cannot describe how far more necessary it is that a man should support his family, than that he should attain to - or preserve - distinction in the arts. But if the pressure comes, through his own fault, he has stolen, and stolen under trust, and stolen (which is the worst of all) in such a way that no law can reach him.

And now you may perhaps ask me, if the debutant artist is to have no thought of money, and if (as is implied) he is to expect no honours from the State, he may not at least look forward to the delights of popularity? Praise, you will tell me, is a savoury dish. And in so far as you may mean the countenance of other artists you would put your finger on one of the most essential and enduring pleasures of the career of art. But in so far as you should have an eye to the commendations of the public or the notice of the newspapers, be sure you would but be cherishing a dream. It is true that in certain esoteric journals the author (for instance) is duly criticised, and that he is often praised a great deal more than he deserves, sometimes for qualities which he prided himself on eschewing, and sometimes by ladies and gentlemen who have denied themselves the privilege of reading his work. But if a man be sensitive to this wild praise, we must suppose him equally alive to that which often accompanies and always follows it - wild ridicule. A man may have done well for years, and then he may fail; he will hear of his failure. Or he may have done well for years, and still do well, but the critics may have tired of praising him, or there may have sprung up some new idol of the instant, some "dust a little gilt," to whom they now prefer to offer sacrifice. Here is the obverse and the reverse of that empty and ugly thing called popularity. Will any man suppose it worth the gaining?

The Nature and Aim of Fiction

Flannery O'Connor

I understand that this is a course called "How the Writer Writes," and that each week you are exposed to a different writer who holds forth on the subject. The only parallel I can think of to this is having the zoo come to you, one animal at a time; and I suspect that what you hear one week from the giraffe is contradicted the next week by the baboon.

My own problem in thinking what I should say to you tonight has been how to interpret such a title as "How the Writer Writes." In the first place, there is no such thing as THE writer, and I think that if you don't know that now, you should by the time such a course as this is over. In fact, I predict that it is the one thing you can be absolutely certain of learning.

But there is a widespread curiosity about writers and how they work, and when a writer talks on this subject, there are always misconceptions and mental rubble for him to clear away before he can even begin to see what he wants to talk about. I am not, of course, as innocent as I look. I know well enough that very few people who are supposedly interested in writing are interested in writing well. They are interested in publishing something, and if possible in making a "killing." They are interested in being a writer, not in writing. They are interested in seeing their names at the top of something printed, it matters not what. And they seem to feel that this can be accomplished by learning certain things about working habits and about markets and about what subjects are currently acceptable.

If this is what you are interested in, I am not going to be of much use to you. I feel that the external habits of the writer will be guided by his common sense or his lack of it and by his personal circumstances; and that these will seldom be alike in two cases. What interests the serious writer is not external habits but what Maritain calls, "the habit of art"; and he explains that "habit" in this sense means a certain quality or virtue of the mind. The scientist has the habit of science; the artist, the habit of art.

Now I'd better stop here and explain how I'm using the word *art*. Art is a word that immediately scares people off, as being a little too grand. But all I mean by art is writing something that is valuable in itself and that works in itself. The basis of art is truth, both in matter and in mode. The person who aims after art in his work aims after truth, in an imaginative sense, no more and no less. St. Thomas said that the artist is concerned with the good of that which is made; and that will have to be the basis of my few words on the subject of fiction.

Now you'll see that this kind of approach eliminates many things from the discussion. It eliminates any concern with the motivation of the writer except as this finds its place inside the work. It also eliminates any concern with the reader in his market sense. It also eliminates that tedious controversy that always rages between people who declare that they write to express themselves and those who declare that they write to fill their pocketbooks, if possible.

In this connection I always think of Henry James. I know of no writer who was hotter after the dollar than James was, or who was more of a conscientious artist. It is true, I think, that these are times when the financial rewards for sorry writing are much greater than those for good writing. There are certain cases in which, if you can only learn to write poorly enough, you can make a great deal of money. But it is not true that if you write well, you won't get published at all. It is true that if you want to write well and live well at the same time, you'd better arrange to inherit money or marry a stockbroker or a rich woman who can operate a typewriter. In any case, whether you write to make money or to express your soul or to insure civil rights or to irritate your grandmother will be a matter for you and your analyst, and the point of departure for this discussion will be the good of the written work.

The kind of written work I'm going to talk about is story-writing, because that's the only kind I know anything about. I'll call any length of fiction a story, whether it be a novel or a shorter piece, and I'll call anything a story in which specific characters and events influence each other to form a meaningful narrative. I find that most people know what a story is until they sit down to write one. Then they find themselves writing a sketch with an essay woven through it, or an essay with a sketch woven through it, or an editorial with a character in it, or a case history with a moral, or some other mongrel thing. When they realize that they aren't writing stories, they decide that the remedy for this is to learn something that they refer to as the "technique of the short story" or "the technique of the novel." Technique in the minds of many is something rigid, something like a formula that you impose on the material; but in the best stories it is something organic, something that grows out of the material, and this being the case, it is different for every story of any account that has ever been written.

I think we have to begin thinking about stories at a much more fundamental level, so I want to talk about one quality of fiction which I think is its least common denominator—the fact that it is concrete—and about a few of the qualities that follow from this. We will be concerned in this with the reader in his fundamental human sense, because the nature of fiction is in large measure determined by the nature of our perceptive apparatus. The beginning of human knowledge is through the senses, and the fiction writer begins where human perception begins. He appeals through the senses, and you cannot appeal to the senses with abstractions. It is a good deal easier for most people to state an abstract idea than to describe and thus re-create some object that they actually see. But the world of the fiction writer is full of matter, and this is what the beginning fiction writers are very loath to create. They are concerned primarily with unfleshed ideas and emotions. They are apt to be reformers and to want to write because they are possessed not by a story but by the bare bones of some abstract notion. They are conscious of problems, not of people, of questions and issues, not of the texture of existence, of case histories and of everything that has a sociological smack, instead of with all those concrete details of life that make actual the mystery of our position on earth.

The Manicheans separated spirit and matter. To them all material things were evil. They sought pure spirit and tried to approach the infinite directly without any mediation of matter. This is also pretty much the modern spirit, and for the sensibility infected with it, fiction is hard if not impossible to write because fiction is so very much an incarnational art.

One of the most common and saddest spectacles is that of a person of really fine sensibility and acute psychological perception trying to write fiction by using these qualities alone. This type of writer will put down one intensely emotional or keenly perceptive sentence after the other, and the result will be complete dullness. The fact is that the materials of the fiction writer are the humblest. Fiction is about everything human and we are made out of dust, and if you scorn getting yourself dusty, then you shouldn't try to write fiction. It's not a grand enough job for you.

Now when the fiction writer finally gets this idea through his head and into his habits, he begins to realize what a job of heavy labor the writing of fiction is. A lady who writes, and whom I admire very much, wrote me that she had learned from Flaubert that it takes at least three activated sensuous strokes to make an object real; and she believes that this is connected with our having five senses. If you're deprived of any of them, you're in a bad way, but if you're deprived of more than two at once, you almost aren't present.

All the sentences in *Madame Bovary* could be examined with wonder, but there is one in particular that always stops me in admiration. Flaubert has just shown us Emma at the piano with Charles watching her. He says, "She struck the notes with aplomb and ran from top to bottom of the keyboard without a break. Thus shaken up, the old instrument, whose strings buzzed, could be heard at the other end of the village when the window was open, and often the bailiff's clerk, passing along the highroad, bareheaded and in list slippers, stopped to listen, his sheet of paper in his hand."

The more you look at a sentence like that, the more you can learn from it. At one end of it, we are with Emma and this very solid instrument "whose strings buzzed," and at the other end of it we are across the village with this very concrete clerk in his list slippers. With regard to what happens to Emma in the rest of the novel, we may think that it makes no difference that the instrument has buzzing strings or that the clerk wears list slippers and has a piece of paper in his hand, but Flaubert had to create a believable village to put Emma in. It's always necessary to remember that the fiction writer is much less *immediately* concerned with grand ideas and bristling emotions than he is with putting list slippers on clerks.

Now of course this is something that some people learn only to abuse. This is one reason that strict naturalism is a dead end in fiction. In a strictly naturalistic work the detail is there because it is natural to life, not because it is natural to the work. In a work of art we can be extremely literal, without being in the least naturalistic. Art is selective, and its truthfulness is the truthfulness of the essential that creates movement.

The novel works by a slower accumulation of detail than the short story does. The short story requires more drastic procedures than the novel because more has to be accomplished in less space. The details have to carry more immediate weight. In good fiction, certain of the details will tend to accumulate meaning from the story itself, and when this happens, they become symbolic in their action.

Now the word *symbol* scares a good many people off, just as the word *art* does. They seem to feel that a symbol is some mysterious thing put in arbitrarily by the writer to frighten the common reader—sort of a literary Masonic grip that is only for the initiated. They seem to think that it is a way of saying something that you aren't actually saying, and so if they can be got to read a reputedly symbolic work at all, they approach it as if it were a problem in algebra. Find *x*. And when they do find or think they find this abstraction, *x*, then they go off with an elaborate sense of satisfaction and the notion that they have "understood" the story. Many students confuse the *process* of understanding a thing with understanding it.

I think that for the fiction writer himself, symbols are something he uses simply as a matter of course. You might say that these are details that, while having their essential place in the literal level of the story, operate in depth as well as on the surface, increasing the story in every direction.

I think the way to read a book is always to see what happens, but in a good novel, more always happens than we are able to take in at once, more happens than meets the eye. The mind is led on by what it sees into the greater depths that the book's symbols naturally suggest. This is what is meant when critics say that a novel operates on several levels. The truer the symbol, the deeper it leads you, the more meaning it opens up. To take an example from my own book, *Wise Blood,* the hero's rat-colored automobile is his pulpit and his coffin as well as something he thinks of as a means of escape. He is mistaken in thinking that it is a means of escape, of course, and does not really escape his predicament until the car is destroyed by the patrolman. The car is a kind of death-in-life symbol, as his blindness is a life-in-death symbol. The fact that these meanings are there makes the book significant. The reader may not see them but they have their effect on him nonetheless. This is the way the modern novelist sinks, or hides, his theme.

The kind of vision the fiction writer needs to have, or to develop, in order to increase the meaning of his story is called anagogical vision, and that is the kind of vision that is able to see different levels of reality in one image or one situation. The medieval commentators on Scripture found three kinds of meaning in the literal level of the sacred text: one they called allegorical, in which one fact pointed to another; one they called tropological, or moral, which had to do with what should be done; and one they called anagogical, which had to do with the Divine life and our participation in it. Although this was a method applied to biblical exegesis, it was also an attitude toward all of creation, and a way of reading nature which included most possibilities, and I think it is this enlarged view of the human scene that the fiction writer has to cultivate if he is ever going to write stories that have any chance of becoming a permanent part of our literature. It seems to be a paradox that the larger and more complex the personal view, the easier it is to compress it into fiction.

People have a habit of saying, "What is the theme of your story?" and they expect you to give them a statement: "The theme of my story is the economic pressure of the machine on the middle class"—or some such absurdity. And when they've got a statement like that, they go off happy and feel it is no longer necessary to read the story.

Some people have the notion that you read the story and then climb out of it into the meaning, but for the fiction writer himself the whole story is the meaning, because it is an experience, not an abstraction.

Now the second common characteristic of fiction follows from this, and it is that fiction is presented in such a way that the reader has the sense that it is unfolding around him. This doesn't mean he has to identify himself with the character or feel compassion for the character or anything like that. It just means that fiction has to be largely presented rather than reported. Another way to say it is that though fiction is a narrative art, it relies heavily on the element of drama.

The story is not as extreme a form of drama as the play, but if you know anything about the history of the novel, you know that the novel as an art form has developed in the direction of dramatic unity.

The major difference between the novel as written in the eighteenth century and the novel as we usually find it today is the disappearance from it of the author. Fielding, for example, was everywhere in his own work, calling the reader's attention to this point and that, directing him to give his special attention here or there, clarifying this and that incident for him so that he couldn't possibly miss the point. The Victorian novelists did this, too. They were always coming in, explaining and psychologizing about their characters. But along about the time of Henry James, the author began to tell his story in a different way. He began to let it come through the minds and eyes of the characters themselves, and he sat behind the scenes, apparently disinterested. By the time we get to James Joyce, the author is nowhere to be found in the book. The reader is on his own, floundering around in the thoughts of various unsavory characters. He finds himself in the middle of a world apparently without comment.

But it is from the kind of world the writer creates, from the kind of character and detail he invests it with, that a reader can find the intellectual meaning of a book. Once this is found, however, it cannot be drained off and used as a substitute for the book. As the late John Peale Bishop said: "You can't say Cézanne painted apples and a tablecloth and have said what Cézanne painted." The novelist makes his statements by selection, and if he is any good, he selects every word for a reason, every detail for a reason, every incident for a reason, and arranges them in a certain time-sequence for a reason. He demonstrates something that cannot possibly be demonstrated any other way than with a whole novel.

Art forms evolve until they reach their ultimate perfection, or until they reach some state of petrifaction, or until some new element is grafted on and a new art form made. But however the past of fiction has been or however the future will be, the present state of the case is that a piece of fiction must be very much a self-contained dramatic unit.

This means that it must carry its meaning inside it. It means that any abstractly expressed compassion or piety or morality in a piece of fiction is only a statement added to it. It means that you can't make an inadequate dramatic action complete by putting a statement of meaning on the end of it or in the middle of it or at the beginning of it. It means that when you write fiction you are speaking *with* character and action, not *about* character and action. The writer's moral sense must coincide with his dramatic sense.

It's said that when Henry James received a manuscript that he didn't like, he would return it with the comment, "You have chosen a good subject and are treating it in a straightforward manner." This usually pleased the person getting the manuscript back, but it was the worst thing that James could think of to say, for he knew, better than anybody else, that the straightforward manner is seldom equal to the complications of the good subject. There may never be anything new to say, but there is always a new way to say it, and since, in art, the way of saying a thing becomes a part of what is said, every work of art is unique and requires fresh attention.

It's always wrong of course to say that you can't do this or you can't do that in fiction. You can do anything you can get away with, but nobody has ever gotten away with much.

I believe that it takes a rather different type of disposition to write novels than to write short stories, granted that both require fundamentally fictional talents. I have a friend who writes both, and she says that when she stops a novel to work on short stories, she feels as if she has just left a dark wood to be set upon by wolves. The novel is a more diffused form and more suited to those who like to linger along the way; it also requires a more massive energy. For those of us who want to get the agony over in a hurry, the novel is a burden and a pain. But no matter which fictional form you are using, you are writing a story, and in a story something has to happen. A perception is not a story, and no amount of sensitivity can make a story-writer out of you if you just plain don't have a gift for telling a story.

But there's a certain grain of stupidity that the writer of fiction can hardly do without, and this is the quality of having to stare, of not getting the point at once. The longer you look at one object, the more of the world you see in it; and it's well to remember that the serious fiction writer always writes about the whole world, no matter how limited his particular scene. For him, the bomb that was dropped on Hiroshima affects life on the Oconee River, and there's not anything he can do about it.

People are always complaining that the modern novelist has no hope and that the picture he paints of the world is unbearable. The only answer to this is that people without hope do not write novels. Writing a novel is a terrible experience, during which the hair often falls out and the teeth decay. I'm always highly irritated by people who imply that writing fiction is an escape from reality. It is a plunge into reality and it's very shocking to the system. If the novelist is not sustained by a hope of money, then he must be sustained by a hope of salvation, or he simply won't survive the ordeal.

People without hope not only don't write novels, but what is more to the point, they don't read them. They don't take long looks at anything, because they lack the courage. The way to despair is to refuse to have any kind of experience, and the novel, of course, is a way to have experience. The lady who only read books that improved her mind was taking a safe course—and a hopeless one. She'll never know whether her mind is improved or not, but should she ever, by some mistake, read a great novel, she'll know mighty well that something is happening to her.

A good many people have the notion that nothing happens in modern fiction and that nothing is supposed to happen, that it is the style now to write a story in which nothing happens. Actually, I think more happens in modern fiction—with less furor on the surface—than has ever happened in fiction before. A good example of this is a story by Caroline Gordon called "Summer Dust." It's in a collection of her stories called *The Forest of the South,* which is a book that repays study.

"Summer Dust" is divided into four short sections, which don't at first appear to have any relation between them and which are minus any narrative connection. Reading the story is at first rather like standing a foot away from an impressionistic painting, then gradually moving back until it comes into focus. When you reach the right distance, you suddenly see that a world has been created—and a world in action—and that a complete story has been told, by a wonderful kind of understatement. It has been told more by showing what happens around the story than by touching directly on the story itself.

You may say that this requires such an intelligent and sophisticated reader that it is not worth writing, but I'm rather inclined to think that it is more a false sophistication that prevents people from understanding this kind of story than anything else. Without being naturalistic in the least, a story like "Summer Dust" is actually much closer in form to life than a story that follows a narrative sequence of events.

The type of mind that can understand good fiction is not necessarily the educated mind, but it is at all times the kind of mind that is willing to have its sense of mystery deepened by contact with reality, and its sense of reality deepened by contact with mystery. Fiction should be both canny and uncanny. In a good deal of popular criticism, there is the notion operating that all fiction has to be about the Average Man, and has to depict average ordinary everyday life, that every fiction writer must produce what used to be called "a slice of life." But if life, in that sense, satisfied us, there would be no sense in producing literature at all.

Conrad said that his aim as a fiction writer was to render the highest possible justice to the visible universe. That sounds very grand, but it is really very humble. It means that he subjected himself at all times to the limitations that reality imposed, but that reality for him was not simply coextensive with the visible. He was interested in rendering justice to the visible universe because it suggested an invisible one, and he explained his own intentions as a novelist in this way:

. . . and if the [artist's] conscience is clear, his answer to those who in the fullness of a wisdom which looks for immediate profit, demand specifically to be edified, consoled, amused; who demand to be promptly improved, or encouraged, or frightened, or shocked or charmed, must run thus: My task which I am trying to achieve is, by the power of the written word, to make you hear, to make you feel—it is, before all, to make you *see*. That—and no more, and it is everything. If I succeed, you shall find there, according to your deserts, encouragement, consolation, fear, charm, all you demand—and, perhaps, also that glimpse of truth for which you have forgotten to ask.

You may think from all I say that the reason I write is to make the reader see what I see, and that writing fiction is primarily a missionary activity. Let me straighten this out.

Last spring I talked here, and one of the girls asked me, "Miss O'Connor, why do you write?" and I said, "Because I'm good at it," and at once I felt a considerable disapproval in the atmosphere. I felt that this was not thought by the majority to be a high-minded answer; but it was the only answer I could give. I had not been asked why I write the way I do, but why I write at all; and to that question there is only one legitimate answer.

There is no excuse for anyone to write fiction for public consumption unless he has been called to do so by the presence of a gift. It is the nature of fiction not to be good for much unless it is good in itself.

A gift of any kind is a considerable responsibility. It is a mystery in itself, something gratuitous and wholly undeserved, something whose real uses will probably always be hidden from us. Usually the artist has to suffer certain deprivations in order to use his gift with integrity. Art is a virtue of the practical intellect, and the practice of any virtue demands a certain asceticism and a very definite leaving-behind of the niggardly part of the ego. The writer has to judge himself with a stranger's eye and a stranger's severity. The prophet in him has to see the freak. No art is sunk in the self, but rather, in art the self becomes self-forgetful in order to meet the demands of the thing seen and the thing being made.

I think it is usually some form of self-inflation that destroys the free use of a gift. This may be the pride of the reformer or the theorist, or it may only be that simple-minded self-appreciation which uses its own sincerity as a standard of truth. If you have read the very vocal writers from San Francisco, you may have got the impression that the first thing you must do in order to be an artist is to loose yourself from the bonds of reason, and thereafter, anything that rolls off the top of your head will be of great value. Anyone's unrestrained feelings are considered worth listening to because they are unrestrained and because they are feelings.

St. Thomas called art "reason in making." This is a very cold and very beautiful definition, and if it is unpopular today, this is because reason has lost ground among us. As grace and nature have been separated, so imagination and reason have been separated, and this always means an end to art. The artist uses his reason to discover an answering reason in everything he sees. For him, to be reasonable is to find, in the object, in the situation, in the sequence, the spirit which makes it itself. This is not an easy or simple thing to do. It is to intrude upon the timeless, and that is only done by the violence of a single-minded respect for the truth.

It follows from all this that there is no technique that can be discovered and applied to make it possible for one to write. If you go to a school where there are classes in writing, these classes should not be to teach you how to write, but to teach you the limits and possibilities of words and the respect due them. One thing that is always with the writer—no matter how long he has written or how good he is—is the continuing process of learning how to write. As soon as the writer "learns to write," as soon as he knows what he is going to find, and discovers a way to say what he knew all along, or worse still, a way to say nothing, he is finished. If a writer is any good, what he makes will have its source in a realm much larger than that which his conscious mind can encompass and will always be a greater surprise to him than it can ever be to his reader.

I don't know which is worse—to have a bad teacher or no teacher at all. In any case, I believe the teacher's work should be largely negative. He can't put the gift into you, but if he finds it there, he can try to keep it from going in an obviously wrong direction. We can learn how not to write, but this is a discipline that does not simply concern writing itself but concerns the whole intellectual life. A mind cleared of false emotion and false sentiment and egocentricity is going to have at least those roadblocks removed from its path. If you don't think cheaply, then there at least won't be the quality of cheapness in your writing, even though you may not be able to write well. The teacher can try to weed out what is positively bad, and this should be the aim of the whole college. Any discipline can help your writing: logic, mathematics, theology, and of course and particularly drawing. Anything that helps you to see, anything that makes you look.

The writer should never be ashamed of staring. There is nothing that doesn't require his attention.

We hear a great deal of lamentation these days about writers having all taken themselves to the colleges and universities where they live decorously instead of going out and getting firsthand information about life. The fact is that anybody who has survived his childhood has enough information about life to last him the rest of his days. If you can't make something out of a little experience, you probably won't be able to make it out of a lot. The writer's business is to contemplate experience, not to be merged in it.

Everywhere I go I'm asked if I think the universities stifle writers. My opinion is that they don't stifle enough of them. There's many a best-seller that could have been prevented by a good teacher. The idea of being a writer attracts a good many shiftless people, those who are merely burdened with poetic feelings or afflicted with sensibility. Granville Hicks, in a recent review of James Jones' novel, quoted Jones as saying, "I was stationed at Hickham Field in Hawaii when I stumbled upon the works of Thomas Wolfe, and his home life seemed so similar to my own, his feelings about himself so similar to mine about myself, that I realized I had been a writer all my life without knowing it or having written." Mr. Hicks goes on to say that Wolfe did a great deal of damage of this sort but that Jones is a particularly appalling example.

Now in every writing class you find people who care nothing about writing, because they think they are already writers by virtue of some experience they've had. It is a fact that if, either by nature or training, these people can learn to write badly enough, they can make a great deal of money, and in a way it seems a shame to deny them this opportunity; but then, unless the college is a trade school, it still has its responsibility to truth, and I believe myself that these people should be stifled with all deliberate speed.

Presuming that the people left have some degree of talent, the question is what can be done for them in a writing class. I believe the teacher's work is largely negative, that it is largely a matter of saying "This doesn't work because . . ." or "This does work because . . ." The *because* is very important. The teacher can help you understand the nature of your medium, and he can guide you in your reading. I don't believe in classes where students criticize each other's manuscripts. Such criticism is generally composed in equal parts of ignorance, flattery, and spite. It's the blind leading the blind, and it can be dangerous. A teacher who tries to impose a way of writing on you can be dangerous too. Fortunately, most teachers I've known were too lazy to do this. In any case, you should beware of those who appear overenergetic.

In the last twenty years the colleges have been emphasizing creative writing to such an extent that you almost feel that any idiot with a nickel's worth of talent can emerge from a writing class able to write a competent story. In fact, so many people can now write competent stories that the short story as a medium is in danger of dying of competence. We want competence, but competence by itself is deadly. What is needed is the vision to go with it, and you do not get this from a writing class.

The Storyteller

John Berger

Now that he has gone down, I can hear his voice in the silence. It carries from one side of the valley to the other. He produces it effortlessly, and, like a yodel, it travels like a lasso. It turns to come back after it has attached the hearer to the shouter. It places the shouter at the centre. His cows respond to it as well as his dog. One evening two cows were missing after we had chained them all in the stable. He went and called. The second time he called the two cows answered from deep in the forest, and a few minutes later they were at the stable door, just as night fell.

The day before he went down, he brought the whole herd back from the valley at about two in the afternoon—shouting at the cows, and at me to open the stable doors. Muguet was about to calve—the two forefeet were already out. The only way to bring her back was to bring the whole herd back. His hands were trembling as he tied the rope round the forefeet. Two minutes pulling and the calf was out. He gave it to Muguet to lick. She moo-ed, making a sound a cow never makes on other occasions—not even when in pain. A high, penetrating, mad sound. A sound stronger than complaint, and more urgent than greeting. A little like an elephant trumpeting. He fetched the straw to bed the calf on. For him these moments are moments of triumph: moments of true gain: moments which unite the foxy, ambitious, hard, indefatigueable, 70 year old cattle-raiser with the universe which sourrounds him.

After working each morning we used to drink coffee together and he would talk about the village. He remembered the date and the day of the week of every disaster. He remembered the month of every marriage of which he had a story to tell. He could trace the family relations of his protagonists to their second cousins by marriage. From time to time I caught an expression in his eyes, a certain look of complicity. About what? About something we share despite the obvious differences Something that joins us together but is never directly referred to. Certainly not the little work I do for him. For a long time I puzzled over this. And suddenly I realised what it was. It was his recognition of our equal intelligence; we are both historians of our time. We both see how events fit together.

In that knowledge there is—for us—both pride and sadness. Which is why the expression I caught in his eyes was both bright and consoling. It was the look of one storyteller to another. I am writing on pages like these which he will not read. He sits in the corner of his kitchen, his dog fed, and sometimes he talks before he goes to bed. He goes to bed early after drinking his last cup of coffee for the day. I am seldom there and unless he were personally telling me the stories I wouldn't understand them because he speaks in patois. The complicity remains however.

I have never thought of writing as a profession. It is a solitary independent activity in which practice can never bestow seniority. Fortunately anyone can take up the activity. Whatever the motives, political or personal, which have led me to undertake to write something, the writing becomes, as soon as I begin, a struggle to give meaning to experience. Every profession has limits to its competence, but also its own territory. Writing, as I know it, has no territory of its own. The act of writing is nothing except the act of approaching the experience written about; just as, hopefully, the act of reading the written text is a comparable act of approach.

To approach experience, however, is not like approaching a house. Experience is indivisible and continuous, at least within a single lifetime and perhaps over many lifetimes. I never have the impression that my experience is entirely my own, and it often seems to me that it preceded me. In any case experience folds upon itself, refers backwards and forwards to itself through the referents of hope and fear; and, by the use of metaphor which is at the origin of language, it is continually comparing like with unlike, what is small with what is large, what is near with what is distant. And so the act of approaching a given moment of experience involves both scrutiny (closeness) and the capacity to connect (distance). The movement of writing resembles that of a shuttlecock: repeatedly it approaches and withdraws, closes in and takes its distance. Unlike a shuttlecock, however, it is not fixed to a static frame. As the movement of writing repeats itself, its nearness to, its intimacy with the experience increases. Finally, if one is fortunate, meaning is the fruit of this intimacy.

For the old man, who talks, the meaning of his stories is more certain but no less mysterious. Indeed the mystery is more openly acknowledged. I will try to explain what I mean by that.

All villages tell stories. Stories of the past, even of the distant past. As I was walking in the mountains with another friend of 70 by the foot of a high cliff, he told me how a young girl had fallen to her death there, whilst haymaking on the alpage above. Was that before the war? I asked. In about 1800 (no misprint), he said. And stories of the very same day. Most of what happens during a day is recounted by somebody before the day ends. The stories are factual, based on observations or on an account given by somebody else. A combination of the sharpest observation of the daily recounting of the day's events and encounters, and of life-long mutual familiarities is what constitutes so-called village *gossip*. Sometimes there is a moral judgment implicit in the story, but this judgment—whether just or unjust—remains a detail: the story *as a whole* is told with some tolerance because it involves those with whom the storyteller and listener are going to go on living.

Very few stories are narrated either to idealise or condemn; rather they testify to the always slightly surprising range of the possible. Although concerned with everyday events, they are mystery stories. How is it that c who is so punctilious in his work, overturned his haycart? How is it that l is able to fleece her lover j of everything, and how is it that j, who normally gives nothing away to anybody, allows himself to be fleeced?

The story invites comment. Indeed it creates it, for even total silence is taken as a comment. The comments may be spiteful or bigoted, but, if so, they themselves will become a story and thus, in turn, become subject to comment. How is it that f never lets a single chance go by of damning her brother? More usually the comments, which add to the story, are intended and taken as the commentator's personal response—in the light of that story—to the riddle of existence. Each story allows everyone to define himself.

The function of these stories which are, in fact, close, oral, daily history, is to allow the whole village to define itself. The life of a village, as distinct from its physical and geographical attributes, is the sum of all the social and personal relationships existing within it, plus the social and economic relations—usually oppressive—which link the village to the rest of the world. But one could say something similar about the life of some large town. Even of some cities. What distinguishes the life of a village is that it is also *a living portrait of itself*: a communal portrait, in that everybody is portrayed and everybody portrays; and this is only possible if everybody knows everybody. As with the carvings on the capitols in a Romanesque church, there is an identity of spirit between what is shown and how it is shown—as if the portrayed were also the carvers. A village's portrait of itself is constructed, not out of stone, but out of words, spoken and remembered: out of opinions, stories, eye-witness reports, legends, comments and hearsay. And it is a continuous portrait; work on it never stops.

Until very recently the only material available to a village and its peasants for defining themselves, were their own spoken words. The village's portrait of itself was—apart from the physical achievements of their work—the only reflection of the meaning of their existence. Nothing and nobody else acknowledged such a meaning. Without such a portrait—and the "gossip" which is its raw material—the village would have been forced to doubt its own existence. Every story and every comment on the story which is a proof that the story has been *witnessed* contributes to the portrait, and confirms the existence of the village.

This continuous portrait, unlike most, is highly realistic, informal and unposed. Like everybody else, and perhaps more so, given the insecurity of their lives, peasants have a need for formality and this formality is expressed in ceremony and ritual, but as makers of their own communal portrait they are informal because this informality corresponds closer to the truth: the truth which ceremony and ritual can only partially control. All weddings are similar but every marriage is different. Death comes to everyone but one mourns alone. That is the truth.

In a village, the difference between what is known about a person and what is unknown is slight. There may be a number of well-guarded secrets but, in general, deceit is rare because impossible. Thus there is little inquisitiveness—in the prying sense of the term, for there is no great need for it. Inquisitiveness is the trait of the city *concierge* who can gain a little power or recognition by telling x what he doesn't know about y. In the village x already knows it. And thus too there is little performing: peasants do not *play roles* as urban characters do.

This is not because they are "simple" or more honest or without guile, it is simply because the space between what is unknown about a person and what is generally known—and this is the space for all performance—is too small. When peasants play, they play practical jokes. As when four men, one Sunday morning when the village was at mass, fetched all the wheelbarrows used for cleaning out the stables and lined them up outside the church porch so that as each man came out he was obliged to find his barrow and wheel it, he in his Sunday clothes, through the village street! This is why the village's continual portrait of itself is mordant, frank, sometimes exagerated but seldom idealised or hypocritical. And the significance of this is that hypocrisy and idealisation close questions, whereas realism leaves them open.

There are two forms of realism. Professional and traditional. Professional realism, as a method chosen by an artist or a writer like myself, is always consciously political; it aims to shatter an opaque part of the ruling ideology, whereby, normally, some aspect of reality is consistently distorted or denied. Traditional realism, always popular in its origins, is in a sense more scientific than political. Assuming a fund of empirical knowledge and experience, it poses the riddle of the unknown. How is it that . . .? Unlike science it can live without the answer. But its experience is too great to allow it to ignore the question.

Contrary to what is usually said, peasants are interested in the world beyond the village. Yet it is rare for a peasant to remain a peasant and be able to move. He has no choice of locality. His place was a given at the very moment of his conception. And so if he considers his village the centre of the world, it is not so much a question of parochialism as a phenomenological truth. His world has a centre (mine does not). He believes that what happens in the village is typical of human experience. This belief is only naive if one interprets it in technological or organisational terms. He interprets it in terms of the species *man*. What fascinates him is the typology of human characters in all their variations, and the common destiny of birth and death, shared by all. Thus the foreground of the village's living portrait of itself is extremely specific whilst the background consists of the most open, general, and never entirely answerable questions. Therein is the acknowledged mystery.

The old man knows that I know this as sharply as he does.

Advice to a Young Writer

Danilo Kiš

Cultivate the suspicion of reigning ideologies and princes.

Keep away from princes.

Do not soil your language with the jargon of ideologies.

Believe you are more powerful than generals, but do not use them as a measuring rod.

Do not believe you are weaker than generals, but do not use them as a measuring rod.

Do not believe in utopian projects other than those you yourself create.

Be equally proud to prince and populace.

Do not allow privileges gained by your literary craft to trouble your conscience.

Do not confuse the curse of your choice with class oppression.

Do not be obsessed by the urgency of history or believe in the metaphor of the train of history.

Do not therefore jump aboard the "train of history": it is merely a foolish metaphor.

Never forget: once you reach your goal, you miss all else.

Do not write articles about countries you have visited as a tourist; do not write articles: you are not a journalist.

Do not believe in statistics, figures, or public statements: reality is what the naked eye cannot see.

Do not visit factories, collective farms, or construction sites: progress is what the naked eye cannot see.

Keep your distance from economics, sociology, and psychoanalysis.

Do not pursue Eastern philosophies such as Zen Buddhism, etc.: you have better things to do.

Bear in mind that imagination is the sister of falsehood and therefore dangerous.

Do not team up with anyone: the writer stands alone.

Do not believe those who say that this is the worst of all possible worlds.

Do not believe in prophets: you are a prophet.

Do not be a prophet: your power is doubt.

Let your conscience rest easy: princes do not concern you, for you are a prince.

Let your conscience rest easy: miners do not concern you, for you are a miner.

Rest assured that what you failed to say in the daily press is not lost forever: it is compost.

Do not write on command.

Do not bet on the moment: you will regret it.

Do not bet on eternity: you will regret it.

Do not be content with your lot: only fools are content.

Do not be discontent with your lot: you are one of the chosen.

Do not seek moral justification for those guilty of betrayal.

Beware of "terrifying consistency."

Beware of false analogies.

Trust those who have paid dearly for their inconsistency.

Do not trust those who make others pay dearly for their inconsistency.

Do not argue that all values are relative: there is a hierarchy of values.

Accept princes' gifts, but impassively, and do nothing to deserve them.

Believe that the language in which you write is the best of all languages, for you have no other.

Believe that the language in which you write is the worst of all languages, though you have no other.

"So then because thou art lukewarm, and neither cold nor hot, I will spew thee out of my mouth" (Revelation 3:16).

Do not be servile: the prince will take you for his gatekeeper.

Do not be arrogant: you will be taken for the prince's gatekeeper.

Do not let anyone tell you that what you write has no "socially redeeming value."

Do not imagine that what you write has "socially redeeming value."

Do not imagine that you yourself are a useful member of society.

Do not let anyone tell you that you are a social parasite.

Believe that your sonnet is worth more than the speeches of politicians and princes.

Believe that your sonnet is worth less than the speeches of politicians and princes.

Have your own opinion about everything.

Do not give your opinion about everything.

Words cost you less than anything.

Your words are priceless.

Do not speak in the name of the nation: who are you to represent anyone but yourself!

Do not side with the opposition: you are below, not against.

Do not side with power and princes: you are above them.

Combat social injustice, but do not make a program of it.

Do not let the fight against social injustice divert you from your path.

Study the thought of others, then reject it.

Invent no political program or any program: your inventions are of the magma and chaos of the universe.

Beware of those who propose final solutions.

Do not be a minority writer.

Question any organization that claims you as its own.

Do not write for the "average reader": all readers are average.

Do not write for an elite that does not exist: you are the elite.

Do not think of death or forget that you are mortal.

Do not believe that writers are immortal: that is academic twaddle.

Do not be tragically serious: that is comic.

Do not play the clown: warlords are used to being amused.

Do not play the court jester.

Do not imagine that writers are "the conscience of humanity": you have seen too many scoundrels among them.

Do not let anyone tell you that you are a nobody: you have seen that warlords fear poets.

Do not die for an idea or encourage others to die.

Do not be a coward; scorn cowards.

Bear in mind that heroism exacts a high price.

Do not write for holidays and anniversaries.

Do not write eulogies: you will regret it.

Do not write funeral orations for national heroes: you will regret it.

If you cannot say the truth, say nothing.

Beware of half-truths.

Do not take part in general rejoicing.

Grant no favors to princes or warlords.

Seek no favors from princes or warlords.

Do not be tolerant out of good manners.

Do not force the truth on people: why argue with fools?

Do not accept the idea that we are all equally right in the end or that there is no accounting for tastes.

"If two interlocutors are wrong, it does not mean they are both right" (Karl Popper).

"Admitting someone else is right does not protect us from another danger: that of believing everyone is right" (Idem).

Do not argue with the ignorant about things they have first heard from you.

Have no mission.

Beware of people with missions.

Do not believe in "scientific thought."

Do not believe in intuition.

Beware of cynicism, your own included.

Beware of ideological platitudes and quotations.

Have the courage to call Aragon's poem in praise of the GPU* an abomination.

Do not seek extenuating circumstances for it.

---

*Predecessor of the KGB, the Soviet Secret Police.

Do not let anyone tell you that in the Sartre—Camus controversy both men were right.

Do not believe in automatic writing or "deliberate vagueness": your goal is clarity.

Reject all literary schools imposed upon you.

Should the term Socialist Realism come up, change the subject.

When asked about "the literature of commitment," keep your lips sealed: leave it to the academics.

Should anyone liken a concentration camp to a prison, tell him where to get off.

Should anyone tell you Kolyma was different from Auschwitz, tell him to go to hell.

Should anyone claim that Auschwitz killed lice not people, ditto.

Should anyone claim that it was all a matter of "historic necessity," ditto.

"Segui il carro e lascia dir la gente" (Dante).

1984

Mentors

Jay Parini

There may be deep psychological reasons for my obsession with mentors and mentoring, but they don't interest me. The fact remains that I've been much influenced by my friendships with Alastair Reid, Robert Penn Warren, and Gore Vidal. Their literary styles, approaches to the craft of writing, even their ways of being in the world, have framed my own development.

I met Alastair Reid in Scotland in 1970. I had first arrived in St. Andrews, an idyllic coastal town on the East Neuk of Fife, in 1968. It was the "home of golf," as their tourist brochures claim, but also the home of Scotland's most ancient university, founded in 1312. The medieval city walls are still, here and there, intact, and the university's granite towers dominate this town beside the North Sea. I spent seven years there, and I still dream about its cobbled byways, steamy pubs, and windswept vistas.

Hearing that I wanted to be a writer, a tutor of mine named Anne Wright said, "Ah, then you should meet Alastair Reid." She and Reid had been students together at St. Andrews in the forties, after the war. It was a heady time, with so many veterans (like Reid, who served in the Pacific with the Royal Navy) returning to student ranks. These men did not feel constrained by the in loco parentis mode characteristic of British higher education in those days, and this made for complex, combustuous relations between administrators and students. "Alastair was a cut-up in those days," Anne Wright recalled, no doubt understating the matter. "You will like him."

I telephoned, and he said to meet him at a pub, the now-defunct Central Tavern, in Market Street. I still remember how tremblingly I went to see him. I had never met a "real" writer. Already, I had checked his books—the slim volumes of idiosyncratic, pellucid, gorgeously musical verse, the collections of essays on travel and ideas—out of the university library. I had never encountered a prose manner like that before, so deeply personal in syntax, image centered, at times almost singing. The tone was so infinitely worldly wise, with a flicker of Celtic charm at every crucial turn. I knew at once that I wanted my poetry and prose to look like that.

Alastair sat at the bar, a man in his mid-forties with a broad ruddy face, big hands, and a whimsical grin. He sipped a pint of bitter with easy familiarity and smoked tobacco as though it were grass, sucking in, holding, then blowing out. His eyes turned on me like headlamps, and I was swept away.

I learned that Alastair lived with his young son, Jasper, at Pilmour Cottage, a house above the West Sands that overlooked the sea. It was nestled in a grove of tall oaks, where hundreds of sooty-winged rooks gathered—"my rookery," as he called it. The house was rented, and Alastair was spending a year or so in St. Andrews after being away for decades. After his graduation (in classics) from the university, he had gone to the United States, where he found a job teaching classics at Sarah Lawrence. After several years, his poems and prose pieces began to appear in *The New Yorker,* and he decided to live by his pen. In the early fifties, he bought a farm in Mallorca, where he apprenticed himself to Robert Graves and became the great man's amanuensis.

He told me about how he learned to write from Graves. He was set the task of bringing into rough English the *Lives of the Noble Caesars* by Suetonius. (Graves had acquired a commission for the translation from Penguin, one of an endless series of small literary tasks that brought in enough money to support his vast family.) At first, Alastair was vaguely offended. He, after all, knew how to write. But when he took his work to Graves, Alastair sat beside him with amazement, watching as weak adjectives disappeared, gathered into the trunks of sturdier nouns, as adverbs evaporated, as verbs grew stronger. He watched the swift hand of the master as he cut and pasted, drawing Alastair's syntax in tightly, as a father might lace a child's boot.

Alastair learned more than the details of a particular craft, although that would have been enough. He learned a way of living, of being, that involved, foremost, a dedication to the job of writing, a commitment to a kind of daily rhythm in which words are cast like a net, gathering and transforming "reality" in a web of prose or verse. He shadowed Graves each day, becoming familiar with his routines. Ever since, he has preferred houses by the sea, and a habit of writing near a kitchen, so that he can keep a pot of soup boiling while a poem or piece of prose boils on the desk nearby. Alastair has found cooking an appropriate analogue to writing: a way of bringing together disparate elements, subjecting them to the heat of imagination, letting them meld, set. The satisfactions of these arts are not dissimilar.

I took to visiting Alastair at Pilmour Cottage in the afternoons, pedaling out along the West Sands to his isolated house through what seemed like perpetual rain. A mug of tea was always waiting, and I would take my poem of the day from a damp rucksack and put it on his kitchen table. Between stirrings of soup, he would sit beside me and do what Graves did for him: add or chop a word, a phrase. Sometimes whole stanzas would disappear or get moved up or down. Once he crumpled a whole poem without a word. He said little. I watched and learned. (This way of teaching reminds me now of those traditional Japanese masters of calligraphy who teach by having a student simply repeat certain patterns, following their brush strokes exactly.)

My poems, not surprisingly, began to sound extremely like Alastair's. I knew this, of course, but it did not worry me. I knew that one day, if lucky, my voice would blend with his, would gradually separate and become distinct. This happens naturally. I think it took longer than I imagined it would, and I can still find myself—decades later—slipping into an Alastairian mode. Yet I don't mind. It's a worthy line, a verse heritage that includes within its folds the voices of Alastair's masters: Graves, Yeats, Hopkins, the anonymous Anglo-Saxon poets.

Alastair also guided my intellectual life. Though I have spent much of my life in the academy, I was never one who could learn from schools. The very idea of a syllabus and reading list put me off, and I always went out of my way to read only those books that were not required. I resisted the formal authority of the classroom and determined to go my own way. But I needed a model, an example of someone who had sought *his* own way and found it. I wanted to know what Alastair was reading, had read. And he obligingly turned me in the direction of certain poets and prose writers whom he admired. Quite literally, he introduced me to the two Latin American writers he was at that time busy translating: Jorge Luis Borges and Pablo Neruda. We met Neruda in London; it was only a year or so before he died of cancer, but the great spirit was there. Borges came to stay in St. Andrews, and my contacts with him—in Alastair's kitchen, mostly—were memorable. With Alastair's help, I made my way carefully through Borges's intricate metaphysical tales and through the poems of Neruda, whose greedy pleasure in the world's alphabet of sensations has been a perpetual light in one corner of my mind.

Alastair's way of being in the world is another matter. He is, as he likes to say, a cat person, moving without dog loyalty from house to house, country to country. His only permanent address since 1953 has been *The New Yorker,* and he has usually lived in other people's houses. The constrictions of conventional marriage have held no appeal for him. As he says in one poem, "Change is where I live." I find this admirable but terrifying. I quickly realized that my own instincts worked against Alastair's here and that I preferred a doglike existence: one house, one wife, a permanent landscape, which for me is always northern New England. But the cat person still calls to me, and— perhaps in obeisance to something I learned from Alastair—I can't resist my forays into the larger world. My wife, Devon, and I regularly go abroad, to Italy or England, where we rent a house for a month, a year, at a time. I entertain fantasies of villas in Mexico or Sicily. I too am drawn to the exhilaration of impermanence, though I retreat for daily life to my wood-frame farmhouse on a hill overlooking the Green Mountains. Unlike Alastair, I want it both ways—a mistake, perhaps.

Alastair embodies, for me, the Taoist way, although he would laugh at this notion. He lives in the moment, utterly, and does not excessively fear mutability. I often think of this verse from the *Tao te ching* as his credo:

Do not be concerned about your place in the world.
Accept misfortune as part of what it means to be human.

What does this mean, to not be concerned about your place?
It means to accept being nobody,
and not to overburden yourself with loss or gain.

What does it mean, to accept misfortune?
Bad luck is natural, part of what it means to have a body.
Without a body, there could be no misfortune.

Give in, with humility.
Then you will be trusted to look after the things of this world.
Consider the world a part of yourself.
Then you will truly love the things of this world.

Alastair has never cared to own things; in fact, most of his clothing is "portable property"—to borrow a phrase from *Great Expectations*. He finds the idea of landownership laughable. He moves lightly in the world, taking no more than he needs. He is attentive to everything, everyone. He listens better than anyone else: taking in what you say, teaching you how to use what you know. Everything in his life is absorbed into an ongoing narrative, and people like his company because he includes everyone in this process of making. No phrase or happening goes unattended, is left dangling; everything is sewn into the larger fabric of a day, a week. He has a childlike sense of play about him.

His dust-jacket note for *Passwords* (1964) best catches this sense of being in the world:

I saw the light in Scotland, and the sharp contrasts, rough and gentle, of its landscape and climate still haunt me strongly enough to keep me from returning. I left Scotland first during the war, when a spell at sea in the East gave me my first taste of strangeness and anonymity. Afterwards, following an irrelevant education, I crossed to the United States out of curiosity, and lived there off and on until the same curiosity propelled me back to Europe, to Spain in particular, which I discovered to be a cranky incarnation of the whole human paradox, joyful, harsh, loving and violent, all at once. I have lived peripherally in France, in Morocco, in Switzerland; the list I hope is not complete—a kind of wistful dissatisfaction keeps me on the move. I have been in and out of trouble; have taken great pleasure in games of all kinds, in friends, in children, in languages, in talking, in running water; and have tried above all to keep a clear eye. Although I am in love with the English language, I have no noticeable accent left. My passport says I am a writer, which has proved a useful cloak for my curiosity. Poems are for me the consequences of the odd epiphanies which from time to time miraculously happen. Prose I keep for a calmer, more reflective everyday attention to the world. I think I have always been a foreigner.

One hears the tone and manner of the man in the syntax, the subtle figuration, of the passage. One can learn a lot from someone like this, and I have. But it remains true of all mentoring relationships that one must take some things and discard others. Mere imitation never lasts. The point of mentoring is that one has an example to follow. One can temporarily "follow the brush," then— ideally, and quite mysteriously—find oneself alone, paradoxically bound to the mentor yet freed from him (even by him) as well.

The passage beyond the mentor relationship is rarely easy, and I found it particularly difficult in this first crucial relationship to move into a more adult form of friendship. It took many years, in fact, and had some difficult passages. Once, for example, we shared a flat in Puerto Rico together (in 1980) for several months. I was just beginning to move into the realm of the published author, and there were strange tensions in me that I took out, like a Prodigal Son, on my literary father. It led to some awkward scenes. But we ironed these tensions out over the next decade. I see Alastair regularly in various places (England, the Dominican Republic, New York, Vermont). Devon and our three boys have come to think of him as a member of the family, and—of course—he is.

I moved from St. Andrews to Hanover, New Hampshire, in the fall of 1975, taking a job at Dartmouth College. Robert Penn Warren had a summer house nearby, in West Wardsboro, Vermont. Before now, I had read only his most celebrated novel, *All the King's Men,* plus a handful of his poems, but I deeply liked what I'd read. After reading through his *New and Selected Poems* (1975) in 1976, two friends and I went to interview him for *New England Review,* and a friendship began that lasted until his death, at eighty-four, in 1989.

Warren had left his native South long ago, although it remained the setting for most of his fiction and much of his poetry. You do not leave the South, of course. It goes with you. But Warren had found a congenial home in New England, moving between a stone barn in Connecticut that he and his wife,

Eleanor Clark, had converted into a house soon after he began teaching at Yale in 1950 and a rustic house in Vermont, where he spent every summer and most winter holidays. Red (as he was called by his friends) and Eleanor invited me to their annual New Year's Eve bash that year, and the tradition continues to this day (carried on by Warren's children, Rosanna and Gabriel).

In my mid-twenties, I was looking for a way to marry teaching and writing. As a writer, I was trying to find a mode of working that allowed for the making of poems, critical essays, and novels. There were few models on the horizon for writers who moved easily between the empires of poetry and fiction, and these were mostly European. Goethe and Victor Hugo came to mind, as did Thomas Hardy and D. H. Lawrence. Beckett wrote just a little poetry but was able to write plays and poems with equal success. For the most part, writers stuck to one genre. I worried that a kind of hubris would bring me down, that I might not develop as a poet or novelist or critic if I kept trying to work in different genres.

What first attracted me to Warren was his example. I saw that he had managed to have a teaching career, to write poems seriously for many decades, and to continue to publish novels well into his seventh decade. He was an old-fashioned man of letters of a type now rare. I knew instinctively that I could learn from him, and I deliberately sought his company.

Fortunately, Red was an extremely accessible man. He and Eleanor actively liked the company of younger people, and it was easy to see them. Devon and I became a part of their regular circle, visiting them whenever they were in Vermont, sometimes venturing south to Connecticut. I always looked forward to these visits, as much for the tactile feel of their house as the good company.

Their place was buried deep in the woods behind Stratton, up an unmarked gravel drive. The house was many-angled and roomy with a huge stone fireplace in the living room and several decks and balconies. We had lunch on a screened-in porch above a deep-throated brook. Drinks, at sundown, were on another porch with mountain views. Dinners were held at a long country table, and the conversation ranged dizzyingly from politics to literature. (Eleanor had once been Trotsky's secretary, and she held her opinions firmly and defended them with rare force of conviction.) One did not speak lightly in their company.

Red and Eleanor each worked in separate "shacks" some distance from the house. Red's shack overlooked a cold pond in which he would swim each afternoon from late May through early September. It was amusing to watch him, a bathing cap drawn tightly over his ears, as he swam, using a peculiar crawl. "Swimming is a regular, boring activity, which makes it ideal for meditation," he told me. "Poems come to me when I swim or walk in the woods. Any form of regular repetitive exercise stimulates the unconscious mind." When he stepped from the water, he looked like some prehistoric monster, his skin loose, his face immensely craggy. He talked rapidly in a high-pitched voice in a barely comprehensible southern accent.

His rituals were important, part of his creative life. These involved getting up early, a round of exercise (lifting weights, even into his eighties), a small breakfast, then several hours of isolation and work before lunch at one. Lunch always began with a glass of sherry on ice, which in summers he often took at the pond. The meal itself was convivial, informal. He usually had a rest after lunch, a solid nap, then a long walk in the woods or a swim, sometimes both. Late afternoon was "a good time for revision," Red told me. He would retreat to his shack for an hour or so before cocktails. Dinner was late, at seven, and—when he had visitors—a visit was always paid to the musty well-stocked wine cellar. Red enjoyed conversation, and dinners would stretch to eleven or so, with long stories by Red about the Old South. He had a perfect memory for Civil War battles and historical details in general. I remember one evening when the conversation (mostly a monologue by Red) ranged from Julius Caesar to Napoleon to Jefferson Davis.

After dinner, I would sit by Red on the ancient yellow couch in the living room and quiz him about the past. I wanted to hear about the Fugitives, the school of poets he once belonged to at Vanderbilt in the twenties. He had known so many writers well: John Crowe Ransom, Randall Jarrell, Allen Tate, Katherine Anne Porter, Eudora Welty, Saul Bellow, on and on. His was a lucky life, with friends galore, with good conversation usually at his elbows. He often repeated himself, but I was glad to hear his stories again and again.

Red was unstinting when it came to advice about writing. I once asked him if writing poetry, then turning to fiction, had posed any problems. "Poetry is the great schoolhouse for fiction," he said. "Think of Hemingway, Faulkner,

Fitzgerald—they all began as poets. Most writers do. Some keep at it, like Lawrence, and the poetry keeps the fiction fresh, supplies details, images, metaphors." He had turned to fiction, he said, "because there is so much pleasure in narrative, in making a whole world." He claimed to have "five or six novels complete" in his head, "if only there were time, and energy." At seventy-five, he had reluctantly abandoned fiction. "I'd be trying to write a novel and the poems kept creeping up in the margins. I couldn't avoid them." In this he resembled Thomas Hardy, one of his great loves. "Hardy gave himself over to poetry in the end," Red said. "But he was a poet in the novels too." In his last years, Red would often reread his favorite writers: Hardy, Eliot, and Shakespeare. "At a certain age, you return to old familiar texts," he told me. "And you see things in them you hadn't noticed or weren't ready to notice."

Red would read my poetry and fiction and make detailed suggestions, offering encouragement and suggesting directions. He urged me to keep a broad view. "It's easy to get lost in details," he said, "but a writer has to think about the shape of his work as a whole—that has to stay at the back of the mind." He also urged me to keep the audience in mind. "Readers are very precious," he said, "and you mustn't disappoint them." He argued that teaching kept one in touch with actual faces and voices. "Too many writers become isolated and lose that immediate relationship with people," he said. "It's lonely work, and the isolation is dangerous." Teaching, as long as it didn't cut too deeply into one's writing time, was an ideal way to maintain contact with a live audience.

Once, when I was going through a dreadful slump and unable to write well, he gave me an essential piece of advice: "Cultivate leisure. That's the best thing a writer can do for himself. Good work never comes from effort. It comes easily. If it doesn't, it isn't ready. Go for a walk, swim, read a book. Learn to wait." He explained that he, like me, was prone to overworking and that his imagination would become "ragged and thin." He said I should actively create an atmosphere of ease and leisure, "a space in your life where nothing special happens but where the ground is fertile, and seeds can take root." He suggested that "empty hours are like water on these seeds." When working, I should "hurry slowly." "It's important to feel the silences in a poem, in a paragraph of prose. Make the white space part of the line or sentence."

Red's manner with people was fetching. He was warm and encouraging to everyone, though one could intuit that he had a high standard. He behaved by the strictest codes of gentlemanliness and expected similar behavior. He never bad-mouthed anyone, although he could deflate pretensions with a wisecrack or sly aside. There was nothing even remotely narcissistic about him: his mind was directed at the world, and ideas were the meat at his table. He read poetry and fiction, history, and philosophy, but history continued to have a great pull on him, and one saw Gibbon and Momsen at his bedside table. "The truth of poetry is greater than the truth of history," he said, "but one depends upon the other. History is an invention that we can't do without. Without it, we'd be like the somebody who wakes up from a deep sleep and can't think where he was." He always refused to think of himself as a "historical novelist." "That phrase would cover just about anybody," he said. "If memory is involved, as it always is, then the work is 'historical.'"

The advent of literary theory in the late seventies and eighties was at times nettling. The New Critics were in bad odor, and Red was considered a founding member of that school. "There was no school," he insisted. "You couldn't possibly see much of a connection among the work of critics as diverse as Cleanth Brooks, [I. A.] Richards, Maynard Mack, [W. K.] Wimsatt, Louis Martz, and so many others. I suppose the one thing we had in common was a wish to look closely at a given text, but the deconstructionists do that, almost to a point of madness." He said that the notion that the New Critics wanted to divorce literature from life was nonsense. "I'm a biographer at heart. It's life that matters, and literature is a part of life."

I read Warren's later poetry with special interest. It was moving to witness a man of his stature as a poet confronting the end of life and using poetry as a way to get a grip on this experience. His poems were philosophical, deeply so, almost religious, if one thinks of religion in its root sense (*religio*), as an attempt to 'link back' to some infinite reservoir of power and being. Warren was able to focus his attention on language as the supreme source of knowledge in this later work, which began with *Audubon: A Vision* (1969) and continued through his final volume of *New and Selected Poems*. But the manner is fully present in *Audubon*, as when he asks: "What is love?" The answer comes: "Our name for it is knowledge." But this is heart knowledge, a kind of visceral understanding of the world's ruthless, dispassionate blend of truth and beauty. In *Audubon,* and successive volumes, one sees what Dave Smith has nicely called "the human need to prevail by witness."

Warren became, in effect, a relentless namer: of memories, experiences, natural objects. He looked around him with childlike wonder, seeing everything fresh. Again and again, he said to himself:

Think hard. Take a deep breath. As the thunder-clap
Dissolves into silence, your nostrils thrill to the

Stunned new electric tang of joy—or pain—like ammonia.

He had a strong desire to see things in their raw glory, including the self and its involvement with fate. As in *Audubon,* where narrator wishes

To wake in some dawn and see,
As though down a rifle barrel, lined up
Like sights, the self that was, the self that is, and there,
Far off but in range, completing that alignment, your fate.

There was something breathtaking about Warren's last push into language, in the nobility of his stance, in the brightness of those sunny particulars that crowd his poems. His language was, like the man, raw boned, expansive, talky, and occasionally nostalgic. He hurled big abstractions like Time and Fate and Knowledge around with abandon. This was ambitious poetry, reaching high for some combination of complete understanding and spiritual grace. Few poets ever try so hard or achieve so much.

Mentors are important in different ways. They can teach by the example of their life or their work or some mixture of the two. I think I got more from Red Warren than even I realized at the time. Some years after his death, I find myself circling back to him, to his work, repeatedly. And I hear his voice in my ear: "Cultivate leisure." I can actually see him, his broad-brimmed hat pulled low, a walking stick in his hand, following a trail through the woods near Stratton. We once stood together on a cliff, looking westward across several mountain ranges, and he said, "That's what we're here for, to look."

In 1985, I spent part of the academic year in Italy, in a small village on the Amalfi coast. Our villa, a white-baked house with colorful tile floors and vaulted ceilings, had a lovely rooftop terrace from which we could see the whole coastline from Salerno to Amalfi. On a clear day, the foothills of Calabria winked in the distance. Above us, through a dense lemon grove, was Ravello, and we could see a magnificent villa clinging to the cliff above. I asked my neighbor (the owner of a local bookstore) who lived there, imagining some Italian nobleman or captain of industry. "Gore Vidal," he said, "an American writer."

I told him I knew Vidal's work well and asked if he ever came down from his perch. "He comes every afternoon to my store to buy the English papers," I was told. I left a note saying that I hoped to meet him one day, if that was agreeable. I gave him my number, and that very evening the phone rang. "Come to dinner," the famously patrician voice said. "Tomorrow night would be fine."

Devon and I were awed by Vidal's villa, La Rondinaia, meaning Swallow's Nest. One walks from the center of a village piazza to a cliffside path with dazzling aerial views. At the end of a private walk, one encounters tall iron gates that are opened electronically from the house. Inside, the garden lures one forward through a walkway of cedars, past a dark blue swimming pool and cabana with a travertine deck, through a loggia, down steep stairs, along another narrow path to the villa itself, which is built into the side of the cliff on five levels, with countless balconies and terraces. "Welcome to the most beautiful view in the world," Gore said, with an undercurrent of irony that made it sound unpretentious.

We met Howard Austen, his companion since the late forties, and settled into the study for drinks. That first night stays in my head, the lively banter, severe politics, the vast social world of high-level Washington pols, Hollywood stars, and writers—all of whom Gore seemed to know intimately. Having come, like most people, from an ordinary background (I did, at the age of twelve, once meet the mayor of Scranton, Pennsylvania, in a hotel lobby), I was impressed and a little frightened but skeptical as well.

Any skepticism toward Gore soon vanished. Despite the glittering world into which he happened to be born, he actually lived in relative isolation. He and Howard were pretty much self-sufficient, and Gore spent most of his time reading and writing. How else would one get so many words down on paper?

By 1985, he had published some twenty novels, as well as a half-dozen books of essays. He had written several immensely popular plays for Broadway, a dozen or more screenplays for Hollywood, and countless original scripts for television. His fiercely sardonic commentaries appeared everywhere from *Esquire* to *The New York Review of Books*. "Work, work, work," Gore said to me. "That's my life. The rest is illusion."

I was taken by Gore's wit, of course, but also moved by his clear signals of friendship. Before long, we met almost every day at a local bar in Amalfi for a drink. We often had dinner together, usually at his place but sometimes at mine or in a restaurant. A friendship grew that has stretched far beyond that year on the Amalfi coast. We have, indeed, become close friends.

Gore's example as a writer is complex. As he has said, "The obvious danger for the writer is the matter of time." He quotes Goethe: "A talent is formed in stillness, a character in the stream of the world." Gore has managed, it seems, to achieve both, although most writers should probably be wary of appearing on television too often or running for public office. One should, however, remain engaged with the world on some level. Perhaps my generation, which came of age during the Vietnam War, takes this for granted.

I remember reading Vidal in college in *The New York Review of Books*. His radical politics were highly persuasive then, as now. Gore argues that the United States has only one party, the Party of Business. That is, the difference between Democrats and Republicans is laughably slight. (There is, for example, no real labor party in this country—something that Europeans find incomprehensible.) Our democracy is a partial affair, because politicians are essentially paid for (if not bought) by special interest groups. It should surprise nobody that less than half the eligible voters actually turn up at the polls; there is deep apathy, even cynicism, everywhere: a natural result of our monolithic politics. What keeps Gore's political analysis from being utterly depressing is the constant wit, as when he called Ronald Reagan "a triumph of the embalmer's art." The situation can't be so bad if it's so funny.

Writers do, in fact, have a responsibility to society. They should actively seek to represent the public conscience. Those who have language and analytical skills at their command have an obligation to use them. A democratic state can function fully only when its people have wide access to a healthy, complex, public discourse—a situation that has been sadly lacking in the United States, where the spectrum of opinion found in most mainstream periodicals is surprisingly narrow. "If I see a pothole in the road, I point to it," Gore once told me. He often alludes to Alfred North Whitehead, who said that one got to the essence of a culture not by looking at what is said but by looking at what is not said, the underlying assumptions of the society, too obvious to be stated. Truth—or some crucial aspect of truth—resides in those silences.

The private job of the writer is another matter, although even here one has responsibilities to what the Romans called the res publica, and to history—that "necessary angel of reality," as Wallace Stevens called it. Gore's work in the historical novel was, for me, a particular inspiration, and my third novel, *The Last Station* (1990)—a novel about Tolstoy—owes something to our conversations about his *Lincoln* (1984). He urged me to put Tolstoy at the still center of the novel and to revolve my characters around him as in a cubist painting. I did as he suggested, and it worked.

The problem with writing fiction that also trades in ideas is how to keep the reader's attention. I recall sitting by Gore's pool one summer and talking about a short story I was writing. I asked him if he thought it possible to hold the reader's attention while two characters discussed Kierkegaard for ten or twelve pages. Gore replied, with a barely restrained smirk: "Only if your characters are sitting in a railway car, and the reader knows there is a bomb under the seat." Now, I always try to keep that bomb under the seat. It's a sure way to create narrative compulsion.

Another tip from Gore that stays in my head concerns reviewing. One often hears that Vidal is the "best reviewer since Edmund Wilson." What is meant, I suppose, is that Gore writes engagingly about books and that he knows a lot. Once I was stuck with reviewing a book that, for reasons now happily forgotten, defeated me. I called Gore to complain, and he said, "Describe the book, that's your job." That advice returns to mind whenever I'm stuck with a difficult book. The work is to describe the textual object coolly and clearly; everything else follows from that.

Gore's reviews, or "bookchat," provide a good model for any novice reviewer. He often begins with a personal anecdote, one related to the subject at hand. His criticism has a vivid sense of the relation of literature to life. He is learned, but he wears this learning lightly. For instance, an essay on Barry Goldwater (*Rocking the Boat* [1962]) opens,

> Julius Caesar stood before a statue of Alexander the Great and wept, for Alexander at twenty-nine had conquered the world and at thirty-two was dead, while Caesar, a late starter of thirty-three, had not yet subverted even his own state. Pascal, contemplating this poignant scene, remarked rather sourly that he could forgive Alexander for wanting to own the earth because of his extreme youth, but Caesar was old enough to have known better.

The sweep of this is breathtaking, and it makes a point about worldly power that is useful throughout the piece.

Whereas Red Warren was, like me, a teacher as well as a writer, Gore is basically anti-academic. Whenever I feel mired in the academy, I call Gore for refreshment. His wit is always sobering. "Teaching has ruined more writers than alcohol," he once told me. "Beware of the scholar-squirrels," of "the hicks and hacks of academe." Having held a professorial job for two decades, I should take offense, but I don't. Gore is a satirist, and satire works by hyperbole. The ideal readers of Gore Vidal should have no personal attachments whatsoever. They should delight in seeing fun poked at anyone, especially those in power.

I was sitting with Gore one summer in the piazza of Ravello, drinking wine, as the cathedral threw a long shadow across the cobbled square. He recalled a visit he had made years before to a nursing home in Rome where George Santayana was living—the husk of the man, one should say. Gore admired the Spanish-born philosopher who had taught generations of Harvard students what aesthetics is all about. "I don't remember anything he said, not specifically, but there was something about him that had an effect," Gore said.

I knew exactly what he meant.

Mentors have an aura, an indefinable yet alluring presence that affects the person under their spell. I have been, to varying degrees, under the spell of Alastair Reid, Robert Penn Warren, and Gore Vidal. Their energies have charged me in different ways. I have benefited from their examples, sometimes defining myself against them. Their styles of writing, subjects, ideas, prejudices, fears, and fondnesses have played into my own. I have sometimes swayed from their headlamps, ducked. Other times, in a dark wood, I have looked for their glow at the edge of the forest; more often than not, it was there. My gratefulness to all three is boundless, and my admiration perpetual.

Create Dangerously: The Immigrant Artist at Work

Edwidge Danticat

On November 12, 1964, in Port-au-Prince, Haiti, a huge crowd gathered to witness an execution. The president of Haiti at that time was the dictator François "Papa Doc" Duvalier, who was seven years into what would be a fifteen-year term. On the day of the execution, he decreed that government offices be closed so that hundreds of state employees could be in the crowd. Schools were shut down and principals ordered to bring their students. Hundreds of people from outside the capital were bused in to watch.

The two men to be executed were Marcel Numa and Louis Drouin. Marcel Numa was a tall, dark-skinned twenty-one-year-old. He was from a family of coffee planters in a beautiful southern Haitian town called Jérémie, which is often dubbed the "city of poets." Numa had studied engineering at the Bronx Merchant Academy in New York and had worked for an American shipping company.

Louis Drouin, nicknamed Milou, was a thirty-one-year-old light-skinned man who was also from Jérémie. He had served in the U.S. army—at Fort Knox, and then at Fort Dix in New Jersey—and had studied finance before working for French, Swiss, and American banks in New York. Marcel Numa and Louis Drouin had been childhood friends in Jérémie.

The men had remained friends when they'd both moved to New York in the 1950s, after François Duvalier came to power. There they had joined a group called Jeune Haiti, or Young Haiti, and were two of thirteen Haitians who left the United States for Haiti in 1964 to engage in a guerrilla war that they hoped would eventually topple the Duvalier dictatorship.

The men of Jeune Haiti spent three months fighting in the hills and mountains of southern Haiti and eventually most of them died in battle. Marcel Numa was captured by members of Duvalier's army while he was shopping for food in an open market, dressed as a peasant. Louis Drouin was wounded in battle and asked his friends to leave him behind in the woods.

"According to our principles I should have committed suicide in that situation," Drouin reportedly declared in a final statement at his secret military trial. "Chandler and Guerdès [two other Jeune Haiti members] were wounded . . . the first one asked . . . his best friend to finish him off; the second committed suicide after destroying a case of ammunition and all the documents. That did not affect me. I reacted only after the disappearance of Marcel Numa, who had been sent to look for food and for some means of escape by sea. We were very close and our parents were friends."

After months of attempting to capture the men of Jeune Haiti and after imprisoning and murdering hundreds of their relatives, Papa Doc Duvalier wanted to make a spectacle of Numa and Drouin's deaths.

So on November 12, 1964, two pine poles are erected outside the national cemetery. A captive audience is gathered. Radio, print, and television journalists are summoned. Numa and Drouin are dressed in what on old black-and-white film seems to be the clothes in which they'd been captured—khakis for Drouin and a modest white shirt and denim-looking pants for Numa. They are both marched from the edge of the crowd toward the poles. Their hands are tied behind their backs by two of Duvalier's private henchmen, Tonton Macoutes in dark glasses and civilian dress. The Tonton Macoutes then tie the ropes around the men's biceps to bind them to the poles and keep them upright.

Numa, the taller and thinner of the two, stands erect, in perfect profile, barely leaning against the square piece of wood behind him. Drouin, who wears brow-line eyeglasses, looks down into the film camera that is taping his final moments. Drouin looks as though he is fighting back tears as he stands there, strapped to the pole, slightly slanted. Drouin's arms are shorter than

Numa's and the rope appears looser on Drouin. While Numa looks straight ahead, Drouin pushes his head back now and then to rest it on the pole.

Time is slightly compressed on the copy of the film I have and in some places the images skip. There is no sound. A large crowd stretches out far beyond the cement wall behind the bound Numa and Drouin. To the side is a balcony filled with schoolchildren. Some time elapses, it seems, as the schoolchildren and others mill around. The soldiers shift their guns from one hand to the other. Some audience members shield their faces from the sun by raising their hands to their foreheads. Some sit idly on a low stone wall.

A young white priest in a long robe walks out of the crowd with a prayer book in his hands. It seems that he is the person everyone has been waiting for. The priest says a few words to Drouin, who slides his body upward in a defiant pose. Drouin motions with his head toward his friend. The priest spends a little more time with Numa, who bobs his head as the priest speaks. If this is Numa's extreme unction, it is an abridged version.

The priest then returns to Drouin and is joined there by a stout Macoute in plain clothes and by two uniformed policemen, who lean in to listen to what the priest is saying to Drouin. It is possible that they are all offering Drouin some type of eye or face cover that he's refusing. Drouin shakes his head as if to say, let's get it over with. No blinders or hoods are placed on either man.

The firing squad, seven helmeted men in khaki military uniforms, stretch out their hands on either side of their bodies. They touch each other's shoulders to position and space themselves. The police and army move the crowd back, perhaps to keep them from being hit by ricocheted bullets. The members of the firing squad pick up their Springfield rifles, load their ammunition, and then place their weapons on their shoulders. Off screen someone probably shouts, "Fire!" and they do. Numa and Drouin's heads slump sideways at the same time, showing that the shots have hit home.

When the men's bodies slide down the poles, Numa's arms end up slightly above his shoulders and Drouin's below his. Their heads return to an upright position above their kneeling bodies, until a soldier in camouflage walks over and delivers the final coup de grace, after which their heads slump forward and their bodies slide further toward the bottom of the pole. Blood spills out of Numa's mouth. Drouin's glasses fall to the ground, pieces of blood and brain matter clouding the cracked lenses.

The next day, *Le Matin,* the country's national newspaper, described the stunned-looking crowd as "feverish, communicating in a mutual patriotic exaltation to curse adventurism and brigandage."

"The government pamphlets circulating in Port-au-Prince last week left little to the imagination," reported the November 27, 1964, edition of the American newsweekly *Time.* "'Dr. François Duvalier will fulfill his sacrosanct mission. He has crushed and will always crush the attempts of the opposition. Think well, renegades. Here is the fate awaiting you and your kind.'"

All artists, writers among them, have several stories—one might call them creation myths—that haunt and obsess them. This is one of mine. I don't even remember when I first heard about it. I feel as though I have always known it, having filled in the curiosity-driven details through photographs, newspaper and magazine articles, books, and films as I have gotten older.

Like many a creation myth, aside from its heartrending clash of life and death, homeland and exile, the execution of Marcel Numa and Louis Drouin involves a disobeyed directive from a higher authority and a brutal punishment as a result. If we think back to the biggest creation myth of all, the world's very first people, Adam and Eve, disobeyed the superior being that fashioned them out of chaos, defying God's order not to eat what must have been the world's most desirable apple. Adam and Eve were then banished from Eden, resulting in everything from our having to punch a clock to spending many long, painful hours giving birth.

The order given to Adam and Eve was not to eat the apple. Their ultimate punishment was banishment, exile from paradise. We, the storytellers of the world, ought to be more grateful than most that banishment, rather than execution, was chosen for Adam and Eve, for had they been executed, there would never have been another story told, no stories to pass on.

In his play *Caligula,* Albert Camus, from whom I borrow part of the title of this essay, has Caligula, the third Roman emperor, declare that it doesn't matter whether one is exiled or executed, but it is much more important that

Caligula has the power to choose. Even before they were executed, Marcel Numa and Louis Drouin had already been exiled. As young men, they had fled Haiti with their parents when Papa Doc Duvalier had come to power in 1957 and had immediately targeted for arrest all his detractors and resistors in the city of poets and elsewhere.

Marcel Numa and Louis Drouin had made new lives for themselves, becoming productive young immigrants in the United States. In addition to his army and finance experience, Louis Drouin was said to have been a good writer and the communications director of Jeune Haiti. In the United States, he contributed to a Haitian political journal called *Lambi*. Marcel Numa was from a family of writers. One of his male relatives, Nono Numa, had adapted the seventeenth-century French playwright Pierre Corneille's *Le Cid*, placing it in a Haitian setting. Many of the young men Numa and Drouin joined with to form Jeune Haiti had had fathers killed by Papa Doc Duvalier, and had returned, Le Cid and Hamlet-like, to revenge them.

Like most creation myths, this one too exists beyond the scope of my own life, yet it still feels present, even urgent. Marcel Numa and Louis Drouin were patriots who died so that other Haitians could live. They were also immigrants, like me. Yet, they had abandoned comfortable lives in the United States and sacrificed themselves for the homeland. One of the first things the despot Duvalier tried to take away from them was the mythic element of their stories. In the propaganda preceding their execution, he labeled them not Haitian, but foreign rebels, good-for-nothing *blans*.

At the time of the execution of Marcel Numa and Louis Drouin, my recently married, twenty-nine-year-old parents lived in Haiti, in a neighborhood called Bel Air, about a thirty-minute walk from the cemetery. Bel Air had a government-sponsored community center, a *centre d'étude*, where young men and women—but mostly young men—went to study in the evenings, especially if they had no electricity at home. Some of these young people— not my parents, but young people who studied at the center—belonged to a book club, a reading group sponsored by the Alliance Française, the French Institute. The book group was called Le Club de Bonne Humeur, or the Good Humor Club. At the time, Le Club de Bonne Humeur was reading Camus' play *Caligula* with an eye to possibly staging it.

In Camus' version of Caligula's life, when Caligula's sister, who is also his lover, dies, Caligula unleashes his rage and slowly unravels. In a preface to an English translation of the play, Camus wrote, "I look in vain for philosophy in these four acts. . . . I have little regard for an art that deliberately aims to shock because it is unable to convince."

After the executions of Marcel Numa and Louis Drouin, as the images of their deaths played over and over in cinemas and on state-run television, the young men and women of the Club de Bonne Humeur, along with the rest of Haiti, desperately needed art that could convince. They needed art that could convince them that they would not die the same way Numa and Drouin did. They needed to be convinced that words could still be spoken, that stories could still be told and passed on. So, as my father used to tell it, these young people donned white sheets as togas and they tried to stage Camus' play—quietly, quietly—in many of their houses, where they whispered lines like:

> Execution relieves and liberates. It is a universal tonic, just in precept as in practice. A man dies because he is guilty. A man is guilty because he is one of Caligula's subjects. Ergo all men are guilty and shall die. It is only a matter of time and patience.

The legend of the underground staging of this and other plays, clandestine readings of pieces of literature, was so strong that years after Papa Doc Duvalier died, every time there was a political murder in Bel Air, one of the young aspiring intellectuals in the neighborhood where I spent the first twelve years of my life might inevitably say that someone should put on a play. And because the uncle who raised me while my parents were in New York for two-thirds of the first twelve years of my life, because that uncle was a minister in Bel Air and had a church and school with some available space, occasionally some of these plays were read and staged, quietly, quietly, in the backyard of his church.

There were many recurrences of this story throughout the country, book and theater clubs secretly cherishing some potentially subversive piece of literature, families burying if not burning their entire libraries, books that might seem innocent but could easily betray them. Novels with the wrong titles. Treatises with the right titles and intentions. Strings of words that, uttered, written, or read, could cause a person's death. Sometimes these words were written by Haitian writers like Marie Vieux-Chauvet and René Depestre, among others. Other times they were written by foreign or *blan* writers, writers like Aimé Césaire, Frantz Fanon, or Albert Camus, who were untouchable because they were either not Haitian or already long dead. The fact that death prevented one from being banished—unlike, say, the English novelist Graham Greene, who was banned from Haiti after writing *The Comedians*—made the "classic" writers all the more appealing. Unlike the country's own citizens, these writers could neither be tortured or murdered themselves nor cause their family members to be tortured or murdered. And no matter how hard he tried, Papa Doc Duvalier could not make their words go away. Their maxims and phrases would keep coming back, buried deep in memories by the rote recitation techniques that the Haitian school system had taught so well. Because those writers who were still in Haiti, not yet exiled or killed, could not freely perform or print their own words outright, many of them turned, or returned, to the Greeks.

When it was a crime to pick up a bloodied body on the street, Haitian writers introduced Haitian readers to Sophocles' *Oedipus Rex* and *Antigone,* which had been rewritten in Creole and placed in Haitian settings by the playwright Franck Fouché and the poet Felix Morisseau Leroy. This is where these writers placed their bets, striking a dangerous balance between silence and art.

How do writers and readers find each other under such dangerous circumstances? Reading, like writing, under these conditions is disobedience to a directive in which the reader, our Eve, already knows the possible consequences of eating that apple but takes a bold bite anyway.

How does that reader find the courage to take this bite, open that book? After an arrest, an execution? Of course he or she may find it in the power of the hushed chorus of other readers, but she can also find it in the writer's courage in having stepped forward, in having written, or rewritten, in the first place.

Create dangerously, for people who read dangerously. This is what I've always thought it meant to be a writer. Writing, knowing in part that no matter how trivial your words may seem, someday, somewhere, someone may risk his or her life to read them. Coming from where I come from, with the history I have—having spent the first twelve years of my life under both dictatorships of Papa Doc and his son, Jean-Claude—this is what I've always seen as the unifying principle among all writers. This is what, among other things, might join Albert Camus and Sophocles to Toni Morrison, Alice Walker, Osip Mandelstam, and Ralph Waldo Emerson to Ralph Waldo Ellison. Somewhere, if not now, then maybe years in the future, a future that we may have yet to dream of, someone may risk his or her life to read us. Somewhere, if not now, then maybe years in the future, we may also save someone's life, because they have given us a passport, making us honorary citizens of their culture.

This is why when I wrote a book called *The Dew Breaker,* a book about a *choukèt lawoze,* or a Duvalier-era torturer, a book that is partly set in the period following the Numa and Drouin executions, I used an epigraph from a poem by Osip Mandelstam, who famously said, "Only in Russia is poetry respected—it gets people killed."

The quotation I used is:

Maybe this is the beginning of madness . . .
Forgive me for what I am saying.
Read it . . . quietly, quietly.

There are many possible interpretations of what it means to create dangerously, and Albert Camus, like the poet Osip Mandelstam, suggests that it is creating as a revolt against silence, creating when both the creation and the reception, the writing and the reading, are dangerous undertakings, disobedience to a directive.

This is a part of my story that I have always wanted to understand better: my family's brief encounters with the pleasures and dangers of reading. I am at a great deficit here because, aside from my much older cousin Maxo, there were not many fanatical readers in my family that I know of, much less people who would risk their lives over a book. Perhaps at a time when one could be shot so easily, assassinated so publicly, not reading or writing was a survival mechanism. Still, sprinkles of other readers' stories continue to intrigue and thrill me. Young men and women who worshipped Euripides and Voltaire,

George Sand and Colette and Haiti's own physician novelist, Jacques Stephen Alexis, who in April 1961, three years before Numa and Drouin were executed, had been ambushed and murdered trying to return from exile, some say, to help topple the Duvalier dictatorship.

No one in my family that I know of had witnessed Numa and Drouin's execution in person. Still they could not help, when it came up, talking about it, even if in the broadest of terms.

"It was a very tragic time," my mother now says.

"It was something that touched a generation," my minister uncle used to say.

They were patriots who died so the rest of us could live, is a line I borrowed from my father. My father was the one who, while lying on his deathbed in early 2005, first told me about the banned books and the plays. Only when he mentioned togas and Caesars, and an author with a name that sounds like *camion*, did I manage to find my way, among many other possible choices, to Camus' *Caligula*. I could be wrong about this too, making connections only I believe are there.

The only book my parents and uncle have read more than once is the Bible. I used to fear their reading my books, worried about disappointing them. My stories do not hold a candle to having lived under a dictatorship for most of your adult life, to having your neighbors disappear and not being able even to acknowledge it, to being forced to act as though these neighbors had never existed at all. Reading, and perhaps ultimately writing, is nothing like living in a place and time where two very young men are killed in a way that is treated like entertainment.

Mourir est beau, to die is beautiful, declares the Haitian national anthem. But writing could never attain that kind of beauty. Or could it? Writing is nothing like dying in, for, and possibly with, your country.

When I first started returning as a public person, as an "author," to Haiti, a place where people trace your failures and successes along family lines, I was often asked if there were any writers in my family. If there were, I do not know. But another thing that has always haunted and obsessed me is trying to write the things that have always haunted and obsessed those who came before me.

Bel Air, now a destitute and earthquake-ravaged slum overlooking Port-au-Prince harbor, was still a poor neighborhood when I was growing up there. But, along with ideological students, our neighborhood also had its intellectuals. The brilliant and compassionate Haitian novelist/poet/playwright/painter Frankétienne grew up in Bel Air, as did the younger novelist and poet Louis Phillipe Dalembert, who later left for Paris and then Rome. There was also Edner Day, a well-known Macoute, who tried to court one of my young cousins, who tried to court everyone's young cousins. He seemed literary for no other reason than that he was sometimes seen in the afternoons sitting on his balcony reading. But he was also a rumored murderer, one of those who may have shot Numa and Drouin.

In "Create Dangerously," Camus writes: "Art cannot be a monologue. We are on the high seas. The artist, like everyone else, must bend to his oar, without dying if possible." In many ways, Numa and Drouin shared the destiny of many Haitian artists, particularly that of the physician-novelist Jacques Stephen Alexis, who wrote such beautiful prose that the first time I read his description of freshly baked bread, I raised the book closer to my nose to sniff it. Perhaps there are no writers in my family because they were too busy trying to find bread. Perhaps there are no writers in my family because they were not allowed to or could barely afford to attend a decrepit village school as children. Perhaps there are no artists in my family because they were silenced by the brutal directives of one dictatorship, or one natural disaster, after another. Perhaps, just as Alice Walker writes of her own forebears in her essay "In Search of Our Mother's Gardens," my blood ancestors—unlike my literary ancestors—were so weather-beaten, terror-stricken, and maimed that they were stifled. As a result, those who somehow managed to create became, in my view, martyrs and saints.

"Instead of being perceived as whole persons," wrote Walker, "their bodies became shrines: what was thought to be their minds became temples suitable for worship. These crazy 'Saints' stared out at the world, wildly, like lunatics—or quietly, like suicides; and the 'God' that was in their gaze was as mute as a great stone."

Of course I could be completely off base. Bel Air's Frankétienne, among others, somehow managed to remain human and alive in Haiti, before, during, and after the Duvalier dictatorship, producing a massive and innovative body of work. Balancing on the metaphorical high seas and bending to their oars without dying is what the majority of Haitians have always done, generation after generation. This legacy of resilience and survival is what had inspired Jacques Stephen Alexis, Marcel Numa and Louis Drouin, and so many others to sacrifice their lives. Their death is possibly among the shocking incidents that eventually motivated so many others, like my parents, for example, to leave. This maybe one of the reasons I live in the United States of America today, writing in this language that is not mine. This could possibly be why I am an immigrant and hopefully an artist, an immigrant artist at work. Even though there is probably no such thing as an immigrant artist in this globalized age, when Algeria and Haiti and even ancient Greece and Egypt are only a virtual visit away. Even without globalization, the writer bound to the reader, under diabolic, or even joyful, circumstances inevitably becomes a loyal citizen of the country of his readers.

My friend the Haitian novelist Dany Laferrière, who was a newspaper journalist during the Duvalier regime and was forced to leave for Canada during the dictatorship, has published a novel called *Je suis un écrivain japonais,* or *I Am a Japanese Writer.* In the book, the fictional author, a stand-in for Dany Laferrière, explains his decision to call himself a Japanese writer, concurring with the French literary critic Roland Barthes that "a text's unity lies not in its origin but in its destination."

> "I am surprised," the fictional Laferrière writes,
>
> to see how much attention is paid to a writer's origins. . . . I repatriated, without giving it a second thought, all the writers I read as a young man. Flaubert, Goethe, Whitman, Shakespeare, Lope de Vega, Cervantes, Kipling, Senghor, Césaire, Roumain, Amado, Diderot, they all lived in the same village that I did. Otherwise, what were they doing in my room? When, years later I myself became a writer and was asked, "Are you a Haitian writer, a Caribbean writer or a Francophone writer?" I would always answer that I took the nationality of my reader, which means that when a Japanese reader reads my books, I immediately become a Japanese writer.

Is there such a thing as an immigrant reader? he wonders.

I too sometimes wonder if in the intimate, both solitary and solidary, union between writers and readers a border can really exist. Is there a border between Antigone's desire to bury her brother and the Haitian mother of 1964 who desperately wants to take her dead son's body out of the street to give him a proper burial, knowing that if she does this she too may die? So perhaps after those executions when those young men and women were reading *Caligula*, Albert Camus became a Haitian writer. When they were reading *Oedipus Rex* and *Antigone*, Sophocles too became a Haitian writer.

"We, as we read," Ralph Waldo Emerson wrote in an essay on history, "must become Greeks, Romans, Turks, priest and king, martyr and executioner; must fasten these images to some reality in our secret experience, or we shall learn nothing rightly."

The nomad or immigrant who learns something rightly must always ponder travel and movement, just as the grief-stricken must inevitably ponder death. As does the artist who comes from a culture that is as much about harnessing life—joyous, jubilant, resilient life—as it is about avoiding death. Since he'd fashioned his dress and persona—a black suit and hat, nasal voice, and glasses—after Baron Samedi, the Vodou guardian spirit of the cemetery, François Duvalier should have known better than anyone that in Haiti people never really die. This is, after all, a place where heroes who are burned at the stake are said to evaporate into a million fireflies, where widows and widowers are advised to wear their nightgowns and pajamas inside out and wear red undergarments to keep their dead spouses out of their beds at night. And where mothers are sometimes advised to wear red bras to keep their dead babies from coming back to nurse at their breasts. Like ancient Egyptians, we Haitians, when a catastrophic disaster does not prevent it, recite spells to launch our dead into the next world, all while keeping them close, building elaborate mausoleums for them in our backyards. In another country, in the cold, with no fireflies, no red underwear or backyard mausoleums, the artist immigrant, or immigrant artist, inevitably ponders the deaths that brought her here, along with the deaths that keep her here, the deaths from hunger and executions and cataclysmic devastation at home, the deaths from paralyzing chagrin in exile, and the other small, daily deaths in between.

The immigrant artist ponders death the way they did in Gabriel Garcia Márquez's Macondo, at the beginning of *One Hundred Years of Solitude*.

"We have still not had a death," Márquez's Colonel says. "A person does not belong to a place until someone is dead under the ground." And the Colonel's wife's reply might have been the same as many an immigrant artist's parents, guardian, or supporter: "If I have to die for the rest of you to stay here, then I will die."

The immigrant artist, to borrow from Toni Morrison's Nobel lecture knows what it is "to live at the edge of towns that cannot bear" our company, hamlets that need our labor but want our children banned from their schools, villages that want our sick shut out from their hospitals, big cities that want our elderly, after a lifetime of impossible labor, to pack up and go off somewhere else to die.

If I have to die for the rest of you to stay here, says the Colonel's wife, then I will die. Like her, the immigrant artist must quantify the price of the American dream in flesh and bone. All this while living with the more "regular" fears of any other artist. Do I know enough about where I've come from? Will I ever know enough about where I am? Even if somebody has died for me to stay here, will I ever truly belong?

Albert Camus once wrote that a person's creative work is nothing but a slow trek to rediscover, through the detours of art, those two or three images in whose presence his or her heart first opened. Over the years, I have tried to explore my two or three images in these rather simple essays. In each of these pieces, though, are several cities, a country, two independent republics in the same hemisphere, but obviously with different destines and goals in the world.

The immigrant artist shares with all other artists the desire to interpret and possibly remake his or her own world. So though we may not be creating as dangerously as our forebears—though we are not risking torture, beatings, execution, though exile does not threaten us into perpetual silence—still, while we are at work bodies are littering the streets somewhere. People are buried under rubble somewhere. Mass graves are being dug somewhere. Survivors are living in makeshift tent cities and refugee camps somewhere, shielding their heads from the rain, closing their eyes, covering their ears, to shut out the sounds of military "aid" helicopters. And still, many are reading, and writing, quietly, quietly.

While I was "at work" at 4:53 p.m., on January 12, 2010, the ground was shaking and killing more than two hundred thousand people in a 7.0 magnitude earthquake in Haiti. And even before the first aftershock, people were calling me asking, "Edwidge, what are you going to do? When are you going back? Could you come on television or on the radio and tell us how you feel? Could you write us fifteen hundred words or less?"

Perhaps this is why the immigrant artist needs to feel that he or she is creating dangerously even though she is not scribbling on prison walls or counting the days until a fateful date with an executioner. Or a hurricane. Or an earthquake.

Self-doubt is probably one of the stages of acclimation in a new culture. It's a staple for most artists. As immigrant artists for whom so much has been sacrificed, so many dreams have been deferred, we already doubt so much. It might have been simpler, safer to have become the more helpful doctors, lawyers, engineers our parents wanted us to be. When our worlds are literally crumbling, we tell ourselves how right they may have been, our elders, about our passive careers as distant witnesses.

Who do we think we are?

We think we are people who risked not existing at all. People who might have had a mother and father killed, either by a government or by nature, even before we were born. Some of us think we are accidents of literacy.

I do.

We think we are people who might not have been able to go to school at all, who might never have learned to read and write. We think we are the children of people who have lived in the shadows for too long. We sometimes even think that we are like the ancient Egyptians, whose gods of death demanded documentation of worthiness and acceptance before allowing them entry into the next world. Might we also be a bit like the ancient Egyptians in the way of their artists and their art, the pyramid and coffin texts, tomb paintings, and hieroglyphic makers?

One of the many ways a sculptor of ancient Egypt was described was as "one who keeps things alive." Before pictures were drawn and amulets were carved for ancient Egyptians tombs, wealthy men and women had their slaves buried with them to keep them company in the next life. The artists who came up with these other types of memorial art, the art that could replace the dead bodies, may also have wanted to save lives. In the face of both external and internal destruction, we are still trying to create as dangerously as they, as though each piece of art were a stand-in for a life, a soul, a future. As the ancient Egyptian sculptors may have suspected, and as Marcel Numa and Louis Drouin surely must have believed, we have no other choice.

Full of It

Charles Baxter

Dear -------,

I am writing this letter to you from a cabin north of Duluth, Minnesota, on Lake Superior. On my left are high windows that face southeast, toward the ledge rock down by the water. I'm typing this letter at the dining room table, and I've positioned myself so that I can gaze out through the windows on the west side of the room. I can see several poplars, a stand of scrubby pines, and, between them and me, the snow that's been falling most of the morning. In the distance I can hear waves breaking on the rocks, and from inside the house, the sound of the water heater clicking on and off. It's quiet and peaceful.

Believe me, it has not always been this way. Writing, in my case, began with exhilaration, misery, and furor.

This time around, I had to travel a day-and-a-half to get to this place, and I lost a pair of reading glasses along the way. Being farsighted, I can't at this moment see clearly the words that I am writing and that are displayed on the laptop. They're almost completely blurred. I'm not even trying to read them. Instead, I am watching the pines and the snow while I type. It's a kind of daydreaming, soul-satisfying and extremely pleasant, like having the gift to be able to write music without having to hear it, except internally.

When I told a friend that I planned to come up here--to this cabin, on the lake, near the woods--for four days just to write, she said, with a pleasant laugh, "That's great. I envy you."

I had to think about this. I don't find it curious that some people should envy writers, but for the most part I think that people don't actually envy them very much (when they think about writers at all), and they probably envy them less now than they used to a few decades ago. People who have to do difficult or meaningless work often envy, with good reason, the life of the artist. Such a life can appear to be fulfilling and, in its way, luxurious. It can also look suspiciously like an escape from reality. As a compensating punishment, outsiders like to imagine the artist being plagued by poverty and unworldliness, which is what artists often have, and get.

Young musicians still starve, fledgling painters starve, writers starve. The idea that they're being self-indulgent and narcissistic is a common accusation, leveled against the would-be artist by friends, lovers, spouses, and family members. You don't often hear investment bankers being accused of self-indulgence, although, as a group, they are often noteworthy for that quality, but their indulgences sometimes make money, thereby exonerating them. The artist who fails, furthermore, has not beaten the odds, because the odds always favor failure and frequently justify the predictions. Fiction writers may have a gift, but they also have an affliction, and this affliction is not often noticed and not much discussed. You need to know about it, and I'll try to describe it, but I have to go out of my way to apologize first.

My trouble is that I don't really believe in most wisdom: not in this letter to you, not my own wisdom, not anybody's. As you must know by now, most "wisdom" is not wisdom. It's bullshit. Too often, what passes for wisdom is simply somebody's personal prejudice masquerading as truth. With good reason, young people often distrust wisdom from the old. They see the effort to justify past mistakes by replicating them in the young. Lars Gustafsson: "We take steps to justify the steps we have already taken . . . stubbornly, we stay on in the bad hotel to justify the fact that we were once stupid enough to check in there."

Most young people can't get away from this scene fast enough. True wisdom is somewhat private, while public wisdom tends to be irrelevant. Wisdom from the middle-aged and the old has a tendency nearly always to miss its mark, to strike the wrong tone (usually one of smug self-importance) and to become fatuous. The fraudulently wise are on stage, figures of comedy and menace, like Hamlet's uncle, Polonius. Audiences are often pleased to see Polonius get what they think he deserves--a knife in the heart.

That's why I'm having trouble writing to you. It's a problem in tone. I keep starting this letter and throwing it away (though, without my reading glasses, I can't find the trash icon). I think you should make your own mistakes, the way that I made mine. Why should you try to avoid failure, mistakes, heartbreak, sorrow, drunkenness, sexual confusion and apathy? I couldn't avoid them, you probably won't, and they will end up serving as resources for your writing. I managed to live through them, though I expect to see those bad friends again, some day.

I myself was both arrogant and insecure as a young writer; I think I must have been insufferable, thanks to my ignorance and knowingness--a dangerous combination, and quite inflammatory, though not all that unusual. Before William Faulkner became the William Faulkner we know, he was of course a young unfamous man, a "writer-about-to-be," to use Walter Abish's wonderful phrase. And what did the people in Faulkner's home town call this young unknown man with great writerly ambitions, who affected to stroll around town with a walking stick, like an aristocrat, or a Count? "Count No-Count," was the name they found for him.

They were the first harbingers of the Fraud Police, who will dog your heels for much of your life. I'll be talking more about those sinister patrolmen later.

Advice is almost as bad as wisdom, especially when it hasn't been asked for. If you've read Rilke's *Letters to a Young Poet,* you'll notice that Rilke takes his young writer-friend very seriously, so seriously, in fact, that Rilke's book achieves a kind of spiritual greatness of an odd sort, as if poetry and genius could be learned from a conduct-manual. At the same time, Rilke's book is almost entirely impractical. It teaches you nothing except how Rilke felt about being a poet. He is explaining to an ordinary person with an ambition to be a poet what it's like to be a genius, and he is pretending for appearance's sake that anyone can aspire to genius. Of course anyone can, but it'll wreck your life if you don't have the capacity for it, and it may wreck your life even if you do. But a life, Rilke might have said, may be a small price to pay for great poems. If you can give up your life for your country, why shouldn't you give it up for poetry? It's like a saint explaining to a house painter the steps to becoming a saint. It's not that the saint is wrong. He is, after all, a saint. (Rilke, after all, is Rilke.) The real problem is that only Rilke could be Rilke. Others have tried to be him, and naturally have failed. They can only succeed at being themselves.

The curse that The Great (like Rilke) leave behind is the curse of their absolutely unfollowable example. Their lives and their work cannot be replicated and they create a bizarre perspective when they seek to offer advice.

Like many other European artists of the early part of the twentieth century, Rilke thought of poetry as a calling, and of art generally as a redemptive spiritual project, though his poetry is never scrupulously clear about what form this redemption would actually take. Still, his message is straightforward: Poetry can save you. You must change your life. Americans, who are at heart pragmatic, have rarely believed that art can solve much of anything or redeem anyone. If you tell them, "Poetry can save you," they are likely to say, "From what?" But they do like to buy how-to books, and, in a general way, they like to be told how to do something. Because fiction is even less transcendent than poetry is, and is more remunerative, Americans, at least, seem to respect it, or used to. There are many how-to-write manuals on the bookstore shelves, most of them quite un-Rilkean and extremely practical. All the same, for fifty years, few people have seriously thought that the writing or reading of fiction is a sacred activity, or even much of an occupation, using the conventional yardsticks.

Nevertheless: here I am in this quiet house. I don't care if I am in a minority. I am writing these words to you, watching the snow fall, happy to think of myself as a writer, someone who has found a calling, and wondering: What can I say that will be of any use?

The first and last thing to say is, "I am happy, despite all my failures." And more: I am almost unbelievably lucky. But the point is not me at all. The point has to do with an art, and a condition.

The condition first.

Probably you are a great or a good noticer. You may well be the one in your family who paid attention to your family members more than the others did. You sometimes knew what they would say before they actually said it. When they were out of the room, their voices sounded in your inner ear. Quite possibly, you were good at imitating all of them. Sometimes, you felt like a spy: you were spying on the whole of life itself. This condition has its own kind of excitement and pathos, but it very clearly carries a feeling of tension, and estrangement. Without quite knowing how, you fell just a bit outside the groups of which you were a member.

And if you were like me, you often sat in the back of the class near the window, daydreaming. Much of the time, while you were observing the world, you yourself were in a fog. You were that fog. You hardly knew who you were. Sometimes you felt like everybody. You may have been very good at telling jokes and stories, keeping the other kids amused or interested for hours, but some part of you watched all this and watched how others were reacting to you. I'm not very good at telling jokes, but I do like to tell stories, and sometimes, in school, when I did so, my friends would say, "Baxter, you're full of it."

I was. I am.

Writers also have an early tendency toward funny and malicious gossip, but in this they are not particularly different from much of anyone else.

It's in the later years of adolescence that writers, as a group, begin to feel a particular affliction, which is also a gift (similarly, a musical gift is often accompanied by the maddening experience of constantly hearing music in one's head, a gift that can also feel like an affliction). This feeling, which I think is peculiar to writers and more specifically to fiction-writers, is that of feeling as if you are carrying a whole landscape of people around inside you. In one of Pynchon's novels this condition is described as "coming on like a whole roomful of people." You may not know who you are (my first book was titled *Chameleon*), but you often do know who these internalized people are, whose tantalizing stories are beginning to press out on you like something growing from the inside out, something extruded. You are full of it; you are full of them.

You are full of the possibility of characters and narrative.

I have not seen this condition described accurately much of anywhere. Kierkegaard, in *Repetition*, remarks on how quickly and how often young men, after falling in love with a woman, draw back slightly and find themselves becoming addicted to the experience they have just had of falling in love, which requires, not the continuation of love itself , but the repetition of the experience of falling-in-love, thus turning the object of love, the loved one, into a pretext, and the lover into a sort of addict. (Don Juan is an addict.) A sign of this, Kierkegaard says, is writing--usually love poems. Writers of fiction are a bit like that. They have fallen into the characters whom they have observed and imagined and loved. And the only way to get out of that feeling is to tell the story of that character. But it's not enough to tell one story. Because there are so many characters buried within the self, the only sensible activity is, to use Gertrude Stein's phrase, "telling it again and again." There is something in this process that resembles the dynamics of addiction. The practice of most arts is very hard to give up once you've started, and few people ever manage to stop doing it.

The young fiction writer--you--carries a burden of sorts. You are lugging something around that seems to be part of your being, but the only way to express it--almost literally, to bring it out--is to write it. What "it" is, in this case, is a piling-up of selves, of beings, and of stories that are being experienced from the inside. What is it like to be you, to be me? You can't answer that question by answering it discursively. You can only answer it by telling a story. That's not therapy. You're probably not sick. You're just a certain kind of human being. It's exactly like the necessity the musician has in humming a tune or playing a piano, or the necessity an artist has in doodling and sketching and drawing and painting. It's almost involuntary. Something needs to get out: Not expressed but extruded. As the composer Camille Saint-Saëns remarked, "I write music the way an apple tree produces apples."

You would feel this necessity even if the novel died, even if there were no audience for fiction (but there always will be), even if it seemed that you might never be published. You would feel the press of stories and characters outward from yourself toward the world, no matter what the conditions might be of publication and distribution. Other literature has simply inspired and inflamed you. In Henry James' words, you are "a reader who has been moved to emulation." It's as if you've been given instructions: Get it all down. The real question is what to do about it, this gift and affliction, how to organize your life so that the conditions of that life don't shape up as a full-fledged disaster. The size of a life-disaster is often proportional to the size of the ambition. Just because you hear the call doesn't mean that you are saved.

Women and men who have decided to be fiction-writers have a certain fanaticism. Sometimes this fanaticism is well-concealed, but more often it isn't. They--you--need it, to get you through the bad times and the long apprenticeship. Learning any craft alters the conditions of your being. Poets, like mathematicians, ripen early, but fiction-writers tend to take longer to get their world on paper because that world has to be observed in predatory detail and because the subtleties of plot, setting, tone and dialogue are, like the mechanics of brain surgery, so difficult to master. Fanaticism ignores current conditions (i.e., you are living in a garage, surviving on peanut butter sandwiches, and writing a Great Novel that no one, so far, has read, or wants to) in the hope of some condition that may arrive at a distant point in the future. Fanaticism and dedication and doggedness and stubbornness are your angels. They keep the demon of discouragement at bay. But, given the demands of the craft, it is no wonder that so many of its practitioners come out at the other end of the process as drunks, bullies, windbags, and assholes. The wonder is that any of them come out as decent human beings. But some do.

A writer's life is tricky to sustain. The debased romanticism that is sometimes associated with it--the sordid glamour of living in an attic, being a drunken oaf or a bully, getting into fistfights à la Bukowski--needs to be discarded, and fast.

I was a late starter, a painfully slow learner. I remember having a great idea for a story while riding a Minneapolis city bus at the age of thirteen. I was on fire with it. The idea was: An inmate of a mental hospital who thinks he is Christ *actually is Christ!* I thought this idea was so good that I was terrified that someone would steal it. I wanted to register this idea in the United States copyright office, though I didn't know how. I kept having ideas like this for years and would walk around in public with a sly, secretive smile on my face.

I first tried to write a novel at the age of twenty-two. I had only taken one creative writing class (insecurity, arrogance), and the single scene of this novel I can remember writing was one in which a man throws himself out of a window of a high-rise building. The man's fall is described in phantasmagoric detail. Everything in my writing was apocalyptic and cataclysmic.

Four years later, armed with an advanced degree and a job, I sat down in my free hours to write my first completed novel, *Ground Zero,* which you will never read because it has never been published and never will be. I think--I hope--no copy of it exists anymore. It was about a world in which everyone starts lying about everything all the time. Remember--in my defense--that this was the era of Johnson and Nixon and the war in Vietnam. I wrote this novel in a state of high excitement. I was exhilarated by almost every one of my sentences. I suspected I was a genius but was careful to keep this stupendous secret to myself. Angels and devils, truth and lying, ultimate realities all found their way into this book. A few people read it, most were mystified by it (I was mystified by their mystification--how could they not see how astoundingly good this book was?), and it found its way to a few editors, all of whom said it was interesting but that it was "not for us."

Undeterred, and now, by a set of bizarre circumstances, armed with an agent, I then sat down and for the next two years wrote my second novel, *Media Event,* which you have not read because it has never been published and never will be. It was about . . . oh, never mind. I wrote this book in a state of high excitement--once again, I was exhilarated by my sentences and by my visionary power. I sent it to the agent I had acquired by writing *Ground Zero* and waited for her excited, blubberingly enthusiastic phone call.

I waited and waited. Finally I decided to call her myself. It was a summer afternoon. In Minnesota, my mother was dying of emphysema and heart failure. I was hoping that I might have some good news for her. Here at home, my wife was pregnant, and we were, despite my job, flat broke. I had spent the last five years of my life trying to become a fiction-writer, to get a foothold. That afternoon, I was in the bedroom, sitting on the bed, and the sun was shining through the west-facing windows, and I was getting up my courage, steeling it, as people say, to the sticking-point.

After I dialed the agency's number, my agent, Julia, answered. I identified myself, and she said hi. There was a brief pause, an expressive air-pocket of dead silence. I explained to her that a friend, a writer who was a visiting professor at my university, had read my new novel manuscript and had said that it might be snapped up at Alfred A. Knopf, his own publisher. I asked what she thought its chances were there.

"Charlie," she said. "Don't you want to know what I think of your new novel? The one you just sent me?"

"Yes, Julie, of course I do."

There was another pause, and I heard her taking a breath. "I hate it," she said, with what seemed to be an odd satisfaction.

"You hate it?" My mouth had turned instantly to cotton.

"Yes, I hate it. Isn't that puzzling? I can't figure it out. How strange. Tell me why I hate it."

"What?"

"Tell me why I hate your novel."

"Julie," I said, trying to hold my head up while the room started to spin, "I have no idea why you hate my novel."

"Of course you do. Oh, sure, you must. You wrote it. Tell me why I hate it."

"I don't know," I said.

"Oh, you must. Please. Give it a try. Help me out here. Tell me why I hate your novel. Is it the characters? Is it the plot? I just don't get it. I don't get any of it. So," she said, cheerfully, "is that it? The whole thing? Is that why I hate your novel?"

That, almost word-for-word, is what she said to me up to that point, but I don't remember the rest of the conversation, except for the news that naturally she no longer wanted to represent me. I went into a sort of shock and can remember nothing else from the rest of the day.

Somewhat deterred by now, but still, after my recovery, brimming with guarded enthusiasm, I subsequently sat down, during those brief moments between child-care and class-preparations, to write my third novel, *In Hibernation,* which you have never read because it was never published . . . etc. Thanks to a new set of bizarre circumstances, I had acquired a different agent. When I finished *In Hibernation,* I gave it to my wife, who seemed unable to finish it. Nevertheless, I bravely sent it to my new agent, who called and told me with great tact and kindness, this time, that no one at the agency thought it was marketable; in other words, they would not be sending it out. I mailed a copy of the manuscript to a literary-minded friend on the West Coast--he's now a book reviewer there--who said to me over the phone a couple weeks later, "Charlie, maybe your imagination is poisoned right at the source."

The condition into which I fell is one that you may discover for yourself. I believed that I knew what I wanted to do with my life. However, I would not be allowed to do it in the way that I had imagined. People seemed to dislike what I produced and could not be persuaded to like it. I carried around within me stories that had, I thought, an aura to them. But these stories struck no chords in anyone else. No one heard the chords, and no one saw the aura. I thought I was reasonably smart. At least: smart enough. And reasonably talented. But none of it was working. I fell down very far into several intellectual and spiritual and emotional abysses, many of them interconnected. I could draw you a map. I felt as if my nerves had moved out to the surface of my skin; I felt humiliated and exposed. I think that, at this point in my life, only my wife and my child and my job kept me anchored to the world of the living.

I was close to being a menace to myself. I decided, among other resolutions, that I would never write another novel.

I also decided that I would never be a writer, in the sense in which that word is commonly used. What I thought was my calling probably wasn't my calling after all--that in fact I didn't have a calling except to be a decent human being, a teacher, a husband, and a father, if indeed I could manage that. I was in my early thirties by this time and felt that I had become an expert on failure and the day-to-day management of despair. Much of the time my mouth was full of ashes. I found that I had a new streak of verbal cruelty that I could not always control. I decided to write one last piece, on my particular subject, about a young man who fails to be a good musician and who becomes a critic instead. It was a story called "Harmony of the World," and I sent it to a local quarterly, *Michigan Quarterly Review*, expecting the usual rejection and scathing comments to which I was becoming accustomed.

A few weeks later I was watching TV in the basement when the phone rang. It was the editor of *Michigan Quarterly Review,* Laurence Goldstein. He told me that he had read my story; he was quite enthusiastic about it. And then he asked me a question. I sometimes remind him of this moment, because it struck me then, and strikes me now, as one of the kindest questions anyone has ever asked me, and because it suggested ever so slightly that I might be somebody, rather than the nobody I had constructed for myself and elaborately resigned myself to being.

"Who are you?" he inquired.

He was a stranger, and yet he asked as if the answer might be worth knowing.

For the next five years I wrote about failure. It had become my subject, my koan, my home base, my infinitely renewable resource. The abyss turned into a mineshaft. My first book, a collection of stories titled with nasty irony *Harmony of the World,* appeared in 1984. The book deals with the failure of characters to do successfully what they have set out to do. It's an interesting subject, though slightly un-American. By the time the book appeared, I was thirty-seven. After my sister-in-law read it, she asked me, over cocktails, "Why do you write about characters with such pathetic little lives?"

Because I know them, I said, or wanted to say. Besides, who are *your* people? These are my people. They're telling. In the title story, there is a character named Luther Stecker who asks the narrator, a pianist, why his playing makes him--Stecker--sick. Why, he asks, do I hate your playing? Tell me. Be courageous. Tell me why I hate your playing. (What I, as a writer, was doing in this story might be called "taking my demons out of the unemployment line and putting them to work.") Thank you, Julie, wherever you are, for your cruelty to me. Now I am an expert on cruelty. Couldn't have done it without you.

In my next book of stories, called *Through the Safety Net,* there is a story called "Media Event," and another story, called "Gryphon," in which an atmosphere of constant lying is created in a classroom, very much as it was in *Ground Zero,* and there is another story called "The Eleventh Floor," in which remnants of *In Hibernation* are visible. As my aunt used to say, "Nothing is ever gained or lost in the universe," and I suppose I had learned that lesson. *Through the Safety Net* is, in part, a massive salvage operation, in which a few moments are retrieved from my personal sunken scrapheap of failures.

It seems a shame to say so, but the hardest part of being a writer is learning how to survive the dark nights of the soul. There are many such nights, far too many, as you will discover. I hate to be the one to bring you this news, but someone should.

Part of the deal of having a soul at all includes the requirement that you go through several dark nights. No soul, no dark nights. But when they come, they have a surprisingly creepy power, and almost no one tells you how to deal with them. You can do illegal drugs or take psychoactive pills, you can have affairs or masturbate, you can watch movies 'til dawn, but that only produces what doctors call "symptomatic relief." In these nights you confront your own doubts, lack of self-confidence, the futility of what you are doing, and the various ways in which you fail to measure up. Feelings of inadequacy are the black-lung disease of writing. These are the nights during which the Fraud Police come to knock on your door.

Psychologists have their own name for this set of feelings. (They have clinical names for most of our emotions by now.) They call it "imposter-syndrome." Imposter-syndrome is endemic to the arts of writing because gifts--the clear evidence of talent--are not so clearly associated with writing as they are with music and graphic art. Not everyone has perfect pitch, not everyone can carry a tune, not everyone can draw or create an interesting representation of something on canvas. But almost every goddamn moron can write prose.

Furthermore, anyone's apprenticeship in the writing of fiction has several stages, at least one of which involves an imposture. To be a novelist or short story writer, you first have to pretend to be a novelist or a short story writer. By great imaginative daring, you start out as Count No-count. Everyone does. Everyone starts as a mere scribbler. Proust got his start as a pesky dandified social layabout with no recognizable talents except for making conversation and noticing everybody. So what do you do? You sit down and pretend to write a novel by actually trying to write one without knowing how to do it. (It is clearly not a rule-governed activity; there are only rules-of-thumb that sometimes work.) As you pretend to write your novel, you learn, if you're lucky, actually how to do it. You learn this intuitively. After you've learned how to do it, you proceed to write another novel, and, if you're lucky, it turns out to be a real novel.

The trouble is that the first stage--of pretending to be a writer--never quite disappears. And there is, in this art, no ultimate validation, again because it's not a rule-governed activity. The ultimate verdict never comes in. God tends to be silent in matters of art and literary criticism. Reviewers and editors who pretend to be God make fools of themselves. Besides, what's the yardstick? It's hard to make a lot of money from writing, and even if you did make a lot of money, what then? You might be labeled as a hack. No one asked you to do what you're doing, so you can't satisfy that person by doing it. You don't find out until much much later that you may have helped some people who have read your work. Reviews may eventually come, and they're good (or bad), and there are prizes, and you get them (or don't). When one of my novels was published, one reviewer said it was destined to be a classic, and another reviewer--Michael Upchurch (how could I forget?)--said the book was a clear sign of my incompetence as a novelist. Someone is always doing better than you are, someone is always being loved a little more, someone is always telling you that the work is not up to snuff, or that it shows incompetence, or a decline.

Compared to poets, however, you have one lucky break. If you write a novel or a book of short stories, most readers will say, "This novel is good (or bad)." They won't deny that at least you've written a novel. Fiction doesn't seem to have an essence in quite the way that poetry does. Having an essence changes everything. The terrible charge of total inauthenticity in the writing of poetry is commonplace as a result of this business of poetry's having an essence. That's why people are always saying, "That's a real poem," or "That's not poetry at all." They're talking about poetry as written material that has some almost indescribable core, a radiant gist. Someone who produces this essence is a poet, or a "real poet." Someone who writes verses but does not produce this essence used to be called a "poetaster." A poetaster is a fraudulent poet, a non-poet.

Luckily for us, there is no such thing as a prosetaster. No such word, at least in English. Because fiction has no essence, any novel that gets written up one way or another is, almost by default, a real novel.

Still, you can wake up at night and feel like a fraud. That probably happens to you now, before anyone has said your work is any good, and it will continue to happen, once you are published and are reviewed. The fraud-feeling is very mysterious and, for most of us, never quite goes away. Prozac and Xanax are sometimes prescribed to banish it. By contrast, bracing self-confidence among writers is a rare commodity and often a sign of psychic instability.

I recently saw Toni Morrison on national television. In front of a large audience, she was asked if she thought she was a great writer. She smiled and laughed, then nodded, and said, well, yes, but she had *always* thought that she was a great writer. Her laughter made the admission appear to be part of an outburst of great good humor, even gaiety, that the audience could share, as in an interview with a good-natured someone who admits that, yes, she won the lottery. It's just a fact. I won the lottery. Toni Morrison was admitting that, indeed, yes, she was Toni Morrison and was lucky and talented and a hard worker, and indeed a great writer, just as, in *Letters to a Young Poet*, Rilke eventually gets around to admitting that he is, indeed, Rilke. This feeling of artistic power--aesthetic triumphalism--seems to me to be increasingly rare in our time, but Toni Morrison has it, and it shows in her work.

Not in mine. The result of my early failures is that I find writing to be almost unimaginably difficult. I always suspect that I am about to make a terrible set of mistakes. Therefore, the writing comes slowly, when it comes at all. I'm not by any stretch of the imagination, *my* imagination, prolific. It's good to be confident, but a lack of self-confidence can be turned to your own purposes if it helps you to take pains, to take care, to avoid glibness. Thomas Mann said, "A writer is someone for whom writing is more difficult than it is for other people."

About four years ago I started to receive anonymous postcards signed "The New Philistine." Almost every time a new story of mine would appear somewhere in print, I'd get a postcard with a withering critical judgment about my efforts inscribed on it, signed by the anonymous Philistine, as he called himself. These cards were postmarked from Detroit. They were soon followed by copies of a 'zine, hand-published every few months, eponymously titled *The New Philistine*. Each issue contained attacks on my work and the work of my contemporaries. The attacks were rabid, funny, intelligent, unfair, wildly accurate and wildly inaccurate (one of the NP's theories was that Tama Janowitz had undergone a sex change of some sort--I was never clear about exactly what it was, or how), maniacal, vicious, crazed, full of spirit and lunacy and anger.

Stung and amused by the 'zines and the postcards, I discovered at the bottom of one of the issues a name and a phone number and an address. After all, the Philistine wanted subscribers. I called him. A man with a somewhat blank voice answered the phone.

"It's Charles Baxter," I said.

"Oh," he said dispiritedly. "It's you?"

"I'm calling because I have a question."

"What?"

"Why me?"

"Why not you?" he said.

"That's no answer."

"Okay. Why you? You personally? Well, because you write about Detroit without knowing anything about it, for one thing. I work there. My life would kill you. And you have all this power."

"That's ridiculous."

"No, it isn't."

We argued about that for a while. We hung up. But we ended up corresponding for a while, and I subscribed to his 'zine and gave him some money. He went on relentlessly attacking me and all my works, though other writers--Jay McInerney in particular--were abused more severely than I was. He wrote some wonderful nonfiction--one essay in particular about American ballparks--that appeared in other magazines, and which I nominated for *The Pushcart Prize Anthology*. He sent me part of his novel, which I read. It was terrible.

He was full of the Holy Spirit, crazed with writing and reading. He worked as a bartender on Cass Avenue, and his interior life resembled that of an eighteenth-century polemicist and pamphleteer at the end of his rope. After a while, he dropped out of sight. I haven't heard from him in years.

Native Americans thought that you couldn't own land, because land wasn't yours to own. Any talent, any gift, any art, can leave you. I've done my best to learn a craft, which is like acquiring a set of tools. And what power anyone can acquire, anyone can lose. Fiction writers don't necessarily get better as they get older. Frequently, they get worse.

You do what you can. You wait, in readiness. You try to be modest. You try not to destroy yourself with drugs and drink and sex and selfishness. You are grateful for what you get, knowing that it could be much, much worse.

It's still very quiet here, and it's still snowing, of course, and the waves are higher, and it's the next day, and as you know perfectly well, I lied to you: I have a second pair of glasses, and I have been watching these words, each letter and phrase, as they appeared on the screen, and I've been changing them and correcting them minute by minute, hour by hour, day by day, because that is who I am, and that is what I do.

Writing in the Cold: The First Ten Years

Ted Solotaroff

During the decade of editing *New American* (later *American*) *Review,* I was often struck by how many gifted young writers there were in America. They would arrive every month, three or four of them, accomplished or close to it, full of wit and panache or a steady power or a fine, quiet complexity. We tried to devote 25 percent of each issue to these new voices and seldom failed to meet the quota. Where are they all coming from? I'd ask myself, though more as an exclamation than a question. They came from everywhere: from Dixon, New Mexico and Seal Rock, Oregon, as well as Chicago and San Francisco, from English departments in community colleges as well as the big creative writing centers. They came amid the twelve hundred or so manuscripts we received each month. America in the late sixties and seventies appeared to be on a writing binge, and eugenics alone would seem to dictate that half of one percent of the writing population would be brilliant.

But what has happened to all that bright promise? When I look through the cumulative index of *NAR/AR,* I see that perhaps one fourth of our discoveries have gone on to have reasonably successful careers; about the same number still have marginal ones, part of the alternative literary community of the little magazines and small presses. And about half have disappeared, or at least their names are again as obscure to me as they were when they came from out of the blue. It's as though some sinister force were at work, a kind of literary population control mechanism that kills off the surplus talent we have been developing or causes it to wither slowly away.

Literary careers are difficult to speculate about. They are so individual, so subject to personal circumstances that are often hidden to the writer himself. Also, what is not hidden is likely to be held so secretly that even the editor who works closely with a writer knows little more about his or her sources of fertility and potency than anyone else does. And those writers who fail are even more inclined to draw a cover of silence or obfuscation over the reasons. Still, it's worth considering why some gifted writers have careers and others don't. It doesn't appear to be a matter of the talent itself—some of the most natural writers, the ones who seemed to shake their prose or poetry out of their sleeves, are among the disappeared. As far as I can tell, the decisive factor is durability. For the gifted writer, durability seems to be directly connected to how one deals with uncertainty, rejection, and disappointment, from within as well as from without, and how effectively one incorporates them into the creative process itself, particularly in the prolonged first stage of a career. In what follows, I'll be writing about fiction writers, the group I know best. But I don't imagine that poets, playwrights, essayists, will find much that is different from their experience.

The gifted young writer will say: I already know about rejection and uncertainty. I know what to expect. Let's get on to surviving. I have to reply: You know about them much as a new immigrant to Alaska knows about cold and ice and isolation. Also, if you come from an enlightened middle-class family that has supported your desire to become a writer and if you have starred in college and then in a graduate writing program, you are like someone who is immigrating from Florida.

Thirty years ago, when I came out of college and went off to become a writer, I expected to remain unknown and unrewarded for ten years or so. So did my few associates in this precarious enterprise. Indeed our low expectations were a measure of our high seriousness. We were hardly going to give ourselves less time and difficulty than our heroes—Joyce, Flaubert, et al.—gave themselves. Also it was such a dubious career that none of our families understood, much less supported, us. Nor were there any universities—except for two, Iowa and Stanford—that wanted us around once we'd gotten a B.A., except as prospective scholars. Not that we knew how to cope with the prolonged uncertainty, isolation, indifference, and likely poverty that faced us—who does until he has been through them?—but at least we expected their likelihood and even understood something of their necessity.

I don't find that our counterparts of the past decade or more are nearly as aware of the struggle to come, or have even begun to be emotionally and mentally prepared for it. As the products of postwar affluence and an undemanding literary education, most of them have very little experience with struggle of any kind. Also their expectations of a writer's life have been formed by the mass marketing and subsidization of culture and by the creative writing industry. Their career models are not, say, Henry Miller or William Faulkner but John Irving or Ann Beattie. Instead of the jazz musicians and painters of thirty years ago somehow making do, the other arts provide them with the model life-styles of rock stars and of the young princes of Soho. Instead of a Guggenheim or Yaddo residency far up the road, there is a whole array of public and private grants, colonies, writing fellowships, that seem just around the corner. And most of all, there is the prospect, no longer as immediate but still only a few significant publications away, of teaching, with its comfortable life and free time. As the poet William Matthews recently remarked, "What our students seem to mainly want to do is to become us, though they have no idea of what we've gone through."

I don't think one can understand the literary situation today without taking into account the one genuine revolutionary development in American letters during the second half of the century: the rise of the creative writing programs. At virtually one stroke we have solved the age-old problem of how literary men and women are to support themselves. Most fiction writers today mainly support themselves by teaching writing. To do so, they place themselves in an insulated and relatively static environment whose main population every year grows a year younger and whose beliefs, attitudes, and privileges become the principal reflection of the society at large. The campus writer also risks disturbing the secret chemistry of his gift by trying to communicate it in class as well as defusing and depersonalizing it in coping with student writing. Then, too, the peculiar institution of tenure prompts the younger writer to publish too quickly and the older one too little. It's no wonder that steady academic employment has done strange things to a number of literary careers and has tended to devitalize the relation between literature, particularly fiction, and society.

The graduate writing program is also a mixed blessing to career-minded young writers by starting them out under extremely favorable—that is to say, unreal—conditions. At a place like Johns Hopkins or Houston or Sarah Lawrence or the twenty or thirty others with prestigious programs, the chances are that several highly accomplished, even famous, writers will be reading a student's work, perhaps even John Barth or Donald Barthelme or Grace Paley. If he is genuinely talented, his work will be taken very seriously because his teachers need to feel that what they are doing for a living isn't entirely a waste of spirit. As well as a dazzling ally or even two, he will also have a responsive and usually supportive audience—the other writers in the program—and a small, intense milieu that envisions the good life as a literary career, particularly the model supplied by his teachers. And of course, he will have a structure of work habits provided by the workshops, degree requirements, and so forth.

For reasons that I shall come to, I think graduate writing programs are mostly wasted on the young. But at their best, they're often good correctives to undergraduate ones in giving the gifted a more realistic sense of where they stand among their peers (there are now three or four others in a class of fifteen), in guiding them in the direction of publishable writing, and in providing a certain amount of validation to a young writer's still green and shaky sense of identity. In general, these programs are a kind of greenhouse that enables certain talents to bloom, particularly those that produce straightforward, well-made stories, the kind that teach well in class, and, depending on the teacher, even certain eccentric ones, particularly those patterned on a prevailing fashion of postmodernism.

At the same time, the graduate writing program makes the next stage, that of being out there by oneself in the cold world, particularly chilling. Instead of a personal and enlightened response to her writing, the young writer now receives mostly rejection slips. Instead of standing out, she now finds herself among the anonymous masses. Instead of being in a literary community, she now has to rely on herself for stimulation, support, and discipline. Also she now has to fit writing into the interstices left by a full-time job or by parenting.

In short, her or his character as a writer will now be tested—and not for a year or two but much more likely for five or ten.

That's how long it generally takes for the gifted young fiction writer to find his way, to come into her own. The two fiction writers whose work appears to be the most admired and influential in the graduate writing programs just now are Bobbie Ann Mason and Raymond Carver. Mason spent some seven years writing an unpublished novel, and then story after story, sending each one to Roger Angell at *The New Yorker,* getting it back, writing another, until finally the twentieth one was accepted. In his essay "Fires," Carver tells about the decade of struggle to write the stories that grew out of his heavily burdened life of "working at crap jobs" and raising two children, until an editor, Gordon Lish, began to beckon from the tower of *Esquire.* (It would be another seven years before Carver's first book appeared.) Three novelists whose "arrival" I witnessed—Lynne Sharon Schwartz, Joan Chase, and Douglas Unger—were by then in their thirties and had already written at least one unpublished novel. My most recent find, Alan Hewat, the author of *Lady's Time* is in his early forties and has written two unpublished novels.

Why this long delay of recognition? Each of the above writers doesn't regard it now as a delay. All of them say the unpublished novel or novels shouldn't have been published. They were mainly part of a protracted effort to find a voice, a more or less individual and stable style which best uncovers and delivers the writer's material. This often requires a period of time for the self to mature and stabilize, particularly the part one writes from. The writer in his middle twenties is not that far removed from adolescence and its insecurities. Indeed the sensitivity he is trying to develop and discipline comes precisely from that side of himself that he likely tried to negate only a few years ago as freakish, unmanly, and unpopular. Hence the painful paradoxes of his new vocation: that his most vulnerable side is now his working one, the one that has to produce, the one that goes forth into the world and represents him; further, that from the side that had been the most uncertain, he must now find his particular clarity about how and why he and others live and his conviction about what is significant in their ways and days as well as in his own. If he is writing a novel, he must also develop a settled and sustainable moral point of view if its meaning is to cohere. And all this from a self that is likely to be rejected each time it looks for confirmation by sending out a manuscript.

The second difficulty is that the typical M.F.A. in creative writing has spent eighteen of his, say, twenty-five years in school. Thus he is likely to be still fairly limited in his grasp of how people live and feel and look at things other than in books and films, sources he still needs to sift out, and other than in his family and its particular culture, from which he is likely still rebelling in typical ways that lead to banal content. Throw in a few love affairs and friendships, a year or two of scattered work experience, perhaps a trip abroad, and his consciousness is still likely to be playing a very limited hand. (There appears to be a long-term psychosocial trend over the past fifty years or so in which each generation takes several years longer to mature: Many of the postwar generation of fiction writers, such as Mailer, Bellow, Styron, Baldwin, Bowles, Flannery O'Connor, Truman Capote, Updike, Roth, Reynolds Price, were highly developed by their mid to late twenties.) As often happens, a young writer's gift itself may fake him out of understanding his true situation by producing a few exceptional stories, part of a novel from the most deeply held experiences of his life. But except for these, he has only his share of the common life of his age, which he must learn to see and think about and depict in a complex and uncommon way. This takes much more time.

A young writer I know won a national award a few years ago for the best short story submitted by the various writing programs. It was one of a group of several remarkable stories that she published, almost all of them about members of her family, gray-collar people finely viewed in their contemporary perplexities from her observation post as the kid sister and the one who would leave. But almost nothing she wrote after that came near their standard; the new fiction was mostly about a difficult love affair that she was still too close to to write about with the same circumspection and touch as her family stories. After they were turned down, she was left low and dry; finally, she went to work reading for a film company and learning script development. Recently she sold an adaptation of one of her early stories, is writing another script, and is looking to take up fiction again. By the time she publishes her first collection, if she does, she'll be in her thirties too.

What she has been going through as a fiction writer is the crisis of rejection from both without and within, and more important from within. For writers are always sending themselves rejection letters, as the late George P. Elliot observed, to this sentence and that paragraph, to this initial characterization and that turn of the story, or, heartbreak time, to the story that has eluded months of tracking it, the hundred pages of a novel that has come to a dead stop.

The gifted young writer has to learn through adversity to separate rejection of one's work from self-rejection, and with respect to the latter, self-criticism (otherwise known as revision and what one might call re-envision) from self-distrust. For the inexperienced writer, a year or two of rejection or a major rejection—say, of a novel—can lead all too easily to self-distrust, and from there to a disabling distrust of the writing process itself. Anxious, depressed, defensive, the writer who is suffering this distrust, whether temporarily or chronically or terminally, gives up her most fundamental and enabling right: the right to write uncertainly, roughly, even badly. A garden in the early stage is not a pleasant or compelling place: it's a lot of arduous, messy, noisome work—digging up the hard ground, putting in the fertilizer, along with the seeds and seedlings. So with beginning a story or novel. The writer can't get her spadework done, can't lay in the bullshit from which something true can grow, can't set her imagination to seeding these dark and fecund places if she is worried about how comely her sentences are, how convincing her characters will be, how viable her plot. But the self-rejecting writer finds herself doing just that. Instead of going from task to task, she goes from creating to judging: from her mind to the typewriter to the wastebasket. In time, her mind forgoes the latter two stages and becomes a ruthless system of self-cancellation.

The longer this goes on, the more writing becomes not a process of planting and cultivating—or, perhaps more accurately, of mining and refining—but an issue of entitlement and prohibition. That is, what the writer sets down or merely thinks about must be so promising that her right to write is suddenly allowed again. But even if she hits upon an exciting first sentence or paragraph or even a whole opening development, just as surely as night follows day, the dull stuff returns, her uncertainty follows, and soon she is back in court again, testifying against herself. To stay in this state too long is to reach the dead end of narcissistic despair known as writer's block, in which one's vanity and guilt have so persecuted one's craft and imagination and so deprived them of their allies—heart, curiosity, will—that they have gone into exile and into the sanctuary of silence.

Unless he is a graphomaniac, the gifted writer is likely to be vulnerable to rejection from without and within, and how well he copes with them is likely to determine whether he has a genuine literary vocation or just a literary flair. To put the matter as directly as I can, rejection and uncertainty and disappointment are as much a part of a writer's life as snow and cold are of an Eskimo's: they are conditions one has to learn not only to live with but also to make use of.

The trouble with most talented first novels is that they lack a prolonged struggle with uncertainty. They typically keep as much as possible to the lived lines of the author's life, which provide the security of a certain factuality and probability but at the expense of depriving the imagination of its authority. Laden with unresolved conflicts, the voice is too insistent here, too vague there. Such a novel is also typically overstuffed and overwritten: the question of what belongs and what doesn't being too easily settled by leaving it in. The writer, particularly if he has some literary sophistication, may also try to quell uncertainty by allying himself with some current literary fashion. At the same time, the struggle with uncertainty may be here and there strongly engaged and won: The material rings true instead of derivatively, whether from experience or books; a power of understanding is abroad in the narrative, however intermittently. If there is enough earned truth and power, the manuscript is probably viable and its deadnesses are relatively detectable. The rest is mostly a matter of the writer's willingness to persist in his gift and its process and to put his ego aside.

This can take some very interesting and illuminating turns. Douglas Unger, whose first novel, *Leaving the Land,* was received with considerable acclaim in 1984, began writing it in 1976. He had already had a previous novel optioned by a major publisher, had rewritten it three times to meet his editor's reservations, only to have it finally rejected. "He literally threw the manuscript at me and told me to get out of his office. Since I didn't know what to do next, I didn't have an agent or anything, I enrolled at the Iowa Writers Workshop."

I met him there the following year when I used the opening section of his next novel to teach a workshop. It began with a young woman named Marge walking through a dusty farm town in the Dakotas, on her way to be fitted for a wedding dress by her prospective mother-in-law and barely able to put one foot after the other. It is just after World War II, in which her two brothers have been killed, and she has chosen the best of a bad lot of local men to help her father and herself to keep the farm going. Unger's writing was remarkably sensitive to the coarse and delicate weave of a farm girl's childhood and adolescence and to the pathos of her love life, in which her spunk and grace are manhandled by a series of misfits left behind by the war. At the same time, he wrote graphically about crops and farm machinery and the special misery of raising turkeys, and he brought the reader close to the local farmers' struggle with Nowell-Safebuy, a turkey-processing plant and part of a giant food trust that drives down their prices and wants their land. Marge's long reverie suddenly ends when a convoy of trucks transporting factory equipment rolls into town. In the midst of it is an attractive man in a snappy roadster. Sensing that her luck may have finally changed, she follows the newcomer into the local café. All in all, it was a terrific beginning.

About eighteen months later, Unger sent me the final manuscript. It was some seven hundred pages long. About one fifth was taken up by a separate story of German prisoners of war operating the turkey plant; the final third jumped ahead thirty years, to tell of the return of Marge's son to Nowell, which is now a ghost town, and then backed and filled. Along with its disconnected narrative line, the writing had grown strangely mock-allegorical and surreal in places, as though Unger's imagination had been invaded by an alien force, perhaps the fiction of Thomas Pynchon. Most disappointing of all, he seemed to have turned away from a story with a great deal of prospective meaning—the eradication of farmers and agrarian values by agribusiness—to make instead the postmodernist point of the pointlessness of it all. I wrote him a long letter, trying to itemize what had gone wrong, and ended by saying that I still felt there was a genuine novel buried inside this swollen one and hoped he would have the courage to find it. When he read the letter, Unger became so enraged he threw down the manuscript and began to jump on it, shouting, "But I've spent so much time on it already."

He didn't write anything for a year and a half. By then he was living on an unworked farm, owned by his wife's family, outside Bellingham, Washington, and had become a commercial fisherman. Then one night he woke up with the people he had written about on his mind, pulled out the manuscript, and began to reread it. His main reaction was a deep chagrin at the distortions he had made in telling their story. "I was running up against people every day who gave the lie to what I'd done to my characters. Then one day my wife's older sister turned up with one of her sons, to try to get the farm going again. I witnessed an incredible scene in which her will to revive the farm ran into his admission that he wanted nothing to do with it. This opened my eyes to the truth that the original version had gone off in the wrong direction. It was really about Marge's efforts all along—through her marriage, her staying in that forsaken community—to hold on to their land with the same tenacity her father had shown and pass it on to her son. Much of this material was already there, lying around undeveloped and untidy. In order to feel easy again, I had to rework it."

It took another three years to do so. I asked Unger what had sustained him, particularly in view of the crushing disappointment after revising his first novel. He told me that after he left Iowa City, he had spent some time in San Francisco with Raymond Carver, to whom he was related by marriage. "Anyone who knows Ray knows that you have to believe that if you write well you'll eventually get published. Also the one thing he kept saying to me was 'A good book is an honest one.' I knew that his whole career had been an effort to write honestly, so those words really sunk in. And they were just the ones I needed to hear. At Iowa I was so desperate to get published, some of the others already were or getting close, and I thought it would help if I put in a lot of postmodernist effects. Also, Barth and Barthelme and Pynchon were all the rage then and it was easy to be influenced by them."

He ended up with three novellas: Marge's early life culminating in her affair and marriage to the man in the roadster, who is the lawyer for the Safebuy Corporation and the farmers' immediate adversary; the prisoners-of-war story; Marge and her son twenty-five years later, her marriage long over, the farm and most of the area abandoned when the Safebuy scheme of "vertical ownership" fails, her life divided between the dying community and the bright lights of Belle Fourche, forty miles away, and her final effort to pass on the deed to her son, who can't wait to get away. A brave, sad, increasingly bleak wind of feeling blew through the final novella, joining it tonally as well as narratively to the first. Were they the buried novel? The prose of all three maintained the straightforward realism of the original opening, but Unger's style had grown diamond hard, with glints of light whichever way it turned. So the three were eminently publishable as they were. Unger decided to go for the novel and set to work revising the first and last to join them more securely together.

What enabled him to persist through all his rewriting and also to let one hundred fifty pages of very good writing go by the board? "By now I'd lost any egotistical involvement in the work. The book was coming together. I was very objective now, almost impersonally watching a process occurring. The book wanted to come together and I was the last person to stand in its way."

There are several morals for the gifted young writer to draw from this account. Perhaps the main one is that Unger needed a period of adversity and silence, not only to recover from my "litany of its flaws," as he put it, but also to reorient himself as a writer and to undo the damage that the frustrated false writer, who wanted to be fashionable and publish as soon as possible, had done to the uncertain true one who had started the project. Once that had been done, the characters, like rejected family or abused friends, began to return.

There is a theory, put forward by D. W. Winnicott and W. R. Fairbairn, that creativity is a mode of play which we do not only for its enjoyment but also to explore the interface of self and world and to make restitution for the damage we do to others and ourselves by our narcissism. The youth tuning up the family car, the man weeding his garden, the woman rewriting a description five times to get it right, are all involved, psychically speaking, in the same activity. Even more overtly was Unger's rewriting an act of restitution ("In order to feel easy again, I had to rework it") for the falsifications he had made about others, and for the harm he had done to his own craft and spirit.

Earlier I wrote of the time that the gifted young writer needs to strengthen and trust the self he writes out of. To put it another way, the struggle with rejection, uncertainty, and disappointment can help him to develop his main defense against the narcissism that prompts him to become a writer in the first place. Writing to a friend, Pushkin tells of reading a canto of *Eugene Onegin* that he had just composed, jumping from his chair, and proudly shouting, "Hey you Pushkin! Hey you son of a bitch!" Anyone who has written knows that feeling, but also knows how easily it can turn over into self-hatred, when the writing or the blank page reflects back one's limitations, failure, deadness. The writer's defense is his power of self-objectivity, his interest in otherness, and his faith in the process itself, which enables him to write on into the teeth of his doubts and then to improve it. In the scars of the struggle between the odd, sensitive side of the self that wants to write and the practical, socialized one that wants results, the gifted young writer is likely to find his true sense of vocation. Moreover, writing itself, if not misunderstood and abused, becomes a way of empowering the writing self. It converts diffuse anger and disappointment into deliberate and durable aggression, the writer's main source of energy. It converts sorrow and self-pity into empathy, the writer's main means of relating to otherness. Similarly, his wounded innocence turns into irony, his silliness into wit, his guilt into judgment, his oddness into originality, his perverseness into his stinger.

Because all this takes time, indeed most of a lifetime, to complete itself, the gifted young writer has to learn that his main task is to persist. This means he must be tough-minded about his fantasies of wealth, fame, and the love of beautiful women or men. However stimulating these motives may be for the social self, for the writing one who perforce needs to stay home and be alone they are trivial and misleading, for they are enacted mostly as fantasies that maintain the adolescent romance of a magically empowered ego that the writer must outgrow if he is to survive. And this is so even if the fantasies come true, and often enough, particularly if they come true. No writer rode these fantasies farther or more damagingly than Scott Fitzgerald did, but it was Fitzgerald who said that inside a novelist there has to be something of a peasant.

Rejection and uncertainty also teach the gifted writer to be firm, kind, and patient, a good parent to his gift if he is to persist in it. As he comes to realize, his gift is partly a skill that is better at some tasks than at others and partly a power that comes and goes. And even when it comes, it is often only partly functioning and its directives are only partly understood. This is why writing a first draft is like ice fishing and building an igloo, as well as like groping one's way into a pitch-dark room, or overhearing a faint conversation, or having prepared for a different exam, or telling a joke whose punch line you've forgotten. As someone said, one writes mainly to rewrite, for rewriting and revising are how one's mind comes to inhabit the material fully.

In its benign form, rewriting is a second, third, and *n*th chance to make something come right, to "fall graciously into place," in Lewis Hyde's phrase. But it is also the testing ground of the writer's conscience, on the one hand, and of his faith, on the other. One has to learn to respect the misgiving that says, This still doesn't ring true, still hasn't touched bottom, still hasn't delivered me. And this means to go back down into the mine again and poke around for the missing ore and find a place for it and let it work its will. Sometimes this may mean re-envisioning the entire work: that is, finding another central idea or image, a new star in the area of the former one to navigate by. Revision is mostly turning loose the editor in oneself, a caretaker who tinkers and straightens out and tidies up and has a steadier hand. At the same time, one must come to the truth of Valéry's remark that no work is ever finished, only at a certain point abandoned. One has to learn to recognize when that point has come from the feel of the work coming together once and for all and of the writing having to be what it is, more or less. For beyond that point, rewriting and revising can turn compulsive and malignant, devouring the vitality and integrity of what one has found to tell and say.

In sum, the gifted young writer needs to learn to trust the writing process itself and, beyond that, to love as well as hate it. For writing is not, of course, always stoop labor and second thoughts and struggling with one's tendency toward negation and despair and accepting one's limits and limitations. There are the exhilarations of finding that the way ahead has opened overnight, that the character who has been so elusive has suddenly walked into the room and started talking, that the figure has been weaving itself into the carpet. But if the gifted young writer persists in believing that for him the latter conditions should be the normal ones, otherwise known as "inspiration" or "natural talent," he will likely decide after a few years that he fatally lacks one or both or that he has developed a writer's block, and may well turn to a more sensible and less threatened mode of expression, such as teaching or editing or writing for one or the other of the media.

There appear to be better and worse ways to get through this long period of self-apprenticeship and to get the most out of it. Of the first novelists and story writers I've been involved with, virtually none of them were teaching writing, at least in a full-time way. Teaching offers the lure of relatively pleasant work and significant free time, but it comes with the snare of using and distorting much of the same energy that goes into writing and tends to fill the mind with the high examples of the models one teaches and the low ones of student work. Moreover, it tends to be insulating and distracting during the period when the young fiction writer should be as open as possible to a range of experience, for the sake of his character as well as his material. A job that makes use of another skill or talent and doesn't come home with one seems to work best over the long haul. It's also well, of course, to give as few hostages as possible to fortune.

What the gifted young writer most needs is time, lots of it. Bobbie Ann Mason says that when she is asked by writing students how to get published, she feels like saying, "Don't sweat it for twenty years or so. It takes experience at life before you really know what you're doing." She began writing fiction in 1971, after she got out of graduate school, and for the next five years or so wrote in a desultory way, finding it hard to get focused. In 1976 she finished a novel about a twelve-year-old girl growing up in western Kentucky who was addicted to Nancy Drew novels. "It took another two years before I began to find my true subject, which was to write about my roots and the kinds of people I'd known, but from a contemporary perspective. It mainly took a lot of living to get to that point. I'd come from such a sheltered and isolated background that I had to go through culture shock by living for years in the North to see the world of Mayfield, Kentucky, in a way I could write about as I was now—in a kind of exile. Also it took me until I was in my thirties to get enough detachment and objectivity to see that many of those people back home were going through culture shock too."

My own sense of things is that young fiction writers should disconnect the necessity to write fiction from what it is often confused with and by, the desire to publish it. This helps to keep one's mind where it belongs—on one's own work—and away from where it doesn't—on the market, which is next to useless, and on writers who are succeeding, which is discouraging. Comparisons with other writers should be inspiring; otherwise they're invidious. Bobbie Ann Mason says that "the writer I was most involved with was Nabokov. It was because he was a stylist and had a peculiar sensibility. In some ways, comparing myself to him is like comparing Willie Nelson to an opera singer, but I felt connected to him because he had the sensibility of an exile, was working with two opposing cultures, which made him peculiar, the same way I felt myself."

If there is no necessity to write fiction, then one should wait and in the meantime write other things. Keeping a journal with some depth to it is a good way to discover and strengthen one's natural style and the best way to talk to oneself about the real issues of one's experience. My other suggestion is to look for other opportunities to write and publish and thereby give one's talent some chance of gainful employment.

Thirty years ago there was a great fear of "selling out," of "prostituting your talent," etc. It was as though your talent was like a beautiful pure virgin whom the philistine world was waiting eagerly to seduce and corrupt. Literary mores no longer place as much stock in the hieratic model of the writer, which is just as well. Unless one is good at self-sacrifice, is endowed with an iron will and a genius-sized gift, it's likely to be a defeating thing to insist on producing Art or nothing.

If one of the primary projects of the gifted young writer is to begin to create a neutral zone between his social self and his literary one, so that the latter can live in peace for a while, it is also true that both need exercise and some degree of satisfaction and toughening. Many novelists-in-progress find it helpful to take their talent at least some of the time out of the rarefied and tenuous realm of literature and put it to work in the marketplace to try to earn some of its keep. Even hack writing has the benefit of putting serious writing into its proper perspective as a privilege rather than a burden. At a respectable professional level, writing for publication makes one into someone who writes rather than, in Robert Louis Stevenson's distinction, someone who wants to have written. Writing without publishing gets to be like loving someone from afar—delicious for fantasies but thin gruel for living. It produces in time what Milan Kundera, in other contexts, calls "the unbearable lightness of being." That is why, to my mind, a strongly written review, profile, piece of reportage in *The Village Voice* or *The Texas Monthly* or *Seattle Magazine* is worth three "Try us again"s from *The New Yorker*. The young writer needs whatever grounding in the vocation she can get. Once in print, her words detach themselves from the fluttering of the ego and become part of the actual world. Along with the reality of type, there is the energy that comes from publication: the "let's see what I can do next" feeling. Unger found that once he began revising his novel, his other cylinders kicked over and he was soon partly supporting himself by writing theater reviews for the local paper and developed a piece for the stage with his wife. The reality of getting paid is also good for one's work habits.

By the same token, the first years the writer is on his own are a good time to let his imagination off the leash and let it sniff and paw into other fields of writing. From journal writing it's only a small Kierkegaardian leap into the personal essay. It's also liberating to get away from term-paper type criticism and begin to try to write about other writers in the way that other writers do, as, say, Updike or Mailer or Sontag does. There is also the possibility of discovering that criticism or reportage or some other mode is for the time being more congenial than fiction. A young fiction writer I know had about come to the end of his rope when he had the wit to turn one of his stories into a one-act play and has been flying as a playwright ever since. Similarly, inside a functioning poet there is often a failed fiction writer. One of the most deforming aspects of American literary culture is the cult of the novel. Another is the decline of the concept of the man of letters, which less specialized times and less academicized literary cultures than ours took for granted. And still do in Europe, where a Graham Greene, a Robbe-Grillet, a Grass, a Kundera, write in three or four modes, depending upon the subject, the occasion, and the disposition of his well-balanced Muse. Even if he doesn't become a triple-threat writer, experimenting with other modes frees up energy and also helps to demystify the writer's vocation, which, like any other, is an ongoing practice rather than a higher state of being. This is particularly so for a prospective novelist. He must get over regarding his medium as a tinted mirror before doing so fakes him out completely. Auden puts it very well when he says that the novelist

> Must struggle out of his boyish gift and learn
> How to be plain and awkward, how to be
> One after whom none think it worth to turn.
> For to achieve his lightest wish, he must
> Become the whole of boredom, subject to
> Vulgar complaints like love, among the Just
> Be just, among the Filthy filthy too.

Hence he must learn to think of his medium as not a flattering mirror but a lens that he must grind and polish himself so that he can see more sharply and closely and powerfully.

Virtually all the fiction writers I've been speaking to about these matters fix the turning point in their writing lives in the period when the intrinsic interest of what they were doing began to take over and to generate a sense of necessity. This is not to say they first had to renounce the world and its painted stages. A little support and recognition from outside tends to go hand in hand with the recognition from within. This seems to be particularly true of women writers. As Lynne Sharon Schwartz explained, "Most women don't give themselves the freedom to pursue their dream. Being brought up a girl has meant just that." She began to write stories when she was seven and did so again during and after college but without taking the enterprise very seriously. "I'd get a letter from *The Paris Review* inviting me to submit other work and I'd think, That's nice, and then put it away in a drawer. Writing fiction was one of several dreams that probably wouldn't be realized." She married, had children, went back to graduate school, which somehow seemed permissible, perhaps because no one does much dreaming in graduate school. "I found, though, that I didn't want to write a dissertation when I got to that point. I just couldn't face the library part of it. Going down into the stacks seemed so alien to my real sources. About that time, a childhood friend who also was married and had children told me she had resolved to give herself five years to become a dance critic. It was the way she did it, putting everything else to the side: it was her fierce tenacity that inspired me. I gave up graduate school and started to write fiction again." "Wasn't it scary," I asked, "giving up something definite and practical for something so uncertain?" "Not really," she said. "Mainly, I felt that I was finally doing what I was intended to do."

Over the next few years she worked on a first novel, which went unpublished. "Just as well," she says, "but it got me an agent and some nice rejection letters, which was encouraging." In time she developed a small network of women fiction writers, published two stories in little magazines and then a satire on Watergate in *The New Republic*. "Doris Grumbach, who was then the literary editor, called me up to tell me and asked me who I was, where I'd been all this time. So I realized I might be someone after all."

Now, four books later, Lynne Schwartz looks back at these years and sees mainly herself at work. "I had to learn to write completely alone. There was no help, no other writer to emulate, no one's influence. It was too private for that. Once I got started I wanted the life of a writer so fiercely that nothing could stop me. I wanted the intensity, the sense of aliveness, that came from writing fiction. I'm still that way. My life is worth living when I've completed a good paragraph."

The development of this sense of necessity seems to be the rock-bottom basis for a career as a novelist. Whatever may feed it, whatever may impede it, finally come to be subsidiary to the simple imperative of being at work. At this point, writing fiction has become one's way, in the religious sense of the term. Not that there are any guarantees that it will continue to be for good or that it will make your inner life easier to bear. The life of published fiction writers is most often the exchange of one level of rejection, uncertainty, and disappointment for another, and to go on means to rely upon the same imperilled and durable trust in the process and the self that got them published in the first place.

The Older Writer in the Underworld

Julia Alvarez

1

At difficult times in my writing life, I tell myself certain stories to remind myself of things I mustn't forget, information which can only be encoded in story form or it won't get where it's going. That place I used to call the heart, and which I now call my soul, the heart you earn as you grow old.

As a younger writer, the story I repeated over and over to myself was that of Scheherazade in the sultan's court. She was fresh out of her apprenticeship, years spent learning stories in her father's library. Now it was time to prove herself by saving her life (Earning a livelihood seemed equivalent at the time) and the lives of other women in the kingdom (Opening paths for Latina writers gave my own struggles meaning). Scheherazade was in full performance mode, and what larger pressure than having to captivate a sultan who was determined to cut her head off in the morning?

I still admire this plucky woman, whom I needed to internalize to get where I was going. But I am relieved that her tenure as my leading muse is over. I could not bear her grueling all-nighters, neither do I have her seductive powers to mesmerize a sultan reader anymore.

Now that I am an older writer, I find myself often in the underworld, burying my dead, getting acquainted with the next stage of my life, my own death. The story I keep returning to for guidance is that of Demeter, Persephone, and Hades.

It is a story of death and rebirth in a life and on the earth. Young Persephone is carried away by Hades, the king of the underworld; her mother, Demeter, goddess of agriculture and the earth's fertility, is bereft. In a fury of self-destructiveness, she punishes her own kingdom with plagues and droughts. Plants, creatures, humans begin to die off. Alarmed, the king of the gods, Zeus, orders that Persephone be returned, provided she hasn't eaten anything in the underworld. But to ensure her stay, Hades has tricked Persephone into eating seven pomegranate seeds. Zeus works out a compromise: Persephone will spend spring and summer and fall with her mother on earth and then descend to the underworld to be with her husband for the rest of the year.

Three quarters of the year is not a bad percentage, but it's all or nothing for Demeter. During her daughter's absence, she inflicts on the earth a short-term version of her earlier punishment. Call it winter.

Because I am entering the wintertime of my life as a woman and a writer, I identify with Demeter. I, too, want to be always producing, summertime year round. I am bereft without my writing, afraid to let go even for a short spell.

But I am also Persephone. That "beginner's mind" self who has to discover how to write each new book. A long journey, she must embark on, again and again, taking risks, including separation from the safety of her mother, her accomplished work. Which is why Persephone swallows those pomegranate seeds. In order to flower she needs to keep returning to the underworld, where those seeds can germinate.

Hades is the character I least want to incorporate into my writing self. What writer doesn't dread those incoherent or silent spells? But terrifying and dangerous as the encounter can be--not every writer returns to tell the tale-- we need his dark energy, Lorca's Duende, Dylan Thomas's "force that through the green fuse drives the flower." Without it, the writing is tidy, lackluster, skimming the surface. It is not writing that can take us far, help us make meaning of our lives, provide string for the labyrinth of being a human being, especially an older human being.

Because I find myself in the underworld, I hold fast to the string of the Demeter-Persephone-Hades story. That is part of the value of stories, reminding us of things we mustn't forget. Not by convincing the discursive mind or seducing the imagination, but by engaging the fully integrated self, our souls, which stories alone know how to powerfully access. This story reminds me that my time this time in Hades will probably come to an end; that my Demeter will probably reunite with her Persephone; that deep inside me, I am carrying one of those pomegranate seeds.

2

My mother died in April, within four months of my father's death. They were old (86 and 96), both afflicted with Alzheimer's. I had been losing them little by little for years. When the final loss came, I thought I would be ready. What I had not foreseen was that their daughter would die with them, and that she was a large part of the writer I had become.

Perhaps because ours is a Latino "we" culture, I always thought of myself as the writer, not *in* the family, but *of* the family. The compulsion for writing at all was to make meaning of our experience, in the belief that the story would hold us together now that we had lost the context of our native country and culture. And so, I was blown away when my first novel was met with intense family disapproval, particularly from my mother, who accused me of betrayal for telling *our* stories to *them*. "But it's fiction," I kept defending myself lamely. The truer statement would have been: There is no *us* and *them*; we become each other in the world of story.

My mother's furious reaction plunged me into a long, painful sojourn in the underworld. I thought I would never write again. That should have been a clue that the writer and the daughter were wedded as tightly together as Demeter and Persephone.

But I found my voice again; I wrote a second novel. And I attribute my endurance to the fact that by the time of my first novel's publication, I was already an older writer, forty-one, who'd been writing seriously since my undergraduate years. I had also survived several decades in that public-sphere underworld that the culture then consigned "minority writers" to. As a woman, a Latina, and an immigrant, I had been sent to the kitchen, where I ate and grew strong in the company of Langston Hughes, Maxine Hong Kingston, Leslie Marmon Silko, Gwendolyn Brooks, and many other muses and mentors, some of them white and male who had strayed from the company of the front rooms (Yeats, Wordsworth, Blake, Roethke) to talk to me (at any rate, their work spoke to me). The hardiness and persistence developed over years of cultural disregard and disappointments allowed my older writing self to survive a familial reaction that I might have crushed my younger writing self.

Daughter and writer did eventually reunite. In her later years, my mother embraced my work. If my books had been babies, they would have assumed pride of place along with photos of her other grandchildren and great grandchildren. In fact, my mother commissioned a Dominican painter to copy an image of the Virgen de la Altagracia from one of my children's books onto a back wall of their property in Santiago, where my parents had returned to spend their last years. The archbishop celebrated a mass in front of the mural and declared the spot a national pilgrimage stop. From banishment to enshrined--my mother's reactions were always, like Demeter's, all or nothing.

The older writer has to bury the daughter who first set out on the journey; whose childhood, horrid or idyllic or a mix of both, provided the gasoline to get her out from under the parental voiceover and into her own voice. She has survived so many endings, including the endings of her books, the death of the writer who wrote the last book, so that she can become the writer who will write the next book; she should be adept at spending these periodic and by now predictable sojourns in the underworld. But death, if it means what it says, means death. If she had the certainty that she will write again, then call it a hiatus, call it research, call it a book tour, but it's not the underworld.

Some writers never do come back from these silences, just as some writers never get near them, refusing engagement with their Duendes, those little deaths. I don't know if their fate is any better, because the writing dies, disconnected from this vital, composting stuff. It becomes fluff, lite, the things whereof many bestsellers are made of. Not a bad fate, if you can be happy with that.

But I am my father's daughter, or was. He was heavily invested in my work. Its intensity, its need to redeem our story. He provided a lot of its fuel: his enormous need to prove himself worthy. My books proved it. He would call from a pay phone on the street afraid to face my mother's ire, and I would come home from a day of not writing in my office, a day in the underworld of silence, to his message on my answering machine: *Your mother will get over this. Don't give up hope. Keep writing.*

Goodbye to that gasoline.

3

The older writer has to find new fuel for the writing. Of course, she can just keep doing the writing out of the habit of writing. But it will show. An empty shell with the life gone out of it. The husk of a seed that does not germinate.

The public sources of fuel--fame, status, "love," money--she'd be lying if she said they are no longer enticing, especially in their older-writer equivalents: esteem, inclusion, affection, security. But they don't hold the same charge anymore. Either she has already gotten some of the above, or she knows that the roots that can nourish her in this next phase of life have to go deeper and the only way she knows to draw up the life force is by writing. Maybe the real work will now be shifting the focus, centering the soul in a larger ground of being. Who knows? The only way for her to find things out is by writing.

Meanwhile, the young ones are coming, the young ones are coming. There is relief in their arrival, for what writer who loves books would want all storytelling to end with her? Après moi, le silence. No way! Let the young ones have their turn.

But they arrive with such noise, albeit so smart and often brilliant, and with all their newfangled toys, their Internet, emails, blogs and tweets and liking on facebook, so many new ways of telling their stories, ways the older writer needs their help to negotiate. And when she confesses that she'd much rather read a book with pages she can turn than a button to turn on, they turn on her and smile benignly or not so benignly, and she can see it in their eyes, tick tock.

The older writer understands their impatience. It is their turn. She has a different role to play now. It's her turn to listen to their Scheherazades, to write introductions to anthologies of writers under-forty, to review first novels or blurb them, all the many ways of being an elder-statesman writer. An earlier generation--or some of the generous ones in that earlier generation--did these things for her.

With the years, as more and more of the people she loves and the parts of her that existed only in relation to them die off, she finds herself frequently in the underworld and for extended spells. It no longer feels seasonal, but a place where she might have to learn how to live from now on. And if there is a pomegranate seed of promise here, it is the knowing that this world, too, needs to be storied.

Part Two

Preparation

Who Would Dare?

Roberto Bolaño

The books that I remember best are the ones I stole in Mexico City, between the ages of sixteen and nineteen, and the ones I bought in Chile when I was twenty, during the first few months of the coup. In Mexico there was an incredible bookstore. It was called the Glass Bookstore and it was on the Alameda. Its walls, even the ceiling, were glass. Glass and iron beams. From the outside, it seemed an impossible place to steal from. And yet prudence was overcome by the temptation to try and after a while I made the attempt.

The first book to fall into my hands was a small volume by [the nineteenth century erotic poet] Pierre Louÿs, with pages as thin as Bible paper, I can't remember now whether it was *Aphrodite* or *Songs of Bilitis*. I know that I was sixteen and that for a while Louÿs became my guide. Then I stole books by Max Beerbohm (*The Happy Hypocrite*), Champfleury, Samuel Pepys, the Goncourt brothers, Alphonse Daudet, and Rulfo and Arreola, Mexican writers who at the time were still more or less practicing, and whom I might therefore meet some morning on

Avenida Niño Perdido, a teeming street that my maps of Mexico City hide from me today, as if Niño Perdido could only have existed in my imagination, or as if the street, with its underground stores and street performers had really been lost, just as I got lost at the age of sixteen.

From the mists of that era, from those stealthy assaults, I remember many books of poetry. Books by Amado Nervo, Alfonso Reyes, Renato Leduc, Gilberto Owen, Heruta and Tablada, and by American poets, like *General William Booth Enters Into Heaven,* by the great Vachel Lindsay. But it was a novel that saved me from hell and plummeted me straight back down again. The novel was *The Fall,* by Camus, and everything that has to do with it I remember as if frozen in a ghostly light, the still light of evening, although I read it, devoured it, by the light of those exceptional Mexico City mornings that shine—or shone—with a red and green radiance ringed by noise, on a bench in the Alameda, with no money and the whole day ahead of me, in fact my whole life ahead of me. After Camus, everything changed.

I remember the edition: it was a book with very large print, like a primary school reader, slim, cloth-covered, with a horrendous drawing on the jacket, a hard book to steal and one that I didn't know whether to hide under my arm or in my belt, because it showed under my truant student blazer, and in the end I carried it out in plain sight of all the clerks at the Glass Bookstore, which is one of the best ways to steal and which I had learned from an Edgar Allan Poe story.

After that, after I stole that book and read it, I went from being a prudent reader to being a voracious reader and from being a book thief to being a book hijacker. I wanted to read everything, which in my innocence was the same as wanting to uncover or trying to uncover the hidden workings of chance that had induced Camus's character to accept his hideous fate. Despite what might have been predicted, my career as a book hijacker was long and fruitful, but one day I was caught. Luckily, it wasn't at the Glass Bookstore but at the Cellar Bookstore, which is—or was—across from the Alameda, on Avenida Juárez, and which, as its name indicates, was a big cellar where the latest books from Buenos Aires and Barcelona sat piled in gleaming stacks. My arrest was ignominious. It was as if the bookstore samurais had put a price on my head. They threatened to have me thrown out of the country, to give me a beating in the cellar of the Cellar Bookstore, which to me sounded like a discussion among neo-philosophers about the destruction of destruction, and in the end, after lengthy deliberations, they let me go, though not before confiscating all the books I had on me, among them *The Fall,* none of which I'd stolen there.

Soon afterwards I left for Chile. If in Mexico I might have bumped into Rulfo and Arreola, in Chile the same was true of Nicanor Parra and Enrique Lihn, but I think the only writer I saw was Rodrigo Lira, walking fast on a night that smelled of tear gas. Then came the coup and after that I spent my time visiting the bookstores of Santiago as a cheap way of staving off boredom and madness. Unlike the Mexican bookstores, the bookstores of Santiago had no clerks and were run by a single person, almost always the owner. There I bought Nicanor Parra's *Obra gruesa* [Complete Works] and the *Artefactos*, and books by Enrique Lihn and Jorge Teillier that I would soon lose and that were essential reading for me; although essential isn't the word: those books helped me breathe. But breathe isn't the right word either.

What I remember best about my visits to those bookstores are the eyes of the booksellers, which sometimes looked like the eyes of a hanged man and sometimes were veiled by a kind of film of sleep, which I now know was something else. I don't remember ever seeing lonelier bookstores. I didn't steal any books in Santiago. They were cheap and I bought them. At the last bookstore I visited, as I was going through a row of old French novels, the bookseller, a tall, thin man of about forty, suddenly asked whether I thought it was right for an author to recommend his own works to a man who's been sentenced to death.

The bookseller was standing in a corner, wearing a white shirt with the sleeves rolled up to the elbows and he had a prominent Adam's apple that quivered as he spoke. I said it didn't seem right. What condemned men are we talking about? I asked. The bookseller looked at me and said that he knew for certain of more than one novelist capable of recommending his own books to a man on the verge of death. Then he said that we were talking about desperate readers. I'm hardly qualified to judge, he said, but if I don't, no one will.

What book would you give to a condemned man? he asked me. I don't know, I said. I don't know either, said the bookseller, and I think it's terrible. What books do desperate men read? What books do they *like*? How do you imagine the reading room of a condemned man? he asked. I have no idea, I said. You're young, I'm not surprised, he said. And then: it's like Antarctica. Not like the North Pole, but like Antarctica. I was reminded of the last days of [Edgar Allan Poe's] Arthur Gordon Pym, but I decided not to say anything. Let's see, said the bookseller, what brave man would drop this novel on the lap of a man sentenced to death? He picked up a book that had done fairly well and then he tossed it on a pile. I paid him and left. When I turned to leave, the bookseller might have laughed or sobbed. As I stepped out I heard him say: What kind of arrogant bastard would dare to do such a thing? And then he said something else, but I couldn't hear what it was.

Unpacking My Library: A Talk about Book Collecting

Walter Benjamin

I am unpacking my library. Yes, I am. The books are not yet on the shelves, not yet touched by the mild boredom of order. I cannot march up and down their ranks to pass them in review before a friendly audience. You need not fear any of that. Instead, I must ask you to join me in the disorder of crates that have been wrenched open, the air saturated with the dust of wood, the floor covered with torn paper, to join me among piles of volumes that are seeing daylight again after two years of darkness, so that you may be ready to share with me a bit of the mood—it is certainly not an elegiac mood but, rather, one of anticipation—which these books arouse in a genuine collector. For such a man is speaking to you, and on closer scrutiny he proves to be speaking only about himself. Would it not be presumptuous of me if, in order to appear convincingly objective and down-to-earth, I enumerated for you the main sections or prize pieces of a library, if I presented you with their history or even their usefulness to a writer? I, for one, have in mind something less obscure, something more palpable than that; what I am really concerned with is giving you some insight into the relationship of a book collector to his possessions, into collecting rather than a collection. If I do this by elaborating on the various ways of acquiring books, this is something entirely arbitrary. This or any other procedure is merely a dam against the spring tide of memories which surges toward any collector as he contemplates his possessions. Every passion borders on the chaotic, but the collector's passion borders on the chaos of memories. More than that: the chance, the fate, that suffuse the past before my eyes are conspicuously present in the accustomed confusion of these books. For what else is this collection but a disorder to which habit has accommodated itself to such an extent that it can appear as order? You have all heard of people whom the loss of their books has turned into invalids, or of those who in order to acquire them became criminals. These are the very areas in which any order is a balancing act of extreme precariousness. "The only exact knowledge there is," said Anatole France, "is the knowledge of the date of publication and the format of books." And indeed, if there is a counterpart to the confusion of a library, it is the order of its catalogue.

Thus there is in the life of a collector a dialectical tension between the poles of disorder and order. Naturally, his existence is tied to many other things as well: to a very mysterious relationship to ownership, something about which we shall have more to say later; also, to a relationship to objects which does not emphasize their functional, utilitarian value—that is, their usefulness—but studies and loves them as the scene, the stage, of their fate. The most profound enchantment for the collector is the locking of individual items within a magic circle in which they are fixed as the final thrill, the thrill of acquisition, passes over them. Everything remembered and thought, everything conscious, becomes the pedestal, the frame, the base, the lock of his property. The period, the region, the craftsmanship, the former ownership—for a true collector the whole background of an item adds up to a magic encyclopedia whose quintessence is the fate of his object. In this circumscribed area, then, it may be surmised how the great physiognomists—and collectors are the physiognomists of the world of objects—turn into interpreters of fate. One has only to watch a collector handle the objects in his glass case. As he holds them in his hands, he seems to be seeing through them into their distant past as though inspired. So much for the magical side of the collector—his old-age image, I might call it.

Habent sua fata libelli: these words may have been intended as a general statement about books. So books like *The Divine Comedy,* Spinoza's *Ethics,* and *The Origin of Species* have their fates. A collector, however, interprets this Latin saying differently. For him, not only books but also copies of books have their fates. And in this sense, the most important fate of a copy is its encounter with him, with his own collection. I am not exaggerating when I say that to a true collector the acquisition of an old book is its rebirth. This is the childlike element which in a collector mingles with the element of old age. For children can accomplish the renewal of existence in a hundred unfailing ways. Among children, collecting is only one process of renewal; other processes are the painting of objects, the cutting out of figures, the application of decals—the whole range of childlike modes of acquisition, from touching things to giving them names. To renew the old world—that is the collector's deepest desire when he is driven to acquire new things, and that is why a collector of older books is closer to the wellsprings of collecting than the acquirer of luxury editions. How do books cross the threshold of a collection and become the property of a collector? The history of their acquisition is the subject of the following remarks.

Of all the ways of acquiring books, writing them oneself is regarded as the most praiseworthy method. At this point many of you will remember with pleasure the large library which Jean Paul's poor little schoolmaster Wutz gradually acquired by writing, himself, all the works whose titles interested him in book-fair catalogues; after all, he could not afford to buy them. Writers are really people who write books not because they are poor, but because they are dissatisfied with the books which they could buy but do not like. You, ladies and gentlemen, may regard this as a whimsical definition of a writer. But everything said from the angle of a real collector is whimsical. Of the customary modes of acquisition, the one most appropriate to a collector would be the borrowing of a book with its attendant non-returning. The book borrower of real stature whom we envisage here proves himself to be an inveterate collector of books not so much by the fervor with which he guards his borrowed treasures and by the deaf ear which he turns to all reminders from the everyday world of legality as by his failure to read these books. If my experience may serve as evidence, a man is more likely to return a borrowed book upon occasion than to read it. And the non-reading of books, you will object, should be characteristic of collectors? This is news to me, you may say. It is not news at all. Experts will bear me out when I say that it is the oldest thing in the world. Suffice it to quote the answer which Anatole France gave to a philistine who admired his library and then finished with the standard question, "And you have read all these books, Monsieur France?" "Not one-tenth of them. I don't suppose you use your Sèvres china every day?"

Incidentally, I have put the right to such an attitude to the test. For years, for at least the first third of its existence, my library consisted of no more than two or three shelves which increased only by inches each year. This was its militant age, when no book was allowed to enter it without the certification that I had not read it. Thus I might never have acquired a library extensive enough to be worthy of the name if there had not been an inflation. Suddenly the emphasis shifted; books acquired real value, or, at any rate, were difficult to obtain. At least this is how it seemed in Switzerland. At the eleventh hour I sent my first major book orders from there and in this way was able to secure such irreplaceable items as *Der blaue Reiter* and Bachofen's *Sage von Tanaquil,* which could still be obtained from the publishers at that time.

Well—so you may say—after exploring all these byways we should finally reach the wide highway of book acquisition, namely, the purchasing of books. This is indeed a wide highway, but not a comfortable one. The purchasing done by a book collector has very little in common with that done in a bookshop by a student getting a textbook, a man of the world buying a present for his lady, or a businessman intending to while away his next train journey. I have made my most memorable purchases on trips, as a transient. Property and possession belong to the tactical sphere. Collectors are people with a tactical instinct; their experience teaches them that when they capture a strange city, the smallest antique shop can be a fortress, the most remote stationery store a key position. How many cities have revealed themselves to me in the marches I undertook in the pursuit of books!

By no means all of the most important purchases are made on the premises of a dealer. Catalogues play a far greater part. And even though the purchaser may be thoroughly acquainted with the book ordered from a catalogue, the individual copy always remains a surprise and the order always a bit of a gamble. There are grievous disappointments, but also happy finds. I remember, for instance, that I once ordered a book with colored illustrations for my old collection of children's books only because it contained fairy tales by Albert

Ludwig Grimm and was published at Grimma, Thuringia. Grimma was also the place of publication of a book of fables edited by the same Albert Ludwig Grimm. With its sixteen illustrations my copy of this book of fables was the only extant example of the early work of the great German book illustrator Lyser, who lived in Hamburg around the middle of the last century. Well, my reaction to the consonance of the names had been correct. In this case too I discovered the work of Lyser, namely *Linas Märchenbuch,* a work which has remained unknown to his bibliographers and which deserves a more detailed reference than this first one I am introducing here.

The acquisition of books is by no means a matter of money or expert knowledge alone. Not even both factors together suffice for the establishment of a real library, which is always somewhat impenetrable and at the same time uniquely itself. Anyone who buys from catalogues must have flair in addition to the qualities I have mentioned. Dates, place names, formats, previous owners, bindings, and the like: all these details must tell him something—not as dry, isolated facts, but as a harmonious whole; from the quality and intensity of this harmony he must be able to recognize whether a book is for him or not. An auction requires yet another set of qualities in a collector. To the reader of a catalogue the book itself must speak, or possibly its previous ownership if the provenance of the copy has been established. A man who wishes to participate at an auction must pay equal attention to the book and to his competitors, in addition to keeping a cool enough head to avoid being carried away in the competition. It is a frequent occurrence that someone gets stuck with a high purchase price because he kept raising his bid—more to assert himself than to acquire the book. On the other hand, one of the finest memories of a collector is the moment when he rescued a book to which he might never have given a thought, much less a wishful look, because he found it lonely and abandoned on the market place and bought it to give it its freedom—the way the prince bought a beautiful slave girl in *The Arabian Nights.* To a book collector, you see, the true freedom of all books is somewhere on his shelves.

To this day, Balzac's *Peau de chagrin* stands out from long rows of French volumes in my library as a memento of my most exciting experience at an auction. This happened in 1915 at the Rümann auction put up by Emil Hirsch, one of the greatest of book experts and most distinguished of dealers. The edition in question appeared in 1838 in Paris, Place de la Bourse. As I pick up my copy, I see not only its number in the Rümann collection, but even the label of the shop in which the first owner bought the book over ninety years ago for one-eightieth of today's price. "Papeterie I. Flanneau," it says. A fine age in which it was still possible to buy such a de luxe edition at a stationery dealer's! The steel engravings of this book were designed by the foremost French graphic artist and executed by the foremost engravers. But I was going to tell you how I acquired this book. I had gone to Emil Hirsch's for an advance inspection and had handled forty or fifty volumes; that particular volume had inspired in me the ardent desire to hold on to it forever. The day of the auction came. As chance would have it, in the sequence of the auction this copy of *La Peau de chagrin* was preceded by a complete set of its illustrations printed separately on India paper. The bidders sat at a long table; diagonally across from me sat the man who was the focus of all eyes at the first bid, the famous Munich collector Baron von Simolin. He was greatly interested in this set, but he had rival bidders; in short, there was a spirited contest which resulted in the highest bid of the entire auction—far in excess of three thousand marks. No one seemed to have expected such a high figure, and all those present were quite excited. Emil Hirsch remained unconcerned, and whether he wanted to save time or was guided by some other consideration, he proceeded to the next item, with no one really paying attention. He called out the price, and with my heart pounding and with the full realization that I was unable to compete with any of those big collectors I bid a somewhat higher amount. Without arousing the bidders' attention, the auctioneer went through the usual routine—"Do I hear more?" and three bangs of his gavel, with an eternity seeming to separate each from the next—and proceeded to add the auctioneer's charge. For a student like me the sum was still considerable. The following morning at the pawnshop is no longer part of this story, and I prefer to speak about another incident which I should like to call the negative of an auction. It happened last year at a Berlin auction. The collection of books that was offered was a miscellany in quality and subject matter, and only a number of rare works on occultism and natural philosophy were worthy of note. I bid for a number of them, but each time I noticed a gentleman in the front row who seemed only to have waited for my bid to counter with his own, evidently prepared to top any offer. After this had been repeated several times, I gave up all hope of acquiring the book which I was most interested in that day. It was the rare *Fragmente aus dem Nachlass eines jungen Physikers* [Posthumous Fragments of a Young Physicist] which Johann Wilhelm Ritter published in two volumes at Heidelberg in 1810. This work has never been reprinted, but I have always considered its preface, in which the author-editor tells the story of his life in the guise of an obituary for his supposedly deceased unnamed friend—with whom he is really identical—as the most important sample of personal prose of German Romanticism. Just as the item came up I had a brain wave. It was simple enough: since my bid was bound to give the item to the other man, I must not bid at all. I controlled myself and remained silent. What I had hoped for came about: no interest, no bid, and the book was put aside. I deemed it wise to let several days go by, and when I appeared on the premises after a week, I found the book in the secondhand department and benefited by the lack of interest when I acquired it.

Once you have approached the mountains of cases in order to mine the books from them and bring them to the light of day—or, rather, of night—what memories crowd in upon you! Nothing highlights the fascination of unpacking more clearly than the difficulty of stopping this activity. I had started at noon, and it was midnight before I had worked my way to the last cases. Now I put my hands on two volumes bound in faded boards which, strictly speaking, do not belong in a book case at all: two albums with stick-in pictures which my mother pasted in as a child and which I inherited. They are the seeds of a collection of children's books which is growing steadily even today, though no longer in my garden. There is no living library that does not harbor a number of booklike creations from fringe areas. They need not be stick-in albums or family albums, autograph books or portfolios containing pamphlets or religious tracts; some people become attached to leaflets and prospectuses, others to handwriting facsimiles or typewritten copies of unobtainable books; and certainly periodicals can form the prismatic fringes of a library. But to get back to those albums: Actually, inheritance is the soundest way of acquiring a collection. For a collector's attitude toward his possessions stems from an owner's feeling of responsibility toward his property. Thus it is, in the highest sense, the attitude of an heir, and the most distinguished trait of a collection will always be its transmissibility. You should know that in saying this I fully realize that my discussion of the mental climate of collecting will confirm many of you in your conviction that this passion is behind the times, in your distrust of the collector type. Nothing is further from my mind than to shake either your conviction or your distrust. But one thing should be noted: the phenomenon of collecting loses its meaning as it loses its personal owner. Even though public collections may be less objectionable socially and more useful academically than private collections, the objects get their due only in the latter. I do know that time is running out for the type that I am discussing here and have been representing before you a bit *ex officio*. But, as Hegel put it, only when it is dark does the owl of Minerva begin its flight. Only in extinction is the collector comprehended.

Now I am on the last half-emptied case and it is way past midnight. Other thoughts fill me than the ones I am talking about—not thoughts but images, memories. Memories of the cities in which I found so many things: Riga, Naples, Munich, Danzig, Moscow, Florence, Basel, Paris; memories of Rosenthal's sumptuous rooms in Munich, of the Danzig Stockturm where the late Hans Rhaue was domiciled, of Süssengut's musty book cellar in North Berlin; memories of the rooms where these books had been housed, of my student's den in Munich, of my room in Bern, of the solitude of Iseltwald on the Lake of Brienz, and finally of my boyhood room, the former location of only four or five of the several thousand volumes that are piled up around me. O bliss of the collector, bliss of the man of leisure! Of no one has less been expected, and no one has had a greater sense of well-being than the man who has been able to carry on his disreputable existence in the mask of Spitzweg's "Bookworm." For inside him there are spirits, or at least little genii, which have seen to it that for a collector—and I mean a real collector, a collector as he ought to be—ownership is the most intimate relationship that one can have to objects. Not that they come alive in him; it is he who lives in them. So I have erected one of his dwellings, with books as the building stones, before you, and now he is going to disappear inside, as is only fitting.

Reading in the Toilet

Henry Miller

There is one theme connected with the reading of books which I think worth dwelling on since it involves a habit which is widespread and about which, to my knowledge, little has been written—I mean, *reading in the toilet*. As a youngster, in search of a safe place wherein to devour the forbidden classics, I sometimes repaired to the toilet. Since that youthful period I have never done any reading in the toilet. Should I be in search of peace and quiet I take my book and go to the woods. I know of no better place to read a good book than in the depths of a forest. Preferably by a running stream.

I immediately hear objections. "But we are not all as fortunate as you! We have jobs, we travel to and from work in crowded trams, buses, subways; we have hardly a minute to call our own."

I was a "worker" myself right up to my thirty-third year. It was in this early period that I did most of my reading. I read under difficult conditions, always. I remember getting the sack once when I was caught reading Nietzsche instead of editing the mail order catalogue, which was then my job. How lucky I was to have been fired, when I think of it now. Was not Nietzsche vastly more important in my life than a knowledge of the mail order business?

For four solid years, on my way to and from the offices of the Everlasting Portland Cement Co., I read the "heaviest" books. I read standing up, squeezed on all sides by straphangers like myself. I not only read during these trips on the "El," I memorized long passages from these too-too-solid tomes. If nothing more, it was a valuable exercise in the art of concentration. At this job I often worked late into the night, and usually without eating lunch—not because I wanted to read during my lunch hour but because I had no money for lunch. Evenings, as soon as I had gulped down my meal, I left the house to join my pals. In those years, and for many a year to come, I rarely slept more than four or five hours a night. Yet I did a vast amount of reading. And, I repeat, I read—for me, at least—the most difficult books, not the easiest ones. I never read to kill time. I seldom read in bed, unless I was indisposed, or pretending to be ill in order to enjoy a brief vacation. As I look back it seems to me I was always reading in an uncomfortable position. (Which is the way most writers write and most painters paint, I find.) But what I read soaked through. The point is, if I must stress it, that when I read I read with undivided attention and with all the faculties I possessed. When I played it was the same thing.

Now and then I would go of an evening to the public library to read. That was like taking a seat in heaven. Often, on leaving the library, I would say to myself: "Why don't you do this oftener?" The reason I did not, of course, was that life came between. One often says "life" when one means pleasure or any foolish distraction.

From what I have gleaned through talks with intimate friends, most of the reading which is done in the toilet is idle reading. The digests, the picture magazines, the serials, detective stories, thrillers, all the tag ends of literature, these are what people take to the toilet to read. Some, I am told, have bookracks in the toilet. Their reading matter awaits them, so to speak, as it does in the dentist's office. Amazing with what avidity people comb through the "reading matter," as it is called, which is piled high in the waiting rooms of professional people. Is it to keep their minds off the painful ordeal ahead? Or is it to make up for lost time, "to catch up," as they say, with current events? My own limited observations tell me that these individuals have already absorbed more than their share of "current events"—i.e. war, accidents, more war, disasters, war again, murders, more war, suicides, war again, bank robberies, war, and again war, hot and cold. Undoubtedly these are the same individuals who keep the radio going most of the day and night, who go to the movies as often as possible—where they get more fresh news, more "current events"—and who buy television sets for their children. All to be informed! But what do they really know that is worth knowing about these dreadfully important, world-shaking events?

People may insist that they devour the papers or glue their ears to the radio (sometimes both at once!) in order to keep abreast of world doings, but that is a sheer delusion. The truth is that the moment these sorry individuals are not active, not busy, they become aware of an awesome, sickening emptiness in themselves. It doesn't matter much, frankly, on what pap they feed, just so long as they can avoid coming face to face with themselves. To *meditate* on the issue of the day, or even on one's personal problems, is the last thing the normal individual wants to do.

Even in the toilet, where you would think it unnecessary to *do* anything, or to *think* anything, where once during the day at least one is alone with himself and whatever happens happens automatically, even this moment of bliss, for it *is* a minor sort of bliss, has to be broken by concentration on printed matter. Each one, I assume, has his own favorite kind of reading matter for the privacy of the toilet. Some wade through long novels, others read only the fluffiest, flimsiest crap. And some, no doubt, just turn the pages and dream. One wonders—what sort of dreams do they dream? With what are their dreams tinged?

There are mothers who will tell you that only in the toilet do they get the chance to read. Poor mothers! Life is indeed hard on you these days. Yet, compared to the mothers of fifty years ago, you have a thousand times more opportunity for self-development. In your complete arsenal of labor-saving devices you have what was lacking even to the empresses of old. If it was really "time" you were eager to save, in acquiring all these gadgets, then you have been cruelly deceived.

There are the children, of course! When all other excuses fail, there are always—"the children!" You have kindergartens, playgrounds, baby-sitters, and God knows what all. You give the kids a nap after lunch and you put them to bed as early as you possibly can, all according to approved "modern" methods. *Bref*, you have as little to do with your young as possible. They get eliminated, just like the odious household chores. All in the name of science and efficiency.

("Francais, encore un tout petit effort . . .!")

Yes, dear mothers, we know that however much you do there is always more waiting to be done. It is true that your job is never finished. Whose is, I wonder? Who rests on the Seventh Day, except God? Who looks upon his work, when it *is* terminated, and finds it good? Only the Creator, apparently.

I wonder sometimes if these conscientious mothers who are always complaining that their work is never finished (an inverted form of self-praise), I wonder, as I say, do they ever think to take with them to the toilet, not reading matter, but the little jobs which they have left undone? Or, to put it another way, does it ever occur to them, I wonder, to sit and meditate upon their lot during these precious moments of complete privacy? Do they ever, in such moments, ask the good Lord for strength and courage to continue in the path of martyrdom?

How did our poor impoverished and woefully handicapped ancestors ever accomplish all they did, is what I often wonder. Some mothers of old, as we know from the lives of great men, managed to do a powerful lot of reading despite these grave "handicaps." Some of them, it would almost seem, had time for everything. Not only did they take care of their own children, teach them all they knew, nurse them, feed them, clean them, play with them, make their clothes (and sometimes the material too), not only did they wash and iron everybody's clothes, but some at least also managed to give their husbands a hand, especially if they were plain country folk. Countless are the big and little things our forbears did unaided—before ever there were labor-saving devices, time-saving devices, before there were short cuts to knowledge, before there were kindergartens, nurseries, recreation centres, welfare workers, moving pictures and Federal relief bureaus of all kinds.

Perhaps the mothers of our great men were also addicted to reading in the toilet. If so, it is not commonly known. Nor have I read that omnivorous readers—like Macaulay, Saintsbury and Rémy de Gourmont, for example—cultivated this habit. I rather suspect that these Gargantuan readers were too active, too intent on the goal, to waste time in this fashion. The very fact that they were such prodigious readers would indicate that their attention was always undivided. It is true, we hear of bibliomaniacs who read while eating or while walking; perhaps some have even been able to read and talk at the same time. There is a breed of men who cannot resist reading whatever falls within range of their eyes; they will read literally anything, even the Lost and Found notices in the newspaper. They are obsessed, and we can only pity them.

A piece of sound advice at this juncture may not be amiss. If your bowels refuse to function, consult a Chinese herb doctor! Don't read in order to divert your mind from the business at hand. What the autonomic system likes, what it responds to, is thorough concentration, whether upon eating, sleeping, evacuating or what you will. If you can't eat, can't sleep, it's because something is bothering you. Something is "on your mind"—where it shouldn't be, in other words. The same is true of the stool. Rid your mind of everything but the business at hand. Whatever you do, tackle it with a free mind and a clear conscience. That's old advice and sound. The modern way is to attempt several things at one and the same time, in order "to make the most of one's time," as it is said. This is thoroughly unsound, unhygienic, and ineffectual. *Easy does it!* "Take care of the little things and the big ones will take care of themselves." Everyone hears that as a child. Few ever practice it.

If it is of vital importance to feed body and mind, it is of equal importance to eliminate from body and mind what has served the purpose. What is unused, "hoarded," becomes poisonous. That's plain horse sense. It follows, therefore, as the night the day that if you go to the toilet to eliminate the waste matter which has accumulated in your system, you are doing yourself a disservice by utilizing these precious moments in filling your mind with "crap." Would you, to save time, think of eating and drinking while using the stool?

If every moment of life is so very precious to you, if you insist on reasoning to yourself that it is no negligible portion of one's life which is spent in the toilet each day—some people prefer the "W.C." or "the John" to toilet—then ask yourself when reaching for your favorite reading matter: *"Do I need this? Why?"* (Cigarette smokers often do just this when trying to break the habit; so do alcoholics. It's a stratagem not to be despised.) Supposing—and this is supposing a good deal!—that you are one who reads only the "world's best literature" on the stool. Even so, I say it will pay to ask yourself: *"Do I need this?"* Let us assume that it is *The Divine Comedy* which you are going to resist reading. Suppose that instead of reading this great classic you meditated on what little you *had* read of it, or on what you had heard about it. That would mark a slight improvement. It would be still better, however, not to meditate on literature at all but simply to keep your mind, as well as your bowels, open. If you must do something, why not offer up a silent prayer to the Creator, a prayer of thanks that your bowels still function? Think what a plight you would be in if they were paralyzed! It takes little time to offer up a prayer of this sort, and with it goes the advantage of being able to take Dante out in the sunlight, where you can commune with him on more equal terms. I am certain that no author, not even a dead one, is flattered by associating his work with the drainage system. Not even scatological works can be enjoyed to the fullest in the water closet. It takes a genuine coprophilist to make the most of such a situation.

Having said some harsh things about the modern mother, what of the modern father? I will confine myself to the American father, because I know him best. This species of pater familias, we know only too well, looks upon himself as a slave-driven, unappreciated wretch. In addition to providing the luxuries, as well as the necessities, of life, he does his utmost to keep to the background as much as possible. Should he have an idle minute or two, he believes it his duty to wash dishes or sing the baby to sleep. Sometimes he feels so driven, so harried, so abused, that when his poor overworked, undernourished, lacklustre wife locks herself in the toilet—or "the John"—for an hour on end he is about ready to break down the door and murder her on the spot.

Let me recommend the following procedure, when such a crisis occurs, to these poor devils who are at a loss to know what their true rôle is. Let us say she has been "in there" a good half hour. She is not constipated, she is not masturbating, and she is not making herself pretty. *"Then what in hell is she doing in there?"* Careful now! I know how it is when you get to talking to yourself. Don't let your temper get the best of you. Just try to imagine that, sitting in there on the stool, is the woman you once loved so madly that nothing would do but hitch up with her for life. Don't be jealous of Dante, Balzac, Dostoievsky, if these be the shades she is communicating with in there. *"Maybe she's reading the Bible!* She's been in there long enough to have read the whole of Deuteronomy." I know. I know how you feel. But it's not the Bible she's reading, and you know it. It's probably not *The Possessed* either, nor *Seraphita,* nor Jeremy Taylor's *Holy Living.* Could be *Gone with the Wind.* But what matter? The thing is—believe me, brother, it's always the thing!—to try a different tack. Try questions and answers. Like this, for example:

"What are you doing in there, *darling*?"

"Reading."

"What, may I ask?"

"About the Battle of the Marne."

(Pretend not to be fazed by this. Continue!)

"I thought perhaps you were brushing up on your Spanish."

"What was that, dear?"

"I said—is it a good yarn?"

"No, it's boring."

"Let me get you something else."

"What's that, dear?"

"I said—would you like a cool drink while you're wading through that stuff?"

"What stuff?"

"The Battle of the Marne."

"Oh, I finished that. I'm on something else now."

"Darling, do you need any reference books?"

"You bet I do. I'd like an abridged dictionary—Webster's, if you don't mind."

"Mind? It's a pleasure. I'll fetch you the unabridged."

"No dear, the abridged will do. It's easier to hold."

(Here run up and down, as if searching for the dictionary.)

"Darling, I can't find either the abridged or the unabridged. Will the encyclopædia do? What is it you're looking for—a word, a date, or . . .?"

"Dearest, what I'm really looking for is peace and quiet."

"Yes, *dear,* of course. I'll just clear the table, wash the dishes, and put the children to bed. Then if you like I'll read to you. I've just discovered a wonderful book on Nostradamus."

"You're *so* thoughtful, dear. But I'd rather just go on reading."

"Reading *what*?"

"It's called *The Memoirs of Marshal Joffre,* with a foreword by Napoleon and a detailed study of the major campaigns by a professor of military strategy—they don't give his name!—at West Point. Does that answer your question, dearest?"

"Perfectly.

(At this point you make for the axe in the woodshed. If there is no woodshed, invent one. Make a noise with your teeth, as if you were grinding the axe—like Minutten in *Mysteries*.)

Here is an alternative suggestion. When she is not looking place a copy of Balzac's *About Catherine de Medici* in the water closet. Put a marker at page 169 and underscore the following passage:

> The Cardinal had just found himself deceived by Catherine. The crafty Italian had seen in the younger branch of the Royal Family an obstacle she could use to check the pretensions of the Guises; and, in spite of the counsel of the two Gondis, who advised her to leave the Guises to act with what violence they could against the Bourbons, she had, by warning the Queen of Navarre, brought to nought the plot to seize Béarn concerted by the Guises with the King of Spain. As this State secret was known only to themselves and to Catherine, the Princes of Lorraine were assured of her betrayal, and they wished to send her back to Florence; but to secure proofs of Catherine's treachery to the State—the House of Lorraine was the State—the Duke and Cardinal had just made her privy to their scheme for making away with the King of Navarre.

The advantage of giving her a text like this to wrestle with is that it will take her mind completely off her houshold duties and put her in a frame of mind to discuss history, prophecy or symbolism with you for the rest of the evening. She may even be tempted to read the introduction written by George Saintsbury, one of the world's greatest readers, a virtue or vice which did not prevent him from writing tedious and superfluous prefaces or introductions to other people's works.

I could, of course, suggest other absorbing books, notably one called *Nature and Man*, by Paul Weiss, a professor of philosophy and a logician, not of the first water merely, but of the "waters reglitterized," a ventriloquist able to twist the brains of a rabbinical pundit into a Gordian knot. One can read at random in this work and not lose a shred of his distillated logic. Everything has been predigested by the author. The text is comprised of nothing but pure thought. Here is a sample, from the section on "Inference":

> A necessary inference differs from a contingent one in that the premise alone suffices to warrant the conclusion. In a necessary inference there is only a logical relation between premise and conclusion; there is no principle which provides content for the conclusion. Such an inference is derivable from a contingent inference by treating the contingent principle as a premise. C. S. Pierce seems to have been the first to discover this truth. 'Let the premises of any argument,' he said, 'be denoted by P, the conclusion by C, and the principle by L. Then if the whole principle be expressed as a premise the argument will become L and P ∴ C. But this new argument must also have its principle which may be denoted by L. Now, as L and P (supposing them to be true), contain all that is requisite to determine the probable or necessary truth of C, they contain L'. Thus L' must be contained in the principle, whether expressed in the premise or not. Hence every argument has, as portion of its principle, a certain principle which cannot be eliminated from its principle. Such a principle may be termed a *logical principle*.' Every principle of inference, Pierce's observation makes dear, contains a logical principle by which one can rigorously proceed from a premise and the original principle to the conclusion. Any result in nature or mind, therefore, is a necessary consequence of some antecedent and of some course which starts from that antecedent and terminates in that result.

The reader may wonder why I have not suggested Hegel's *Phenomenology of Mind,* which is the acknowledged cornerstone of the whole nutcracker suite of intellectual hocus-pocus, or Wittgenstein, Korzybski, Gurdjieff & Co. Why not, indeed! Why not Vaihinger's *Philosophy of As If?* Or *The Alphabet* by David Diringer? Why not *The Ninety-Five Theses* of Luther or Sir Walter Raleigh's *Preface to the History of the World?* Why not Milton's *Areopagitica?* All lovely books. So edifying, so instructive.

Ah me, if our poor American *pater familias* were to take this problem of reading in the toilet to heart, if he were to give serious thought to the most effective means of breaking this habit, what a list of books might he not devise for a Five-Foot Privy Shelf! With a little ingenuity he would manage either to cure his wife of the habit or break her mind in the process.

If he were truly ingenious he might think up a substitute for this pernicious reading habit. He might, for example, line the walls of the "watt*erre*," as the French call it, with paintings. How pleasant soothing, lenitive and *educational*, while answering the call of Nature, to let the eye roam over a few choice masterpieces of art! For a starter—Romney, Gainsborough, Watteau, Dali, Grant Wood, Soutine, Breughel the Elder and the Albright brothers. (Works of art, incidentally, are no affront to the autonomic system.) Or, if her taste did not run in these directions, he could line the walls of the "watt*erre*" with *Saturday Evening Post* covers or the covers of *Time*, than which nothing could be more "basic-basic," to use the language of dianetics. Or he might, in his off-moments, busy himself embroidering in many colored silks a quaint motto to be hung at the level of her eyes when she takes her accustomed place in the "watt*erre*," a motto such as: *Home is wherever you hang your hat.* This, since it involves a moral, might captivate her in ways unimaginable. Who knows, it might free her from the cloying clutches of the stool in record time!

At this point I think it important to mention the fact that SCIENCE has just discovered the efficacy, the therapeutic efficacy, of Love. The Sunday supplements are full of this subject. Next to Dianetics, the Flying Saucers and Cybernetics, is is apparently the great discovery of the age. The fact that even psychiatrists now recognize the validity of love gives the stamp of approval which (seemingly) Jesus the Christ, *The Light of the World*, was unable to provide. Mothers, now awakened to this ineluctable fact, will no longer have a problem in dealing with their children, nor, "ipso facto," in dealing with their husbands. Wardens will be emptying the prisons of their inmates; generals will be ordering their men to throw away their arms. The millennium is just around the corner.

Nevertheless, and despite the approach of the millennium, human beings will still be obliged to repair to the water closet daily. They will still be confronted with the problem of how to use the time spent therein most profitably. This problem is virtually a metaphysical one. To give oneself up completely to the emptying of one's bowels would, at first blush, seem the easiest and the most natural thing in the world. To perform this function Nature asks nothing of us but complete abeyance. The only collaboration she demands is the willingness on our part to let go. Evidently the Creator, when designing the human organism, realized that it were better for us if certain functions were allowed to take care of themselves; it is only too obvious that if such vital functions as breathing, sleeping, defecating were left to our disposition, some of us would cease to breathe, sleep, or go to the toilet. There are plenty of people, and they are not all in the asylum either, who see no reason why we should eat, sleep, breathe or defecate. They not only question the laws which govern the universe, they question the intelligence of their own organism. They ask why, not to know, but to render absurd what is beyond their limited intelligence to grasp. They look upon the demands of the body as so much time wasted. How then do they spend their time, these superior beings? Are they completely at the service of mankind? Is it because there is so much "good work" to do that they cannot see the sense of spending time eating, drinking, sleeping and defecating? It would indeed be interesting to know what these people mean when they speak of "wasting time."

Time, time . . . I have often wondered, if suddenly we were all privileged to function perfectly, what we *would* do with our time. For the moment we think of perfect functioning we can no longer retain the image of society as it is now constituted. We spend the greater part of our life in contending against maladjustments of all sorts; everything is out of whack, from the human body to the body politic. Assuming the smooth functioning of the human body, with the correlative smooth functioning of the social body, I ask: "What *would* we do with our time?" To limit the problem for the moment to one phase only—*reading*—try, I beg you, to imagine what books, what sort of books, one would then consider necessary or worth while giving time to. The moment one studies the reading problem from this angle almost the whole of literature falls away. We read now, as I see it, primarily for these reasons: one, to get away from ourselves; two, to arm ourselves against real or imaginary dangers; three, to "keep up" with our neighbors, or to impress them, one and the same thing; four, to know what is going on in the world; five, to enjoy ourselves, which means to be stimulated to greater, higher activity and richer being. Other reasons might be added, but these five appear to me to be the principal ones— and I have given them in the order of their *current* importance, if I know my fellow man. It does not take much reflection to conclude that, if one were right with himself and all was well with the world, only the last reason, the one which holds least sway at present, would be valid. The others would fade away, because there would be no reason for their existence. And even the last-named, given the ideal conditions mentioned, would have little or no hold over us. There are, and always have been, a few rare individuals who no longer have need of books, not even "holy" books. And these are precisely the enlightened, the awakened ones. They know full well what is going on in the world. They do not regard life as a problem or an ordeal but as a privilege and a blessing. They seek not to fill themselves with knowledge but with wisdom. They are not riddled with fear, anxiety, ambition, envy, greed, hatred or rivalry. They are deeply involved, and at the same time detached. They enjoy everything they do because they participate directly. They have no need to read sacred books or act in a holy way because they see life whole and are themselves thoroughly whole—and thus everything to them is whole and holy.

How do these unique individuals spend their time?

Ah, there have been many answers given to this query, many. And the reason why there have been many answers is because whoever is able to put such a question to himself has a different type of "unique" individual in mind. Some view these rare individuals as passing their life in prayer and meditation; some see them moving in the midst of life, performing any and all tasks, but never making themselves conspicuous. But no matter how one looks upon these rare souls, no matter how much or how little disagreement there may be as to the validity or the efficacy of their way of life, one quality these men have in common, one which distinguishes them utterly from the rest of mankind and gives the key to their personality, their raison d'être: *they have all time on their hands!* These men are never in a hurry, never too busy to respond to a call. The problem of time is simply nonexistent for them. They live in the moment and they are aware that each moment is an eternity. Every other type of individual that we know puts limits on his "free" time. These other men have nothing but free time.

If I could give you a thought to take with you daily to the water closet, it would be: "Meditate on free time!" Should this thought bear no fruit, then go back to your books, your magazines, your newspapers, your digests, your comic strips, your thriller-dillers. Arm yourselves, inform yourselves, prepare yourselves, amuse yourselves, forget yourselves, divide yourselves. And when you have done all these things (including the burnishing of gold, as Cennini recommends), ask yourselves if you are stronger, wiser, happier, nobler, more contented beings. I know you will *not* be, but that is for *you* to discover . . .

It is a curious thing, but the best kind of water closet—according to the medicos—is one in which only an equilibrist could manage to read. I refer to the kind one finds in Europe, France especially, and which makes the ordinary American tourist quail. There is no seat, no bowl, just a hole in the floor with two footpads and a handrail on either side for support. One doesn't sit, one squats. (Les vraies chiottes, quoi!) In these quaint retreats the thought of reading never enters one's head. One wants to get done with it as soon as possible—and not get one's feet wet! We Americans, through disguising whatever has to do with the vital functions, end up by making "the John" so attractive that we linger there long after we have done our business. The combination of toilet-and-bath is to us just ducky. To take a bath in a separate part of the house would strike us as absurd. It might not seem so to people with truly delicate susceptibilities.

Break . . . A few moments ago I was taking a nap outdoors in a heavy fog. It was a light sleep broken by the buzzing of a torpid fly. In one of my fitful starts, half-asleep half-awake, there came to me the remembrance of a dream, or to be exact, the fragment of a dream. It was an old, old dream, and a very wonderful one, which comes back to me—in parts—again and again. At times it comes back so vividly, even though through a chink, that I doubt if it ever was a dream. And then I begin to rack my brain to recall the title of a series of books which I once kept safely hidden away in a little vault. At this present moment the nature and content of this recurrent dream is not as clear as it has been on previous occasions. Nevertheless, the aura of it is still strong, as well as the associations which usually accompany the recall.

A moment ago I was wondering why it was that I thought of this dream in connection with the toilet, but then suddenly I recalled that in coming out of my fitful sleep, or half out of it, I brought with me, so to speak, the frightful odor of the toilet which was secreted in "the storm shed" at home in that neighborhood which I always telescope into "the street of early sorrows."

In winter it was a veritable ordeal to take refuge in this air-tight, sub-zero cubicle which was never illuminated, not even by a flickering wax taper in sweet oil.

But there was something else which precipitated the remembrance of these days long past. Just this morning I was glancing over the index given in the last volume of The Harvard Classics, in order to refresh my memory. As always, the mere thought of this collection awakens memories of gloomy days spent in the parlor upstairs with these bloody volumes. Considering the morose frame of mind I usually was in when I retreated to this funereal wing of the house, I cannot help but marvel that I ever waded through such literature as *Rabbi Ben Ezra, The Chambered Nautilus, Ode to a Waterfowl, I Promessi Sposi, Samson Agonistes, William Tell, The Wealth of Nations, The Chronicles* of Froissart, John Stuart Mill's *Autobiography* and such like. I believe now that it was not the cold fog but the leaden weight of those days upstairs in the parlor, when I was struggling with authors for whom I had no relish, that made me sleep so fitfully just a little while ago. If so, I must thank their departed spirits for making me recall this dream which has to do with a set of magic books I prized so highly that I hid them away—in a little vault—and never have been able to find them again. Is it not strange that these books, books belonging to my youth, should be of more importance to me than anything I have read subsequently? Obviously I must have read them in my sleep, inventing titles, contents, author, everything. Now and then, as I mentioned before, with flashes of the dream there come sometimes vivid recollections of the very texture of the narrative. At such moments I go almost frantic, for there is one book among the series which holds the clue to the entire work, and this particular book, its title, contents, meaning, comes at times to the very threshold of consciousness.

One of the hazier, fuzzier, more tormenting aspects connected with the recall is that I am always reminded—by whom? by what?—that it was in the neighborhood of Fort Hamilton (Brooklyn) that I read these magic books. The conviction is forced upon me that they are still secreted in the house wherein I read them, but where this house is exactly, whom it belonged to, what business brought me there, I have not the faintest notion. All that I can recollect today about Fort Hamilton are the bike rides to and in the vicinity which I took on lonely Saturday afternoons when consumed with a forlorn love for my first sweetheart. Like a ghost on wheels, I covered the same routine trajectory—Dyker Heights, Bensonhurst, Fort Hamilton—whenever I left the house thinking of her. So engrossed was I in thoughts of her that I was absolutely unconscious of my body: I might be hugging the rear right fender of a car at forty miles an hour or trailing along like a somnambulist. I can't say that time hung heavy on my hands. The heaviness was entirely in my heart. Occasionally I would be roused from my reverie by the whizzing of a golf ball over my head. Occasionally the sight of the barracks would bring me to, for whenever I espy military quarters, quarters where men are herded like cattle, I experience a feeling almost of nausea. But there were also pleasant intermissions—or "remissions"—if you like. Always, for instance, when swinging into Bensonhurst where, as a boy, I had spent such marvelous days with Joey and Tony. How time had changed everything! I was now, on these Saturday afternoons, a young man hopelessly in love, an absolute mooncalf utterly indifferent to everything else in the world. If I threw myself into a book it was only to forget the pain of a love which was too much for me. The bike was my refuge. Astride the bike, I had the sensation of taking my painful love for an airing. The panorama which unrolled before me, or receded behind me, was thoroughly dreamlike: I might just as well have been riding a treadmill before a stage set. Whatever I looked at served only to mind me of *her.* Sometimes, in order I suppose not to tumble off the wheel in sheer despair and chagrin, I would encourage those fatuous fancies which assail the lovelorn, the wisp of a hope, let us say, that in making a bend in the road who should be standing there to greet me—and with such a warm, gracious, lovely smile!—but *she.* If she failed to "materialize" at this point I would lead myself to believe that it would be at some other point, towards which, with prayers and propitiations, I would proceed to rush full speed, only to arrive there breathless and again deceived.

Undoubtedly the mysterious magical nature of those dream books had to do, and were inspired by, my pent-up longing for this girl I could never catch up with. Undoubtedly, somewhere in the neighbourhood of Fort Hamilton, in brief moments so black, so grief-ridden, so desolate, so uniquely my very own, my heart must have broken again and again. Yet—of this I am certain!—*those books had nothing to do with the subject of love.* They were beyond such . . . such what? They dealt with unutterable things. Even now, foggy and time-bitten as the dream is in remembrance, I can recall such dim, shadowy, yet revelatory elements as these: a hoary, wizard-like figure seated on a throne (as in ancient stone chess pieces), holding in his hands a bunch of large, heavy keys (like ancient Swedish money), and he resembles neither Hermes Trismegistus nor Apollonius of Tyana, nor even dread Merlin, but is more like Noah or Methuselah. He is trying, it is so clear, to tell me something beyond my comprehension, something I have been longing and aching to know. (A cosmic secret, doubtless.) This figure is out of the key book which, as I have emphasized, is the missing link in the whole series. Up to this point in the narrative, if it may be called that—that is to say, throughout the preceding volumes of the dream collection—it has been a series of unearthly, interplanetary, and, for want of a better word, "forbidden" adventures of the most dazzling variety and nature. As if legend, history and myth, combined with supra-sensual flights beyond description, had been telescoped and compressed into one long sustained moment of godlike fancy. And of course—for my especial benefit! *But*—what aggravates the situation, in the dream, is that I can always recall the fact that I *did* begin the reading of the missing volume but—ah, think of it!—for no obvious, apparent, or even hidden reason, certainly for no *good* reason, I dropped it. A sense of irreparable loss smothers, literally flattens out, any rising sense of guilt. Why, why, I ask myself, had I not continued the reading of this book? Had I done so, the book would never have been lost, nor the others either. In the dream the double loss—loss of contents, loss of book itself—is accentuated and presented as one.

There is still another feature connected with this dream: my mother's part in it. In *The Rosy Crucifixion* I have described my visits to the old home, visits made expressly to recover my youthful belongings—particularly certain books which would, for some unaccountable reason, suddenly become on these occasions very precious to me. As I relate it, my mother seems to have taken a perverse delight in telling me that she had "long ago" given these old books away. *"To whom?"* I would demand, beside myself. She could never remember, it was always so long ago. Or, if she did remember, the brats to whom she had given them had long since moved away, and of course she no longer knew where they lived, nor did she think—and this was ever gratuitous on her part—that they would have kept these childish books all this time. And so on. Some she had given, so she confessed, to the Good Will Society or to the Society of Saint Vincent de Paul. This sort of talk always drove me frantic. Sometimes, in waking moments, I would actually wonder to myself if those missing dream books whose titles had vanished from memory utterly were not real flesh-and-blood books which my mother had thoughtlessly, recklessly given away.

Of course, all the time I was up there in the parlor wading through the dreary five-foot shelf, my mother was just as baffled by this behavior as by everything which it struck me to do. She could not understand how I could "waste" a beautiful afternoon reading those soporific tomes. That I was miserable she knew, but as to why I was miserable she had never the faintest idea. Occasionally she would express the thought that it was the books which depressed me. And of course they did help to depress me more deeply—since they contained no remedy for what ailed me. I wanted to drown myself in my sorrows, and the books were like so many fat, buzzing flies keeping me awake, making my very scalp itch with boredom.

How I jumped the other day when I read in one of Marie Corelli's now forgotten books: "'Give us something that will endure!' is the exclamation of weary humanity. The things we have pass, and by reason of their ephemeral nature are worthless. Give us what we can keep and call our own forever!' This is why we try and test all things that *appear* to give proof of the supersensual element in man, and when we find ourselves deceived by impostors and conjurors, our disgust and disappointment are too bitter to even find vent in words."

There is another dream, concerning another book, which I tell of in *The Rosy Crucifixion*. It is a very, very strange dream, and in it there appears a big book which this girl I loved (the same one!) and another person (her unknown lover probably) are reading over my shoulder. It is my own book—I mean a book which I wrote myself. I mention it only to suggest that by all the laws of logic it *would* come about that the missing dream book, the key to the whole series—*what whole series?*—was written by myself and no other. If I had been able to write it in a dream why could I not rewrite it in a waking dream? Is one state so different from another? Since I have ventured to hazard this much, why not complete the thought and add that my whole purpose in writing has been to clear up a mystery. (What this mystery is I have never given overtly.) Yes, from the time I began to write in earnest my one desire has been to unload this book which I have carried about with me, deep under my belt, in all latitudes and longitudes, in all travails and vicissitudes. To dig this book out of my guts, make it warm, living, palpable—that has been my whole aim and preoccupation . . . That hoary wizard who appears in onirific flashes hidden away in a tiny vault—a dream of a vault, you might say—who is he but myself, my most ancient, ancient self? He holds a bunch of keys in his hands, does he not? And he is situated in the key center of the whole mysterious edifice. Well, what is that missing book, then, if not "the story of my heart," as Jefferies so beautifully names it. Is there any other story a man has to tell but this? And is this not the most difficult one of all to tell, the one which is most hidden, most abstruse, most mystifying?

That we read even in our dreams is a signal thing. What are we reading, what *can* we be reading in the darkness of unconsciousness, save our inmost thoughts? Thoughts never cease to stir the brain. Occasionally we perceive a difference between thoughts and thought, between that which thinks and the mind which is all thought. Sometimes, as if through a tiny crevice, we catch a glimpse of our dual self. Brain is not mind, that we may be certain of. If it *were* possible to localize the seat of mind, then it would be truer to situate it in the heart. But the heart is merely a receptacle, or transformer, by means of which thought becomes recognizable and effective. Thought has to pass through the heart to be made active and meaningful.

There is a book which is part of our being, contained in our being, and is the record of our being. Our being, I say, and not our becoming. We commence the writing of this book at birth and we continue it after death. It is only when we are about to be reborn that we bring it to a close and write "Finis." Thus there is a whole series of books which, from birth to birth, continue the tale of identity. We are all authors, but we are not all heralds and prophets. What we bring to light of the hidden record we sign with our baptismal name, which is never the real name. But it is only a tiny, tiny fraction of the record which even the best of us, the strongest, the most courageous, the most gifted, ever bring to light. What cramps our style, what falsifies the narrative, are those portions of the record which we can no longer decipher. The art of writing we never lose, but what we do lose sometimes is the art of reading. When we encounter an adept in this art the gift of sight is restored to us. It is the gift for interpretation, naturally, for to read is always to interpret.

The universality of thought is supreme and paramount. Nothing is beyond comprehension or understanding. What fails us is the desire to know, the desire to read or interpret, the desire to give meaning to whatever thought be voiced. *Acedia:* the great sin against The Holy Ghost. Drugged by the pain of deprivation, in whatever form it manifests itself, and it assumes many, many forms, we take refuge in mystification. Humanity is, in the deepest sense, an orphan—not because it has been *abandoned,* but because it obstinately refuses to recognize its divine parentage. We terminate the book of life in the afterworld because we refuse to understand what we have written here and now . . .

But let us return to *les cabinets,* which is the French for toilet and, for some baffling reason, used always in the plural. Some of my readers may recall a passage, one in which I give tender reminiscences of France, concerning a hurried visit to the toilet and the wholly unexpected view of Paris which I had from the window of this tight place.* Would it not be fetching, some people think, to so build one's home that from the toilet seat itself one could command a breath-taking panorama? My thought is that it does not matter in the least what the view from the toilet may be. If, in going to the toilet, you have to take something else with you besides yourself, besides your own vital need to eliminate and cleanse the system, then perhaps a beautiful or a breath-taking view from the toilet window is a desideratum. In that case you may as well build a book shelf, hang paintings, and otherwise beautify this *lieu d'aisance.* Then, instead of going outdoors and seeking a bo-tree, one may as well sit in "the bathroom" and meditate. If necessary, build your whole world around "the John." Let the rest of the house remain subordinate to the seat of this supreme function. Bring forth a race which, highly conscious of

---

*See the chapter called "Remember to Remember" from my book, *Remember to Remember;* New Directions, New York.

the art of elimination, will make it its business to eliminate all that is ugly, useless, evil and "deleterious" in everyday life. Do that and you will raise the toilet to a heavenly place. But do not, while making use of this sacred retreat, waste your time reading *about* the elimination of this or that, nor even about elimination itself. The difference between the people who secrete themselves in the toilet, whether to read, pray or meditate, and those who go there only to do their business, is that the former always find themselves with unfinished business on hand and the latter are always ready for the next move, the next act.

The old saying is: "Keep your bowels open and trust in the Lord!" There's wisdom in it. Broadly speaking, it means that if you keep your system free of poison you will be able to keep your mind free and clear, open and receptive; you will cease worrying about matters which are not your concern—such as how the cosmos should be run, for example—and you will do what has to be done in peace and tranquillity. There is no hint or suspicion contained in this homely piece of advice that, in keeping your bowels open, you should also struggle to keep up with world events, or keep abreast of current books and plays, or familiarize yourself with the latest fashions, the most glamorous cosmetics, or the fundamentals of basic English. Indeed, the whole implication of this curt maxim is—the less done about it the better. I say "it," meaning the very serious—and neither absurd nor disgusting—business of going to the toilet. The key words are "open" and "trust." Now, if it be argued that to read while sitting on the stool is an aid to loosening the bowels, then I say—read the most lenitive literature possible. Read the Gospels, for the Gospels are of the Lord—and the second injunction is "to trust in the Lord." Myself, I am convinced that it is possible to have faith and trust in the Lord without reading Holy Writ in the toilet. Indeed, I am convinced that one is apt to have more faith and trust in the Lord if one reads nothing at all in the toilet.

When you visit your analyst does he ask you what you read when using the stool? He should, you know. To an analyst it should make a great difference whether you read one kind of literature in the toilet and another elsewhere. It should even make a difference to him whether you read or do not read— in the toilet. Such matters are unfortunately not widely enough discussed.

It is assumed that what one does in the toilet is one's own private affair. It is not. The whole universe is concerned. If, as we are led to believe more and more, there are creatures from other planets who are keeping tabs on us, be certain that they are prying into our most secret doings. If they are able to penetrate the atmosphere of this earth, what is to stop them from penetrating the locked doors of our toilets? Give that a thought when you have nothing better to meditate upon—in there. Let me urge those who are experimenting with rockets and other interstellar means of communication and transportation to think for a brief moment of how they must appear to the denizens of other worlds when reading *Time* or *The New Yorker,* let us say, in "the John." What you read tells a good deal about your inmost being, but it does not tell everything. The fact, however, that you are *reading* when you should be *doing* has a certain importance. It is a characteristic which men alien to this planet would remark immediately. It might well influence their judgment of us.

And if, to change the tune, we limit ourselves to the opinion of merely terrestrial beings, but beings who are alert and discriminating, the picture does not alter much. There is not only something grotesque and ridiculous about poring over the printed page while seated on the stool, there is something mad about it. This pathological element evinces itself clearly enough when reading is combined with eating, for example, or with taking a promenade. Why is it not equally arresting when we observe it connected with the act of defecation? Is there anything natural about doing these two things simultaneously? Supposing that, though you never intended to become an opera singer, every time you went to the toilet you began practicing the scales. Supposing that, though singing was all in all to you, you insisted that the only time you could sing was when you went to "the John." Or supposing you simply said that you sang in the toilet because you had nothing better to do. Would that hold water in an alienist's cabinet? But this is the sort of alibi people give when they are pressed to explain why they *must* read in the toilet.

To merely open the bowels, then, is not enough? Must one include Shakespeare, Dante, William Faulkner and the whole galaxy of pocket-book authors? Dear me, how complicated life has become! Once upon a time any old place would do. For company one had the sun or the stars, the song of the birds or the hooting of an owl. There was no question of killing time, nor of killing two birds with one stone. It was just a matter of letting go. There wasn't even the thought of trust in the Lord. This trusting in the Lord was so implicit a part of man's nature that to connect it with the movement of the bowels would have seemed blasphemous and absurd. Nowadays it takes a higher mathematician, who is also a metaphysician and an astrophysicist, to explain the simple functioning of the autonomic system. Nothing is simple any more. Through analysis and experiment the slightest things have assumed such complicated proportions that it is a wonder any one can be said to know anything about anything. Even instinctive behavior now appears to be highly complex. Primitive emotions, such as fear, hate, love, anguish, all prove to be terribly complex.

And we are the people, heaven forbid, who in the next fifty years are going to conquer space! We are the creatures who, though scorning to become angels, are going to develop into interplanetary beings! Well, one thing is certainly predictable: even out there in space we shall have our water closets! Wherever we go, "the John" accompanies us, I notice. Formerly we used to ask: "What if cows could fly?" That joke has become antediluvian. The question which now imposes, in view of projected voyages beyond the gravitational pull, is: "How will our organs function when we are no longer subject to the sway of gravity?" Traveling at a rate faster than the speed of thought—it has been hazarded that we may be able to accomplish this!—will we be able to read at all out there between the stars and planets? I ask because I assume that the model space ship will be equipped with lavatories as well as laboratories, and, if so, our new time-space explorers will undoubtedly bring with them their toilet literature.

There is something to conjure upon—the nature of this interspatial literature! We used to see questionnaires from time to time demanding to know what we would read if we were going to take refuge on a deserted island. No one, to my knowledge, has yet framed a questionnaire as to what would make good reading on the stool in space. If we are going to get the same old answers to this coming questionnaire, i.e., Homer, Dante, Shakespeare, et Cie, I shall indeed be cruelly disappointed.

That first ship to leave the earth, and possibly never return—what I would not give to know the titles of the books it will contain! Methinks the books have not been written which will offer mental, moral and spiritual sustenance to these daring pioneers. The great possibility, as I see it, is that these men may not care to read at all, not even in the toilet: they may be content to tune in on the angels, to listen to the voices of the dear departed, to cock their ears to catch the ceaseless celestial song.

My First Speech*: On Writing

Katherine Anne Porter

I have always had a fixed notion that a writer should lead a private life and keep silent in so far as writing is concerned and let published works speak for themselves, so, in trying to tell you something of what I think and believe about certain aspects of writing, I speak strictly as an individual and not as the spokesman for one school or the enemy of another.

Legend and memory is the title of the first section of a long novel I am now working on, and I called it that because it is from these two sources I am attempting to recreate a history of my family, which begins almost with the beginnings of the settlement of America. I have for this only legend, those things I have been told or that I read as a child; and I may say here that I consider most of our published history available to children quite as legendary as the siege of Troy: and my own memory of events taking place around me at the same time. And there is a third facet: my present memory and explanation to myself of my then personal life, the life of a child, which is in itself a mystery, while being living and legendary to that same child grown up. All this is working at once in my mind, in a confusion of dimensions. This may not sound so simple, and I believe it is less simple even than it sounds. But I feel that to give a true testimony it is necessary to know and remember what I was, what I felt, and what I knew then, and not confuse it with what I know or

---

*These are short hand notes taken of a lecture I made before the American Women's Club in Paris, 1934.—K.A.P.

think I know now. So, I shall try to tell the truth, but the result will be fiction. I shall not be at all surprised at this result: it is what I mean to do; it is, to my way of thinking, the way fiction is made.

It is a curious long process, roundabout to the last degree, like a slow chemical change, and I believe it holds true as much when one is not recreating one's own life and past but the life-history of another person. I think there are very few living characters in fiction who were not founded on a real living original. I think of Anna Karenina, Madame Bovary, and the tragic characters in *The Possessed*. Thackeray, so far as I know, never admitted that there had ever lived an Englishwoman like Becky Sharp. He was far too chivalrous for that. But that he did know, disapprove of, and admire such a person seems to me by the internal evidence fairly certain. I believe she could not have had so much vitality, if nature had not first created her for Thackeray to transmute into a work of art.

I should dare to say that none of these characters so living in fiction would have recognized their own portraits, for if the transformation is successful the character becomes something else in its own right, as alive as the person who posed for the portrait.

This is not a particularly easy thing to do, and I think of late a great many writers have found what they consider a way out, which leads really to an impasse. I mean the very thinly disguised autobiographical novel. It is an old saying that every human being possesses in his own life and experience the material for one novel. This may be true. It is one of those generalities hard to prove or disprove. It has been accepted a shade too literally, I think, by a great group of recent writers. This tendency is to make one's self the hero or heroine of one's own adventure, in literature as in life. It is only, I think, when the writer is adult enough to face the rather disheartening truth that he is not by any means always the hero of his own little history, much less the center of the universe, that we can begin to get near a human chronicle that could be worth reading. If writers, and not always professional writers, but anyone who really has a story to tell, could only tell the facts in such matters: the plain facts, it would be worth hearing. The novel is not really the vehicle for autobiography. It grows even more confusing when literary people live in such close-knitted groups that all of them have only one experience in common, and each one sits down to give his version of it, with himself as the hero and the others either pallid, minor figures, fools, or outright villains. For in the anxiety of each one to justify himself, he hardly takes care to disguise his characters other than in a kind of distortion.

Most certainly the artist is present in all he creates. He is his own work; and, if he were not, then there could be, I think, no true creation. But it is a confession of failure of what I shall call imaginative honesty to make one's self always the shining protagonist of one's own novels. It is true there do exist, I can't name one off hand, heroes who are the wishfulfillment of the author. Everyone knows that Stendhal (Henri Beyle) was a short, lumpy, timid fellow, unattractive, and unlucky in love. He had a kind of minor official post under Napoleon, a dull job that he detested—we know from internal evidence that Stendhal was brilliant, witty, a great sober artist. He dreamed of himself and created to his heart's desire a hero whom I consider one of the most detestable in all fiction: Julien Sorel. But Julien Sorel is nonetheless a superb creation, a work of art beyond a doubt. Still, as I follow the adventures of Julien Sorel, the workings of his pretentious, disorderly, shallow mind and heart, I am beset by the uneasy feeling that Stendhal meant him to be an admirable, complicated, unusually sensitive young man: portrait of Stendhal, the handsome French mask of little Henri Beyle—in a word. Too many quite promising young writers have been misled by the same vanity, but with less adroitness, along this same path; and how many little books do I know written by rather drab young men whose experience has not been unusual but who make themselves always the golden hero, and how many young women of ordinary charm cannot resist being either the spangle-eyed heroine or much the brightest girl in the class.

In America there is a great deal of excitement about the importance of being American. Even the writers have taken it up. When I was in America, all my writing friends were here,* sending me word that Paris, or some city in Europe, was to be their final choice of a dwelling place; when I finally came here, it was only to begin receiving letters from them all, now back in America,

---

*In France.

telling me that I was wrong to expatriate myself. The discussion runs on and on about "typical" and "not typical" American writers. So far as I am able to remember, for such classifications mean little to me, Bret Harte, Mark Twain, Sara Orne Jewett, Ralph Waldo Emerson, and other such diverse personalities are mentioned most frequently as American; while such strangely different writers as Hemingway and Hergesheimer, let us say, are called "not typical."

This may seem a digression, yet it belongs to what I am trying to say.

What is a typical American? In any profession? or state of life? I believe that different periods produce a certain typical mode of thought, or habit of mind, and the causes for this habit of mind are so complicated, so much a matter of the converging of a thousand influences to a given point, that I, for one, could never attempt to account for them. I think that artists are quite often not prophets, and there is very little reason why they should be. They have a way of being formed by their epoch, as other people are. Their code of morals, their religions, their mode of dress, even their styles in writing, can usually be dated and placed without much trouble. Now there was a time, or so legend insists, when there was a stable, settled world of society, when everybody thought, felt, and believed the same thing. This was never true, but it has become the fashion to say so; and in America we also had our golden age, which seems to have ended around 1910. Now, to a great many of us, and this includes the larger number of our so-called modern writers, there have been varieties of experience, historical changes. For some of them, life dates from the great war.* Their independent life, if that after-war life could be said to have had any independence (it had revolt, and disillusion, and hardship, and the privilege of sinking or swimming); but that is hardly independence, and above all there is nothing solid or comfortable about it. Also, with the new mixture of races, the breaking up of caste to some extent, economic upheavals, is it not possible that the author is merely again being the child of his time and is running to variety instead of to type? But we have always had variety.

We have always had variety, and an American writer who, thirsting for change, imitates Joyce is at least stating a point of view and a preference

*1914–1918.

not likely to make his fortune; but he had better do that than to write slick fiction for a slick weekly or attempt to return to an America and an American mode of thought which no longer exists except possibly in a past which is too recent to be appropriately revived. What we look upon now as typical may simply have been, once, one thing among many but was chosen as a type. You might say that Buffalo Bill was a typical American, or that Mark Twain was typical, or that Charles Francis Adams is, or that Nathan Hale was, or Jesse James. I believe that these men were not typical at all. They were individuals, who by the mysterious workings of environment and education in blood and tradition became the finished products of a certain sort of society; more than that, a certain section or region of America. They became typical in two ways, by being distinguished enough to be imitated and by being so admired or hated that their lives became symbols: but there was really, let us remember, only one of each of these men; and, different as they are, they were all Americans. Our blood has become pretty well mixed by now, and it was fairly well mixed before we came here. It is European or Oriental blood, transplanted to a new Continent, our roots are here; and our types are as varied. I dare say there is no man living who can with certainty name *all* the bloods that flow in his veins.

Lately the mixing process has speeded up and is now going through a new phase. The changes that are taking place will end by giving us a new set of features, so that I, for one, would be puzzled to say just what is a typical American. Think of our American writers. Let me name a few of them at random. They come on all levels of talent and achievement, from several periods, and from all parts of that tremendous country. Herman Melville, Sherwood Anderson, Edgar Allan Poe, Henry Adams, Stephen Crane, Sinclair Lewis, Ralph Waldo Emerson, Henry James, Walt Whitman, John Dos Passos, Ernest Hemingway, Washington Irving. Think of these last two together. But how can we say that they are not all Americans, and each one typically, oh quite typically, exactly himself and nobody else. They are typical as Chekhov, Dostoievsky, and Tolstoy are typical Russians, and each one a unique creature. I should think, one might very well say that Joyce is not a typical Irishman. No, but now that he has done it it is hard to imagine any other than an Irishman reacting in just such a way against his particular country, time, and society. It is fairly easy to say that now, because it just happens that no one but this one Irishman has ever behaved in just that way. Whether you like him or not, I fancy he is here to stay for some time. He will be there in the road: you may walk around him, climb over him, or dig under; but he will be there. I admire him immensely, but one of him is enough. Indeed, that is all there *can* be of him. I know better than to try to imitate him, and I wouldn't be influenced by him for the world; but I think he is going to begin a tradition, indeed has already. Now when one speaks of tradition even American tradition, which we are in the habit of speaking of as new, it is better to remember that there are already a great many different traditions and most of them quite feasible. The artist, after having served his apprenticeship, may discover in what tradition he belongs. But the artist is usually too busy and too preoccupied with his own undertaking to worry much about whether he has got into the right tradition, or, indeed, into any at all. There have been more of them lately worrying about how they were going to get out of the beaten track. I think they were mistaken. An artist does better to leave all such classifications to the critics. He had better follow the bent of his own mind, whether it is for the moment fashionable or not; and it isn't for him to worry about whether he is really great or a true genius: that throws him off most frightfully, and his audience too. I should say that a major work of art occurs in any medium when a first-rate creative intelligence gets hold of a great theme and does something hitherto unexampled with it. And if this happens in our time we had better bless our luck and not worry about whether this marks the beginning or the end of a tradition. The other day a young writing friend of mine burst out suddenly: "I am going to write like Racine!" Now this is an American boy, an Irish-American boy with a very good talent. He added, in a moment: "I am Racine." Well, of course, the only possible answer to that was: "You're nothing of the sort." And then he explained, and it wasn't so foolish as all that: he meant he admired the qualities of clearness and directness in the style of Racine, what he called Racine's coldness. He meant, after all, that he feels a sympathy in his mind for that kind of writing; and if he goes on writing and his mind goes on working that way he may develop a good measured spare style. But I feel pretty certain no one will even be reminded of Racine by it; above all, not if our American boy does a really good job.

It is my belief that the less typical a writer is the less you are able to catalogue him, the more apt he is to be a writer worth your attention. We don't need any more types. We need individuals. We always did need them. The value of a writer can be measured best, probably, by his capacity to express what he feels, knows, is, has been, has seen, and experienced, by means of this paraphrase which is art, this process of taking his own material and making what he wants to make of it. He cannot do this, indeed he is not an artist, if he allows himself to be hampered by any set of conventions outside of the severe laws and limitations of his own medium. No one else can tell him what life is like to him, in what colors he sees the world. He cannot sit down and say, Go to, I will be a writer because it's an interesting career! Even less can he say, I must be an American writer; or French, or whatever. He has already been born one kind of person or another, and taking thought about it cannot change much. He cannot even worry about whether the publishers are going to accept his work or not; if he does, he is as good as done for: he may as well never have begun. He may be interpreter, critic, rebel, prophet, conformist, devil, or angel, or he may be all these things in turn, or all of them a little at once; but he can be none of these things to order: nobody's order, not even his own.

Simply stated, maybe too simply, it is the writer's business first to have something of his own to say; second, to say it in his own language and style. You must have heard this many times before; but I think it is one of the primary rules to keep in mind. The great thing is to convey to you, in this saying, a sense of the reality and the truth of what he tells you, with some new light thrown upon it that gives you a glimpse into some wider world not built with hands. It is like the dizzying blue in the upper right-hand corner of some of Brueghel's paintings. I remember especially the two versions of the fall of Icarus. The lower left-hand corner is real, no doubt about it: we have all seen such fields, such figures of men, such furrows and animals; but the upper right-hand corner is true too, though it is this vast transfiguration of blue such as we may never have seen in the sky over us, but it exists for us because Brueghel has made it. Artists create monsters and many different sorts of landscapes;

and they are true, if the artists are great enough to show you what they have seen. Matisse has said: the painter should paint the thing he knows. So far as it goes, this is good advice. The question is, how much more does any artist know imaginatively than factually? That is his test; for Dante knew both heaven and hell without ever having seen them; and described them for us so that we know them too: and Shakespeare, taking legends and his own great fertility, created for us countries which did not exist until then: but they exist now, and we may travel in them when we please. Only yesterday, I was looking again at some of Dürer's scenes representing St. John's revelations, and I am glad Dürer chose not to stick by the thing he knew with the eye of the flesh even though that was an exceptionally clear and magical eye too. But I have his view of the Apocalypse, and it is mine: I was there.

So the reader, whether with pleasure, pain, or even disgust (it is not necessary for you always to be pleased), must still find himself in the atmosphere created for him by the artists, and the artists do not always create a pleasant world, because that is not their business. If they do that, you will be right not to trust them in anything. We must leave all that to people whose affair it is, to smooth our daily existence a little. Great art is hardly ever agreeable; the artist should remind you that, for some, experience is a horror in this world, and that the human imagination also knows horror. He should direct you to points of view you have not examined before, or cause you to comprehend, even if you do not sympathize with predicaments not your own, ways of life, manners of speech, even of dress, above all of the unique human heart, outside of your normal experience. And this can better be done by presentation than by argument. This presentation must be real, with a truth beyond the artist's own prejudices, loves, hates; I mean his personal ones. The outright propagandist sets up in me such a fury of opposition I am not apt to care much whether he has got his facts straight or not. He is like someone standing on your toes, between you and an open window, describing the view to you. All I ask of him to do is to open the window, stand out of the way, and let me look at the view for myself. Now truth is a very tall word, and we are rather apt to tag our pet theories and beliefs with this abused word. Let me reconsider a moment and say, the writer must have honesty, he should not wilfully distort and obscure. Now I have said always that honesty in any case is not enough, but it is an indispensable element in the arts. No legend is ever true, but I believe all of them are founded on some germ of truth; and even these truths appear in different lights to every mind they are presented to, and the legend is that work of art which goes on in the human mind, adding to and arranging, harmonizing and rounding out, making larger or smaller than life, and holding the entire finished product in a good light and asking you to believe it. And it is true. No memory is really faithful. It has too far to go, too many changing landscapes of the human mind and heart, to bear any sort of really trustworthy witness, except in part. So the truth in art is got by change. In the work of art, nothing can be accidental: the sprawling, chaotic sense of that word as we use it in everyday life, where so many things happen to us that we by no means plan, it takes craftsmanship quite often beyond our powers to manage by plan even a short day for ourselves. The craftsmanship of the artist can make what he wishes of anything that excites his imagination. Craftsmanship is a homely, workaday thing. It is a little like making shoes, or weaving cloth. A writer may be inspired occasionally: that's his good luck; but he doesn't learn to write by inspiration: he works at it. In that sense the writer is a worker, a workingman, a workingwoman. Writing is not an elegant pastime, it is a sober and hardworked trade, which gives great joy to the worker. The artist is first a worker. He must roll up his sleeves and get to work like a bricklayer. The romantic notion of the artist—persons who live their romances, those who depend on the gestures, the dress, the habits, of what they hope is genius—hoping by presenting the appearance of genius, genius would be added to them.

It is not a career, it is a vocation; it is not a means to fame and glory—it is a discipline of living—and unless you think this, it is better not to take it up. It is not the sort of thing one "takes up" as one might take up knitting and put it down again.

All this you can learn about the mechanics, the technique, and it is all to the good for your education. It cannot make you an artist. But it will make of you a better reader, a cleverer critic, it will make of you some one the artist must look out for, and it will make for him an audience that he can't trifle with even if he would.

Literary Pleasure

Jorge Luis Borges

I suspect that the detective novels of Eduardo Gutiérrez and a volume of Greek mythology and *The Student of Salamanca* and the reasonable and not at all fanciful fantasies of Jules Verne and Stevenson's grandiose romances and the first serial novel ever written, *The Thousand and One Nights,* are the greatest literary joys I have experienced. The list is diverse and cannot claim any unity other than the early age at which I read them. I was a hospitable reader in those days, a polite explorer of the lives of others, and I accepted everything with providential and enthusiastic resignation. I believed everything, even errata and poor illustrations. Each story was an adventure, and I sought worthy and prestigious places to live it: the highest step of a staircase, an attic, the roof of the house.

Then I discovered words: I discovered their receptive and even memorable readability, and harbored many printed in prose and verse. Some—still—accompany my solitude; the pleasure they inspired has become a second nature to me. Others have fallen mercifully from my memory, like *Don Juan Tenorio,* which I once knew by heart, and which the years and my indifference have uprooted. Gradually, through ineffable leaps of taste, I became familiar with literature. I am unable to remember the first time I read Quevedo, who is now the writer I most frequent. On the other hand, my first encounter with *Sartor Resartus* by the maniacal Thomas Carlyle was passionate—a book now huddled in some corner, which has been reading itself for years in my library. Later, I became worthy of writerly friendships that still honor me: Schopenhauer, Unamuno, Dickens, De Quincey, again Quevedo.

And today? I have turned into a writer, a critic, and I must confess (not without remorse and conscious of my deficiency) that I reread with the pleasure of remembering and that new readings do not enthrall me. Now I tend to dispute their novelty, to translate them into schools, influences, composites. I suspect that if they were sincere, all the critics in the world (and even some in Buenos Aires) would say the same. It is only normal: intelligence is economical and orderly, and a miracle strikes it as a bad habit. By admitting this I already disqualify myself.

Menéndez y Pelayo writes: "If poetry was not read with the eyes of history, so few poems would survive!" (*Historia de la poesía americana* II, 103). What seems a warning is a confession. Those often resurrected eyes of history, are they not but a network of sympathies, generosities, or simply courtesies? You may reply that without them, we would confuse the plagiarist with the inventor, the shadow with the body. Certainly, but one thing is the equitable distribution of glories, and another, pure aesthetic pleasure. I have observed with regret that any man, by merely perusing many volumes in order to judge them (and the critic's task is nothing else) can become a genealogist of styles and detective of influences. He inhabits this terrifying and almost inexpressible truth: Beauty in literature is accidental, depending on the harmony or discord of the words manipulated by the writer, and is not tied to eternity. Epigones, those who frequent already lyricized themes, usually achieve it; innovators, almost never.

Our indolence speaks of classical books, eternal books. If only some eternal book existed, primed for our enjoyment and whims, no less inventive in the populous morning as in the secluded night, oriented toward all hours of the world. Your favorite books, reader, are like the rough drafts of that book without a final reading.

If the attainments of the verbal beauty that art can provide us were infallible, non-chronological anthologies would exist, or even ones that would not mention the names of authors or of literary schools. The single evidence of each composition's beauty would be enough to justify it. Of course this behavior would be bizarre and even dangerous for those anthologies in use. How can we admire the sonnets of Juan Boscán if we do not know that they are the first to be borne by our language? How can we endure so-and-so's verse if we do not know that he has perpetrated many others that are even more flawed and that, moreover, he is a friend of the anthologist?

I fear you will not understood my point here, and so, at the risk of over-simplifying the matter, I will find an example. Let our illustration be this unfamiliar metaphor: "The fire, with ferocious jaws, devours the countryside." Is this phrase censurable or legitimate? That depends, I insist, solely on the one who forged it, and this is not a paradox. Let us suppose that in a café on the Calle Corrientes or on the Avenida 9 de Julio, a man of letters presents it to me as his own. I will think: Making metaphors is now a vulgar pastime; to substitute *swallow* for *burn* is not an auspicious exchange; the matter of jaws may amaze some people, but it is weak of the poet to allow himself to be carried away by the mechanical phrase "devouring fire"; in brief, nil. . . . Let us now suppose that it is presented to me as originating from a Chinese or Siamese poet. I will think: The Chinese turn everything into a dragon, and it will represent to me a clear fire like a celebration, slithering, which I will like. Let us suppose that the witness to a fire uses it, or even better, someone whose life was threatened by the flames. I will think: This concept of a fire with jaws is really a nightmarish horror, and adds a ghastly human evil to an unconscious event; the phrase is very strong, almost mythological. Let us suppose I am told that the father of this figure of speech is Aeschylus, and that it was uttered by Prometheus (which is true), and that the shackled titan, tied to a precipice of rocks by Force and Violence, those harsh ministers, declaimed it to the Ocean, an old gentleman who came to visit his misfortune on a winged chariot. Then the sentence would seem good, even perfect, given the extravagant nature of the speakers and its (already poetic) remote origin. I shall do as the reader, who has doubtlessly suspended his judgment, does, until confirming whose phrase it was.

I speak without intending any irony. Distance and antiquity (the emphases of space and time) pull on our hearts. Novalis has already uttered this truth, and Spengler was its grandiose advocate in his famous book. I want to discuss its relevance to literature, which is a paltry thing. If we are already sobered by the thought that men lived two thousand five hundred years ago, how could we not be moved to know that they made verses, were spectators of the world, that they sheltered in light, lasting words something of their ponderous, fleeting life, words that fulfill a long destiny?

Time, such a respected subversive, so famous for its demolitions and Italic ruins, also constructs. Upon Cervantes's lofty verse:

¡Vive Dios, que me espanta esta grandeza!
[By God, this greatness terrifies me!]

we see time refashioned and even notably widened. When the inventor and storyteller of *Don Quixote* wrote it, *"vive Dios"* was as ordinary an exclamation as "my goodness!" and "terrify" meant "astonish." I suspect that his contemporaries would have felt it to mean: "How this device astonishes me!" or something similar. It is firm and tidy in our eyes. Time—Cervantes's friend—has sagely revised his drafts.

Immortals have, generally, another destiny. The details of their feelings or thoughts tend to vanish or lie invisibly in their work, irretrievable and unsuspected. In contrast, their individuality (that simplified Platonic idea which they never purely possessed) fastens upon souls like a root: they become as impoverished and perfect as a cipher; they become abstractions. They are barely a bit of shadow, but they are so eternally. They fit too neatly into this phrase: Echoes remained, in the void of their majesty, not a whole voice, but merely the lingering absence of a word (Quevedo, *La hora de todos y la fortuna con seso,* episode XXXV). But there are many different immortalities.

A tender and sure immortality (attained sometimes by men who are ordinary but have an honest dedication and a lifelong fervor) is that of the poet whose name is linked to a place in the world. Such is the case of Burns, over the grazing lands of Scotland and unhurried rivers and little lambs; such is our Carriego's, prevailing in the shameful, furtive, almost buried outskirts of Palermo on the Southside, where an extravagant archeological effort can reconstruct the vacant lot whose current ruin is the house and the beverage store which has become an Emporium. Some are also immortalized in eternal things. The moon, springtime, the nightingales, all manifest the glory of Heinrich Heine; the sea that suffers grey skies, Swinburne; the long railway platforms and docks, Walt Whitman. But the best immortalities—those in the domain of passion—are still vacant. There is no poet who is the total voice of love, hate, or despair. That is, the great verses of humanity have still not been written. This imperfection should raise our hopes.

Of Books

Michel de Montaigne

I make no doubt but that I often happen to speak of things that are much better and more truly handled by those who are masters of the trade. You have here purely an essay of my natural parts, and not of those acquired: and whoever shall catch me tripping in ignorance, will not in any sort get the better of me; for I should be very unwilling to become responsible to another for my writings, who am not so to myself, nor satisfied with them. Whoever goes in quest of knowledge, let him fish for it where it is to be found; there is nothing I so little profess. These are fancies of my own, by which I do not pretend to discover things but to lay open myself; they may, peradventure, one day be known to me, or have formerly been, according as fortune has been able to bring me in place where they have been explained; but I have utterly forgotten it; and if I am a man of some reading, I am a man of no retention; so that I can promise no certainty, more than to make known to what point the knowledge I now have has risen. Therefore, let none lay stress upon the matter I write, but upon my method in writing it. Let them observe, in what I borrow, if I have known how to choose what is proper to raise or help the invention, which is always my own. For I make others say for me, not before but after me, what, either for want of language or want of sense, I cannot myself so well express. I do not number my borrowings, I weigh them; and had I designed to raise their value by number, I had made them twice as many; they are all, or within a very few, so famed and ancient authors, that they seem, methinks, themselves sufficiently to tell who they are, without giving me the trouble. In reasons, comparisons, and arguments, if I transplant any into my own soil, and confound them amongst my own, I purposely conceal the author, to awe the temerity of those precipitate censors who fall upon all sorts of writings, particularly the late ones, of men yet living; and in the vulgar tongue which puts every one into a capacity of criticising and which seem to convict the conception and design as vulgar also. I will have them give Plutarch a fillip on my nose, and rail against Seneca when they think they rail at me. I must shelter my own weakness under these great reputations. I shall love any one that can unplume me, that is, by clearness of understanding and judgment, and by the sole distinction of the force and beauty of the discourse. For I who, for want of memory, am at every turn at a loss to, pick them out of their national livery, am yet wise enough to know, by the measure of my own abilities, that my soil is incapable of producing any of those rich flowers that I there find growing; and that all the fruits of my own growth are not worth any one of them. For this, indeed, I hold myself responsible; if I get in my own way; if there be any vanity and defect in my writings which I do not of myself perceive nor can discern, when pointed out to me by another; for many faults escape our eye, but the infirmity of judgment consists in not being able to discern them, when by another laid open to us. Knowledge and truth may be in us without judgment, and judgment also without them; but the confession of ignorance is one of the finest and surest testimonies of judgment that I know. I have no other officer to put my writings in rank and file, but only fortune. As things come into my head, I heap them one upon another; sometimes they advance in whole bodies, sometimes in single file. I would that every one should see my natural and ordinary pace, irregular as it is; I suffer myself to jog on at my own rate. Neither are these subjects which a man is not permitted to be ignorant in, or casually and at a venture, to discourse of. I could wish to have a more perfect knowledge of things, but I will not buy it so dear as it costs. My design is to pass over easily, and not laboriously, the remainder of my life; there is nothing that I will cudgel my brains about; no, not even knowledge, of what value soever.

I seek, in the reading of books, only to please myself by an honest diversion; or, if I study, 'tis for no other science than what treats of the knowledge of myself, and instructs me how to die and how to live well.

"Has meus ad metas sudet oportet equus."

["My horse must work according to my step."
—*Propertius, iv.]*

I do not bite my nails about the difficulties I meet with in my reading; after a charge or two, I give them over. Should I insist upon them, I should both lose myself and time; for I have an impatient understanding, that must be satisfied at first: what I do not discern at once is by persistence rendered more obscure. I do nothing without gaiety; continuation and a too obstinate endeavour, darkens, stupefies, and tires my judgment. My sight is confounded and dissipated with poring; I must withdraw it, and refer my discovery to new attempts; just as, to judge rightly of the lustre of scarlet, we are taught to pass the eye lightly over it, and again to run it over at several sudden and reiterated glances. If one book do not please me, I take another; and I never meddle with any, but at such times as I am weary of doing nothing. I care not much for new ones, because the old seem fuller and stronger; neither do I converse much with Greek authors, because my judgment cannot do its work with imperfect intelligence of the material.

Amongst books that are simply pleasant, of the moderns, Boccaccio's Decameron, Rabelais, and the Basia of Johannes Secundus (if those may be ranged under the title) are worth reading for amusement. As to the Amadis, and such kind of stuff, they had not the credit of arresting even my childhood. And I will, moreover, say, whether boldly or rashly, that this old, heavy soul of mine is now no longer tickled with Ariosto, no, nor with the worthy Ovid; his facility and inventions, with which I was formerly so ravished, are now of no more relish, and I can hardly have the patience to read them. I speak my opinion freely of all things, even of those that, perhaps, exceed my capacity, and that I do not conceive to be, in any wise, under my jurisdiction. And, accordingly, the judgment I deliver, is to show the measure of my own sight, and not of the things I make so bold to criticise. When I find myself disgusted with Plato's 'Axiochus', as with a work, with due respect to such an author be it spoken, without force, my judgment does not believe itself: it is not so arrogant as to oppose the authority of so many other famous judgments of antiquity, which it considers as its tutors and masters, and with whom it is rather content to err; in such a case, it condemns itself either to stop at the outward bark, not being able to penetrate to the heart, or to consider it by sortie false light. It is content with only securing itself from trouble and disorder; as to its own weakness, it frankly acknowledges and confesses it. It thinks it gives a just interpretation to the appearances by its conceptions presented to it; but they are weak and imperfect. Most of the fables of AEsop have diverse senses and meanings, of which the mythologists chose some one that quadrates well to the fable; but, for the most part, 'tis but the first face that presents itself and is superficial only; there yet remain others more vivid, essential, and profound, into which they have not been able to penetrate; and just so 'tis with me.

But, to pursue the business of this essay, I have always thought that, in poesy, Virgil, Lucretius, Catullus, and Horace by many degrees excel the rest; and signally, Virgil in his Georgics, which I look upon as the most accomplished piece in poetry; and in comparison of which a man may easily discern that there are some places in his AEneids, to which the author would have given a little more of the file, had he had leisure: and the fifth book of his AEneids seems to me the most perfect. I also love Lucan, and willingly read him, not so much for his style, as for his own worth, and the truth and solidity of his opinions and judgments. As for good Terence, the refined elegance and grace of the Latin tongue, I find him admirable in his vivid representation of our manners and the movements of the soul; our actions throw me at every turn upon him; and I cannot read him so often that I do not still discover some new grace and beauty. Such as lived near Virgil's time complained that some should compare Lucretius to him. I am of opinion that the comparison is, in truth, very unequal: a belief that, nevertheless, I have much ado to assure myself in, when I come upon some excellent passage in Lucretius. But if they were so angry at this comparison, what would they say to the brutish and barbarous stupidity of those who, nowadays, compare him with Ariosto? Would not Ariosto himself say?

"*O seclum insipiens et inficetum!*"
[*"O stupid and tasteless age."*—*Catullus, xliii. 8.*]

I think the ancients had more reason to be angry with those who compared Plautus with Terence, though much nearer the mark, than Lucretius with Virgil. It makes much for the estimation and preference of Terence, that the father of Roman eloquence has him so often, and alone of his class, in his mouth; and the opinion that the best judge of Roman poets —[Horace, De Art. Poetica, 279.]—has passed upon his companion. I have often observed that those of our times, who take upon them to write comedies (in imitation of the Italians, who are happy enough in that way of writing), take three or four plots of those of Plautus or Terence to make one of their own, and , crowd five or six of Boccaccio's novels into one single comedy. That which makes them so load themselves with matter is the diffidence they have of being able to support themselves with their own strength. They must find out something to lean to; and not having of their own stuff wherewith to entertain us, they bring in the story to supply the defect of language. It is quite otherwise with my author; the elegance and perfection of his way of speaking makes us lose the appetite of his plot; his refined grace and elegance of diction everywhere occupy us: he is so pleasant throughout,

"Liquidus, puroque simillimus amni,"

["Liquid, and likest the pure river."
—Horace, Ep., ii. s, 120.]

and so possesses the soul with his graces that we forget those of his fable. This same consideration carries me further: I observe that the best of the ancient poets have avoided affectation and the hunting after, not only fantastic Spanish and Petrarchic elevations, but even the softer and more gentle touches, which are the ornament of all succeeding poesy. And yet there is no good judgment that will condemn this in the ancients, and that does not incomparably more admire the equal polish, and that perpetual sweetness and flourishing beauty of Catullus's epigrams, than all the stings with which Martial arms the tails of his. This is by the same reason that I gave before, and as Martial says of himself:

"Minus illi ingenio laborandum fuit,
in cujus locum materia successerat:"

["He had the less for his wit to do that the subject itself
supplied what was necessary."—Martial, praef. ad lib. viii.]

The first, without being moved, or without getting angry, make themselves sufficiently felt; they have matter enough of laughter throughout, they need not tickle themselves; the others have need of foreign assistance; as they have the less wit they must have the more body; they mount on horseback, because they are not able to stand on their own legs. As in our balls, those mean fellows who teach to dance, not being able to represent the presence and dignity of our noblesse, are fain to put themselves forward with dangerous jumping, and other strange motions and tumblers tricks; and the ladies are less put to it in dance; where there are various coupees, changes, and quick motions of body, than in some other of a more sedate kind, where they are only to move a natural pace, and to represent their ordinary grace and presence. And so I have seen good drolls, when in their own everyday clothes, and with the same face they always wear, give us all the pleasure of their art, when their apprentices, not yet arrived at such a pitch of perfection, are fain to meal their faces, put themselves into ridiculous disguises, and make a hundred grotesque faces to give us whereat to laugh. This conception of mine is nowhere more demonstrable than in comparing the AEneid with Orlando Furioso; of which we see the first, by dint of wing, flying in a brave and lofty place, and always following his point: the latter, fluttering and hopping from tale to tale, as from branch to branch, not daring to trust his wings but in very short flights, and perching at every turn, lest his breath and strength should fail.

> *"Excursusque breves tentat."*

> *["And he attempts short excursions."*
> *—Virgil, Georgics, iv. 194.]*

These, then, as to this sort of subjects, are the authors that best please me.

As to what concerns my other reading, that mixes a little more profit with the pleasure, and whence I learn how to marshal my opinions and conditions, the books that serve me to this purpose are Plutarch, since he has been translated into French, and Seneca. Both of these have this notable convenience suited to my humour, that the knowledge I there seek is discoursed in loose pieces, that do not require from me any trouble of reading long, of which I am incapable.

Such are the minor works of the first and the epistles of the latter, which are the best and most profiting of all their writings. 'Tis no great attempt to take one of them in hand, and I give over at pleasure; for they have no sequence or dependence upon one another. These authors, for the most part, concur in useful and true opinions; and there is this parallel betwixt them, that fortune brought them into the world about the same century: they were both tutors to two Roman emperors: both sought out from foreign countries: both rich and both great men. Their instruction is the cream of philosophy, and delivered after a plain and pertinent manner. Plutarch is more uniform and constant; Seneca more various and waving: the last toiled and bent his whole strength to fortify virtue against weakness, fear, and vicious appetites; the other seems more to slight their power, and to disdain to alter his pace and to stand upon his guard. Plutarch's opinions are Platonic, gentle, and accommodated to civil society; those of the other are Stoical and Epicurean, more remote from the common use, but, in my opinion, more individually commodious and more firm. Seneca seems to lean a little to the tyranny of the emperors of his time, and only seems; for I take it for certain that he speaks against his judgment when he condemns the action of the generous murderers of Caesar. Plutarch is frank throughout: Seneca abounds with brisk touches and sallies; Plutarch with things that warm and move you more; this contents and pays you better: he guides us, the other pushes us on.

As to Cicero, his works that are most useful to my design are they that treat of manners and rules of our life. But boldly to confess the truth (for since one has passed the barriers of impudence, there is no bridle), his way of writing appears to me negligent and uninviting: for his prefaces, definitions, divisions, and etymologies take up the greatest part of his work: whatever there is of life and marrow is smothered and lost in the long preparation. When I have spent an hour in reading him, which is a great deal for me, and try to recollect what I have thence extracted of juice and substance, for the most part I find nothing but wind; for he is not yet come to the arguments that serve to his purpose, and to the reasons that properly help to form the knot I seek. For me, who only desire to become more wise, not more learned or eloquent, these logical and Aristotelian dispositions of parts are of no use. I would have a man begin with the main proposition. I know well enough what death and pleasure are;

let no man give himself the trouble to anatomise them to me. I look for good and solid reasons, at the first dash, to instruct me how to stand their shock, for which purpose neither grammatical subtleties nor the quaint contexture of words and argumentations are of any use at all. I am for discourses that give the first charge into the heart of the redoubt; his languish about the subject; they are proper for the schools, for the bar, and for the pulpit, where we have leisure to nod, and may awake, a quarter of an hour after, time enough to find again the thread of the discourse. It is necessary to speak after this manner to judges, whom a man has a design to gain over, right or wrong, to children and common people, to whom a man must say all, and see what will come of it. I would not have an author make it his business to render me attentive: or that he should cry out fifty times Oyez! as the heralds do. The Romans, in their religious exercises, began with 'Hoc age' as we in ours do with 'Sursum corda'; these are so many words lost to me: I come already fully prepared from my chamber. I need no allurement, no invitation, no sauce; I eat the meat raw, so that, instead of whetting my appetite by these preparatives, they tire and pall it. Will the licence of the time excuse my sacrilegious boldness if I censure the dialogism of Plato himself as also dull and heavy, too much stifling the matter, and lament so much time lost by a man, who had so many better things to say, in so many long and needless preliminary interlocutions? My ignorance will better excuse me in that I understand not Greek so well as to discern the beauty of his language. I generally choose books that use sciences, not such as only lead to them. The two first, and Pliny, and their like, have nothing of this Hoc age; they will have to do with men already instructed; or if they have, 'tis a substantial Hoc age; and that has a body by itself. I also delight in reading the Epistles to Atticus, not only because they contain a great deal of the history and affairs of his time, but much more because I therein discover much of his own private humours; for I have a singular curiosity, as I have said elsewhere, to pry into the souls and the natural and true opinions of the authors, with whom I converse. A man may indeed judge of their parts, but not of their manners nor of themselves, by the writings they exhibit upon the theatre of the world. I have a thousand times lamented the loss of the treatise Brutus wrote upon Virtue, for it is well to learn the theory from those who best know the practice.

But seeing the matter preached and the preacher are different things, I would as willingly see Brutus in Plutarch, as in a book of his own. I would rather choose to be certainly informed of the conference he had in his tent with some particular friends of his the night before a battle, than of the harangue he made the next day to his army; and of what he did in his closet and his chamber, than what he did in the public square and in the senate. As to Cicero, I am of the common opinion that, learning excepted, he had no great natural excellence. He was a good citizen, of an affable nature, as all fat, heavy men, such as he was, usually are; but given to ease, and had, in truth, a mighty share of vanity and ambition. Neither do I know how to excuse him for thinking his poetry fit to be published; 'tis no great imperfection to make ill verses, but it is an imperfection not to be able to judge how unworthy his verses were of the glory of his name. For what concerns his eloquence, that is totally out of all comparison, and I believe it will never be equalled. The younger Cicero, who resembled his father in nothing but in name, whilst commanding in Asia, had several strangers one day at his table, and, amongst the rest, Cestius seated at the lower end, as men often intrude to the open tables of the great. Cicero asked one of his people who that man was, who presently told him his name; but he, as one who had his thoughts taken up with something else, and who had forgotten the answer made him, asking three or four times, over and over again; the same question, the fellow, to deliver himself from so many answers and to make him know him by some particular circumstance; "'tis that Cestius," said he, "of whom it was told you, that he makes no great account of your father's eloquence in comparison of his own." At which Cicero, being suddenly nettled, commanded poor Cestius presently to be seized, and caused him to be very well whipped in his own presence; a very discourteous entertainer! Yet even amongst those, who, all things considered, have reputed his, eloquence incomparable, there have been some, who have not stuck to observe some faults in it: as that great Brutus his friend, for example, who said 'twas a broken and feeble eloquence, 'fyactam et elumbem'. The orators also, nearest to the age wherein he lived, reprehended in him the care he had of a certain long cadence in his periods, and particularly took notice of these words, 'esse videatur', which he there so often makes use of. For my part, I more approve of a shorter style, and that comes more roundly off. He does, though, sometimes shuffle his parts more briskly together, but 'tis very seldom. I have myself taken notice of this one passage:

"*Ego vero me minus diu senem mallem,*
quam esse senem, antequam essem."

[*"I had rather be old a brief time, than be old before old age.*
—"Cicero, De Senect., c. 10.]

The historians are my right ball, for they are pleasant and easy, and where man, in general, the knowledge of whom I hunt after, appears more vividly and entire than anywhere else:

[*The easiest of my amusements, the right ball at tennis being that*
which coming to the player from the right hand, is much easier
played with.—Coste.]

the variety and truth of his internal qualities, in gross and piecemeal, the diversity of means by which he is united and knit, and the accidents that threaten him. Now those that write lives, by reason they insist more upon counsels than events, more upon what sallies from within, than upon what happens without, are the most proper for my reading; and, therefore, above all others, Plutarch is the man for me. I am very sorry we have not a dozen Laertii,—[Diogenes Laertius, who wrote the Lives of the Philosophers]—or that he was not further extended; for I am equally curious to know the lives and fortunes of these great instructors of the world, as to know the diversities of their doctrines and opinions. In this kind of study of histories, a man must tumble over, without distinction, all sorts of authors, old and new, French or foreign, there to know the things of which they variously treat. But Caesar, in my opinion, particularly deserves to be studied, not for the knowledge of the history only, but for himself, so great an excellence and perfection he has above all the rest, though Sallust be one of the number. In earnest, I read this author with more reverence and respect than is usually allowed to human writings; one while considering him in his person, by his actions and miraculous greatness, and another in the purity and inimitable polish of his language, wherein he not only excels all other historians, as Cicero confesses, but, peradventure, even Cicero himself; speaking of his enemies with so much sincerity in his judgment, that, the false colours with which he strives to palliate his evil cause, and the ordure of his pestilent ambition excepted, I think there is no fault to be objected against him, saving this, that he speaks too sparingly of himself, seeing so many great things could not have been performed under his conduct, but that his own personal acts must necessarily have had a greater share in them than he attributes to them.

I love historians, whether of the simple sort, or of the higher order. The simple, who have nothing of their own to mix with it, and who only make it their business to collect all that comes to their knowledge, and faithfully to record all things, without choice or discrimination, leave to us the entire judgment of discerning the truth. Such, for example, amongst others, is honest Froissart, who has proceeded in his undertaking with so frank a plainness that, having committed an error, he is not ashamed to confess and correct it in the place where the finger has been laid, and who represents to us even the variety of rumours that were then spread abroad, and the different reports that were made to him; 'tis the naked and inform matter of history, and of which every one may make his profit, according to his understanding. The more excellent sort of historians have judgment to pick out what is most worthy to be known; and, of two reports, to examine which is the most likely to be true: from the condition of princes and their humours, they conclude their counsels, and attribute to them words proper for the occasion; such have title to assume the authority of regulating our belief to what they themselves believe; but certainly, this privilege belongs to very few. For the middle sort of historians, of which the most part are, they spoil all; they will chew our meat for us; they take upon them to judge of, and consequently, to incline the history to their own fancy; for if the judgment lean to one side, a man cannot avoid wresting and writhing his narrative to that bias; they undertake to select things worthy to be known, and yet often conceal from us such a word, such a private action, as would much better instruct us; omit, as incredible, such things as they do not understand, and peradventure some, because they cannot express good French or Latin. Let them display their eloquence and intelligence, and judge according to their own fancy: but let them, withal, leave us something to judge of after them, and neither alter nor disguise, by their abridgments and at their own choice, anything of the substance of the matter, but deliver it to us pure and entire in all its dimensions.

For the most part, and especially in these latter ages, persons are culled out for this work from amongst the common people, upon the sole consideration of well-speaking, as if we were to learn grammar from them; and the men so chosen have fair reason, being hired for no other end and pretending to nothing but babble, not to be very solicitous of any part but that, and so, with a fine jingle of words, prepare us a pretty contexture of reports they pick up in the streets. The only good histories are those that have been written themselves who held command in the affairs whereof they write, or who participated in the conduct of them, or, at least, who have had the conduct of others of the same nature. Such are almost all the Greek and Roman histories: for, several eye-witnesses having written of the same subject, in the time when grandeur and learning commonly met in the same person, if there happen to be an error, it must of necessity be a very slight one, and upon a very doubtful incident. What can a man expect from a physician who writes of war, or from a mere scholar, treating of the designs of princes? If we could take notice how scrupulous the Romans were in this, there would need but this example: Asinius Pollio found in the histories of Caesar himself something misreported, a mistake occasioned; either by reason he could not have his eye in all parts of his army at once and had given credit to some individual persons who had not delivered him a very true account; or else, for not having had too perfect notice given him by his lieutenants of what they had done in his absence.—[Suetonius, Life of Caesar, c. 56.]—By which we may see, whether the inquisition after truth be not very delicate, when a man cannot believe the report of a battle from the knowledge of him who there commanded, nor from the soldiers who were engaged in it, unless, after the method of a judicial inquiry, the witnesses be confronted and objections considered upon the proof of the least detail of every incident. In good earnest the knowledge we have of our own affairs, is much more obscure: but that has been sufficiently handled by Bodin, and according to my own sentiment —[In the work by jean Bodin, entitled "Methodus ad facilem historiarum cognitionem." 1566.]—A little to aid the weakness of my memory (so extreme that it has happened to me more than once, to take books again into my hand as new and unseen, that I had carefully read over a few years before, and scribbled with my notes) I have adopted a custom of late, to note at the end of every book (that is, of those I never intend to read again) the time when I made an end on't, and the judgment I had made of it, to the end that this might, at least, represent to me the character and general idea I had conceived of the author in reading it; and I will here transcribe some of those annotations.

I wrote this, some ten years ago, in my Guicciardini (of what language soever my books speak to me in, I always speak to them in my own): "He is a diligent historiographer, from whom, in my opinion, a man may learn the truth of the affairs of his time, as exactly as from any other; in the most of which he was himself also a personal actor, and in honourable command. There is no appearance that he disguised anything, either upon the account of hatred, favour, or vanity; of which the free censures he passes upon the great ones, and particularly those by whom he was advanced and employed in commands of great trust and honour, as Pope Clement VII., give ample testimony. As to that part which he thinks himself the best at, namely, his digressions and discourses, he has indeed some very good, and enriched with fine features; but he is too fond of them: for, to leave nothing unsaid, having a subject so full, ample, almost infinite, he degenerates into pedantry and smacks a little of scholastic prattle. I have also observed this in him, that of so many souls and so many effects, so many motives and so many counsels as he judges, he never attributes any one to virtue, religion, or conscience, as if all these were utterly extinct in the world: and of all the actions, how brave soever in outward show they appear in themselves, he always refers the cause and motive to some vicious occasion or some prospect of profit. It is impossible to imagine but that, amongst such an infinite number of actions as he makes mention of, there must be some one produced by the way of honest reason. No corruption could so universally have infected men that some one would not escape the contagion which makes me suspect that his own taste was vicious, whence it might happen that he judged other men by himself."

In my Philip de Commines there is this written: "You will here find the language sweet and delightful, of a natural simplicity, the narration pure, with the good faith of the author conspicuous therein; free from vanity, when speaking of himself, and from affection or envy, when speaking of others: his discourses and exhortations rather accompanied with zeal and truth, than with any exquisite sufficiency; and, throughout, authority and gravity, which bespeak him a man of good extraction, and brought up in great affairs."

Upon the Memoirs of Monsieur du Bellay I find this: "'Tis always pleasant to read things written by those that have experienced how they ought to be carried on; but withal, it cannot be denied but there is a manifest decadence in these two lords—[Martin du Bellay and Guillaume de Langey, brothers, who jointly wrote the Memoirs.]—from the freedom and liberty of writing that shine in the elder historians, such as the Sire de Joinville, the familiar companion of St. Louis; Eginhard, chancellor to Charlemagne; and of later date, Philip de Commines. What we have here is rather an apology for King Francis, against the Emperor Charles V., than history. I will not believe that they have falsified anything, as to matter of fact; but they make a common practice of twisting the judgment of events, very often contrary to reason, to our advantage, and of omitting whatsoever is ticklish to be handled in the life of their master; witness the proceedings of Messieurs de Montmorency and de Biron, which are here omitted: nay, so much as the very name of Madame d'Estampes is not here to be found. Secret actions an historian may conceal; but to pass over in silence what all the world knows and things that have drawn after them public and such high consequences, is an inexcusable defect. In fine, whoever has a mind to have a perfect knowledge of King Francis and the events of his reign, let him seek it elsewhere, if my advice may prevail. The only profit a man can reap from these Memoirs is in the special narrative of battles and other exploits of war wherein these gentlemen were personally engaged; in some words and private actions of the princes of their time, and in the treaties and negotiations carried on by the Seigneur de Langey, where there are everywhere things worthy to be known, and discourses above the vulgar strain."

Deciding to Write in English

Ha Jin

Transcript of Lecture at the University of San Francisco given on February 26, 2000

When I decided to write in English, I didn't know how far I could go. In the English language, there has been a grand tradition in the prose established by the writers whose mother tongues are not English, writers like Conrad and Nabokov.

But I started writing poetry and I was hired as a poet by Emory University. So there was a lot of uncertainty involved. I think there was also a kind of confusion as well. The major condition is at whom do you write? For whom? In whose interest? These basic questions were not clear to me. I made some assumptions but they were wrong.

I thought I would remain a Chinese person writing English exclusively, so I treated the English language as an instrument. But if what I want is to write literature, how could I not care about the language? How can you achieve anything without a regard for the language?

I think that was the misconception on my part. In addition to that, there was—I didn't know how far I could go especially as a person with my background. I had served in the army. Life had been difficult to me. In China, life at the time, in the case of myself, life physically was harsh, difficult. But mentally, it was very reliable. Everything was clear, secure.

So once I decided to stay in this country and to write in English, everything became uncertain. It took a long time for me to get used to the certainty. I don't mean now it is certain; still it is uncertain. But gradually, I realized that certainty is not a human condition. For a writer, uncertainty is good because that means there is a risk that has to be taken.

In most cases, the more risk you take, the better. The work may turn out to be better. So gradually, I think, uncertainty becomes a part of the writing process. I think I have developed the ability to accept it and to endure it as a part of the process.

Another problem in my writing life, I think, is frustration. At the very beginning, it was very difficult, especially when I began to write creatively. I had to relearn the language. Before I came to the States, I knew some English and I could manage to write academic papers but that was a different kind of language. For instance, if we write fiction, we need a different kind of language, a different diction. Also the nuances, each character is supposed to speak slightly differently from others. So the language has to be more subtle, richer.

So there is a lot of frustration, in the practical sense, just to get the work published. Send out work and receive the rejection is a very busy process. In fact, the year after Emory hired me, I realized I had to publish a lot in order to keep my job. So basically, I sent out routinely poems and stories and, as a result, I received for some time, two years, I almost received rejection letters every day. Every day. To the point that my wife made a rule: before dinner nobody was allowed to check the mail.

So she got very emotionally involved in this. But I think that is also very valuable, in fact; if some of the works had been accepted, I would have felt very embarrassed. Every time I received the returned manuscript, I would rework it and really try my best to revise it, to edit it, to the point I felt I couldn't do anything but send it out.

So the whole process, in a way, is a way to develop myself, my ability as a writer. I think the frustration basically is kind of, in a way, nourishment to develop myself. As a result, I always advise my students to send out their work. If you get embarrassed, that's fine. Embarrassment is part of the education, the apprenticeship.

Approaches to What?

Georges Perec

What speaks to us, seemingly, is always the big event, the untoward, the extra-ordinary: the front-page splash, the banner headlines. Railway trains only begin to exist when they are derailed, and the more passengers that are killed, the more the trains exist. Aeroplanes achieve existence only when they are hijacked. The one and only destiny of motor-cars is to drive into plane trees. Fifty-two weekends a year, fifty-two casualty lists: so many dead and all the better for the news media if the figures keep on going up! Behind the event there has to be a scandal, a fissure, a danger, as if life reveals itself only by way of the spectacular, as if what speaks, what is significant, is always abnormal: natural cataclysms or historical upheavals, social unrest, political scandals.

In our haste to measure the historic, significant and revelatory, let's not leave aside the essential: the truly intolerable, the truly inadmissible. What is scandalous isn't the pit explosion, it's working in coalmines. 'Social problems' aren't 'a matter of concern' when there's a strike, they are intolerable twenty-four hours out of twenty-four, three hundred and sixty-five days a year.

Tidal waves, volcanic eruptions, tower-blocks that collapse, forest fires, tunnels that cave in, the Drugstore des Champs-Elysées burns down. Awful! Terrible! Monstrous! Scandalous! But where's the scandal? The true scandal? Has the newspaper told us anything except: not to worry, as you can see life exists, with its ups and its downs, things happen, as you can see.

The daily papers talk of everything except the daily. The papers annoy me, they teach me nothing. What they recount doesn't concern me, doesn't ask me questions and doesn't answer the questions I ask or would like to ask.

What's really going on, what we're experiencing, the rest, all the rest, where is it? How should we take account of, question, describe what happens every day and recurs every day: the banal, the quotidian, the obvious, the common, the ordinary, the infra-ordinary, the background noise, the habitual?

To question the habitual. But that's just it, we're habituated to it. We don't question it, it doesn't question us, it doesn't seem to pose a problem, we live it without thinking, as if it carried within it neither questions nor answers, as if it weren't the bearer of any information. This is no longer even conditioning, it's anaesthesia. We sleep through our lives in a dreamless sleep. But where is our life? Where is our body? Where is our space?

How are we to speak of these 'common things', how to track them down rather, flush them out, wrest them from the dross in which they remain mired, how to give them a meaning, a tongue, to let them, finally, speak of what is, of what we are.

What's needed perhaps is finally to found our own anthropology, one that will speak about us, will look in ourselves for what for so long we've been pillaging from others. Not the exotic any more, but the endotic.

To question what seems so much a matter of course that we've forgotten its origins. To rediscover something of the astonishment that Jules Verne or his readers may have felt faced with an apparatus capable of reproducing and transporting sounds. For that astonishment existed, along with thousands of others, and it's they which have moulded us.

What we need to question is bricks, concrete, glass, our table manners, our utensils, our tools, the way we spend our time, our rhythms. To question that which seems to have ceased forever to astonish us. We live, true, we breathe, true; we walk, we open doors, we go down staircases, we sit at a table in order to eat, we lie down on a bed in order to sleep. How? Where? When? Why?

Describe your street. Describe another street. Compare.

Make an inventory of your pockets, of your bag. Ask yourself about the provenance, the use, what will become of each of the objects you take out.

Question your tea spoons.

What is there under your wallpaper?

How many movements does it take to dial a phone number? Why?

Why don't you find cigarettes in grocery stores? Why not?

It matters little to me that these questions should be fragmentary, barely indicative of a method, at most of a project. It matters a lot to me that they should seem trivial and futile: that's exactly what makes them just as essential, if not more so, as all the other questions by which we've tried in vain to lay hold on our truth.

The Lesson of the Master

Cynthia Ozick

There was a period in my life—to purloin a famous Jamesian title, "The Middle Years"—when I used to say, with as much ferocity as I could muster, "I hate Henry James and I wish he was dead."

I was not to have my disgruntled way. The dislike did not last and turned once again to adoration, ecstasy, and awe; and no one is more alive than Henry James, or more likely to sustain literary immortality. He is among the angels, as he meant to be.

But in earlier days I felt I had been betrayed by Henry James. I was like the youthful writer in "The Lesson of the Master" who believed in the Master's call to live immaculately, unspoiled by what we mean when we say "life"—relationship, family mess, distraction, exhaustion, anxiety, above all disappointment. Here is the Master, St. George, speaking to his young disciple, Paul Overt:

> "One has no business to have any children," St. George placidly declared. "I mean, of course, if one wants to do anything good."
>
>> "But aren't they an inspiration—an incentive?"
>
>> "An incentive to damnation, artistically speaking."

And later Paul inquires:

> "Is it deceptive that I find you living with every appearance of domestic felicity—blest with a devoted, accomplished wife, with children whose acquaintance I haven't yet had the pleasure of making, but who *must* be delightful young people, from what I know of their parents?"

St. George smiled as for the candour of his question. "It's all excellent, my dear fellow—heaven forbid I should deny it. . . . I've got a loaf on the shelf; I've got everything in fact but the great thing."

"And the great thing?" Paul kept echoing.

"The sense of having done the best—the sense which is the real life of the artist and the absence of which is his death, of having drawn from his intellectual instrument the finest music that nature had hidden in it, of having played it as it should be played. He either does that or he doesn't—and if he doesn't he isn't worth speaking of."

Paul pursues the matter:

"Then what did you mean. . . by saying that children are a curse?"

"My dear youth, on what basis are we talking?" and St. George dropped upon the sofa at a short distance from him. . . . "On the supposition that a certain perfection's possible and even desirable—isn't it so? Well, all I say is that one's children interfere with perfection. One's wife interferes. Marriage interferes."

"You think, then, the artist shouldn't marry?"

"He does so at his peril—he does so at his cost."

Yet the Master who declares all this is himself profoundly, inextricably, married; and when his wife dies, he hastens to marry again, choosing Life over Art. Very properly James sees marriage as symbol and summary of the passion for ordinary human entanglement, as experience of the most commonplace, most fated kind.

But we are also given to understand, in the desolation of this comic tale, that the young artist, the Master's trusting disciple, is left both perplexed and bereft: the Master's second wife is the young artist's first love, and the Master has stolen away his disciple's chance for ordinary human entanglement.

So the Lesson of the Master is a double one: choose ordinary human entanglement, and live; or choose Art, and give up the vitality of life's passions and panics and endurances. What I am going to tell now is a stupidity, a misunderstanding, a great Jamesian life-mistake: an embarrassment and a life-shame. (Imagine that we are in one of those lavishly adorned Jamesian chambers where intimate confessions not accidentally but suspensefully take place.) As I have said, I felt myself betrayed by a Jamesian trickery. Trusting in James, believing, like Paul Overt, in the overtness of the Jamesian lesson, I chose Art, and ended by blaming Henry James. It seemed to me James had left out the one important thing I ought to have known, even though he was saying it again and again. The trouble was that I was listening to the Lesson of the Master at the wrong time, paying powerful and excessive attention at the wrong time; and this cost me my youth.

I suppose a case can be made that it is certainly inappropriate for anyone to moan about the loss of youth and how it is all Henry James's fault. All of us will lose our youth, and some of us, alas, have lost it already; but not all of us will pin the loss on Henry James.

I, however, do. I blame Henry James.

Never mind the sublime position of Henry James in American letters. Never mind the Jamesian prose style—never mind that it, too, is sublime, nuanced, imbricated with a thousand distinctions and observations (the reason H.G. Wells mocked it), and as idiosyncratically and ecstatically redolent of the spirals of past and future as a garlic clove. Set aside also the Jamesian impatience with idols, the moral seriousness active both in the work and the life. (I am thinking, for example, of Edith Wharton's compliance in the face of their mutual friend Paul Bourget's anti-Semitism, and James's noble and definitive dissent.) Neglect all this, including every other beam that flies out from the stupendous Jamesian lantern to keep generations reading in rapture (which is all right), or else scribbling away at dissertation after dissertation (which is not so good). I myself, after all, committed a Master's thesis, long ago, called "Parable in Henry James," in which I tried to catch up all of James in the net of a single idea. Before that, I lived many months in the black hole of a microfilm cell, transcribing every letter James ever wrote to Mr. Pinker, his London agent, for a professorial book; but the professor drank, and died, and after thirty years the letters still lie in the dark.

All that while I sat cramped in that black bleak microfilm cell, and all that while I was writing that thesis, James was sinking me and despoiling my youth, and I did not know it.

I want, parenthetically, to recommend to the Henry James Society—there is such an assemblage—that membership be limited: no one under age forty-two-and-three-quarters need apply. Proof of age via birth certificate should be mandatory; otherwise the consequences may be harsh and horrible. I offer myself as an Extreme and Hideous Example of Premature Exposure to Henry James. I was about seventeen, I recall, when my brother brought home from the public library a science-fiction anthology, which, through an odd perspective that perplexes me still, included "The Beast in the Jungle." It was in this anthology, and at that age, that I first read James—fell, I should say, into the jaws of James. I had never heard of him before. I read "The Beast in the Jungle" and creepily thought: here, here is my autobiography.

From that time forward, gradually but compellingly—and now I yield my scary confession—I became Henry James. Leaving graduate school at the age of twenty-two, disdaining the PhD as an acquisition surely beneath the concerns of literary seriousness, I was already Henry James. When I say I "became" Henry James, you must understand this: though I was a near-sighted twenty-two-year-old young woman infected with the commonplace intention of writing a novel, I was *also* the elderly bald-headed Henry James. Even without close examination, you could see the light glancing off my pate; you could see my heavy chin, my watch chain, my walking stick, my tender paunch.

I had become Henry James, and for years and years I remained Henry James. There was no doubt about it: it was my own clear and faithful truth. Of course, there were some small differences: for one thing, I was not a genius. For another, even in my own insignificant scribbler class, I was not prolific. But I carried the Jamesian idea. I was of his cult, I was a worshiper of literature, literature was my single altar; I was, like the elderly bald-headed James, a priest at that altar; and that altar was all of my life. Like John Marcher in "The Beast in the Jungle," I let everything pass me by for the sake of waiting for the Beast to spring—but unlike John Marcher, I knew what the Beast was, I knew exactly, I even knew the Beast's name: the Beast was literature itself, the sinewy grand undulations of some unraveling fiction, meticulously dreamed out in a language of masterly resplendence, which was to pounce on me and turn me into an enchanted and glorious Being, as enchanted and glorious as the elderly baldheaded Henry James himself.

But though the years spent themselves extravagantly, that ambush never occurred: the ambush of Sacred and Sublime Literature. The great shining Beast of Sacred and Sublime Literature did not pounce. Instead, other beasts, lesser ones, unseemly and misshapen, sprang out—all the beasts of ordinary life: sorrow, disease, death, guilt, responsibility, envy, grievance, grief, disillusionment—the beasts that are chained to human experience, and have nothing to do with Art except to interrupt and impede it, exactly according to the Lesson of the Master.

It was not until I read a certain vast and subtle book that I understood what had happened to me. The book was not by Henry James, but about him. Nowadays we give this sort of work a special name: we call it a nonfiction novel. I am referring, of course, to Leon Edel's ingenious and beautiful biography of Henry James, which is as much the possession of Edel's imagination as it is of the exhilaratingly reported facts of James's life. In Edel's rendering, I learned what I had never before taken in—but the knowledge came, in the Jamesian way, too late. What I learned was that Henry James himself had not always been the elderly bald-headed Henry James—that he, too, had once been twenty-two years old.

This terrible and secret knowledge instantly set me against James. From that point forward I was determined to eradicate him. And for a long while I succeeded.

What had happened was this: in early young womanhood I believed, with all the rigor and force and stunned ardor of religious belief, in the old Henry James, in his scepter and his authority. I believed that what *he* knew at sixty I was to encompass at twenty-two; at twenty-two I lived like the elderly baldheaded Henry James. I thought it was necessary—it was imperative, there was no other path!—to be, all at once, with no progression or evolution, the author of the equivalent of *The Ambassadors* or *The Wings of the Dove,* just as if "A Bundle of Letters," or "Four Meetings," or the golden little *The Europeans* had never preceded the great late Master.

For me, the Lesson of the Master was a horror, a Jamesian tale of a life of mishap and mistake and misconceiving. Though the Master himself was saying, in *The Ambassadors,* in Gloriani's garden, to Little Bilham, through the urgent cry of Strether, "Live, live!"—and though the Master himself was saying, in "The Beast in the Jungle," through May Bartram, how ghastly, how ghostly, it is to eschew, to evade, to turn from, to miss absolutely and irrevocably what is all the time there for you to seize—I mistook him, I misheard him, I missed, absolutely and irrevocably, his essential note. What I heard instead was: *Become a Master.*

Now the truth is it could not have been done, even by a writer of genius; and what a pitiful flicker of the flame of high ambition for a writer who is no more than the ordinary article! No one—not even James himself—springs all at once in early youth into full Mastery, and no writer, whether robustly gifted, or only little and pale, should hope for this implausible fate.

All this, I suppose, is not at all a "secret" knowledge, as I have characterized it, but is, rather, as James named it in the very person of his naïve young artist, most emphatically *overt*—so obvious that it is a mere access of foolishness even to talk about it. Still, I offer the implausible and preposterous model of myself to demonstrate the proposition that the Lesson of the Master is not a lesson about genius, or even about immense ambition; it is a lesson about misreading—about what happens when we misread the great voices of Art, and suppose that because they speak of Art, they *mean* Art. The great voices of Art never mean *only* Art; they also mean Life, they always mean Life, and Henry James, when he evolved into the Master we revere, finally meant nothing else.

The true Lesson of the Master, then, is, simply, never to venerate what is complete, burnished, whole, in its grand organic flowering or finish—never to look toward the admirable and dazzling end; never to be ravished by the goal; never to worship ripe Art or the ripened artist; but instead to seek to be young while young, primitive while primitive, ungainly when ungainly—to look for crudeness and rudeness, to husband one's own stupidity or ungenius.

There *is* this mix-up most of us have between ourselves and what we admire or triumphantly cherish. We see this mix-up, this mishap, this mishmash, most often in writers: the writer of a new generation ravished by the genius writer of a classical generation, who begins to dream herself, or himself, as powerful, vigorous, and original—as if being filled up by the genius writer's images, scenes, and stratagems were the same as having the capacity to pull off the identical magic. To be any sort of competent writer one must keep one's psychological distance from the supreme artists.

If I were twenty-two now, I would not undertake a cannibalistically ambitious Jamesian novel to begin with; I would look into the eyes of Henry James at twenty-two, and see the diffident hope, the uncertainty, the marveling tentativeness, the dream that is still only a dream; the young man still learning to fashion the Scene. Or I would go back still further, to the boy of seventeen, misplaced in a Swiss polytechnic school, who recalled in old age that "I so feared and abhorred mathematics that the simplest arithmetical operation had always found and kept me helpless and blank." It is not to the Master in his fullness I would give my awed, stricken, desperate fealty, but to the faltering, imperfect, dreaming youth.

If these words should happen to reach the ears of any young writer dumbstruck by the elderly bald-headed Henry James, one who has hungrily heard and ambitiously assimilated the voluptuous cathedral tones of the developed organ master, I would say to her or him: put out your lean and clumsy forefinger and strike your paltry, oafish, feeble, simple, skeletal, single note. Try for what Henry James at sixty would scorn—just as he scorned the work of his own earliness, and revised it and revised it in the manner of his later pen in that grand chastisement of youth known as the New York Edition. Trying, in youth, for what the Master in his mastery would condemn—that is the only road to modest mastery. Rapture and homage are not the way. Influence is perdition.

Part Three

Creation

Not-Knowing

Donald Barthelme

Let us suppose that someone is writing a story. From the world of conventional signs he takes an azalea bush, plants it in a pleasant park. He takes a gold pocket watch from the world of conventional signs and places it under the azalea bush. He takes from the same rich source a handsome thief and a chastity belt, places the thief in the chastity belt and lays him tenderly under the azalea, not neglecting to wind the gold pocket watch so that its ticking will, at length, awaken the now-sleeping thief. From the Sarah Lawrence campus he borrows a pair of seniors, Jacqueline and Jemima, and sets them to walking in the vicinity of the azalea bush and the handsome, chaste thief. Jacqueline and Jemima have just failed the Graduate Record Examination and are cursing God in colorful Sarah Lawrence language. What happens next?

Of course, I don't know.

It's appropriate to pause and say that the writer is one who, embarking upon a task, does not know what to do. I cannot tell you, at this moment, whether Jacqueline and Jemima will succeed or fail in their effort to jimmy the chastity belt's lock, or whether the thief, whose name is Zeno and who has stolen the answer sheets for the next set of Graduate Record Examinations, will pocket the pocket watch or turn it over to the nearest park employee. The fate of the azalea bush, whether it will bloom or strangle in a killing frost, is unknown to me.

A very conscientious writer might purchase an azalea at the Downtown Nursery and a gold watch at Tiffany's, hire a handsome thief fresh from Riker's Island, obtain the loan of a chastity belt from the Metropolitan, inveigle Jacqueline and Jemima in from Bronxville, and arrange them all under glass for study, writing up the results in honest, even fastidious prose. But in so doing he places himself in the realm of journalism or sociology. The not-knowing is crucial to art, is what permits art to be made. Without the scanning process engendered by not-knowing, without the possibility of having the mind move in unanticipated directions, there would be no invention.

This is not to say that I don't know anything about Jacqueline or Jemima, but what I do know comes into being at the instant it's inscribed. Jacqueline, for example, loathes her mother, whereas Jemima dotes on hers—I discover this by writing the sentence that announces it. Zeno was fathered by a—what? Polar bear? Roller skate? Shower of gold? I opt for the shower of gold, for Zeno is a hero (although he's just become one by virtue of his golden parent). Inside the pocket watch there is engraved a legend. Can I make it out? I think so: *Drink me,* it says. No no, can't use it, that's Lewis Carroll's. But could Zeno be a watch swallower rather than a thief? No again, Zeno'd choke on it, and so would the reader. There are rules.

Writing is a process of dealing with not-knowing, a forcing of what and how. We have all heard novelists testify to the fact that, beginning a new book, they are utterly baffled as to how to proceed, what should be written and how it might be written, even though they've done a dozen. At best there's a slender intuition, not much greater than an itch. The anxiety attached to this situation is not inconsiderable. "Nothing to paint and nothing to paint with," as Beckett says of Bram van Velde. The not-knowing is not simple, because it's hedged about with prohibitions, roads that may not be taken. The more serious the artist, the more problems he takes into account and the more considerations limit his possible initiatives—a point to which I shall return.

What kind of a fellow is Zeno? How do I know until he's opened his mouth?

"Gently, ladies, gently," says Zeno, as Jacqueline and Jemima bash away at the belt with a spade borrowed from a friendly park employee. And to the park employee: "Somebody seems to have lost this-here watch."

Let us change the scene.

Alphonse, the park employee from the preceding episode, he who lent the spade, is alone in his dismal room on West Street (I could position him as well in a four-story townhouse on East Seventy-second, but you'd object, and rightly so; verisimilitude forbids it, nothing's calculated quicker than a salary).

Alphonse, like so many toilers in the great city, is not as simple as he seems. Like those waiters who are really actors and those cab drivers who are really composers of electronic music, Alphonse is sunlighting as a Parks Department employee although he is, in reality, a literary critic. We find him writing a letter to his friend Gaston, also a literary critic although masquerading *pro tem* as a guard at the Whitney Museum. Alphonse poises paws over his Smith-Corona and writes:

Dear Gaston,

Yes, you are absolutely right—Postmodernism is dead. A stunning blow, but not entirely surprising. I am spreading the news as rapidly as possible, so that all of our friends who are in the Postmodernist "bag" can get out of it before their cars are repossessed and the insurance companies tear up their policies. Sad to see Postmodernism go (and so quickly!). I was fond of it. As fond, almost, as I was of its grave and noble predecessor, Modernism. But we cannot dwell in the done-for. The death of a movement is a natural part of life, as was understood so well by the partisans of Naturalism, which is dead.

I remember exactly where I was when I realized that Postmodernism had bought it. I was in my study with a cup of tequila and William Y's new book, *One-Half.* Y's work is, we agree, good—*very* good. But who can make the leap to greatness while dragging after him the burnt-out boxcars of a dead aesthetic? Perhaps we can find new employment for him. On the roads, for example. When the insight overtook me, I started to my feet, knocking over the tequila, and said aloud (although there was no one to hear), "What? Postmodernism, too?" So many, so many. I put Y's book away on a high shelf and turned to the contemplation of the death of Plainsong, A.D. 958.

By the way: Structuralism's tottering. I heard it from Gerald, who is at Johns Hopkins and thus in the thick of things. You don't have to tell everybody. Frequently, idle talk is enough to give a movement that last little "push" that topples it into its grave. I'm convinced that's what happened to the New Criticism. I'm persuaded that it was Gerald, whispering in the corridors.

On the bright side, one thing that is dead that I don't feel too bad about is Existentialism, which I never thought was anything more than

Phenomenology's bathwater anyway. It had a good run, but how peeving it was to hear all those artists going around talking about "the existential moment" and similar claptrap. Luckily, they have stopped doing that now. Similarly, the Nouveau Roman's passing did not disturb me overmuch. "Made dreariness into a religion," you said, quite correctly. I know this was one of your pared-to-the-bone movements and all that, but I didn't even like what they left out. A neat omission usually raises the hairs on the back of my neck. Not here. Robbe-Grillet's only true success, for my money, was with *Jealousy,* which I'm told he wrote in a fit of.

Well, where are we? Surrealism gone, got a little sweet toward the end, you could watch the wine of life turning into Gatorade. Sticky. Altar Poems—those constructed in the shape of an altar for the greater honor and glory of God—have not been seen much lately: missing and presumed dead. The Anti-Novel is dead; I read it in the *Times.* The Anti-Hero and the Anti-Heroine had a thing going which resulted in three Anti-Children, all of them now at M.I.T. The Novel of the Soil is dead, as are Expressionism, Impressionism, Futurism, Imagism, Vorticism, Regionalism, Realism, the Kitchen Sink School of Drama, the Theatre of the Absurd, the Theatre of Cruelty, Black Humor, and Gongorism. You know all this; I'm just totting up. To be a Pre-Raphaelite in the present era is to be somewhat out of touch. And, of course, Concrete Poetry—sank like a stone.

So we have a difficulty. What shall we call the New Thing, which I haven't encountered yet but which is bound to be out there somewhere? Post-Postmodernism sounds, to me, a little lumpy. I've been toying with the Revolution of the Word, II, or the New Revolution of the Word, but I'm afraid the Jolas estate may hold a copyright. It should have the word *new* in it somewhere. The New Newness? Or maybe the Post-New? It's a problem. I await your comments and suggestions. If we're going to slap a saddle on this rough beast, we've got to get moving.

Yours,

Alphonse

If I am slightly more sanguine than Alphonse about Postmodernism, however dubious about the term itself and not altogether clear as to who is supposed to be on the bus and who is not, it's because I locate it in relation to a series of problems, and feel that the problems are durable ones. Problems are a comfort. Wittgenstein said, of philosophers, that some of them suffer from "loss of problems," a development in which everything seems quite simple to them and what they write becomes "immeasurably shallow and trivial." The same can be said of writers. Before I mention some of the specific difficulties I have in mind, I'd like to at least glance at some of the criticisms that have been leveled at the alleged Postmodernists—let's say John Barth, William Gass, John Hawkes, Robert Coover, William Gaddis, Thomas Pynchon, and myself in this country, Calvino in Italy, Peter Handke and Thomas Bernhard in Germany, although other names could be invoked. The criticisms run roughly as follows: that this kind of writing has turned its back on the world, is in some sense not about the world but about its own processes, that it is masturbatory, certainly chilly, that it excludes readers by design, speaks only to the already tenured, or that it does not speak at all, but instead, like Frost's Secret, sits in the center of a ring and Knows.

I would ardently contest each of these propositions, but it's rather easy to see what gives rise to them. The problems that seem to me to define the writer's task at this moment (to the extent that he has chosen them as his problems) are not of a kind that make for ease of communication, for work that rushes toward the reader with out-flung arms—rather, they're the reverse. Let me cite three such difficulties that I take to be important, all having to do with language. First, there is art's own project, since Mallarmé, of restoring freshness to a much-handled language, essentially an effort toward finding a language in which making art is possible at all. This remains a ground theme, as potent, problematically, today as it was a century ago. Secondly, there is the political and social contamination of language by its use in manipulation of various kinds over time and the effort to find what might be called a "clean" language, problems associated with the Roland Barthes of *Writing Degree Zero* but also discussed by Lukács and others. Finally, there is the pressure on language from contemporary culture in the broadest sense—I mean our devouring commercial culture—which results in a double impoverishment: theft of complexity from the reader, theft of the reader from the writer.

These are by no means the only thorny matters with which the writer has to deal, nor (allowing for the very great differences among the practitioners under discussion) does every writer called Postmodern respond to them in the same way and to the same degree, nor is it the case that other writers of quite different tendencies are innocent of these concerns. If I call these matters "thorny," it's because any adequate attempt to deal with them automatically creates barriers to the ready assimilation of the work. Art is not difficult because it wishes to be difficult, but because it wishes to be art. However much the writer might long to be, in his work, simple, honest, and straightforward, these virtues are no longer available to him. He discovers that in being simple, honest, and straightforward, nothing much happens: he speaks the speakable, whereas what we are looking for is the as-yet unspeakable, the as-yet unspoken.

With Mallarmé the effort toward mimesis, the representation of the external world, becomes a much more complex thing than it had been previously. Mallarmé shakes words loose from their attachments and bestows new meanings upon them, meanings which point not toward the external world but toward the Absolute, acts of poetic intuition. This is a fateful step; not for nothing does Barthes call him the Hamlet of literature. It produces, for one thing, a poetry of unprecedented difficulty. You will find no Mallarmé in Bartlett's *Familiar Quotations*. Even so ardent an admirer as Charles Mauron speaks of the sense of alienation enforced by his work. Mauron writes: "All who remember the day when first they looked into the *Poems* or the *Divagations* will testify to that curious feeling of *exclusion* which put them, in the face of a text written with *their* words (and moreover, as they could somehow feel, magnificently written), suddenly outside their own language, deprived of their rights in a common speech, and, as it were, rejected by their oldest friends." Mallarmé's work is also, and perhaps most importantly, a step toward establishing a new ontological status for the poem, as an object in the world rather than a representation of the world. But the ground seized is dangerous ground. After Mallarmé the struggle to renew language becomes a given for the writer, his exemplary quest an imperative. Mallarmé's work, "this whisper that is so close to silence," as Marcel Raymond calls it, is at once a liberation and a loss to silence of a great deal of territory.

The silencing of an existing rhetoric (in Harold Rosenberg's phrase) is also what is at issue in Barthes's deliberations in *Writing Degree Zero* and after—in this case a variety of rhetorics seen as actively pernicious rather than passively inhibiting. The question is, what is the complicity of language in the massive crimes of Fascism, Stalinism, or (by implication) our own policies in Vietnam? In the control of societies by the powerful and their busy functionaries? If these abominations are all in some sense facilitated by, made possible by, language, to what degree is that language ruinously contaminated (considerations also raised by George Steiner in his well-known essay "The Hollow Miracle" and, much earlier, by George Orwell)? I am sketching here, inadequately, a fairly complex argument; I am not particularly taken with Barthes's tentative solutions but the problems command the greatest respect. Again, we have language deeply suspicious of its own behavior; although this suspicion is not different in kind from Hemingway's noticing, early in the century, that words like *honor, glory,* and *country* were perjured, bought, the skepticism is far deeper now, and informed as well by the investigations of linguistic philosophers, structuralists, semioticians. Even conjunctions must be inspected carefully. "I read each word with the feeling appropriate to it," says Wittgenstein. "The word 'but' for example with the but-feeling. . . ." He is not wrong. Isn't the but-feeling, as he calls it, already sending us headlong down a greased slide before we've had the time to contemplate the proposition it's abutting? Quickly now, quickly—when you hear the phrase "our vital interests" do you stop to wonder whether you were invited to the den, Zen, Klan, or coven meeting at which these were defined? Did you speak?

In turning to the action of contemporary culture on language, and thus on the writer, the first thing to be noticed is a loss of reference. If I want a world of reference to which all possible readers in this country can respond, there is only one universe of discourse available, that in which the Love Boat sails on seas of passion like a Flying Dutchman of passion and the dedicated men in white of *General Hospital* pursue, with evenhanded diligence, triple bypasses and the nursing staff. This limits things somewhat. The earlier newspaper culture, which once dealt in a certain amount of nuance and zestful, highly literate hurly-burly, has deteriorated shockingly. The newspaper I worked for as a raw youth, thirty years ago, is today a pallid imitation of its former self.

Where once we could put spurious quotes in the paper and attribute them to Ambrose Bierce and be fairly sure that enough readers would get the joke to make the joke worthwhile, from the point of view of both reader and writer, no such common ground now exists. The situation is not peculiar to this country. Steiner remarks of the best current journalism in Germany that, read against an average number of the *Frankfurter Zeitung* of pre-Hitler days, it's difficult at times to believe that both are written in German. At the other end of the scale much of the most exquisite description of the world, discourse about the world, is now being carried on in mathematical languages obscure to most people—certainly to me—and the contributions the sciences once made to our common language in the form of coinages, new words and concepts, are now available only to specialists. When one adds the ferocious appropriation of high culture by commercial culture—it takes, by my estimate, about forty-five minutes for any given novelty in art to travel from the Mary Boone Gallery on West Broadway to the display windows of Henri Bendel on Fifty-seventh Street—one begins to appreciate the seductions of silence.

Problems in part define the kind of work the writer chooses to do, and are not to be avoided but embraced. A writer, says Karl Kraus, is a man who can make a riddle out of an answer.

Let me begin again.

Jacqueline and Jemima are instructing Zeno, who has returned the purloined GRE documents and is thus restored to dull respectability, in Postmodernism. Postmodernism, they tell him, has turned its back on the world, is not about the world but about its own processes, is masturbatory, certainly chilly, excludes readers by design, speaks only to the already tenured, or does not speak at all, but instead—

Zeno, to demonstrate that he too knows a thing or two, quotes the critic Perry Meisel on semiotics. "Semiotics," he says, "is in a position to claim that no phenomenon has any ontological status outside its place in the particular information system from which it draws its meaning"—he takes a large gulp of his Gibson—"and therefore, all language is finally groundless." I am eavesdropping and I am much reassured. This insight is one I can use. Gaston, the critic who is a guard at the Whitney Museum, is in love with an IRS agent named Madelaine, the very IRS agent, in fact, who is auditing my return for the year 1982. "Madelaine," I say kindly to her over lunch, "semiotics is in a position to claim that no phenomenon has any ontological status outside its place in the particular information system from which it draws its meaning, and therefore, all language is finally groundless, including that of those funny little notices you've been sending me." "Yes," says Madelaine kindly, pulling from her pocket a large gold pocket watch that Alphonse has sold Gaston for twenty dollars, her lovely violet eyes atwitter, "but some information systems are more enforceable than others." Alas, she's right.

If the writer is taken to be the work's way of getting itself written, a sort of lightning rod for an accumulation of atmospheric disturbances, a St. Sebastian absorbing in his tattered breast the arrows of the Zeitgeist, this changes not very much the traditional view of the artist. But it does license a very great deal of critical imperialism.

This is fun for everyone. A couple of years ago I received a letter from a critic requesting permission to reprint a story of mine as an addendum to the piece he had written about it. He attached the copy of my story he proposed to reproduce, and I was amazed to find that my poor story had sprouted a set of tiny numbers—one to eighty-eight, as I recall—an army of tiny numbers marching over the surface of my poor distracted text. Resisting the temptation to tell him that all the tiny numbers were in the wrong places, I gave him permission to do what he wished, but I did notice that by a species of literary judo the status of my text had been reduced to that of footnote.

There is, in this kind of criticism, an element of aggression that gives one pause. Deconstruction is an enterprise that announces its intentions with startling candor. Any work of art depends upon a complex series of interdependences. If I wrench the rubber tire from the belly of Rauschenberg's famous goat to determine, in the interest of a finer understanding of same, whether the tire is a B. F. Goodrich or a Uniroyal, the work collapses, more or less behind my back. I say this not because I find this kind of study valueless but because the mystery worthy of study, for me, is not the signification of parts but how they come together, the tire wrestled over the goat's hind legs. Calvin Tomkins tells us in *The Bride and the Bachelors* that Rauschenberg himself says that the tire seemed "something as unavoidable as the goat." To see both goat and tire as "unavoidable" choices, in the context of art-making, is to illuminate just how strange the combinatorial process can be. Nor was the choice a hasty one; Tomkins tells us that the goat had been in the studio for three years and had appeared in two previous versions (the final version is titled "Monogram") before it met the tire.

Modern-day critics speak of "recuperating" a text, suggesting an accelerated and possibly strenuous nursing back to health of a basically sickly text, very likely one that did not even know itself to be ill. I would argue that in the competing methodologies of contemporary criticism, many of them quite rich in implications, a sort of tyranny of great expectations obtains, a rage for final explanations, a refusal to allow a work that mystery which is essential to it. I hope I am not myself engaging in mystification if I say, not that the attempt should not be made, but that the mystery exists. I see no immediate way out of the paradox—tear a mystery to tatters and you have tatters, not mystery—I merely note it and pass on.

We can, however, wonder for a moment why the goat girdled with its tire is somehow a magical object, rather than, say, only a dumb idea. Harold Rosenberg speaks of the contemporary artwork as "anxious," as wondering: Am I a masterpiece or simply a pile of junk? (If I take many of my examples here from the art world rather than the world of literature it is because the issues are more quickly seen in terms of the first: "goat" and "tire" are standing in for pages of prose, pounds of poetry.) What precisely is it in the coming together of goat and tire that is magical? It's not the surprise of seeing the goat attired, although that's part of it. One might say, for example, that the tire *contests* the goat, *contradicts* the goat, as a mode of being, even that the tire *reproaches* the goat, in some sense. On the simplest punning level, the goat is *tired.* Or that the unfortunate tire has *been caught by* the goat, which has been fishing in the Hudson—goats eat anything, as everyone knows—or that the goat is being *consumed by* the tire; it's outside, after all, mechanization takes command. Or that the goateed goat is protesting the fatigue of its friend, the tire, by wearing it as a sort of STRIKE button. Or that two contrasting models of infinity are being presented, tires and goats both being infinitely reproducible, the first depending on the good fortunes of the B. F. Goodrich company and the second upon the copulatory enthusiasm of goats—parallel production lines suddenly met. And so on. What is magical about the object is that it at once invites and resists interpretation. Its artistic worth is measurable by the degree to which it remains, after interpretation, vital—no interpretation or cardiopulmonary push-pull can exhaust or empty it.

In what sense is the work "about" the world, the world that Jacqueline and Jemima have earnestly assured Zeno the work has turned its scarlet rump to? It is to this vexing question that we shall turn next.

Let us discuss the condition of my desk. It is messy, mildly messy. The messiness is both physical (coffee cups, cigarette ash) and spiritual (unpaid bills, unwritten novels). The emotional life of the man who sits at the desk is also messy—I am in love with a set of twins, Hilda and Heidi, and in a fit of enthusiasm I have joined the Bolivian army. The apartment in which the desk is located seems to have been sublet from Moonbeam McSwine. In the streets outside the apartment melting snow has revealed a choice assortment of decaying et cetera. Furthermore, the social organization of the country is untidy, the world situation in disarray. How do I render all this messiness, and if I succeed, what have I done?

In a commonsense way we agree that I attempt to find verbal equivalents for whatever it is I wish to render. The unpaid bills are easy enough. I need merely quote one: FINAL DISCONNECT NOTICE. Hilda and Heidi are somewhat more difficult. I can say that they are beautiful—why not?—and you will more or less agree, although the bald statement has hardly stirred your senses. I can describe them—Hilda has the map of Bolivia tattooed on her right cheek and Heidi habitually wears, on her left hand, a set of brass knuckles wrought of solid silver—and they move a step closer. Best of all, perhaps, I can permit them to speak, for they speak much as we do.

"On Valentine's Day," says Hilda, "he sent me oysters, a dozen and a half."

"He sent me oysters too," said Heidi, "two dozen."

"Mine were long-stemmed oysters," says Hilda, "on a bed of the most wonderful spinach."

"Oh yes, spinach," says Heidi, "he sent me spinach too, miles and miles of spinach, wrote every bit of it himself."

To render "messy" adequately, to the point that you are enabled to feel it—it should, ideally, frighten your shoes—I would have to be more graphic than the decorum of the occasion allows. What should be emphasized is that one proceeds by way of particulars. If I know how a set of brass knuckles feels on Heidi's left hand it's because I bought one once, in a pawnshop, not to smash up someone's face but to exhibit on a pedestal in a museum show devoted to cultural artifacts of ambivalent status. The world enters the work as it enters our ordinary lives, not as world-view or system but in sharp particularity: a tax notice from Madelaine, a snowball containing a résumé from Gaston.

The words with which I attempt to render "messy," like any other words, are not inert, rather they are furiously busy. We do not mistake the words *the taste of chocolate* for the taste of chocolate itself, but neither do we miss the tease in *taste,* the shock in *chocolate.* Words have halos, patinas, overhangs, echoes. The word *halo,* for instance, may invoke St. Hilarius, of whom we've seen too little lately. The word *patina* brings back the fine pewtery shine on the saint's halo. The word *overhang* reminds us that we have, hanging over us, a dinner date with St. Hilarius, that crashing bore. The word *echo* restores us to Echo herself, poised like the White Rock girl on the overhang of a patina of a halo—infirm ground, we don't want the poor spirit to pitch into the pond where Narcissus blooms eternally, they'll bump foreheads, or maybe other parts closer to the feet, a scandal. There's chocolate smeared all over Hilarius' halo—messy, messy. . . .

The combinatorial agility of words, the exponential generation of meaning once they're allowed to go to bed together, allows the writer to surprise himself, makes art possible, reveals how much of Being we haven't yet encountered. It could be argued that computers can do this sort of thing for us, with critic-computers monitoring their output. When computers learn how to make jokes, artists will be in serious trouble. But artists will respond in such a way as to make art impossible for the computer. They will redefine art to take into account (that is, to exclude) technology—photography's impact upon painting and painting's brilliant response being a clear and comparatively recent example.

The prior history of words is one of the aspects of language the world uses to smuggle itself into the work. If words can be contaminated by the world, they can also carry with them into the work trace elements of world which can be used in a positive sense. We must allow ourselves the advantages of our disadvantages.

A late bulletin: Hilda and Heidi have had a baby, with which they're thoroughly displeased, it's got no credit cards and can't speak French, they'll send it back. . . . Messy.

Style is not much a matter of choice. One does not sit down to write and think: Is this poem going to be a Queen Anne poem, a Biedermeier poem, a Vienna Secession poem, or a Chinese Chippendale poem? Rather it is both a response to constraint and a seizing of opportunity. Very often a constraint is an opportunity. It would seem impossible to write *Don Quixote* once again, yet Borges has done so with great style, improving on the original (as he is not slow to tell us) while remaining faithful to it, faithful as a tick on a dog's belly. I don't mean that whim does not intrude. Why do I avoid, as much as possible, using the semicolon? Let me be plain: the semicolon is ugly, ugly as a tick on a dog's belly. I pinch them out of my prose. The great German writer Arno Schmidt, punctuation-drunk, averages eleven to a page.

Style is of course *how*. And the degree to which *how* has become *what*—since, say, Flaubert—is a question that men of conscience wax wroth about, and should. If I say of my friend that on this issue his marbles are a little flat on one side, this does not mean that I do not love my friend. He, on the other hand, considers that I am ridden by strange imperatives, and that the little piece I gave to the world last week, while nice enough in its own way, would have been vastly better had not my deplorable aesthetics caused me to score it for banjulele, cross between a banjo and a uke. Bless Babel.

Let us suppose that I am the toughest banjulele player in town and that I have contracted to play "Melancholy Baby" for six hours before an audience that will include the four next-toughest banjulele players in town. We imagine the smoky basement club, the hustling waiters (themselves students of the jazz banjulele), Jacqueline, Jemima, Zeno, Alphonse, Gaston, Madelaine, Hilda, and Heidi forming a congenial group at the bar. There is one thing of which you may be sure: I am not going to play "Melancholy Baby" as written. Rather I will play something that is parallel, in some sense, to "Melancholy Baby," based upon the chords of "Melancholy Baby," made out of "Melancholy Baby," *having to do with* "Melancholy Baby"—commentary, exegesis, elaboration, contradiction. The interest of my construction, if any, is to be located in the space between the new entity I have constructed and the "real" "Melancholy Baby," which remains in the mind as the horizon which bounds my efforts.

This is, I think, the relation of art to world. I suggest that art is always a meditation upon external reality rather than a representation of external reality or a jackleg attempt to "be" external reality. If I perform even reasonably well, no one will accuse me of not providing a true, verifiable, note-for-note reproduction of "Melancholy Baby"—it will be recognized that this was not what I was after. Twenty years ago I was much more convinced of the autonomy of the literary object than I am now, and even wrote a rather persuasive defense of the proposition that I have just rejected: that the object is itself world. Beguiled by the rhetoric of the time—the sculptor Phillip Pavia was publishing a quite good magazine called *It Is*, and this was typical—I felt that the high ground had been claimed and wanted to place my scuffed cowboy boots right there. The proposition's still attractive. What's the right answer? Bless Babel.

A couple of years ago I visited Willem de Kooning's studio in East Hampton, and when the big doors are opened one can't help seeing—it's a shock—the relation between the rushing green world outside and the paintings. Precisely how de Kooning manages to distill nature into art is a mystery, but the explosive relation is there, I've seen it. Once when I was in Elaine de Kooning's studio on Broadway, at a time when the metal sculptor Herbert Ferber occupied the studio immediately above, there came through the floor a most horrible crashing and banging. "What in the world is that?" I asked, and Elaine said, "Oh, that's Herbert thinking."

Art is a true account of the activity of mind. Because consciousness, in Husserl's formulation, is always consciousness *of* something, art thinks ever of the world, cannot not think of the world, could not turn its back on the world even if it wished to. This does not mean that it's going to be honest as a mailman; it's more likely to appear as a drag queen. The problems I mentioned earlier, as well as others not taken up, enforce complexity. "We do not spend much time in front of a canvas whose intentions are plain," writes Cioran, "music of a specific character, unquestionable contours, exhausts our patience, the overexplicit poem seems . . . incomprehensible." Flannery O'Connor, an artist of the first rank, famously disliked anything that looked funny on the page, and her distaste has widely been taken as a tough-minded put-down of puerile experimentalism. But did she also dislike anything that looked funny on the wall? If so, a severe deprivation. Art cannot remain in one place. A certain amount of movement, up, down, across, even a gallop toward the past, is a necessary precondition.

Style enables us to speak, to imagine again. Beckett speaks of "the long sonata of the dead"—where on earth did the word *sonata* come from, imposing as it does an orderly, even exalted design upon the most disorderly, distressing phenomenon known to us? The fact is not challenged, but understood, momentarily, in a new way. It's our good fortune to be able to imagine alternative realities, other possibilities. We can quarrel with the world, constructively (no one alive has quarreled with the world more extensively or splendidly than Beckett). "Belief in progress," says Baudelaire, "is a doctrine of idlers and Belgians." Perhaps. But if I have anything unorthodox to offer here, it's that I think art's project is fundamentally meliorative. The aim of meditating about the world is finally to change the world. It is this meliorative aspect of literature that provides its ethical dimension. We are all Upton Sinclairs, even that Hamlet, Stéphane Mallarmé.

Levels of Reality in Literature

Italo Calvino

Paper read at an international conference on "Levels of Reality,"
Florence, September 1978.

Different levels of reality also exist in literature; in fact literature rests precisely on the distinction among various levels, and would be unthinkable without an awareness of this distinction. A work of literature might be defined as an operation carried out in the written language and involving several levels of reality at the same time. From this point of view, some consideration of works of literature might not be completely useless even to the scientist or philosopher of science.

In a work of literature, various levels of reality may meet while remaining distinct and separate, or else they may melt and mingle and knit together, achieving a harmony among their contradictions or else forming an explosive mixture. Shakespeare's plays provide us with a number of clear examples. For distinction between the different levels we might think of *A Midsummer Night's Dream,* in which the complications in the plot occur where three levels of reality intersect, though these remain quite distinct: (1) the aristocratic characters at the court of Theseus and Hippolyta; (2) the supernatural characters Titania, Oberon, and Puck; (3) the rustic comic characters, Bottom and his friends. This third level borders on the animal kingdom, which may be seen as a fourth level, entered by Bottom when he is changed into an ass. In addition there is one further level to consider, that of the performance of the story of Pyramus and Thisbe, the play within the play.

Hamlet, on the other hand, constitutes a sort of short circuit, or a whirlpool that sucks in all the various levels of reality; it is from their very irreconcilability that the drama comes into being. There is the ghost of Hamlet's father with his demand for justice, which is the level of archaic values, of knightly virtues, with its moral code and supernatural beliefs; there is the level we might call realistic, that of "Something is rotten in the state of Denmark" (i.e., the court at Elsinore); there is the level of Hamlet's inner life, of the modern psychological and intellectual awareness that is the great novelty of the play. To hold these three levels together, Hamlet disguises himself in a fourth, the linguistic barrier of his feigned madness. But, as if by induction, this feigned madness leads to real madness, and the level of madness seizes and eliminates one of the few positive elements remaining in the play: the delicate figure of Ophelia. This drama also has a play within the play, the performance of the troupe of strolling players; and this constitutes a level of reality on its own, separate from the rest, though interacting with them.

Up till now I have confined myself to distinguishing the various levels of reality within the work of art considered as a world of its own, but we cannot stop there. We have to consider the work as a product, in its relation to the outside world in the age when it was created and the age when we received it. In all periods and in all literatures we find works that at a certain time turn around on themselves, look at themselves in the act of coming into being, and become aware of the materials they are made of. Just to stick to Shakespeare, in the last act of *Antony and Cleopatra,* before killing herself, Cleopatra imagines her fate as a prisoner taken to Rome for Caesar's triumph, mocked by the crowds; even now she thinks that her love for Antony will become the subject of theatrical performances:

> . . . the quick comedians
> Extemporally will stage us, and present
> Our Alexandrian revels. Antony
> Shall be brought drunken forth, and I shall see

Some squeaking Cleopatra boy my greatness
I' the posture of a whore.

There is a fine passage by Middleton Murry about this dazzling piece of mental acrobatics. On the stage of the Globe theatre a piping boy dressed up as Cleopatra represents the real, majestic Queen Cleopatra in the act of imagining herself being represented by a boy dressed up as Cleopatra.

These are the tangles we have to start with in saying anything about the levels of reality in a work of literature. We cannot lose sight of the fact that these levels are part of the *written* world.

"I write." This statement is the one and only real "datum" a writer can start from. "At this moment I am writing." Which is also the same as saying: "You who are reading are obliged to believe only one thing: that what you are reading is something that at some previous time someone has written; what you are reading takes place in one particular world, that of the written word. It may be that likenesses can be established between the world of the written word and other worlds of experience, and that you will be called on to judge upon these likenesses, but your judgment would in any case be wrong if while reading you hoped to enter into a direct relationship with the experience of worlds other than that of the written word." I have spoken here of "worlds of experience," not of "levels of reality," because within the world of the written word one can discern many levels of reality, as in any other world of experience.

Let us then agree that the statement "I write" serves the purpose of pinning down a first level of reality, which I have, explicitly or otherwise, to take account of in any operation that creates a rapport between diverse levels of reality in writing, and even between things written and things not written. This first level may be useful to me as a platform on which to erect a second level, which may even belong to a reality utterly different from the first, and indeed refer to a different stratum of experience.

For example, I might write, "I write that Ulysses listens to the song of the Sirens," an incontrovertible statement that bridges the gap between two worlds that are not contiguous: the immediate and empirical world in which I am and am writing, and the mythical one in which it always happens that Ulysses, tied to the ship's mast, is listening to the Sirens' song.

The same thing might also be written, "Ulysses listens to the song of the Sirens," leaving the "I write" understood. But if we do leave this understood we must be prepared to risk the reader's getting confused between two levels of reality, and believing that the act of listening on the part of Ulysses takes place on the same level of reality as my act of writing this sentence.

I have said "the reader believes," but it is clear enough that the credibility of what is written can be understood in very different ways, each one corresponding to more than one level of reality. There is nothing to prevent anyone from believing in the encounter of Ulysses with the Sirens as a historical fact, in the same way as one believes in the landing of Christopher Columbus on October 12, 1492. Or else we may believe it by feeling ourselves struck by the revelation of a truth beyond perception that is contained in the myth. But here we enter a field of religious phenomenology in which the written word would merely act as a spur to meditation. However, the credibility that interests us here is neither of these, but the kind of credibility peculiar to the literary text, in parentheses, as it were, matched on the reader's part by an attitude Coleridge defined as "suspension of disbelief." This suspension of disbelief is the condition on which the success of every literary invention depends, even if it is admittedly within the realm of the fabulous and incredible.

We have considered the possibility that the level of "Ulysses listens" might be put on a par with that of "I write." But this balance between the two levels could occur only if you, the reader, believed that the statement "I write" also belonged on a literary or mythological level. The "I" that is the subject of "I write" would then become the "I" of a fictional or mythological character— such as Homer, in fact. For clarity's sake, let us put our sentence in the following manner: "I write that Homer tells that Ulysses listens to the Sirens." The statement "Homer tells" may be placed on a level of mythical reality, in which case we will have two levels of mythical reality, that of the fable narrated and that of the legendary blind bard inspired by the Muses. But the same statement might be placed on a level of historical or (better) philological reality. In that case, by "Homer" we mean the individual or collective author with whom scholars busy themselves over the "Homeric question," and the level of reality would then be identical or contiguous to that of "I write." (Notice that I have not written "Homer writes" or "Homer sings," but "Homer tells," so as to leave both possibilities open.)

The way in which I have formulated the sentence makes it natural to think that Homer and I are two distinct persons, but this could be a wrong impression. The phrase would be exactly the same if it had been written by Homer in person, or in any case by the real author of the *Odyssey,* who at the moment of writing splits into two first persons: the empirical "I" who pens the words on the page (or dictates them to a scribe) and the mythical character of the blind bard, visited by divine inspiration, with whom he identifies himself.

In the same way, nothing would change if the "I" were the "I" who is speaking to you, while Homer, of whom I speak, were also "I": that is, if what I attribute to Homer were my own invention. This procedure would be clear at once if the phrase ran: "I write that Homer tells that Ulysses discovers that the Sirens are mute." In this case, in order to obtain a particular literary effect, I apocryphally attribute to Homer my own inversion, or distortion, or interpretation of the Homeric narrative. (In fact, the idea of the silent Sirens is Kafka's, and we must realize that the "I" who is the subject of the sentence is Kafka.) But even without turning things upside down, the countless authors who in recasting an earlier author have rewritten or interpreted a mythical (or at least a traditional) tale have done this to communicate something new, while still remaining faithful to the image of the original; and with all of them, in the "I" of the writing first person one can distinguish one or more levels of mythical or epic reality that draw material from the collective imagination.

Let us go back to the sentence we started with. Every reader of the *Odyssey* knows that more exactly it ought to be written, "I write that Homer tells that Ulysses says: I have listened to the song of the Sirens."

In the *Odyssey,* in fact, the adventures of Ulysses in the third person surround and contain other adventures of Ulysses in the first person, narrated by him to Alcinoüs, king of the Phaeacians. If we compare one with the other, we find that the difference between them is not simply grammatical. The adventures told in the third person have a psychological and emotional dimension that the others lack, and in them the supernatural presence consists in appearances of the Olympian gods in the guise of ordinary mortals. On the other hand, the adventures of Ulysses in the first person belong to a more primitive repertoire of myth, in which ordinary mortals and supernatural beings meet face to face; a world peopled by monsters, Cyclopes, Sirens, enchantresses who change men into pigs, and in fact the whole pre-Olympian pagan world of the supernatural. We may therefore define these as two different levels of mythical reality, to which there are two corresponding geographical realities. One corresponds to the historical knowledge of the time (the voyages of Telemachus and the homecoming to Ithaca), while the other belongs to fable and results from a juxtaposition of the most heterogeneous traditions (the travels of Ulysses as told by Ulysses himself). We may add that between the two levels is the island of the Phaeacians, which was the ideal place that gave birth to the narrative—a utopia of human perfection, outside the bounds of history and geography.

I have dwelt on this point because it serves to show how the different levels of reality may be matched by different levels of credibility—or, to put it better, a different suspension of disbelief. Assuming that a reader "believes" in the adventures of Ulysses as told by Homer, this same reader might judge Ulysses to be a mere braggart in all that Homer makes him say in the first person. But let us be careful not to confuse levels of reality (within the work) with levels of truth (referring to things outside it). For this reason we ought always to bear in mind the entire sentence: "I write that Homer tells that Ulysses says: I have listened to the song of the Sirens."

This is the formula that I put forward as the most complete, and at the same time the most compact, model of the connecting links between levels of reality in works of literature. Every part of this sentence may be linked to various sets of problems. I shall now give a number of suggestions, starting again from the beginning.

I write

This statement, "I write" (or "I am writing"), is connected with the whole field of problems—particularly fertile in this century—concerning what has been called metaliterature, and the analogous problems of metatheatre, metapainting, and so on. We already mentioned the play within the play while speaking of Shakespeare; there is no dearth of examples in the work of other playwrights, from Corneille's *Illusion comique* to Pirandello's *Six Characters in Search of an Author*. But in the last few decades these metatheatrical and metaliterary processes have acquired fresh importance, with foundations of a moral or epistemological nature, in opposition to the illusoriness of art, to the claim made by realism to lead the reader or spectator to forget that what he has before his eyes is an operation performed by means of language, a fiction worked out with an eye toward a strategy of effects.

The moral and indeed pedagogical motive is dominant in Brecht, with his theory of the epic theatre of alienation: the spectator must not abandon himself passively and emotionally to the illusion on the stage, but must be urged to think and to participate.

A process of theorization based on structural linguistics, on the other hand, forms the background to research carried out in French literature during the past fifteen years, and in both critical thought and creative practice this puts the material side of writing—the text itself—firmly in the foreground. We need only mention the name of Roland Barthes.

I write that Homer tells

Here we enter a very extensive field, the splitting or multiplication of the subject of the verb "to write"; and it is a field in which any really exhaustive theoretical work has yet to be done.

We might begin with a habit characteristic of the writers of chivalric romances, that of claiming a hypothetical manuscript as a source. Even Ariosto pretends to refer back to the authority of Turpin. And Cervantes introduces the figure of an Arab writer, Cid Hamet Benengeli, between himself and Don Quixote. Not only that, but Cervantes supposes a kind of contemporaneousness between the action narrated and the writing of the Arabic manuscript, so that Don Quixote and Sancho Panza are aware that the adventures they are having are those written by Benengeli, and not the ones written about by Avellaneda in his apocryphal second part of *Don Quixote*.

A still simpler method is that of suggesting that the book is written in the first person by the protagonist. The first novel that may be considered entirely *modern* was not published under the name of the author, Daniel Defoe, but as the memoirs of an obscure sailor from York, a certain Robinson Crusoe.

All this brings me little by little to the heart of the problem: the successive layers of subjectivity and feigning that we can discern underneath the author's name, and the various "I"'s that go to make up the "I" who is writing. The preliminary condition of any work of literature is that the person who is writing has to invent that first character, who is the author of the work. That a person puts his whole self into the work he is writing is something we often hear said, but it is never true. It is always only a projection of himself that an author calls into play while he is writing; it may be a projection of a real part of himself or the projection of a fictitious "I"—a mask, in short. Writing always presupposes the selection of a psychological attitude, a rapport with the world, a tone of voice, a homogeneous set of linguistic tools, the data of experience and the phantoms of the imagination—in a word, a *style*. The author is an author insofar as he enters into a role the way an actor does and identifies himself with that projection of himself at the moment of writing.

The author-*cum*-character is both something less and something more than the "I" of the individual as an empirical subject. He is something less because (for example) Gustave Flaubert the author of *Madame Bovary* excludes the language and visions of Gustave Flaubert the author of *La Tentation de Saint Antoine* or *Salammbô*. He rigorously cuts down his inner world to the set of data that make up the world of *Madame Bovary*. And he is something more because the Gustave Flaubert who exists only in relation to the manuscript of *Madame Bovary* partakes of a far more compact and well-defined state of being than does the Gustave Flaubert who, while writing *Madame Bovary*, knows that he was the author of *La Tentation* and is about to be the author of *Salammbô*. He knows that he is continually oscillating between one world and another, and that in the end all these worlds flow together and unify in his mind.

The example of Flaubert may be used to verify the formula I have suggested if we translate this into a series of projections or lantern slides. Gustave Flaubert the author of the complete works of Gustave Flaubert projects outside himself the Gustave Flaubert who is the author of *Madame Bovary*, who in turn projects from himself the character of a middle-class married woman in

Rouen, Emma Bovary, who projects from herself that Emma Bovary whom she dreams of being.

$$\{G\,F\} \rightarrow \boxed{G\,F} \rightarrow \boxed{E\,B} \rightarrow \{E\,B\}$$

Each element projected reacts in its turn on the element that projects it; it transforms and conditions it. So the arrows go not in one direction only, but in both:

$$\{G\,F\} \rightleftarrows \boxed{G\,F} \rightleftarrows \boxed{E\,B} \rightleftarrows \{E\,B\}$$

All we then have to do is connect the last term with the first—that is, establish the circular movement of these projections. It was Flaubert himself who gave us a precise clue to this with his famous phrase *"Madame Bovary, c'est moi."*

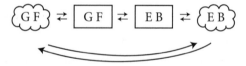

How much of the "I" who shapes the characters is in fact an "I" who has been shaped by the characters? The further we go toward distinguishing the various levels that go to make up the "I" of the author, the more we realize that many of these levels do not belong to the author as an individual but to collective culture, to the historical period or the deep sedimentary layers of the species. The starting point of the chain, the real primary subject of the verb "to write," seems ever more distant from us, more rarefied and indistinct. Perhaps it is a phantom "I," an empty space, an absence.

In order to acquire more solid substance, the "I" can become a character, and indeed the protagonist of the written work. But we need only think of the extremely subtle pages that Gianfranco Contini devotes to the "I" of the *Divine Comedy* to realize that it, too, can be split into a number of persons, rather like the "I" who is speaking in Proust's *A la recherche du temps perdu.*

With the "I" who becomes a character we are shifting our focus from "I write that Homer tells" to "Homer tells that Ulysses . . ."

Homer tells that Ulysses

The author-protagonist brings an internal subjectivity to the written world, a figure endowed with a distinctness of his own—often a visual and iconic distinctness—which seizes the imagination of the reader and acts as a device to connect the different levels of reality, or even to bring them into being and enable them to take on form in the course of writing.

The character Don Quixote clears the way for the clash and encounter of two antithetical languages, or, rather, of two literary worlds without any ground in common: the chivalric-supernatural and the picaresquecomic. It opens up a new dimension, or, rather, two: an extremely complex level of mental reality and a representation of the environment which we might call realistic, but in a completely new sense compared with picaresque "realism," which consisted of a repertoire of stereotyped images of poverty and squalor. The sundrenched country roads on which Don Quixote and Sancho Panza meet with friars carrying parasols, muleteers, ladies in sedan chairs, and flocks of sheep constitute a world that had never before been written about. It had never before been written about because there had never been a reason for writing about it, whereas here it fulfills a need: it is the reverse of the inner reality of Don Quixote, or, better still, the background against which Don Quixote projects his own codified interpretation of the world.

Don Quixote is a character endowed with an unmistakable iconic quality and inexhaustible inner riches. But this does not mean that to perform the function of protagonist a character necessarily has to have such depth. The function of the character may be likened to that of an "operator," in the mathematical sense of the word. As long as his function is well defined, he can be merely a name, a profile, a hieroglyphic, a sign.

When we read *Gulliver's Travels* we know very little about Dr. Lemuel Gulliver, ship's doctor in the Royal Navy. His substance as a character is infinitely scantier than that of Don Quixote, yet his is the personality that we follow throughout the book, and the one that brings it into being. This is because, even though it is hard to define Lemuel Gulliver psychologically or facially, his function as an "operator" is very clear, in the first place as a giant in a world of dwarfs and then as a dwarf in a world of giants. And this operation in terms of size is the easier interpretation, whereby Gulliver "works" as a character even for children who read Swift's book in simplified texts. But the real operation which he manifests (and here I am thinking of a very persuasive essay on this subject by an Italian scholar, Giuseppe Sertoli, published this year) is that of the contrast between the world of logico-mathematical reason and the world of bodies, of their physiological materiality and various cognitive experiences and various ethical and theological concepts.

Ulysses says:

Punctuated with a colon. This colon is a very important articulated "joint," and I would call it the headstone of narrative at all times in all lands. Not only because one of the most widespread structures of written narrative has always been that of stories inserted into another story that acts as a frame, but also because where the frame does not exist we may infer an invisible colon that starts off the discourse and introduces the whole work.

I will confine myself to touching on the salient problem. In the West, the novel was born in Hellenistic Greece, taking the form of a main narrative into which secondary narratives, told by the various characters, were inserted. This method is characteristic of ancient Indian narrative, where, however, the structure of the story in relation to the point of view of the narrator obeys rules far more complicated than in the West. (I am here relying on a monograph published in 1914, *Sur l'origine indienne du roman grec,* by F. Lacôte, an expert on Indian literature.) Also based on Indian models are those collections of stories inserted into a narrative that acts as a frame, both in the Islamic world and in medieval and Renaissance Europe.

All of us have in mind *The Arabian Nights,* in which all the stories are contained within the general framework of the tale of the Persian king, Shahryar, who kills his brides after their wedding night, and of his bride Scheherazade, who succeeds in postponing this fate by telling wonderful stories and stopping just at the climax. Besides the tales told by Scheherazade, there are others narrated by characters in her tales. In other words, the stories are like boxes within boxes—as many as five of them at a time. Here I am relying on an essay called *Les Hommes-récits* by Tzvetan Todorov, who has studied the *enchâssement* of the tales in *The Arabian Nights* and in Potocki's *Manuscrit trouvé à Saragosse* (*Poétique de la prose* [Paris: Seuil, 1971]).

Borges speaks of one of the *Arabian Nights,* number 602, the most magical of all, in which Scheherazade tells Shahryar a tale in which Scheherazade tells Shahryar a tale, etc., etc. In the translations of *The Arabian Nights* that I have at hand, I have never been able to find this 602nd Night. But even if Borges invented it he did well, because it represents the natural culmination of the *enchâssement* of the tales.

From the point of view of levels of reality, I should say that the *enchâssement* of *The Arabian Nights* does indeed create a structure in perspective, but to my reading, at least in the only way we can read them, these tales appear to be all on the same plane. In them we can distinguish two very different types of narrative: the magical type of Indian and Persian origin, with its genies, flying horses, and metamorphoses, and the Arab-Islamic storytelling type of the Baghdad cycle, with the caliph Harun-al-Rashid and Jafar the vizier. But the tales of both types are put on the same plane, both structurally and stylistically, and as we read we slide from one type to the other, as the eye slides over the surface of a tapestry.

In the prototype of literary storytelling in the West, Giovanni Boccaccio's *Decameron,* between the tales and the framework there is a clean stylistic split that highlights the distance between the two planes. The framework of the ten days of the *Decameron* describes the pleasant life lived in their country abode by the seven women and three men of this happy band of storytellers. We are on a plane of stylized reality, uniformly pleasant, refined in a mannered fashion, without contrasts, without characterization; nothing but descriptions of the weather and the landscape, of the pastimes and conversations of this playful little court that every day elects a queen and ends the day with a poem. The tales narrated, however, constitute a catalogue of the narrative possibilities becoming available to language and culture at a time when the variety of living forms was a new thing, coming into its own at that very moment. Each novella reveals an intensity of writing and of representation that radiates outward in all sorts of different directions in such a way as to stress these directions in comparison with the frame. Does this mean that the frame is a merely decorative element? If we said this, we would be forgetting that the framework of the tales, that earthly paradise of the elegant court, is itself contained within another frame, tragic, deathly, hellish: the plague in Florence in 1348, described in the introduction to the *Decameron*. It is the stark reality of a world at the end of the world, the plague as a biological and social catastrophe, that makes sense of the utopia of an idyllic society governed by beauty, gentleness, and intelligence. The chief product of this utopian society is the short story, and the story reproduces the variety and nervous intensity of a world that is lost, the laughter and tears by now erased by Death the Leveler.

Let us now see what is inside the frame.

I have listened to the Sirens' song

I could also have said: I have blinded Polyphemus the Cyclops, or: I have eluded the enchantments of Circe. But if I have chosen the episode of the Sirens it is because this enables me to introduce a further transition in perspective with the narrative of Ulysses, a further level of reality, contained in the Sirens' song.

What do the Sirens sing? One possible hypothesis is that their song is nothing more or less than the *Odyssey*. The tendency of the poem to incorporate itself, to reflect itself as in a mirror, appears a number of times in the *Odyssey*, especially at banquets when the bards sing. And who better than the Sirens could endow their own song with this function of magic looking glass?

In this case we would have a case of the literary process that André Gide defined by the heraldic term *mise en abyme*. This occurs when a work of literature includes another work resembling the first—that is, when a part of it reproduces the whole. We have already mentioned the play within the play in *Hamlet* and the 602nd Night according to Borges. Examples also extend to painting, as in the mirror effects in the pictures of van Eyck. I will not dwell on the *mise en abyme*, because I need only refer you to an exhaustive study published a few months ago: Lucien Dällenbach, *Le Récit spéculaire* (Paris: Seuil, 1977).

But what the text of the *Odyssey* tells us about the Sirens' song is that the Sirens say they are singing and wish to be heard, and that their song is the best that can be sung. The final experience taken into account in the narrative of Ulysses is a lyrical and musical experience on the borders of the ineffable. One of the finest passages in Maurice Blanchot interprets the Sirens' song as a "beyond" of expressive possibilities from which Ulysses, having experienced its ineffability, withdraws, falling back from the song itself to his account of the song.

In order to verify my formula I have so far made use of narrative examples, choosing from the classics in verse or prose or in the theatre, but always with a story to tell. Now that I have got to the Sirens' song, I ought to go back over my entire argument to see if it can be applied, as I think it can, point by point to lyric poetry, and shed light on the various levels of reality that the "operation" of poetry traverses. I am convinced that this formula, with very small modifications, can be transcribed with Mallarmé in Homer's place. Such a formulation might perhaps enable us to pursue the Sirens' song, the ultimate point writing can attain, the final core of the written word, and perhaps in the wake of Mallarmé we would arrive at the blank page, at silence, at absence.

The path that we have followed—the levels of reality evoked by literature, the whole gamut of veils and shields—may perhaps stray off into infinity, may perhaps encounter nothingness. As we have witnessed the disappearance of the "I," the primary subject of the verb "to write," so the ultimate object eludes us. Perhaps it is in the field of tension between one vacuum and another that literature multiplies the depths of a reality that is inexhaustible in forms and meanings.

Now, right at the end of my talk, it occurs to me that I have been speaking throughout of "levels of reality," whereas the topic of this conference reads "The Levels of Reality." Perhaps the fundamental point of my talk is exactly this: literature does not recognize Reality as such, but only *levels.* Whether there is such a thing as Reality, of which the various levels are only partial aspects, or whether there are only the levels, is something that literature cannot decide. Literature recognizes the *reality of the levels,* and this is a reality (or "Reality") that it knows all the better, perhaps, for not having come to understand it by other cognitive processes. And that is already a great deal.

The Novel Démeublé

Willa Cather

The novel, for a long while, has been over-furnished. The property-man has been so busy on its pages, the importance of material objects and their vivid presentation have been so stressed, that we take it for granted whoever can observe, and can write the English language, can write a novel. Often the latter qualification is considered unnecessary.

In any discussion of the novel, one must make it clear whether one is talking about the novel as a form of amusement, or as a form of art; since they serve very different purposes and in very different ways. One does not wish the egg one eats for breakfast, or the morning paper, to be made of the stuff of immortality. The novel manufactured to entertain great multitudes of people must be considered exactly like a cheap soap or a cheap perfume, or cheap furniture. Fine quality is a distinct disadvantage in articles made for great numbers of people who do not want quality but quantity, who do not want a thing that "wears," but who want change, — a succession of new things that are quickly threadbare and can be lightly thrown away. Does anyone pretend that if the Woolworth store windows were piled high with Tanagra figurines at ten cents, they could for a moment compete with Kewpie brides in the popular esteem? Amusement is one thing; enjoyment of art is another.

Every writer who is an artist knows that his "power of observation," and his "power of description," form but a low part of his equipment. He must have both, to be sure; but he knows that the most trivial of writers often have a very good observation. Mérimée said in his remarkable essay on Gogol: "L'art de choisir parmi les innombrables traits que nous offre la nature est, après tout, bien plus difficile que celui de les observer avec attention et de les rendre avec exactitude."

There is a popular superstition that "realism" asserts itself in the cataloguing of a great number of material objects, in explaining mechanical processes, the methods of operating manufactories and trades, and in minutely and unsparingly describing physical sensations. But is not realism, more than it is anything else, an attitude of mind on the part of the writer toward his material, a vague indication of the sympathy and candour with which he accepts, rather than chooses, his theme? Is the story of a banker who is unfaithful to his wife and who ruins himself by speculation in trying to gratify the caprices of his mistresses, at all reinforced by a masterly exposition of banking, our whole system of credits, the methods of the Stock Exchange? Of course, if the story is thin, these things do reinforce it in a sense, — any amount of red meat thrown into the scale to make the beam dip. But are the banking system and the Stock Exchange worth being written about at all? Have such things any proper place in imaginative art?

The automatic reply to this question is the name of Balzac. Yes, certainly, Balzac tried out the value of literalness in the novel, tried it out to the uttermost, as Wagner did the value of scenic literalness in the music drama. He tried it, too, with the passion of discovery, with the inflamed zest of an unexampled curiosity. If the heat of that furnace could not give hardness and sharpness to material accessories, no other brain will ever do it. To reproduce on paper the actual city of Paris; the houses, the upholstery, the food, the wines, the game of pleasure, the game of business, the game of finance: a stupendous ambition — but, after all, unworthy of an artist. In exactly so far as he succeeded in pouring out on his pages that mass of brick and mortar and furniture and proceedings in bankruptcy, in exactly so far he defeated his end. The things by which he still lives, the types of greed and avarice and ambition and vanity and lost innocence of heart which he created — are as vital today as they were then. But their material surroundings, upon which he expended such labour and pains . . . the eye glides over them. We have had too much of the interior decorator and the "romance of business" since his day. The city he built on paper is already crumbling. Stevenson said he wanted to blue-pencil a great deal of Balzac's "presentation" — and he loved him beyond all modern novelists. But where is the man who could cut one sentence from the stories of Mérimée? And who wants any more detail as to how Carmencita and her fellow factory-girls made cigars? Another sort of novel? Truly. Isn't it a better sort?

In this discussion another great name naturally occurs. Tolstoi was almost as great a lover of material things as Balzac, almost as much interested in the way dishes were cooked, and people were dressed, and houses were furnished. But there is this determining difference: the clothes, the dishes, the haunting interiors of those old Moscow houses, are always so much a part of the emotions of the people that they are perfectly synthesized; they seem to exist, not so much in the author's mind, as in the emotional penumbra of the characters themselves. When it is fused like this, literalness ceases to be literalness — it is merely part of the experience.

If the novel is a form of imaginative art, it cannot be at the same time a vivid and brilliant form of journalism. Out of the teeming, gleaming stream of the present it must select the eternal material of art. There are hopeful signs that some of the younger writers are trying to break away from mere verisimilitude, and, following the development of modern painting, to interpret imaginatively the material and social investiture of their characters; to present their scene by suggestion rather than by enumeration. The higher processes of art are all processes of simplification. The novelist must learn to write, and then he must unlearn it; just as the modern painter learns to draw, and then learns when utterly to disregard his accomplishment, when to subordinate it to a higher and truer effect. In this direction only, it seems to me, can the novel develop into anything more varied and perfect than all the many novels that have gone before.

One of the very earliest American romances might well serve as a suggestion to later writers. In *The Scarlet Letter* how truly in the spirit of art is the mise-en-scène presented. That drudge, the theme-writing high-school student, could scarcely be sent there for information regarding the manners and dress and interiors of Puritan society. The material investiture of the story is presented as if unconsciously; by the reserved, fastidious hand of an artist, not by the gaudy fingers of a showman or the mechanical industry of a department-store window-dresser. As I remember it, in the twilight melancholy of that book, in its consistent mood, one can scarcely see the actual surroundings of the people; one feels them, rather, in the dusk.

Whatever is felt upon the page without being specifically named there – that, one might say, is created. It is the inexplicable presence of the thing not named, of the overtone divined by the ear but not heard by it, the verbal mood, the emotional aura of the fact or the thing or the deed, that gives high quality to the novel or the drama, as well as to poetry itself.

Literalness, when applied to the presenting of mental reactions and of physical sensations, seems to be no more effective than when it is applied to material things. A novel crowded with physical sensations is no less a catalogue than one crowded with furniture. A book like *The Rainbow* by D. H. Lawrence sharply reminds one how vast a distance lies between emotion and mere sensory reactions. Characters can be almost dehumanized by a laboratory study of the behaviour of their bodily organs under sensory stimuli — can be reduced, indeed, to mere animal pulp. Can one imagine anything more terrible than the story of *Romeo and Juliet* rewritten in prose by D. H. Lawrence?

How wonderful it would be if we could throw all the furniture out of the window; and along with it, all the meaningless reiterations concerning physical sensations, all the tiresome old patterns, and leave the room as bare as the stage of a Greek theatre, or as that house into which the glory of Pentecost descended; leave the scene bare for the play of emotions, great and little — for the nursery tale, no less than the tragedy, is killed by tasteless amplitude. The elder Dumas enunciated a great principle when he said that to make a drama, a man needed one passion, and four walls.

The Personal and the Individual

Leonard Michaels

Nothing should be easier than talking about ways in which I write about myself, but I find it isn't easy at all. Indeed, I want to say before anything else that a great problem for me, in writing about myself, is how not to write *merely* about myself. I think the problem is very common among writers even if they are unaware of it. Basic elements of writing—diction, grammar, tone, imagery, the patterns of sound made by your sentences—will say a good deal about you (whether you are conscious of it or not) so that it is possible for you to be writing about yourself before you even know you are writing about yourself. Regardless of your subject, these basic elements, as well as countless and immeasurable qualities of mind, are at play in your writing and will make your presence felt to a reader as palpably as your handwriting. You virtually write your name, as it were, before you literally sign your name, every time you write.

Spinoza wrote his *Ethics* in Latin, a language nobody spoke anymore, using a severely logical method of argument. The last thing he wanted was to make his presence felt, or to write about himself. The way he wrote his *Ethics* was rather like the way he lived—determined to remain obscure, uncompromised by a recognizable personal identity in the public world. The impersonal purity of his *Ethics,* then, couldn't have been more self-expressive. The book wasn't published in his lifetime partly because it would have been recognized as his book. He was, in his obscurity, too well known.

Shakespeare isn't discoverable in a personal way in anything he wrote, and yet it is generally agreed that we know what Shakespeare personally wrote, or what only he is likely to have written. His sonnets, which are among the most personal poems ever written, are remarkably artificial in their quatrains, couplets, puns, and paradoxes—devices that are manifestly impersonal. It is curiously relevant that, in Shakespeare's various signatures, he never spelled his name the same way twice, rather as if he thought his personal identity had very little to do with any particular way of spelling his name. A particular way, always the same, would simply be individual.

Montaigne said of his own essays, "I have no more made this book than this book has made me." I think he meant his writing revealed him to himself, and the revelations weren't always consciously intended. Again and again in his essays he seems to discover himself inadvertently, though he says he wrote his essays for his family to help them remember him as he was in life. All this is to say only that your radically personal identity, with or without your consent, is made evident in your writing. Like a fingerprint. Or what is even more personally telling, a face print—according to experts there are eighty places in the human face that can be used to identify a person.

One rainy night many years ago, I went with a friend to a jazz club called Basin Street in Greenwich Village to hear a Miles Davis quartet. There was a small, sophisticated crowd. You could tell the crowd was sophisticated because it applauded in the right places. At a certain point Miles Davis began turning his back to the crowd whenever he played a solo. I don't know what he thought he was doing, but the effect was to absent himself from the tune, as though he were saying, "Don't look at me. I'm not here. Listen to it." He gave us a lesson in music appreciation, or the appreciation of any art. With Davis's back turned, the music seemed to become more personal.

A professor of mathematics at Berkeley told me that, while reading a newspaper article about the Unabomber, he suddenly realized the man had been his student. The professor then went to his files, pulled out the Unabomber's math papers and reviewed them. He said, "B/B+." Mathematics couldn't be further from the kinds of self-presentation and self-revelation to which all of us are constantly susceptible, but even in the absolutely neutral language of equations, the Unabomber had declared his identity. From the point of view of a mathematician, B/B+ was the man.

I think we name ourselves, more or less, whenever we write, and we always tend to write about ourselves. When people ask if you write by hand or use a typewriter or a computer, they are interested to know how personal your writing is. But even now in the age of electronic writing, when the immediate revelations of handwriting have become rare, a ghostly electronic residue of persons remains faintly discernible in words and sentence structure. A more familiar example of what I'm getting at is phone calls. Imagine answering the phone and hearing a voice you haven't heard in years, a voice that says only your name or even only hello, and you say instantly, "Aunt Molly, it's been so long since you phoned." There's a joke that touches on this experience: The phone rings, Molly says, "Hello," and a man's voice says, "Molly, I know you and I know what you want. I'm coming over there and I'm going to throw you on the floor and do every dirty thing to you." Molly says, "You know all this from hello?"

In another kind of personal revelation, you see a painting you've never seen before and you say: "Hokusai," or "Guercino," or "Cranach." With the names you announce that you have recognized a unique presence or personal being. The existence of any human being or personal presence tends to be an announcement, virtually a name, and this is just as true of my uncelebrated and obscure Aunt Molly as the very great and famous Hokusai. Adam was required to name the animals, but how could he have done that unless their names were already implicit in their individual being? "Obviously, this beast is Lion, and this can only be Pig." In regard to animals, the case is more individual than personal, as far as we know. If an animal could spell its name, it would be spelled the same way every time. Existence moves in the direction of names.

Diction, grammar, imagery, the sound of a person's voice on the phone, the way an animal looks—if a thing has any sort of sensational existence, a name is being announced, and this is true even if it goes unrecognized. It is only God who can say "I am that I am" and remain nameless, accessible only through the *via negativa*. As Spinoza puts it, substance is conceived only in and through itself; that is, only in terms of itself. As for us folks, or any other finite individual entity, we are among the modes of substance and, ultimately,

"Rolled round in earth's diurnal course with rocks and stones and trees." This mournful line is from Wordsworth's profoundly personal poem "A Slumber Did My Spirit Seal" about a woman who is never named. In fact, what makes the poem so haunting in its desperation is that it is almost entirely about Wordsworth himself. Inevitably, we are names. To say Henry IV or John Smith III is to say a name that precedes the being it names—the fourth Henry, the third John Smith.

In a story I wrote long ago, I quoted a freshman paper that had been submitted to my class. The student wrote: "Karl Marx, for that was his name. . . ." It's as if Marx's father had said to his wife, "I've decided to name our boy Karl," and his wife said, "No, no, anything but Karl," and the father said, "I'm afraid I have no choice, for that is his name."

For reasons I understand very imperfectly, though I suppose they might be obvious to anyone else by this point, it has always been more difficult for me to write about myself than any other subject. What I know for sure is that writing about myself always entails writing about other people, and there is a chance someone will be embarrassed or hurt even if my intentions are innocent.

One of my brightest and most likeable students was named Canterbury. He wanted me to direct his dissertation. I told him that wasn't a good idea, and that he ought to ask one of my colleagues who is well known as a scholar and critic, and has clout and will be able to help him get a job. No. Canterbury wanted me to be the director. Finally, I agreed. Canterbury wrote a brilliant prospectus, and then became amazingly casual about the prospect of writing anymore. Upon graduation he left for West Virginia (his home state) where he made a name for himself in politics. It was as if, like Miles Davis, he'd turned his back on the audience—which was me. Canterbury had to escape individual distinction, in my eyes, to achieve the personal. Before he left for West Virginia, I asked if he would try to find a certain kind of old handmade tool, an adze, and bring it to me when he visited California. About six months later, he visited California and presented me with a handmade adze from West Virginia—the tool used to make the coffin in *As I Lay Dying*. I was very touched. Nothing remained of our former relationship of professor and student. We had become purely friends.

When I was writing my novel *The Men's Club,* it occurred to me that Canterbury was the right name for one of the characters in my novel. The character looked nothing like the real Canterbury, and his personality couldn't be more different, but my friend, the real Canterbury, was shocked. How could I have done this to him? "So that's what you think about me," he said. He went on and on reminding me of what I had done to him. I couldn't tell if he were serious or joking.

Usually, when writing about myself, I will disguise the people I talk about and never use their real names. Occasionally, when I want to say something innocuous or affectionate, I'll ask permission to use their real name. One of my writer friends, also a former student, found it mysteriously impossible not to use real names when writing about herself, though it could make no difference to the quality or the sales of her book. She simply couldn't bring herself to change the names. As a result, people were hurt and family relations were irreparably damaged. There is something horrific about seeing your name in print. For some of us, it's almost as disturbing as a photograph. Even when writing only about myself, I'm very reluctant to use my name in a sentence, I do it only when I have no choice. It gives me the creeps to write "Leonard" or "Lenny."

I think I know why my student couldn't help using real names despite the consequences for her family relations. From my experience when writing about myself, the moment I begin making up names for the real people in my life, there seems to be a loss of seriousness, and then I can't get rid of the feeling and everything begins to seem like a lie even if everything—except for a few names—is entirely true. The impulse toward truth is built into our existence just as the shape of our eyes is built into our genes, and the truth, like murder, wants out. Of course there are different kinds of truth. My friend should have changed the real names of the people in her book, but she couldn't do it. She was possessed by a sort of demonic righteousness. "I'm writing the truth and nothing but. These are the true names." People often say when accused of slanderous gossip, "But it's the truth," as if that were a justification. The truth is in the heart of the speaker.

Another reason I have trouble writing about myself, aside from what it entails in regard to other people, has to do with the essential nature of writing.

According to Freud, "Writing is the record of an absent person." This is a condensation of what Socrates said about not writing. He said, if you have something to say, you ought to be present to answer questions from your audience, because truth lies only in the practice of the dialectic, which is a very difficult thing to arrive at, or to experience. When it happens it is like a sudden flame. In Plato's *Seventh Letter,* he goes on about the frivolousness that is inevitable in writing, and says that any man who tries to write the absolute truth, as it is known to himself, must be insane. There is no better definition of insanity.

Freud's way of restating Socrates's point, "the record of an absent person," is very suggestive. If you are absent when you write, you must be absent to the second power when you write about yourself. It's time for me to confess that I'm trying to reconcile the idea of presence in one's writing with the idea of absence, which is what I intend to do, finally, in talking about how I write about myself. First, I'd like to tell a joke that touches on this complexity of simultaneous presence and absence:

> The king and his court are out hunting elk in the royal forest. A poacher sees them coming and becomes terrified. He leaps from behind a bush and cries, "I am not an elk." Immediately, the king shoots him. One of the courtiers says, "But your majesty, he said, 'I am not an elk.'" The king slaps his forehead and says, "I thought he said 'I am an elk.'"

Whenever I write anything, my presence and absence are in constant tension—especially when writing about myself. What makes things worse for me is that because of this excruciating tension, I always feel very much out of fashion, since it is now very common for writers to be more than usually present—even outrageously present—in their writing, whether or not they are writing about themselves. Some writers don't know how to be otherwise than fully present. There has never been such extraordinary directness and candor. The effect is comparable to pornography, not because of explicit sexual content, but rather because the directness and candor tend to be shockingly impersonal. The way I write about myself or anything else is, I'm afraid, personal or it's nothing. This means I must always find some appropriate form. One relation of being personal and finding an appropriate form can be seen in Hamlet's famous soliloquy where he thinks about suicide. He says, "That it should come to this." As opposed to Hamlet, a contemporary in the same situation would say, "Incredible," or some version of incredible, which is a cry of me-feeling.

The difference between the contemporary speaker and Hamlet isn't simply in the loss of the subjunctive mood, but rather the loss of a significant intervening form between speaker and audience. When Hamlet says "That it should come to this," he is noticing the convergence of terrific forces outside himself. One force is justice. The other is necessity. A grammatical form, the subjunctive mood, makes it possible for the reader and Hamlet to convene in the understanding of his personal situation. This convening is the experience of the personal. In order for it to have happened, Hamlet absents himself in the sentence as definitively as Miles Davis turning his back to the audience.

You might argue that Hamlet isn't using the subjunctive. He is stating a fact; so his comment has indicative force. I'm not a grammarian, but insofar as what Hamlet says implies that it could have come to something other than this, he is using the subjunctive in a peculiarly delicate and personal way.

When the contemporary says "Incredible," we are forbidden to convene in any understanding and obliged merely to notice a figure of emotion, all of which emotion is locked within his cry, "Incredible." This kind of expression in which all meaning and feeling are at once sensationally apparent and completely unavailable to you, which I take to be emblematic of contemporary writing and much else that is contemporary, resembles greed. It's probably somehow related to the culture of capitalism, where we are constantly assaulted by images that demand attention to what we can't have, mainly beautiful faces and bodies, but also a lot of other things—vast fortunes, celebrity, power, love—almost anything you might suppose people want.

The haiku, a poem of three lines and seventeen syllables, which is usually about nature, offers a form in which writer and reader personally convene. I can't write haiku, but when writing about myself, I feel the impulse to write in that terse and essentializing way. This should be apparent in my book, *Time Out of Mind,* a selection of journal entries made over thirty years. In these entries I say more about myself personally than in any other place. I also say less since the entries contain far more implication than explication. For example, I wrote an entry on December 12, 1993, in Hawaii, that reads:

> Birdcalls wake me, a sound like names, like
> the trees repeating themselves in the dawn mist, each
> holding its place, awaiting recognition, like names.

The context for this entry is omitted. A reader could figure it out from things said in other entries, though many autobiographical details that might seem relevant to a biographer or a gossip aren't given. In this entry I don't say that I had awakened lying beside my girlfriend and that we had been together for almost three years. Not long after this moment she would leave me. I don't say that I knew she would leave me, and I don't mention the fact that she was twenty-seven years younger than me. I don't say that I knew the age difference was of concern to her, or that it somehow hadn't yet troubled me as much. I don't say our backgrounds and interests were nothing alike. I don't say that she didn't enjoy lectures given by visiting scholars at Berkeley where we lived during our three years together, or that she hated Berkeley dinner parties with academic or literary celebrities. I don't say that I was crazy about her. I don't say that I would have happily not gone to lectures and dinner parties and stayed home with her and watched Monday Night Football, or, if she insisted, I'd even have gone bowling. I don't say that what she found interesting— running small businesses, investment banking, managing the finances and personnel of an office—didn't much interest me. I don't say that I tried to be interested, and I would ask her questions about her work, but I would end up feeling more intrusive than properly engaged. The innerness of business life, and the whole realm of action and money were never accessible to my brain. I don't say that once, after a lecture in Berkeley given by the chairman of the Harvard English department, she said, "We're basically different. You listened to the lecture and I wondered how much it cost the university for the lighting and janitorial service that made the lecture possible. Now you want to talk about the lecture, but I'm still wondering about the maintenance of the building. All that glass had to be washed, the floors polished. Someone had to take care of the garden outside, the landscaping." I don't say that I woke up beside my girlfriend who was twenty-seven years younger than I was and would soon leave me, which I knew, though I didn't know she would leave me for a businessman.

My girlfriend and I had gone to Hawaii, the Puna coast of the Big Island. We were staying in one room of a primitive but elegant shack in an artist colony. The shack had no windows. You could sense the magnificent luxuriance and vitality outside, the trees, the weather, the light, the ocean. In the other room of the shack, there were three men. One of them coughed all night. He had AIDS and so did several other men at the colony. The wall between our rooms was a thin sheet of wood. Listening to him cough, and knowing my girlfriend would leave me, are elements in the journal entry, and a reader might get a sense of them from other entries, but they aren't emphasized. I don't say that her youth didn't make me feel young, but rather the opposite, and I don't say that the coughing all night was heartbreaking and that it intensified the heartbreak I'd begun to feel, knowing I was much closer to the end than my girlfriend and knowing she would soon leave me. I don't say that in the beginning of our love affair she said she would never leave me. I don't say that I didn't pity myself. I felt an overwhelming melancholy. I don't know a word for it in English. In German, I think it is called *Weltschmerz*. I say only that the birdcalls and the trees were like names. I watched the trees emerging in the mist, and I listened to the birdcalls. I was struck by the repetition of things and by the pathos there is in the way individual being is always emerging and calling its name as if to distinguish itself amid the mindless proliferation and density of life in general. I don't say much of this in the journal. When writing about myself, I find that I am interested in the expressive value of form and its relation to the personal more than I am interested in particular revelations of my individual life.

Grief

Colm Tóibín

When I came to Dublin as a student in 1972, the writer Mary Lavin was a familiar presence in the city. I watched her as she moved with a sort of stateliness between the desks in the National Library on her way to the main desk, or as she sat in a small cafe known as the Country Shop, or as she drank coffee in Bewley's in Grafton Street. She was usually alone. She wore black. Her hair was parted in the middle and pulled untidily into a bun at the back. Her gaze was kind and sad and oddly distracted, but it had a funny strength to it as well. She had spent her life describing others, and finding strategies to create versions of herself; it was not easy to categorise her or ever be sure about her just from looking.

I have no clear memory of how I knew that she had been left a widow with children at a young age, but I certainly knew it before I came to the city. I was interested in the word 'widow' and I would have paid real attention to a writer, or anyone at all indeed, who was a widow, since my mother was one. It may have been when we studied a story by Mary Lavin in school called 'The Widow's Son'.

I had read a good deal of her work by the time I saw her. Some of her stories meant nothing to me. The scenes of upper middle-class life in County Meath, north of Dublin, were too rarefied. But the ones which dealt with the life of a widow were almost too close to the space between how we lived then in our house and what was unmentionable - the business of silence around grief, the life of a woman alone, the palpable absence of a man, a husband, a father, our father, my father, the idea of conversation as a way of concealing loss rather than revealing anything, least of all feeling - for me not to have read her with full recognition. The recognition was so clear, in fact, that I do not remember recognising anything. I was reading with too much rawness.

But I must have sat up when I came to this passage in Mary Lavin's story 'Happiness': 'When Father went to hospital Mother went with him and stayed in a small hotel across the street so she could be with him all day from early to late. "Because it was so awful for him, being in Dublin," she said. "You have no idea how he hated it." Maybe I thought this would be in other books in the future, the precise image of what had happened to us being lived now by fictional people, but I never found it again. It was only there. It is in the novel I have written, 'Nora Webster', but it took me a long time between from hearing those words, or words like them, said in our own house, and finding a dramatic form for them.

In Mary Lavin's stories about solitude and widowhood, her characters live in a twilight time. They barely manage. One of her stories about grief and its aftermath, controlled grief, is 'In the Middle of the Fields'. In the first sentence she establishes that her heroine is alone in an isolated rural place. And then the next sentence reads: 'And yet she was less lonely for him here in Meath than elsewhere.'

The loss is complex, or it comes in a complex guise. People think she wants to talk about her dead husband, or be reminded of what she has lost. 'They thought she hugged tight every memory she had of him. What did they know about memory?' She hopes for a time when she had 'forgotten him for a minute.' It is clear that the grief does not have to be named as 'grief', or brought out for inspection. All she knows is that how she feels is not stable, it cannot be trusted. It is wayward.

In Lavin's stories about loss the newly widowed woman has to remake the rules for herself, including the most ordinary rules of behaviour. Emotions dart, fresh longings emerge; what her characters do can easily become irrational and hard to explain; they often do the very opposite of what they intend. Being unmoored by loss affects their every thought, even when they are not thinking about loss, and, indeed, affects their every action.

This idea of the personality as suddenly protean under the pressure of loss belongs fundamentally to the literature of grief because, of course, it belongs to the experience.

I remember in school sitting at the back of the class soon after my father had died and listening to a discussion about Hamlet's madness and Hamlet's character and everyone wondering why Hamlet could in one second be in love, and the next out of love, and then angry and ready for revenge and then ready to procrastinate, the next minute melancholy and the next putting an antic disposition on, and why his tone could be so wise and then also so bitter and sharply sarcastic and rude. How could he be so many things, and how could we define his character?

I wish I had put up my hand to say that I thought I understood what was at the root of all his antics. His father had died not long before. That was all. He had been unmoored. While those around him were trying to explain that what had happened was normal, a part of nature, and were trying to get on with things, Hamlet had become wayward and, luckily, Shakespeare had seen the dramatic possibilities of this.

In the Preface to her book 'Grief Lessons', translations of four plays by Euripides, Anne Carson muses on grief. 'Why does tragedy exist?' she asks. And then replies: 'Because you are full of rage.' Then she asks: 'Why are you full of rage?' The answer is: 'Because you are full of grief. Ask a headhunter why he cuts off human heads. He'll say that rage impels him and rage is born of grief. The act of severing and tossing away the victim's head enables him to throw away the anger of all his bereavements. Perhaps you think this does not apply to you. Yet you recall the day your wife, driving you to your mother's funeral, turned left instead of right at the intersection and you had to scream at her so loud other drivers turned to look. When you tore off her head and threw it out the window they nodded, changed gears, drove away.'

A few years later, in her introduction to her translation of Sophocles' 'Elektra', one of the great plays about grief, Carson's tone seemed less certain as she wrote about the scene in which Orestes returns and hands his sister an urn with ashes which he says are of her dead brother Orestes. Orestes listens to Elektra mourn at some length before he announces that he was just fooling and that he has, in fact, been alive all the time and is now in front of her. Carson quotes the actress Fiona Shaw saying that she found the 'deception/ recognition scene between Elektra and Orestes "unspeakably impossible to play."'

'Critics and scholars (and translators),' Carson goes on, 'agree, this scene is a hard nut to crack. Why does Orestes decide to trick his sister into thinking he's dead? Why does he give it up in the middle? What does Sophocles want to achieve here? The alternation of lies and truth, high emotions and low, is bewildering and cruel, the tug-of-war over an empty urn almost bizarre.' So, too, Philip Vellacott, who translated Euripides's version of the play, wonders about this scene and identifies the point 'where Orestes should reveal himself... He does not reveal himself. Why?'

Surely the solution is simple. Surely Orestes' trickery is the very currency of grief. Orestes, having lost his father, is unable to come clean. The issues of life and death have entered his spirit and poisoned him so that his approach to re-meeting his sister will be all gnarled. He cannot deal simply with emotion. As Carson writes about Euripides's version of him: 'All in all, Orestes is a peculiar customer – not exactly insane but strange and unknowable. His consciousness is entirely his own.' Thus his response will be filled with double-speak and trickery about the very things – the difference between being dead and being alive - that he cannot manage to come to terms with. Becoming 'bewildering and cruel', as Anne Carson puts it, and 'bizarre', are what has happened to his personality under pressure. While his sister has been doing all the shouting, Orestes has let the pain seep silently into the very core of his being so that nothing he does will ever be easy to explain. While people are busy avoiding his sister because of what she says, they have been perhaps even busier avoiding Orestes because of his silence.

Some weeks after my father died, I went with my aunt into a house of an old friend of hers and my mother's to collect something. When my aunt said that my mother was in the car outside, the friend stepped backwards, making clear, without saying anything, that she was not prepared for this and would prefer if my mother remained in the car. I watched this and moved into the shadows. No one knows what to do in presence of someone who has suffered loss, or what to say.

In his book 'A Grief Observed', published in 1961 after the death of his wife, C.S. Lewis described this very sense, in the aftermath of loss, of being someone to avoid. 'An odd by-product of my loss is that I'm aware of being an embarrassment to everyone I meet...Some funk it altogether. R. has been avoiding me for a week...Perhaps the bereaved ought to be isolated in special settlements like lepers.' In Julian Barnes's 'Levels of Life', written after the death of his wife, he writes: 'So how do you feel? As if you have been dropped from a height of several hundred feet, conscious all the time, have landed feet first in a rose bed with an impact that has driven you in up to the knees, and whose shock has caused your internal organs to rupture and burst forth from your body. That is what it feels like, and why should it look any different? No wonder some want to swerve away to a safer topic of conversation. And perhaps they are not avoiding death, and her; they are avoiding you.'

In Joyce Carol Oates's 'A Widow's Story', written after the death of her husband, she describes the efforts of her friend C. to have an enormous dinner party for her, inviting many of her friends, to help ease the pain. 'I envision,' Oates writes, 'a thirty-foot dining room table and at the farther end the widow placed like a leper, as far from the lovely C. as possible.' Despite Oates's asking for a smaller event, C. persists, only to find of course that the friends are not free on any of the suggested nights. Oates writes: 'I am beginning to realise that though C. has said that she and her husband are "eager" to see me they are in fact dreading to see me.'

The writing of Lewis and Barnes and Oates about grief is deeply personal, precise and particular. The feeling they describe is unique because the person grieved over was unique. The loss happened only once. But the writing is also public; it does not come in diary form with many cryptic references. Its source is perhaps the very source of fiction itself – the mysterious and compulsive need to find a rhythm and an artful tone to suggest and communicate the most private feelings and imaginings and facts to someone else, to make sentences which will move from mirroring the writer to allowing the reader to catch a more intense glimpse of the world.

Novelists make things up, but the things, or the feelings surrounding them, come from the world; they have a shape like the world's shape, or the shape, indeed, of experience, including the writer's experience or the writer's pressing concerns. Thus the experience of grief for a novelist makes its way into work in the same way as the waters from the flood may be channelled into a living stream. Joan Didion's 'The Year of Magical Thinking' and 'Blue Nights,' the books about losing her husband and her daughter, and Francisco Goldman's

'Say Her Name', his book about the death of his wife, use with skill and subtlety the very gift for narrative which distinguishes the authors as novelists.

The novelists have become characters in their own books. By the urgency of the tone, they make clear, however, that, in the aftermath of loss, nothing they can invent compares to it. And that, since they are writers, what happened needs to be written down so that it can be known and shared and understood, so that it can lose its incoherence. And so that they, in their powerlessness and helplessness, can at least still do this, can at least write down what it was like.

For other writers, grief comes into the work more strangely and hesitantly, as though the flood water got trapped and began to seep into things. In the fiction of both Nadine Gordimer and Juan Goytisolo there is a steely emotional distance made palpable by the writers' intelligence and political concerns. How strange then to find in Gordimer's last book of stories a story called 'Dreaming of the Dead', in which she dreams that she is having a meal with her old friends Anthony Samson, Edward Said and Susan Sontag, but all the time she is waiting for her recently dead husband, to whom the book is dedicated. 'Did you come back last night? I try to dream you into materialisation but you don't appear,' the story begins. And it ends: 'I sat at the table, you didn't turn up, too late. You will not come. Never.' And in between, his absence hovers over every gesture, every word, every thought.

Juan Goytisolo's novel 'The Blind Rider' is filled with the absence of his wife of many years, an absence mentioned in the opening pages merely as 'her departure'. Slowly, the glancing references to the loss, her death, give way to the most abject grief. As with Gordimer, the personal tone and the helplessness are all the most sharp and surprising because of their non-presence in most of Goytisolo's other fiction.

I began my novel 'Nora Webster' in the spring of 2000. Even though I wrote other books over the next thirteen and a half years, I added to 'Nora Webster' every year, or deleted something from it. I thought about it almost every day. Although some of the details are invented, including the details of the place where Nora goes to work, there is nothing invented about the atmosphere in the house in the small town where myself and my younger brother lived with my mother in the years after my father died.

I thought at first of writing the book from my own perspective, rather than my mother's, but when I tried to set some of that down, I found there was nothing, or not enough for a novel. It was as though the experience had hollowed me out and was, from my perspective, too filled with silence and distance for me to able to harness it for a novel's purposes.

My father was a teacher in the town's secondary school. I knew the rooms he taught in because, as a student in the primary school, I often went over to his part of the school and waited for him to finish class. Now, five or six weeks after his death, I began for the first time to attend the school where he had taught. I sat in the classrooms where he had been at the blackboard. What is strange is that I have no memory of feeling anything; there was no drama, no obvious grief, just a blankness.

Slowly, his name ceased to be mentioned in the house. C.S. Lewis has a description of the same silence after his wife's death: 'I cannot talk to the children about her. The moment I try, there appears on their faces neither grief, nor love, nor fear, nor pity, but the most fatal of non-conductors, embarrassment. They look as if I were committing an indecency. They are longing for me to stop. I felt just the same after my mother's death when my father mentioned her. I can't blame them. It's the way boys are.'

What grows then is a strange and insistent watchfulness which gave me, among other things, total recall, so that there are scenes in 'Nora Webster' which, down to the smallest detail – who was in the room, who said what, who looked at whom, who said nothing – is what happened. Once I realised that I could not tell the story from my own perspective, that I had no story, or one so filled with chaos and silence that it could not be rendered, then I saw that I could, because I had been watching and listening so fiercely, dramatise things from my mother's perspective, see things from her side. I could combine the tricks and strategies of fiction with the insistent business of fact. I knew enough to be able to imagine everything.

In the first chapter I wrote, Nora Webster decides never again to go back to the place on the Wexford coast where the family had spent the summers. I wrote a good deal of the book in that very place, not far from the house where we stayed then, the house we never went back to. The last chapter of the book has the most difficult and emotional scene. On a Saturday in the

August of last year I got up at first light to write the scene. It had been in my head for so long.

I remember afterwards swimming in the sea, staying in the water for as long as I could. The scene was written. It would be lovely to say that I felt free of it all then, that by writing it down I had somehow erased it, or dealt with it properly for once, broken the silence. But writing requires such an amount of technical care, such cold deliberation, that it is not a form of self-help. The page is blank when you start; it is not a mirror. I wrote the novel because it was on my mind. I wrote it because what is on my mind has a habit of becoming rhythm almost of its own accord. But I knew, nonetheless, that this was probably something I would not come back to, so it should have been a relief when it was over, when it was written. But, as other writers who have described grief and loss must know, things are never as simple as that.

Character in Fiction

Virginia Woolf

It seems to me possible, perhaps desirable, that I may be the only person in this room who has committed the folly of writing, trying to write, or failing to write, a novel. And when I asked myself, as your invitation to speak to you about modern fiction made me ask myself, what demon whispered in my ear and urged me to my doom, a little figure rose before me — the figure of a man, or of a woman, who said, 'My name is Brown. Catch me if you can.'

Most novelists have the same experience. Some Brown, Smith, or Jones comes before them and says in the most seductive and charming way in the world, 'Come and catch me if you can.' And so, led on by this will-o'-the-wisp, they flounder through volume after volume, spending the best years of their lives in the pursuit, and receiving for the most part very little cash in exchange. Few catch the phantom; most have to be content with a scrap of her dress or a wisp of her hair.

My belief that men and women write novels because they are lured on to create some character which has thus imposed itself upon them has the sanction of Mr Arnold Bennett. In an article from which I will quote he says: 'The foundation of good fiction is character-creating and nothing else . . . Style counts; plot counts; originality of outlook counts. But none of these counts anything like so much as the convincingness of the characters. If the characters are real the novel will have a chance; if they are not, oblivion will be its portion . . .'[2] And he goes on to draw the conclusion that we have no young novelists of first-rate importance at the present moment, because they are unable to create characters that are real, true, and convincing.

These are the questions that I want with greater boldness than discretion to discuss tonight. I want to make out what we mean when we talk about 'character' in fiction; to say something about the question of reality which Mr Bennett raises; and to suggest some reasons why the younger novelists fail to create characters, if, as Mr Bennett asserts, it is true that fail they do. This will lead me, I am well aware, to make some very sweeping and some very vague assertions. For the question is an extremely difficult one. Think how little we know about character — think how little we know about art. But, to make a clearance before I begin, I will suggest that we range Edwardians and Georgians into two camps; Mr Wells, Mr Bennett, and Mr Galsworthy I will call the Edwardians; Mr Forster, Mr Lawrence, Mr Strachey, Mr Joyce, and Mr Eliot I will call the Georgians.[3] And if I speak in the first person, with intolerable egotism, I will ask you to excuse me. I do not want to attribute to the world at large the opinions of one solitary, ill-informed, and misguided individual.

My first assertion is one that I think you will grant — that every one in this room is a judge of character. Indeed it would be impossible to live for a year without disaster unless one practised character-reading and had some skill in the art. Our marriages, our friendships depend on it; our business largely depends on it; every day questions arise which can only be solved by its help. And now I will hazard a second assertion, which is more disputable perhaps, to the effect that on or about December 1910 human character changed.

I am not saying that one went out, as one might into a garden, and there saw that a rose had flowered, or that a hen had laid an egg. The change was not sudden and definite like that. But a change there was, nevertheless; and since one must be arbitrary, let us date it about the year 1910.[4] The first signs of it are recorded in the books of Samuel Butler, in *The Way of All Flesh* in particular; the plays of Bernard Shaw continue to record it.[5] In life one can see the change, if I may use a homely illustration, in the character of one's cook. The Victorian cook lived like a leviathan in the lower depths, formidable, silent, obscure, inscrutable; the Georgian cook is a creature of sunshine and fresh air; in and out of the drawing room, now to borrow the *Daily Herald*,[6] now to ask advice about a hat. Do you ask for more solemn instances of the power of the human race to change? Read the *Agamemnon*, and see whether, in process of time, your sympathies are not almost entirely with Clytemnestra.

Or consider the married life of the Carlyles,[7] and bewail the waste, the futility, for him and for her, of the horrible domestic tradition which made it seemly for a woman of genius to spend her time chasing beetles, scouring saucepans, instead of writing books. All human relations have shifted — those between masters and servants, husbands and wives, parents and children. And when human relations change there is at the same time a change in religion, conduct, politics and literature. Let us agree to place one of these changes about the year 1910.

I have said that people have to acquire a good deal of skill in character-reading if they are to live a single year of life without disaster. But it is the art of the young. In middle age and in old age the art is practised mostly for its uses, and friendships and other adventures and experiments in the art of reading character are seldom made. But novelists differ from the rest of the world because they do not cease to be interested in character when they have learnt enough about it for practical purposes. They go a step further; they feel that there is something permanently interesting in character in itself. When all the practical business of life has been discharged, there is something about people which continues to seem to them of overwhelming importance, in spite of the fact that it has no bearing whatever upon their happiness, comfort, or income. The study of character becomes to them an absorbing pursuit; to impart character an obsession. And this I find it very difficult to explain: what novelists mean when they talk about character, what the impulse is that urges them so powerfully every now and then to embody their view in writing.

So, if you will allow me, instead of analysing and abstracting, I will tell you a simple story which, however pointless, has the merit of being true, of a journey from Richmond to Waterloo, in the hope that I may show you what I mean by character in itself; that you may realise the different aspects it can wear; and the hideous perils that beset you directly you try to describe it in words.

One night some weeks ago, then, I was late for the train and jumped into the first carriage I came to. As I sat down I had the strange and uncomfortable feeling that I was interrupting a conversation between two people who were already sitting there. Not that they were young or happy. Far from it. They were both elderly, the woman over sixty, the man well over forty. They were sitting opposite each other, and the man, who had been leaning over and talking emphatically to judge by his attitude and the flush on his face, sat back and became silent. I had disturbed him, and he was annoyed. The elderly lady, however, whom I will call Mrs Brown, seemed rather relieved. She was one of those clean, threadbare old ladies whose extreme tidiness – everything buttoned, fastened, tied together, mended and brushed up – suggests more extreme poverty than rags and dirt. There was something pinched about her – a look of suffering, of apprehension, and, in addition, she was extremely small. Her feet, in their clean little boots, scarcely touched the floor. I felt that she had nobody to support her; that she had to make up her mind for herself; that, having been deserted, or left a widow, years ago, she had led an anxious, harried life, bringing up an only son, perhaps, who, as likely as not, was by this time beginning to go to the bad. All this shot through my mind as I sat down, being uncomfortable, like most people, at travelling with fellow passengers unless I have somehow or other accounted for them. Then I looked at the man. He was no relation of Mrs Brown's I felt sure; he was of a bigger, burlier, less refined type. He was a man of business I imagined, very likely a respectable corn-chandler from the North, dressed in good blue serge with a pocket-knife and a silk handkerchief, and a stout leather bag. Obviously, however, he had an unpleasant business to settle with Mrs Brown; a secret, perhaps sinister business, which they did not intend to discuss in my presence.

'Yes, the Crofts have had very bad luck with their servants,' Mr Smith (as I will call him) said in a considering way, going back to some earlier topic, with a view to keeping up appearances.

'Ah, poor people,' said Mrs Brown, a trifle condescendingly. 'My grandmother had a maid who came when she was fifteen and stayed till she was eighty' (this was said with a kind of hurt and aggressive pride to impress us both perhaps).

'One doesn't often come across that sort of thing nowadays,' said Mr Smith in conciliatory tones.

Then they were silent.

'It's odd they don't start a golf club there – I should have thought one of the young fellows would,' said Mr Smith, for the silence obviously made him uneasy.

Mrs Brown hardly took the trouble to answer.

'What changes they're making in this part of the world,' said Mr Smith looking out of the window, and looking furtively at me as he did do.

It was plain, from Mrs Brown's silence, from the uneasy affability with which Mr Smith spoke, that he had some power over her which he was exerting disagreeably. It might have been her son's downfall, or some painful episode in her past life, or her daughter's. Perhaps she was going to London to sign some document to make over some property. Obviously against her will she was in Mr Smith's hands. I was beginning to feel a great deal of pity for her, when she said, suddenly and inconsequently.

'Can you tell me if an oak tree dies when the leaves have been eaten for two years in succession by caterpillars?'

She spoke quite brightly, and rather precisely, in a cultivated, inquisitive voice.

Mr Smith was startled, but relieved to have a safe topic of conversation given him. He told her a great deal very quickly about plagues of insects. He told her that he had a brother who kept a fruit farm in Kent. He told her what fruit farmers do every year in Kent, and so on, and so on. While he talked a very odd thing happened. Mrs Brown took out her little white handkerchief and began to dab her eyes. She was crying. But she went on listening quite composedly to what he was saying, and he went on talking, a little louder, a little angrily, as if he had seen her cry often before; as if it were a painful habit. At last it got on his nerves. He stopped abruptly, looked out of the window, then leant towards her as he had been doing when I got in, and said in a bullying, menacing way, as if he would not stand any more nonsense.

'So about that matter we were discussing. It'll be all right? George will be there on Tuesday?'

'We shan't be late,' said Mrs Brown, gathering herself together with superb dignity.

Mr Smith said nothing. He got up, buttoned his coat, reached his bag down, and jumped out of the train before it had stopped at Clapham Junction. He had got what he wanted, but he was ashamed of himself; he was glad to get out of the old lady's sight.

Mrs Brown and I were left alone together. She sat in her corner opposite, very clean, very small, rather queer, and suffering intensely. The impression she made was overwhelming. It came pouring out like a draught, like a smell of burning. What was it composed of – that overwhelming and peculiar impression? Myriads of irrelevant and incongruous ideas crowd into one's head on such occasions; one sees the person, one sees Mrs Brown, in the centre of all sorts of different scenes. I thought of her in a seaside house, among queer ornaments: sea-urchins, models of ships in glass cases. Her husband's medals were on the mantelpiece. She popped in and out of the room, perching on the edges of chairs, picking meals out of saucers, indulging in long, silent stares. The caterpillars and the oak trees seemed to imply all that. And then, into this fantastic and secluded life, in broke Mr Smith. I saw him blowing in, so to speak, on a windy day. He banged, he slammed. His dripping umbrella made a pool in the hall. They sat closeted together.

And then Mrs Brown faced the dreadful revelation. She took her heroic decision. Early, before dawn, she packed her bag and carried it herself to the station. She would not let Smith touch it. She was wounded in her pride, unmoored from her anchorage; she came of gentlefolks who kept servants – but details could wait. The important thing was to realise her character, to steep oneself in her atmosphere. I had no time to explain why I felt it somewhat tragic, heroic, yet with a dash of the flighty, and fantastic, before the train stopped, and I watched her disappear, carrying her bag, into the vast blazing station. She looked very small, very tenacious; at once very frail and very heroic. And I have never seen her again, and I shall never know what became of her.

The story ends without any point to it. But I have not told you this anecdote to illustrate either my own ingenuity or the pleasure of travelling from Richmond to Waterloo. What I want you to see in it is this. Here is a character imposing itself upon another person. Here is Mrs Brown making someone begin almost automatically to write a novel about her. I believe that all novels begin with an old lady in the corner opposite. I believe that all novels, that is to say, deal with character, and that it is to express character – not to preach doctrines, sing songs, or celebrate the glories of the British Empire, that the form of the novel, so clumsy, verbose, and undramatic, so rich, elastic, and alive, has been evolved. To express character, I have said; but you will at once reflect that the very widest interpretation can be put upon those words. For example, old Mrs Brown's character will strike you very differently according to the age and country in which you happen to be born. It would be easy enough to write three different versions of that incident in the train, an English, a French, and a Russian. The English writer would make the old lady in to a 'character'; he would bring out her oddities and mannerisms; her buttons and wrinkles; her ribbons and warts. Her personality would dominate the book. A French writer would rub out all that; he would sacrifice the individual Mrs Brown to give a more general view of human nature; to make a more abstract, proportioned, and harmonious whole. The Russian would pierce through the flesh; would reveal the soul – the soul alone, wandering out into the Waterloo Road, asking of life some tremendous question which would sound on and on in our ears after the book was finished. And then there is the writer's temperament to be considered.* You see one thing in character, and I another. You say it means this, and I that. And when it comes to writing each makes a further selection on principles of his own. Thus Mrs Brown can be treated in an infinite variety of ways, according to the age, country, and temperament of the writer.

But now I must recall what Mr Arnold Bennett says. He says that it is only if the characters are real that the novel has any chance of surviving. Otherwise, die it must. But, I ask myself, what is reality? And who are the judges of reality? A character may be real to Mr Bennett and quite unreal to me. For instance, in this article he says that Dr Watson in *Sherlock Holmes* is real to him:[8] to me Dr Watson is a sack stuffed with straw, a dummy, a figure of fun. And so it is with character after character–in book after book. There is nothing that people differ about more than the reality of characters, especially in contemporary books. But if you take a larger view I think that Mr Bennett is perfectly right. If, that is, you think of the novels which seem to you great novels – *War and Peace, Vanity Fair, Tristram Shandy, Madame Bovary, Pride and Prejudice, The Mayor of Casterbridge, Villette*[9] – if you think of these books, you do at once think of some character who has seemed to you so real (I do not by that mean so lifelike) that it has the power to make

---

*HP Essay: 'And then besides age and country there is the writer's temperament to be considered.'

you think not merely of it itself, but of all sorts of things through its eyes – of religion, of love, of war, of peace, of family life, of balls in county towns, of sunsets, moonrises, the immortality of the soul. There is hardly any subject of human experience that is left out of *War and Peace* it seems to me. And in all these novels all these great novelists have brought us to see whatever they wish us to see through some character. Otherwise, they would not be novelists; but poets, historians, or pamphleteers.

But now let us examine what Mr Bennett went on to say—he said that there was no great novelist among the Georgian writers because they cannot create characters who are real, true, and convincing. And there I cannot agree. There are reasons, excuses, possibilities which I think put a different colour upon the case. It seems to to me at least, but I am well aware that this is a matter about which I am likely to be prejudiced, sanguine, and near-sighted. I will put my view before you in the hope that you will make it impartial, judicial, and broad-minded. Why, then, is it so hard for novelists at present to create characters which seem real, not only to Mr Bennett, but to the world at large? Why, when October comes round, do the publishers always fail to supply us with a masterpiece?

Surely one reason is that the men and women who began writing novels in 1910 or thereabouts had this great difficulty to face–that there was no English novelist living from whom they could learn their business. Mr Conrad is a Pole; which sets him apart, and makes him, however admirable, not very helpful. Mr Hardy has written no novel since 1895.[10] The most prominent and successful novelists in the year 1910 were, I suppose, Mr Wells, Mr Bennett, and Mr Galsworthy. Now it seems to me that to go to these men and ask them to teach you how to write a novel – how to create characters that are real – is precisely like going to a bootmaker and asking him to teach you how to make a watch. Do not let me give you the impression that I do not admire and enjoy their books. They seem to me of great value, and indeed of great necessity. There are seasons when it is more important to have boots than to have watches. To drop metaphor, I think that after the creative activity of the Victorian age it was quite necessary, not only for literature but for life, that someone should write the books that Mr Wells, Mr Bennett, and Mr Galsworthy have written. Yet what odd books they are! Sometimes I wonder if we are right to call them books at all. For they leave one with so strange a feeling of incompleteness and dissatisfaction. In order to complete them it seems necessary to do something – to join a society, or, more desperately, to write a cheque. That done, the restlessness is laid, the book finished; it can be put upon the shelf, and need never be read again. But with the work of other novelists it is different. *Tristram Shandy* or *Pride and Prejudice* is complete in itself; it is self-contained; it leaves one with no desire to do anything, except indeed to read the book again, and to understand it better. The difference perhaps is that both Sterne and Jane Austen were interested in things in themselves; in character in itself; in the book in itself. Therefore everything was inside the book, nothing outside. But the Edwardians were never interested in character in itself; or in the book in itself. They were interested in something outside. Their books, then, were incomplete as books, and required that the reader should finish them, actively and practically, for himself.

Perhaps we can make this clearer if we take the liberty of imagining a little party in the railway carriage — Mr Wells, Mr Galsworthy, Mr Bennett are travelling to Waterloo with Mrs Brown. Mrs Brown, I have said, was poorly dressed and very small. She had an anxious, harassed look. I doubt whether she was what you call an educated woman. Seizing upon all these symptoms of the unsatisfactory condition of our primary schools with a rapidity to which I can do no justice, Mr Wells would instantly project upon the window-pane a vision of a better, breezier, jollier, happier, more adventurous and gallant world, where these musty railway carriages and fusty old women do not exist; where miraculous barges bring tropical fruit to Camberwell by eight o'clock in the morning; where there are public nurseries, fountains, and libraries, dining rooms, drawing rooms, and marriages; where every citizen is generous and candid, manly and magnificent, and rather like Mr Wells himself. But nobody is in the least like Mrs Brown. There are no Mrs Browns in Utopia. Indeed I do not think that Mr Wells, in his passion to make her what she ought to be, would waste a thought upon her as she is. And what would Mr Galsworthy see? Can we doubt that the walls of Doulton's factory would take his fancy? There are women in that factory who make twenty-five dozen earthenware pots every day. There are mothers in the Mile End Road who depend upon the farthings which those women earn. But there are employers in Surrey who are even now smoking rich cigars while the nightingale sings. Burning with indignation, stuffed with information, arraigning civilisation, Mr Galsworthy would only see in Mrs Brown a pot broken on the wheel and thrown into the corner.

Mr Bennett, alone of the Edwardians, would keep his eyes in the carriage. He, indeed, would observe every detail with immense care. He would notice the advertisements; the pictures of Swanage and Portsmouth; the way in which the cushion bulged between the buttons; how Mrs Brown wore a brooch which had cost three-and-ten-three at Whitworth's bazaar; and had mended both gloves — indeed the thumb of the left-hand glove had been replaced. And he would observe, at length, how this was the non-stop train from Windsor which calls at Richmond for the convenience of middle-class residents, who can afford to go to the theatre but have not reached the social rank which can afford motorcars, though it is true, there are occasions (he would tell us what), when they hire them from a company (he would tell us which). And so he would gradually sidle sedately towards Mrs Brown, and would remark how she had been left a little copyhold, not freehold, property at Datchet, which, however, was mortgaged to Mr Bungay the solicitor – but why should I presume to invent Mr Bennett? Does not Mr Bennett write novels himself? I will open the first book that chance puts in my way – *Hilda Lessways*.[11] Let us see how he makes us feel that Hilda is real, true, and convincing, as a novelist should. She shut the door in a soft, controlled way, which showed the constraint of her relations with her mother. She was fond of reading *Maud*;[12] she was endowed with the power to feel intensely. So far, so good; in his leisurely, surefooted way Mr Bennett is trying in these first pages, where every touch is important, to show us the kind of girl she was.

But then he begins to describe, not Hilda Lessways, but the view from her bedroom window, the excuse being that Mr Skellorn, the man who collects rents, is coming along that way. Mr Bennett proceeds:

The bailiwick of Turnhill lay behind her; and all the murky district of the Five Towns, of which Turnhill is the northern outpost, lay to the south. At the foot of Chatterley Wood the canal wound in large curves on its way towards the undefiled plains of Cheshire and the sea. On the canal-side, exactly opposite to Hilda's window, was a flour-mill, that sometimes made nearly as much smoke as the kilns and the chimneys closing the prospect on either hand. From the flour-mill a bricked path, which separated a considerable row of new cottages from their appurtenant gardens, led straight into Lessways Street, in front of Mrs Lessways' house. By this path Mr Skellorn should have arrived, for he inhabited the farthest of the cottages.[13]

One line of insight would have done more than all those lines of description; but let them pass as the necessary drudgery of the novelist. And now — where is Hilda? Alas. Hilda is still looking out of the window. Passionate and dissatisfied as she was, she was a girl with an eye for houses. She often compared this old Mr Skellorn with the villas she saw from her bedroom window. Therefore the villas must be described. Mr Bennett proceeds:

The row was called Freehold Villas: a consciously proud name in a district where much of the land was copyhold and could only change owners subject to the payment of 'fines', and to the feudal consent of a 'court' presided over by the agent of a lord of the manor. Most of the dwellings were owned by their occupiers, who, each an absolute monarch of the soil, niggled in his sooty garden of an evening amid the flutter of drying shirts and towels. Freehold Villas symbolised the final triumph of Victorian economics, the apotheosis of the prudent and industrious artisan. It corresponded with a Building Society Secretary's dream of paradise. And indeed it was a very real achievement. Nevertheless, Hilda's irrational contempt would not admit this.[14]

Heaven be praised, we cry! At last we are coming to Hilda herself. But not so fast. Hilda may have been this, that, and the other; but Hilda not only looked at houses, and thought of houses; Hilda lived in a house. And what sort of a house did Hilda live in? Mr Bennett proceeds:

It was one of the two middle houses of a detached terrace of four houses built by her grandfather Lessways, the teapot manufacturer; it was the chief of the four, obviously the habitation of the proprietor of the terrace. One of the corner houses comprised a grocer's shop, and this house had been robbed of its just proportion of garden so that the seigncurial garden-plot might be triflingly larger than the other. The terrace was not a terrace of cottages, but of houses rated at from twenty-six to thirty-six pounds a year; beyond the means of artisans and petty insurance agents and rent-collectors. And further, it was well built, generously built; and its architecture, though debased, showed some faint traces of Georgian amenity. It was admittedly the best row of houses in that newly settled quarter of the town. In coming to it out of Freehold Villas Mr Skellorn obviously came to something superior, wider, more liberal. Suddenly Hilda heard her mother's voice . . .[15]

But we cannot hear her mother's voice, or Hilda's voice; we can only hear Mr Bennett's voice telling us facts about rents and freeholds and copyholds and fines. What can Mr Bennett be about? I have formed my own opinion of what Mr Bennett is about – he is trying to make us imagine for him; he is trying to hypnotise us into the belief that, because he has made a house, there must be a person living there. With all his powers of observation, which are marvellous, with all his sympathy and humanity, which are great, Mr Bennett has never once looked at Mrs Brown in her corner. There she sits in the corner of the carriage – that carriage which is travelling, not from Richmond to Waterloo, but from one age of English literature to the next, for Mrs Brown is eternal, Mrs Brown is human nature, Mrs Brown changes only on the surface, it is the novelists who get in and out – there she sits and not one of the Edwardian writers has so much as looked at her. They have looked very powerfully, searchingly, and sympathetically out of the window; at factories, at Utopias, even at the decoration and upholstery of the carriage; but never at her, never at life, never at human nature. And so they have developed a technique of novel-writing which suits their purpose; they have made tools and established conventions which do their business. But those tools are not our tools, and that business is not our business. For us those conventions are ruin, those tools are death.

You may well complain of the vagueness of my language. What is a convention, a tool, you may ask, and what do you mean by saying that Mr Bennett's and Mr Wells's and Mr Galsworthy's conventions are the wrong conventions for the Georgians? The question is difficult: I will attempt a short cut. A convention in writing is not much different from a convention in manners. Both in life and in literature it is necessary to have some means of bridging the gulf between the hostess and her unknown guest on the one hand, the writer and his unknown reader on the other. The hostess bethinks her of the weather, for generations of hostesses have established the fact that this is a subject of universal interest in which we all believe. She begins by saying that we are having a wretched May, and, having thus got into touch with her unknown guest, proceeds to matters of greater interest. So it is in literature. The writer must get into touch with his reader by putting before him something which he recognises, which therefore stimulates his imagination, and makes him willing to co-operate in the far more difficult business of intimacy. And it is of the highest importance that this common meeting-place should be reached easily, almost instinctively, in the dark, with one's eyes shut. Here is Mr Bennett making use of this common ground in the passage which I have quoted. The problem before him was to make us believe in the reality of Hilda Lessways. So he began, being an Edwardian, by describing accurately and minutely the sort of house Hilda lived in, and the sort of house she saw from the window. House property was the common ground from which the Edwardians found it easy to proceed to intimacy. Indirect as it seems to us, the convention worked admirably, and thousands of Hilda Lessways were launched upon the world by this means. For that age and generation, the convention was a good one.

But now, if you will allow me to pull my own anecdote to pieces, you will see how keenly I felt the lack of a convention, and how serious a matter it is when the tools of one generation are useless for the next. The incident had made a great impression on me. But how was I to transmit it to you? All I could do was to report as accurately as I could what was said, to describe in detail what was worn, to say, despairingly, that all sorts of scenes rushed into my mind, to proceed to tumble them out pell-mell, and to describe this vivid, this overmastering impression by likening it to a draught or a smell of burning. To tell you the truth, I was also strongly tempted to manufacture a three-volume novel about the old lady's son, and his adventures crossing the Atlantic, and her daughter, and how she kept a milliner's shop in Westminster, the past life of Smith himself, and his house at Sheffield, though such stories seem to me the most dreary, irrelevant, and humbugging affairs in the world.

But if I had done that I should have escaped the appalling effort of saying what I meant. And to have got at what I meant, I should have had to go back and back and back; to experiment with one thing and another; to try this sentence and that, referring each word to my vision, matching it as exactly as possible, and knowing that somehow I had to find a common ground between us, a convention which would not seem to you too odd, unreal, and far-fetched to believe in. I admit that I shirked that arduous undertaking. I let my Mrs Brown slip through my fingers. I have told you nothing whatever about her. But that is partly the great Edwardians' fault. I asked them – they are my elders and betters – How shall I begin to describe this woman's character? And they said, 'Begin by saying that her father kept a shop in Harrogate. Ascertain the rent. Ascertain the wages of shop assistants in the year 1878, Discover what her mother died of. Describe cancer. Describe calico. Describe –' But I cried, 'Stop! Stop!' and I regret to say that I threw that ugly, that clumsy, that incongruous tool out of the window, for I knew that if I began describing the cancer and the calico my Mrs Brown,* that vision to which I cling though I know no way of imparting it to you, would have been dulled and tarnished and vanished for ever.

That is what I mean by saying that the Edwardian tools are the wrong ones for us to use. They have laid an enormous stress upon the fabric of things. They have given us a house in the hope that we may be able to deduce the human beings who live there. To give them their due, they have made that house much better worth living in. But if you hold that novels are in the first place about people, and only in the second about the houses they live in, that is the wrong way to set about it. Therefore, you see, the Georgian writer had to begin by throwing away the method that was in use at the moment. He was left alone there facing Mrs Brown without any method of conveying her to the reader. But that is inaccurate. A writer is never alone. There is always the public with him – if not on the same seat, at least in the compartment next door. Now the public is a strange travelling companion. In England it is a very suggestible and docile creature, which, once you get it to attend, will believe implicitly what it is told for a certain number of years. If you say to the public with sufficient

---

*HP Essay: 'if I began describing the cancer and the calico, my Mrs Brown'.

convinction, 'All women have tails, and all men have humps', it will actually learn to see women with tails and men with humps, and will think it very revolutionary and probably improper if you say 'Nonsense. Monkeys have tails and camels humps. But men and women have brains, and they have hearts; they think and they feel', – that will seem to it a bad joke, and an improper into the bargain.*

But to return. Here is the British public sitting by the writer's side and saying in its vast and unanimous way, 'Old women have houses. They have fathers. They have incomes. They have servants. They have hot water bottles. That is how we know that they are old women. Mr Wells and Mr Bennett and Mr Galsworthy have always taught us that this is the way to recognise them. But now with your Mrs Brown – how are we to believe in her? We do not even know whether her villa was called Albert or Balmoral; what she paid for her gloves; or whether her mother died of cancer or of consumption. How can she be alive? No; she is a mere figment of your imagination.'

And old women of course ought to be made of freehold villas and copyhold estates, not of imagination.

The Georgian novelist, therefore, was in an awkward predicament. There was Mrs Brown protesting that she was different, quite different, from what people made out, and luring the novelist to her rescue by the most fascinating if fleeting glimpse of her charms; there were the Edwardians handing out tools appropriate to house building and house breaking; and there was the British public asseverating that they must see the hot water bottle first. Meanwhile the train was rushing to that station where we must all get out.

Such, I think, was the predicament in which the young Georgians found themselves about the year 1910. Many of them – I am thinking of Mr Forster and Mr Lawrence in particular – spoilt their early work because, instead of throwing away those tools, they tried to use them. They tried to compromise. They tried to combine their own direct sense of the oddity and significance of some character with Mr Galsworthy's knowledge of the Factory Acts, and Mr Bennett's knowledge of the Five Towns. They tried it, but they had too keen, too overpowering a sense of Mrs Brown and her peculiarities to go on trying

---

*HP Essay: '–that will seem to it a bad joke, and an improper one into the bargain'.

it much longer. Something had to be done. At whatever cost of life, limb, and damage to valuable property Mrs Brown must be rescued, expressed, and set in her high relations to the world before the train stopped and she disappeared for ever. And so the smashing and the crashing began. Thus it is that we hear all round us, in poems and novels and biographies, even in newspaper articles and essays, the sound of breaking and falling, crashing and destruction. It is the prevailing sound of the Georgian age – rather a melancholy one if you think what melodious days there have been in the past, if you think of Shakespeare and Milton and Keats or even of Jane Austen and Thackeray and Dickens;[16] if you think of the language, and the heights to which it can soar when free, and see the same eagle captive, bald, and croaking.

In view of these facts, with these sounds in my ears and these fancies in my brain, I am not going to deny that Mr Bennett has some reason when he complains that our Georgian writers are unable to make us believe that our characters are real. I am forced to agree that they do not pour out three immortal masterpieces with Victorian regularity every autumn. But instead of being gloomy, I am sanguine. For this state of things is, I think, inevitable whenever from hoar old age or callow youth the convention ceases to be a means of communication between writer and reader, and becomes instead an obstacle and an impediment. At the present moment we are suffering, not from decay, but from having no code of manners which writers and readers accept as a prelude to the more exciting intercourse of friendship. The literary convention of the time is so artificial – you have to talk about the weather and nothing but the weather throughout the entire visit – that, naturally, the feeble are tempted to outrage, and the strong are led to destroy the very foundations and rules of literary society. Signs of this are everywhere apparent. Grammar is violated; syntax disintegrated, as a boy staying with an aunt for the weekend rolls in the geranium bed out of sheer desperation as the solemnities of the sabbath wear on. The more adult writers do not, of course, indulge in such wanton exhibitions of spleen. Their sincerity is desperate, and their courage tremendous; it is only that they do not know which to use, a fork or their fingers. Thus, if you read Mr Joyce and Mr Eliot you will be struck by the indecency of the one, and the obscurity of the other. Mr Joyce's indecency in *Ulysses*[17] seems to me the conscious and calculated indecency of a desperate man who feels that in order to breathe he must break the windows. At moments, when the window is broken, he is magnificent. But what a waste of energy! And, after all, how dull indecency is, when it is not the overflowing of a superabundant energy or savagery, but the determined and public-spirited act of a man who needs fresh air! Again, with the obscurity of Mr Eliot. I think that Mr Eliot has written some of the loveliest lines in modern poetry.* 'But how intolerant he is of the old usages and politenesses of society – respect for the weak, consideration for the dull! As I sun myself upon the intense and ravishing beauty of one of his lines, and reflect that I must make a dizzy and dangerous leap to the next, and so on from line to line, like an acrobat flying precariously from bar to bar, I cry out, I confess, for the old decorums, and envy the indolence of my ancestors who, instead of spinning madly through mid-air, dreamt quietly in the shade with a book. Again, in Mr Strachey's books, *Eminent Victorians* and *Queen Victoria*,[19] the effort and strain of writing against the grain and current of the times is visible too. It is much less visible, of course, for not only is he dealing with facts, which are stubborn things, but he has fabricated, chiefly from eighteenth-century material, a very discreet code of manners of his own, which allows him to sit at table with the highest in the land and to say a great many things under cover of that exquisite apparel which, had they gone naked, would have been chased by the men-servants from the room. Still, if you compare *Eminent Victorians* with some of Lord Macaulay's essays,[20] though you will feel that Lord Macaulay is always wrong, and Mr Strachey always right, you will also feel a body, a sweep, a richness in Lord Macaulay's essays which show that his age was behind him; all his strength went straight into his work; none was used for purposes of concealment or of conversion. But Mr Strachey has had to open our eyes before he made us see; he has had to search out and sew together a very artful manner of speech; and the effort, beautifully though it is concealed, has robbed his work of some of the force that should have gone into it, and limited his scope.

For these reasons, then, we must reconcile ourselves to a season of failures and fragments. We must reflect that where so much strength is spent on finding a way of telling the truth the truth itself is bound to reach us in rather an

---

HP Essay: 'I think that Mr Eliot has written some of the loveliest single lines in modern poetry'.

exhausted and chaotic condition. Ulysses, Queen Victoria, Mr Prufrock – to give Mrs Brown some of the names she has made famous lately – is a little pale and dishevelled by the time her rescuers reach her. And it is the sound of their axes that we hear – a vigorous and stimulating sound in my ears – unless of course you wish to sleep, when in the bounty of his concern, Providence has provided a host of writers anxious and able to satisfy your needs.

Thus I have tried, at tedious length, I fear, to answer some of the questions which I began by asking. I have given an account of some of the difficulties which in my view beset the Georgian writer in all his forms. I have sought to excuse him. May I end by venturing to remind you of the duties and responsibilities that are yours as partners in this business of writing books, as companions in the railway carriage, as fellow travellers with Mrs Brown? For she is just as visible to you who remain silent as to us who tell stories about her. In the course of your daily life this past week you have had far stranger and more interesting experiences than the one I have tried to describe. You have overheard scraps of talk that filled you with amazement. You have gone to bed at night bewildered by the complexity of your feelings. In one day thousands of ideas have coursed through your brains; thousands of emotions have met, collided, and disappeared in astonishing disorder. Nevertheless, you allow the writers to palm off upon you a version of all this, an image of Mrs Brown, which has no likeness to that surprising apparition whatsoever. In your modesty you seem to consider that writers are of different blood and bone from yourselves; that they know more of Mrs Brown than you do. Never was there a more fatal mistake. It is this division between reader and writer, this humility on your part, these professional airs and graces on ours, that corrupt and emasculate the books which should be the healthy offspring of a close and equal alliance between us. Hence spring those sleek, smooth novels, those portentous and ridiculous biographies, that milk and watery criticism, those poems melodiously celebrating the innocence of roses and sheep which pass so plausibly for literature at the present time.

Your part is to insist that writers shall come down off their plinths and pedestals, and describe beautifully if possible, truthfully at any rate, our Mrs Brown. You should insist that she is an old lady of unlimited capacity and infinite variety; capable of appearing in any place; wearing any dress; saying anything and doing heaven knows what. But the things she says and the things she does and her eyes and her nose and her speech and her silence have an overwhelming fascination, for she is, of course, the spirit we live by, life itself.

But do not expect just at present a complete and satisfactory presentment of her. Tolerate the spasmodic, the obscure, the fragmentary, the failure. Your help is invoked in a good cause. For I will make one final and surpassingly rash prediction – we are trembling on the verge of one of the great ages of English literature. But it can only be reached if we are determined never, never to desert Mrs Brown.

The Art of Fiction

Henry James

I should not have affixed so comprehensive a title to these few remarks, necessarily wanting in any completeness, upon a subject the full consideration of which would carry us far, did I not seem to discover a pretext for my temerity in the interesting pamphlet lately published under this name by Mr. Walter Besant. Mr. Besant's lecture at the Royal Institution—the original form of his pamphlet—appears to indicate that many persons are interested in the art of fiction and are not indifferent to such remarks as those who practise it may attempt to make about it. I am therefore anxious not to lose the benefit of this favourable association, and to edge in a few words under cover of the attention which Mr. Besant is sure to have excited. There is something very encouraging in his having put into form certain of his ideas on the mystery of story-telling.

It is a proof of life and curiosity—curiosity on the part of the brotherhood of novelists, as well as on the part of their readers. Only a short time ago it might have been supposed that the English novel was not what the French call *discutable*. It had no air of having a theory, a conviction, a consciousness of itself behind it—of being the expression of an artistic faith, the result of choice and comparison. I do not say it was necessarily the worse for that; it would take much more courage than I possess to intimate that the form of the novel, as Dickens and Thackeray (for instance) saw it, had any taint of incompleteness. It was, however, *naïf* (if I may help myself out with another French word); and, evidently, if it is destined to suffer in any way for having lost its *naïveté*, it has now an idea of making sure of the corresponding advantages. During the period I have alluded to there was a comfortable, good-humoured feeling abroad that a novel is a novel, as a pudding is a pudding, and that this was the end of it. But within a year or two, for some reason or other, there have been signs of returning animation—the era of discussion would appear to have been to a certain extent opened. Art lives upon discussion, upon experiment, upon curiosity, upon variety of attempt, upon the exchange of views and the comparison of standpoints; and there is a presumption that those times when no one has anything particular to say about it, and has no reason to give for practice or preference, though they may be times of genius, are not times of development, are times, possibly even, a little, of dulness. The successful application of any art is a delightful spectacle, but the theory, too, is interesting; and though there is a great deal of the latter without the former, I suspect there has never been a genuine success that has not had a latent core of conviction. Discussion, suggestion, formulation, these things are fertilizing when they are frank and sincere. Mr. Besant has set an excellent example in saying what he thinks, for his part, about the way in which fiction should be written, as well as about the way in which it should be published; for his view of the 'art,' carried on into an appendix, covers that too. Other labourers in the same field will doubtless take up the argument, they will give it the light of their experience, and the effect will surely be to make our interest in the novel a little more what it had for some time threatened to fail to be—a serious, active, inquiring interest, under protection of which this delightful study may, in moments of confidence, venture to say a little more what it thinks of itself.

It must take itself seriously for the public to take it so. The old superstition about fiction being 'wicked' has doubtless died out in England; but the spirit of it lingers in a certain oblique regard directed toward any story which does not more or less admit that it is only a joke. Even the most jocular novel feels in some degree the weight of the proscription that was formerly directed against literary levity; the jocularity does not always succeed in passing for gravity. It is still expected, though perhaps people are ashamed to say it, that a production which is after all only a 'make believe' (for what else is a 'story?') shall be in some degree apologetic—shall renounce the pretension of attempting really to compete with life. This, of course, any sensible wide-awake story declines to do, for it quickly perceives that the tolerance granted to it on such a condition is only an attempt to stifle it, disguised in the form of generosity. The old Evangelical hostility to the novel, which was as explicit as it was narrow, and which regarded it as little less favourable to our immortal part than a stage-play, was in reality far less insulting. The only reason for the existence of a novel is that it *does* compete with life. When it ceases to compete as the canvas of the painter competes, it will have arrived at a very strange pass. It is not expected of the picture that it will make itself humble in order to be forgiven; and the analogy between the art of the painter and the art of the novelist is, so far as I am able to see, complete. Their inspiration is the same, their process (allowing for the different quality of the vehicle) is the same, their success is the same. They may learn from each other, they may explain and sustain each other. Their cause is the same, and the honour of one is the honour of another. Peculiarities of manner, of execution, that correspond on either side, exist in each of them and contribute to their development. The Mahometans think a picture an unholy thing, but it is a long time since any Christian did, and it is therefore the more odd that in the Christian mind the traces (dissimulated though they may be) of a suspicion of the sister art should linger to this day. The only effectual way to lay it to rest is to emphasize the analogy to which I just alluded——to insist on the fact that as the picture is reality, so the novel is history. That is the only general description (which does it justice) that we may give of the novel. But history also is allowed to compete with life, as I say; it is not, any more than painting, expected to apologize. The subject-matter of fiction is stored up likewise in documents and records, and if it will not give itself away, as they say in California, it must speak with assurance, with the tone of the historian. Certain accomplished novelists have a habit of giving themselves away which must often bring tears to the eyes of people who take their fiction seriously. I was lately struck, in reading over many pages of Anthony Trollope, with his want of discretion in this particular. In a digression, a parenthesis or an aside, he concedes to the reader that he and this trusting friend are only 'making believe.' He admits that the events he narrates have not really happened, and that he can give his narrative any turn the reader may like best. Such a betrayal of a sacred office seems to me, I confess, a terrible crime; it is what I mean by the attitude of apology, and it shocks me every whit as much in Trollope as it would have shocked me in Gibbon or Macaulay. It implies that the novelist is less occupied in looking for the truth than the historian, and in doing so it deprives him at a stroke of all his standing-room. To represent and illustrate the past, the actions of men, is the task of either writer, and the only difference that I can see is, in proportion as he succeeds, to the honour of the novelist, consisting as it does in his having more difficulty in collecting his evidence, which is so far from being purely literary. It seems to me to give him a great character, the fact that he has at once so much in common with the philosopher and the painter; this double analogy is a magnificent heritage.

It is of all this evidently that Mr. Besant is full when he insists upon the fact that fiction is one of the *fine* arts, deserving in its turn of all the honours and emoluments that have hitherto been reserved for the successful profession of music, poetry, painting, architecture. It is impossible to insist too much on so important a truth, and the place that Mr. Besant demands for the work of the novelist may be represented, a trifle less abstractly, by saying that he demands not only that it shall be reputed artistic, but that it shall be reputed very artistic indeed. It is excellent that he should have struck this note, for his doing so indicates that there was need of it, that his proposition may be to many people a novelty. One rubs one's eyes at the thought; but the rest of Mr. Besant's essay confirms the revelation. I suspect, in truth, that it would be possible to confirm it still further, and that one would not be far wrong in saying that in addition to the people to whom it has never occurred that a novel ought to be artistic, there are a great many others who, if this principle were urged upon them, would be filled with an indefinable mistrust. They would find it difficult to explain their repugnance, but it would operate strongly to put them on their guard. 'Art,' in our Protestant communities, where so many things have got so strangely twisted about, is supposed, in certain circles, to have some vaguely injurious effect upon those who make it an important consideration, who let it weigh in the balance. It is assumed to be opposed in some mysterious manner to morality, to amusement, to instruction. When it is embodied in the work of the painter (the sculptor is another affair!) you know what it is; it stands there before you, in the honesty of pink and green and a gilt frame; you can see the worst of it at a glance, and you can be on your guard. But when it is introduced into literature it becomes more insidious—there is danger of its hurting you before you know it. Literature should be either instructive or amusing, and there is in many minds an impression that these artistic preoccupations, the search for form, contribute to neither end, interfere indeed with both. They are too frivolous to be edifying, and too serious to be diverting; and they are, moreover, priggish and paradoxical and superfluous. That, I think, represents the manner in which the latent thought of many people who read novels as an exercise in skipping would explain itself if it were to become articulate. They would argue, of course, that a novel ought to be 'good,' but they would interpret this term in a fashion of their own, which, indeed, would vary considerably from one critic to another. One would say that being good means representing virtuous and aspiring characters, placed in prominent positions; another would say that it depends for a 'happy ending' on a distribution at the last of prizes, pensions, husbands, wives, babies, millions, appended paragraphs and cheerful remarks. Another still would say that it means being full of incident and movement, so that we shall wish to jump ahead, to see who was the mysterious stranger, and if the stolen will was ever found, and shall not be distracted from this pleasure by any tiresome analysis or 'description.' But they would all agree that the 'artistic' idea would spoil some of their fun. One would hold it accountable for all the description, another would see it revealed in the absence of sympathy. Its hostility to a happy ending would be evident, and it might even, in some cases, render any ending at all impossible. The 'ending' of a novel is, for many persons, like that of a good dinner, a course of dessert and ices, and the artist in fiction is regarded as a sort of meddlesome doctor who forbids agreeable aftertastes. It is therefore true that this conception of Mr. Besant's, of the novel as a superior form, encounters not only a negative but a positive indifference. It matters little that, as a work of art, it should really be as little or as much concerned to supply happy endings, sympathetic characters, and an objective tone, as if it were a work of mechanics; the association of ideas, however incongruous, might easily be too much for it if an eloquent voice were not sometimes raised to call attention to the fact that it is at once as free and as serious a branch of literature as any other.

Certainly, this might sometimes be doubted in presence of the enormous number of works of fiction that appeal to the credulity of our generation, for it might easily seem that there could be no great substance in a commodity so quickly and easily produced. It must be admitted that good novels are somewhat compromised by bad ones, and that the field, at large, suffers discredit from overcrowding. I think, however, that this injury is only superficial, and that the superabundance of written fiction proves nothing against the principle itself. It has been vulgarised, like all other kinds of literature, like everything else, to-day, and it has proved more than some kinds accessible to vulgarisation. But there is as much difference as there ever was between a good novel and a bad one: the bad is swept, with all the daubed canvases and spoiled marble, into some unvisited limbo or infinite rubbish-yard, beneath the back-windows of the world, and the good subsists and emits its light and stimulates our desire for perfection. As I shall take the liberty of making but a single criticism of Mr. Besant, whose tone is so full of the love of his art, I may as well have done with it at once. He seems to me to mistake in attempting to say so definitely beforehand what sort of an affair the good novel will be. To indicate the danger of such an error as that has been the purpose of these few pages; to suggest that certain traditions on the subject, applied *a priori,* have already had much to answer for, and that the good health of an art which undertakes so immediately to reproduce life must demand that it be perfectly free. It lives upon exercise, and the very meaning of exercise is freedom. The only obligation to which in advance we may hold a novel without incurring the accusation of being arbitrary, is that it be interesting. That general responsibility rests upon it, but it is the only one I can think of. The ways in which it is at liberty to accomplish this result (of interesting us) strike me as innumerable and such as can only suffer from being marked out, or fenced in, by prescription. They are as various as the temperament of man, and they are successful in proportion as they reveal a particular mind, different from others. A novel is in its broadest definition a personal impression of life; that, to begin with, constitutes its value, which is greater or less according to the intensity of the impression. But there will be no intensity at all, and therefore no value, unless there is freedom to feel and say. The tracing of a line to be followed, of a tone to be taken, of a form to be filled out, is a limitation of that freedom and a suppression of the very thing that we are most curious about. The form, it seems to me, is to be appreciated after the fact; then the author's choice has been made, his standard has been indicated; then we can follow lines and directions and compare tones. Then, in a word, we can enjoy one of the most charming of pleasures, we can estimate quality, we can apply the test of execution. The execution belongs to the author alone;

it is what is most personal to him, and we measure him by that. The advantage, the luxury, as well as the torment and responsibility of the novelist, is that there is no limit to what he may attempt as an executant—no limit to his possible experiments, efforts, discoveries, successes. Here it is especially that he works, step by step, like his brother of the brush, of whom we may always say that he has painted his picture in a manner best known to himself. His manner is his secret, not necessarily a deliberate one. He cannot disclose it, as a general thing, if he would; he would be at a loss to teach it to others. I say this with a due recollection of having insisted on the community of method of the artist who paints a picture and the artist who writes a novel. The painter *is* able to teach the rudiments of his practice, and it is possible, from the study of good work (granted the aptitude), both to learn how to paint and to learn how to write. Yet it remains true, without injury to the *rapprochement,* that the literary artist would be obliged to say to his pupil much more than the other, 'Ah, well, you must do it as you can!' It is a question of degree, a matter of delicacy. If there are exact sciences there are also exact arts, and the grammar of painting is so much more definite that it makes the difference.

I ought to add, however, that if Mr. Besant says at the beginning of his essay that the 'laws of fiction may be laid down and taught with as much precision and exactness as the laws of harmony, perspective, and proportion,' he mitigates what might appear to be an over-statement by applying his remark to 'general' laws, and by expressing most of these rules in a manner with which it would certainly be unaccommodating to disagree. That the novelist must write from his experience, that his 'characters must be real and such as might be met with in actual life;' that 'a young lady brought up in a quiet country village should avoid descriptions of garrison life,' and 'a writer whose friends and personal experiences belong to the lower middle-class should carefully avoid introducing his characters into Society;' that one should enter one's notes in a common-place book; that one's figures should be clear in outline; that making them clear by some trick of speech or of carriage is a bad method, and 'describing them at length' is a worse one; that English Fiction should have a 'conscious moral purpose;' that 'it is almost impossible to estimate too highly the value of careful workmanship—that is, of style;' that 'the most important point of all is the story,' that 'the story is everything'—these are principles with most of which it is surely impossible not to sympathise. That remark about the lower middle-class writer and his knowing his place is perhaps rather chilling; but for the rest, I should find it difficult to dissent from any one of these recommendations. At the same time I should find it difficult positively to assent to them, with the exception, perhaps, of the injunction as to entering one's notes in a common-place book. They scarcely seem to me to have the quality that Mr. Besant attributes to the rules of the novelist—the 'precision and exactness' of 'the laws of harmony, perspective, and proportion.' They are suggestive, they are even inspiring, but they are not exact, though they are doubtless as much so as the case admits of; which is a proof of that liberty of interpretation for which I just contended. For the value of these different injunctions—so beautiful and so vague—is wholly in the meaning one attaches to them. The characters, the situation, which strike one as real will be those that touch and interest one most, but the measure of reality is very difficult to fix. The reality of Don Quixote or of Mr. Micawber is a very delicate shade; it is a reality, so coloured by the author's vision that, vivid as it may be, one would hesitate to propose it as a model; one would expose one's self to some very embarrassing questions on the part of a pupil. It goes without saying that you will not write a good novel unless you possess the sense of reality; but it will be difficult to give you a recipe for calling that sense into being. Humanity is immense and reality has a myriad forms; the most one can affirm is that some of the flowers of fiction have the odour of it, and others have not; as for telling you in advance how your nosegay should be composed, that is another affair. It is equally excellent and inconclusive to say that one must write from experience; to our supposititious aspirant such a declaration might savour of mockery. What kind of experience is intended, and where does it begin and end? Experience is never limited and it is never complete; it is an immense sensibility, a kind of huge spider-web, of the finest silken threads, suspended in the chamber of consciousness and catching every air-borne particle in its tissue. It is the very atmosphere of the mind; and when the mind is imaginative—much more when it happens to be that of a man of genius—it takes to itself the faintest hints of life, it converts the very pulses of the air into revelations. The young lady living in a village has only to be a damsel upon whom nothing is lost to make it quite unfair (as it seems to me) to declare to her that she shall have nothing to say about the military. Greater miracles have been seen than that, imagination assisting, she should speak the truth about some of these gentlemen. I remember an English novelist, a woman of genius, telling me that she was much commended for the impression she had managed to give in one of her tales of the nature and way of life of the French Protestant youth. She had been asked where she learned so much about this recondite being, she had been congratulated on her peculiar opportunities. These opportunities consisted in her having once, in Paris, as she ascended a staircase, passed an open door where, in the household of a *pasteur,* some of the young Protestants were seated at table round a finished meal. The glimpse made a picture; it lasted only a moment, but that moment was experience. She had got her impression, and she evolved her type. She knew what youth was, and what Protestantism; she also had the advantage of having seen what it was to be French; so that she converted these ideas into a concrete image and produced a reality. Above all, however, she was blessed with the faculty which when you give it an inch takes an ell, and which for the artist is a much greater source of strength than any accident of residence or of place in the social scale. The power to guess the unseen from the seen, to trace the implication of things, to judge the whole piece by the pattern, the condition of feeling life, in general, so completely that you are well on your way to knowing any particular corner of it—this cluster of gifts may almost be said to constitute experience, and they occur in country and in town, and in the most differing stages of education. If experience consists of impressions, it may be said that impressions *are* experience, just as (have we not seen it?) they are the very air we breathe. Therefore, if I should certainly say to a novice, 'Write from experience, and experience only,' I should feel that this was a rather tantalising monition if I were not careful immediately to add, 'Try to be one of the people on whom nothing is lost!'

I am far from intending by this to minimise the importance of exactness— of truth of detail. One can speak best from one's own taste, and I may therefore venture to say that the air of reality (solidity of specification) seems to me to be the supreme virtue of a novel—the merit in which all its other merits (including that conscious moral purpose of which Mr. Besant speaks) helplessly and submissively depend. If it be not there, they are all as nothing, and if these be there, they owe their effect to the success with which the author has produced the illusion of life. The cultivation of this success, the study of this exquisite process, form, to my taste, the beginning and the end of the art of the novelist. They are his inspiration, his despair, his reward, his torment, his delight. It is here, in very truth, that he competes with life; it is here that he competes with his brother the painter, in *his* attempt to render the look of things, the look that conveys their meaning, to catch the colour, the relief, the expression, the surface, the substance of the human spectacle. It is in regard to this that Mr. Besant is well inspired when he bids him take notes. He cannot possibly take too many, he cannot possibly take enough. All life solicits him, and to 'render' the simplest surface, to produce the most momentary illusion, is a very complicated business. His case would be easier, and the rule would be more exact, if Mr. Besant had been able to tell him what notes to take. But this I fear he can never learn in any hand-book; it is the business of his life. He has to take a great many in order to select a few, he has to work them up as he can, and even the guides and philosophers who might have most to say to him must leave him alone when it comes to the application of precepts, as we leave the painter in communion with his palette. That his characters 'must be clear in outline,' as Mr. Besant says— he feels that down to his boots; but how he shall make them so is a secret between his good angel and himself. It would be absurdly simple if he could be taught that a great deal of 'description' would make them so, or that, on the contrary, the absence of description and the cultivation of dialogue, or the absence of dialogue and the multiplication of 'incident,' would rescue him from his difficulties. Nothing, for instance, is more possible than that he be of a turn of mind for which this odd, literal opposition of description and dialogue, incident and description, has little meaning and light. People often talk of these things as if they had a kind of internecine distinctness, instead of melting into each other at every breath and being intimately associated parts of one general effort of expression. I cannot imagine composition existing in a series of blocks, nor conceive, in any novel worth discussing at all, of a passage of description that is not in its intention narrative, a passage of dialogue that is not in its intention descriptive, a touch of truth of any sort that does not partake of the nature of incident, and an incident that derives its interest from any other source than the general and only source of the success of a work of art—that of being illustrative. A novel is a living thing, all one and continuous, like every other organism, and in proportion as it lives will it be found, I think, that in each of the parts there is something of each of the other parts. The critic who over the close texture of a finished work will pretend to trace a geography of items will mark some frontiers as artificial, I fear, as any that have been known to history. There is an old-fashioned distinction between the novel of character and the novel of incident, which must have cost many a smile to the intending romancer who was keen about his work. It appears to me as little to the point as the equally celebrated distinction between the novel and the romance—to answer as little to any reality. There are bad novels and good novels, as there are bad pictures and good pictures; but that is the only distinction in which I see any meaning, and I can as little imagine speaking of a novel of character as I can imagine speaking of a picture of character. When one says picture, one says of character, when one says novel, one says of incident, and the terms may be transposed. What is character but the determination of incident? What is incident but the illustration of character? What is a picture or a novel that is *not* of character? What else do we seek in it and find in it? It is an incident for a woman to stand up with her hand resting on a table and look out at you in a certain way; or if it be not an incident, I think it will be hard to say what it is. At the same time it is an expression of character. If you say you don't see it (character in *that—allons done!*) this is exactly what the artist who has reasons of his own for thinking he *does* see it undertakes to show you. When a young man makes up his mind that he has not faith enough, after all, to enter the Church, as he intended, that is an incident, though you may not hurry to the end of the chapter to see whether perhaps he doesn't change once more. I do not say that these are extraordinary or startling incidents. I do not pretend to estimate the degree of interest proceeding from them, for this will depend upon the skill of the painter. It sounds almost puerile to say that some incidents are intrinsically much more important than others, and I need not take this precaution after having professed my sympathy for the major ones in remarking that the only classification of the novel that I can understand is into the interesting and the uninteresting.

The novel and the romance, the novel of incident and that of character—these separations appear to me to have been made by critics and readers for their own convenience, and to help them out of some of their difficulties, but to have little reality or interest for the producer, from whose point of view it is, of course, that we are attempting to consider the art of fiction. The case is the same with another shadowy category, which Mr. Besant apparently is disposed to set up— that of the 'modern English novel;' unless, indeed, it be that in this matter he has fallen into an accidental confusion of standpoints. It is not quite clear whether he intends the remarks in which he alludes to it to be didactic or historical. It is as difficult to suppose a person intending to write a modern English, as to suppose him writing an ancient English, novel; that is a label which begs the question. One writes the novel, one paints the picture, of one's language and of one's time, and calling it modern English will not, alas! make the difficult task any easier. No more, unfortunately, will calling this or that work of one's fellow artist a romance—unless it be, of course, simply for the pleasantness of the thing, as, for instance, when Hawthorne gave this heading to his story of Blithedale. The French, who have brought the theory of fiction to remarkable completeness, have but one word for the novel, and have not attempted smaller things in it, that I can see, for that. I can think of no obligation to which the 'romancer' would not be held equally with the novelist; the standard of execution is equally high for each. Of course it is of execution that we are talking—that being the only point of a novel that is open to contention. This is perhaps too often lost sight of, only to produce interminable confusions and cross-purposes. We must grant the artist his subject, his idea, what the French call his *donnée*; our criticism is applied only to what he makes of it. Naturally I do not mean that we are bound to like it or find it interesting: in case we do not our course is perfectly simple—to let it alone. We may believe that of a certain idea even the most sincere novelist can make nothing at all, and the event may perfectly justify our belief; but the failure will have been a failure to execute, and it is in the execution that the fatal weakness is recorded. If we pretend to respect the artist at all we must allow him his freedom of choice, in the face, in particular cases, of innumerable presumptions that the choice will not fructify. Art derives a considerable part of its beneficial exercise from flying in the face of presumptions, and some of the most interesting experiments of which it is capable are hidden in the bosom of

common things. Gustave Flaubert has written a story about the devotion of a
servant-girl to a parrot, and the production, highly finished as it is, cannot on
the whole be called a success. We are perfectly free to find it flat, but I think it
might have been interesting; and I, for my part, am extremely glad he should
have written it; it is a contribution to our knowledge of what can be done—or
what cannot. Ivan Turgénieff has written a tale about a deaf and dumb serf and a
lap-dog, and the thing is touching, loving, a little masterpiece. He struck the note
of life where Gustave Flaubert missed it—he flew in the face of a presumption
and achieved a victory.

Nothing, of course, will ever take the place of the good old fashion of 'liking'
a work of art or not liking it; the more improved criticism will not abolish
that primitive, that ultimate, test. I mention this to guard myself from the
accusation of intimating that the idea, the subject, of a novel or a picture, does
not matter. It matters, to my sense, in the highest degree, and if I might put up
a prayer it would be that artists should select none but the richest. Some, as I
have already hastened to admit, are much more substantial than others, and it
would be a happily arranged world in which persons intending to treat them
should be exempt from confusions and mistakes. This fortunate condition
will arrive only, I fear, on the same day that critics become purged from error.
Meanwhile, I repeat, we do not judge the artist with fairness unless we say to
him, 'Oh, I grant you your starting-point, because if I did not I should seem
to prescribe to you, and heaven forbid I should take that responsibility. If I
pretend to tell you what you must not take, you will call upon me to tell you
then what you must take; in which case I shall be nicely caught! Moreover, it
isn't till I have accepted your data that I can begin to measure you. I have the
standard; I judge you by what you propose, and you must look out for me
there. Of course I may not care for your idea at all; I may think it silly, or stale,
or unclean; in which case I wash my hands of you altogether. I may content
myself with believing that you will not have succeeded in being interesting, but
I shall of course not attempt to demonstrate it, and you will be as indifferent to
me as I am to you. I needn't remind you that there are all sorts of tastes: who
can know it better? Some people, for excellent reasons, don't like to read about
carpenters; others, for reasons even better, don't like to read about courtesans.
Many object to Americans. Others (I believe they are mainly editors and

publishers) won't look at Italians. Some readers don't like quiet subjects; others don't like bustling ones. Some enjoy a complete illusion; others revel in a complete deception. They choose their novels accordingly, and if they don't care about your idea they won't, *a fortiori,* care about your treatment.'

So that it comes back very quickly, as I have said, to the liking; in spite of M. Zola, who reasons less powerfully than he represents, and who will not reconcile himself to this absoluteness of taste, thinking that there are certain things that people ought to like, and that they can be made to like. I am quite at a loss to imagine anything (at any rate in this matter of fiction) that people *ought* to like or to dislike. Selection will be sure to take care of itself, for it has a constant motive behind it. That motive is simply experience. As people feel life, so they will feel the art that is most closely related to it. This closeness of relation is what we should never forget in talking of the effort of the novel. Many people speak of it as a factitious, artificial form, a product of ingenuity, the business of which is to alter and arrange the things that surround us, to translate them into conventional, traditional moulds. This, however, is a view of the matter which carries us but a very short way, condemns the art to an eternal repetition of a few familiar *clichés,* cuts short its development, and leads us straight up to a dead wall. Catching the very note and trick, the strange irregular rhythm of life, that is the attempt whose strenuous force keeps Fiction upon her feet. In proportion as in what she offers us we see life *without* rearrangement do we feel that we are touching the truth; in proportion as we see it *with* rearrangement do we feel that we are being put off with a substitute, a compromise and convention. It is not uncommon to hear an extraordinary assurance of remark in regard to this matter of rearranging, which is often spoken of as if it were the last word of art. Mr. Besant seems to me in danger of falling into this great error with his rather unguarded talk about 'selection.' Art is essentially selection, but it is a selection whose main care is to be typical, to be inclusive. For many people art means rose-coloured windows, and selection means picking a bouquet for Mrs. Grundy. They will tell you glibly that artistic considerations have nothing to do with the disagreeable, with the ugly; they will rattle off shallow commonplaces about the province of art and the limits of art, till you are moved to some wonder in return as to the province and the limits of ignorance. It appears to me that no one can ever have made a seriously artistic attempt without becoming conscious of an immense increase—a kind of revelation—of freedom. One perceives, in that case—by the light of a heavenly ray—that the province of art is all life, all feeling, all observation, all vision. As Mr. Besant so justly intimates, it is all experience. That is a sufficient answer to those who maintain that it must not touch the painful, who stick into its divine unconscious bosom little prohibitory inscriptions on the end of sticks, such as we see in public gardens—'It is forbidden to walk on the grass; it is forbidden to touch the flowers; it is not allowed to introduce dogs, or to remain after dark; it is requested to keep to the right.' The young aspirant in the line of fiction, whom we continue to imagine, will do nothing without taste, for in that case his freedom would be of little use to him; but the first advantage of his taste will be to reveal to him the absurdity of the little sticks and tickets. If he have taste, I must add, of course he will have ingenuity, and my disrespectful reference to that quality just now was not meant to imply that it is useless in fiction. But it is only a secondary aid; the first is a vivid sense of reality.

Mr. Besant has some remarks on the question of 'the story,' which I shall not attempt to criticise, though they seem to me to contain a singular ambiguity, because I do not think I understand them. I cannot see what is meant by talking as if there were a part of a novel which is the story and part of it which for mystical reasons is not—unless indeed the distinction be made in a sense in which it is difficult to suppose that anyone should attempt to convey anything. 'The story,' if it represents anything, represents the subject, the idea, the data of the novel; and there is surely no 'school'—Mr. Besant speaks of a school—which urges that a novel should be all treatment and no subject. There must assuredly be something to treat; every school is intimately conscious of that. This sense of the story being the idea, the starting-point, of the novel is the only one that I see in which it can be spoken of as something different from its organic whole; and since, in proportion as the work is successful, the idea permeates and penetrates it, informs and animates it, so that every word and every punctuation-point contribute directly to the expression, in that proportion do we lose our sense of the story being a blade which may be drawn more or less out of its sheath. The story and the novel, the idea and the form, are the needle and thread, and I never heard of a guild of tailors who recommended the use of the thread without the needle or the needle without the thread. Mr. Besant is not the only critic who may be observed to have spoken as if there were certain things in life which constitute stories and certain others which do not. I find the same odd implication in an entertaining article in the *Pall Mall Gazette,* devoted, as it happens, to Mr. Besant's lecture. 'The story is the thing!' says this graceful writer, as if with a tone of opposition to another idea. I should think it was, as every painter who, as the time for 'sending in' his picture looms in the distance, finds himself still in quest of a subject—as every belated artist, not fixed about his *donnée,* will heartily agree. There are some subjects which speak to us and others which do not, but he would be a clever man who should undertake to give a rule by which the story and the no-story should be known apart. It is impossible (to me at least) to imagine any such rule which shall not be altogether arbitrary. The writer in the *Pall Mall* opposes the delightful (as I suppose) novel of 'Margot la Balafrée' to certain tales in which 'Bostonian nymphs' appear to have 'rejected English dukes for psychological reasons.' I am not acquainted with the romance just designated, and can scarcely forgive the *Pall Mall* critic for not mentioning the name of the author, but the title appears to refer to a lady who may have received a scar in some heroic adventure. I am inconsolable at not being acquainted with this episode, but am utterly at a loss to see why it is a story when the rejection (or acceptance) of a duke is not, and why a reason, psychological or other, is not a subject when a cicatrix is. They are all particles of the multitudinous life with which the novel deals, and surely no dogma which pretends to make it lawful to touch the one and unlawful to touch the other will stand for a moment on its feet. It is the special picture that must stand or fall, according as it seems to possess truth or to lack it. Mr. Besant does not, to my sense, light up the subject by intimating that a story must, under penalty of not being a story, consist of 'adventures.' Why of adventures more than of green spectacles? He mentions a category of impossible things, and among them he places 'fiction without adventure.' Why without adventure, more than without matrimony, or celibacy, or parturition, or cholera, or hydropathy, or Jansenism? This seems to me to bring the novel back to the hapless little *rôle* of being an artificial, ingenious thing—bring it down from its large, free character of an immense and exquisite correspondence with life. And what *is* adventure, when it comes to that, and by what sign is the listening pupil to recognise it? It is an adventure—an immense one—for me to write this little article; and for a Bostonian nymph to reject an English duke is an adventure only less stirring, I should say, than for an English duke to be rejected by a Bostonian nymph. I see dramas within dramas in that, and innumerable points of view. A psychological reason is, to my imagination, an object adorably pictorial; to catch the tint of its complexion—I feel as if that idea might inspire one to Titianesque efforts. There are few things more exciting to me, in short, than a psychological reason, and yet, I protest, the novel seems to me the most magnificent form of art. I have just been reading, at the same time, the delightful story of 'Treasure Island,' by Mr. Robert Louis Stevenson, and the last tale from M. Edmond de Goncourt, which is entitled 'Chérie.' One of these works treats of murders, mysteries, islands of dreadful renown, hairbreadth escapes, miraculous coincidences and buried doubloons. The other treats of a little French girl who lived in a fine house in Paris and died of wounded sensibility because no one would marry her. I call 'Treasure Island' delightful, because it appears to me to have succeeded wonderfully in what it attempts; and I venture to bestow no epithet upon 'Chérie,' which strikes me as having failed in what it attempts—that is, in tracing the development of the moral consciousness of a child. But one of these productions strikes me as exactly as much of a novel as the other, and as having a 'story' quite as much. The moral consciousness of a child is as much a part of life as the islands of the Spanish Main, and the one sort of geography seems to me to have those 'surprises' of which Mr. Besant speaks quite as much as the other. For myself (since it comes back in the last resort, as I say, to the preference of the individual), the picture of the child's experience has the advantage that I can at successive steps (an immense luxury, near to the 'sensual pleasure' of which Mr. Besant's critic in the *Pall Mall* speaks) say Yes or No, as it may be, to what the artist puts before me. I have been a child, but I have never been on a quest for a buried treasure, and it is a simple accident that with M. de Goncourt I should have for the most part to say No. With George Eliot, when she painted that country, I always said Yes.

The most interesting part of Mr. Besant's lecture is unfortunately the briefest passage—his very cursory allusion to the 'conscious moral purpose' of the novel. Here again it is not very clear whether he is recording a fact or laying down a principle; it is a great pity that in the latter case he should not have developed his idea. This branch of the subject is of immense importance, and Mr. Besant's few words point to considerations of the widest reach, not to be lightly disposed of. He will have treated the art of fiction but superficially who is not prepared to go every inch of the way that these considerations will carry him. It is for this reason that at the beginning of these remarks I was careful to notify the reader that my reflections on so large a theme have no pretension to be exhaustive. Like Mr. Besant, I have left the question of the morality of the novel till the last, and at the last I find I have used up my space. It is a question surrounded with difficulties, as witness the very first that meets us, in the form of a definite question, on the threshold. Vagueness, in such a discussion, is fatal, and what is the meaning of your morality and your conscious moral purpose? Will you not define your terms and explain how (a novel being a picture) a picture can be either moral or immoral? You wish to paint a moral picture or carve a moral statue; will you not tell us how you would set about it? We are discussing the Art of Fiction; questions of art are questions (in the widest sense) of execution; questions of morality are quite another affair, and will you not let us see how it is that you find it so easy to mix them up? These things are so clear to Mr. Besant that he has deduced from them a law which he sees embodied in English Fiction and which is 'a truly admirable thing and a great cause for congratulation.' It is a great cause for congratulation, indeed, when such thorny problems become as smooth as silk. I may add that, in so far as Mr. Besant perceives that in point of fact English Fiction has addressed itself preponderantly to these delicate questions, he will appear to many people to have made a vain discovery. They will have been positively struck, on the contrary, with the moral timidity of the usual English novelist; with his (or with her) aversion to face the difficulties with which, on every side, the treatment of reality bristles. He is apt to be extremely shy (whereas the picture that Mr. Besant draws is a picture of boldness), and the sign of his work, for the most part, is a cautious silence on certain subjects. In the English novel (by which I mean the American as well), more than in any other, there is a traditional difference between that which people know and that which they agree to admit that they know, that which they see and that which they speak of, that which they feel to be a part of life and that which they allow to enter into literature. There is the great difference, in short, between what they talk of in conversation and what they talk of in print. The essence of moral energy is to survey the whole field, and I should directly reverse Mr. Besant's remark, and say not that the English novel has a purpose, but that it has a diffidence. To what degree a purpose in a work of art is a source of corruption I shall not attempt to inquire; the one that seems to me least dangerous is the purpose of making a perfect work. As for our novel, I may say, lastly, on this score, that, as we find it in England to-day, it strikes me as addressed in a large degree to 'young people,' and that this in itself constitutes a presumption that it will be rather shy. There are certain things which it is generally agreed not to discuss, not even to mention, before young people. That is very well, but the absence of discussion is not a symptom of the moral passion. The purpose of the English novel—'a truly admirable thing, and a great cause for congratulation'—strikes me, therefore, as rather negative.

There is one point at which the moral sense and the artistic sense lie very near together; that is, in the light of the very obvious truth that the deepest quality of a work of art will always be the quality of the mind of the producer. In proportion as that mind is rich and noble will the novel, the picture, the statue, partake of the substance of beauty and truth. To be constituted of such elements is, to my vision, to have purpose enough. No good novel will ever proceed from a superficial mind; that seems to me an axiom which, for the artist in fiction, will cover all needful moral ground; if the youthful aspirant take it to heart it will illuminate for him many of the mysteries of 'purpose.' There are many other useful things that might be said to him, but I have come to the end of my article, and can only touch them as I pass. The critic in the *Pall Mall Gazette,* whom I have already quoted, draws attention to the danger, in speaking of the art of fiction, of generalizing. The danger that he has in mind is rather, I imagine, that of particularizing, for there are some comprehensive remarks which, in addition to those embodied in Mr. Besant's suggestive lecture, might, without fear of misleading him, be addressed to the ingenuous student. I should remind him first of the magnificence of the form that is open to him, which offers to sight so few restrictions and such innumerable opportunities. The other arts, in comparison, appear confined and hampered; the various conditions under which they are exercised are so rigid and definite.

But the only condition that I can think of attaching to the composition of the novel is, as I have already said, that it be interesting. This freedom is a splendid privilege, and the first lesson of the young novelist is to learn to be worthy of it. 'Enjoy it as it deserves,' I should say to him; 'take possession of it, explore it to its utmost extent, reveal it, rejoice in it. All life belongs to you, and don't listen either to those who would shut you up into corners of it and tell you that it is only here and there that art inhabits, or to those who would persuade you that this heavenly messenger wings her way outside of life altogether, breathing a superfine air and turning away her head from the truth of things. There is no impression of life, no manner of seeing it and feeling it, to which the plan of the novelist may not offer a place; you have only to remember that talents so dissimilar as those of Alexandre Dumas and Jane Austen, Charles Dickens and Gustave Flaubert, have worked in this field with equal glory. Don't think too much about optimism and pessimism; try and catch the colour of life itself. In France to-day we see a prodigious effort (that of Emile Zola, to whose solid and serious work no explorer of the capacity of the novel can allude without respect), we see an extraordinary effort vitiated by a spirit of pessimism on a narrow basis. M. Zola is magnificent, but he strikes an English reader as ignorant; he has an air of working in the dark; if he had as much light as energy his results would be of the highest value. As for the aberrations of a shallow optimism, the ground (of English fiction especially) is strewn with their brittle particles as with broken glass. If you must indulge in conclusions let them have the taste of a wide knowledge. Remember that your first duty is to be as complete as possible—to make as perfect a work. Be generous and delicate, and then, in the vulgar phrase, go in!'

Writing American Fiction

Philip Roth

Several winters back, while I was living in Chicago, the city was shocked and mystified by the death of two teen-age girls. So far as I know the populace is mystified still; as for the shock, Chicago is Chicago, and one week's dismemberment fades into the next's. The victims this particular year were sisters. They went off one December night to see an Elvis Presley movie, for the sixth or seventh time we are told, and never came home. Ten days passed and fifteen and twenty, and then the whole bleak city, every street and alley, was being searched for the missing Grimes girls, Pattie and Babs. A girl friend had seen them at the movie, a group of boys had had a glimpse of them afterwards getting into a black Buick; another group said a green Chevy, and so on and so forth, until one day the snow melted and the unclothed bodies of the two girls were discovered in a roadside ditch in a forest preserve on the West Side of Chicago. The coroner said he didn't know the cause of death and then the newspapers took over. One paper, I forget which one, ran a drawing of the girls on the back page, in bobby socks and levis and babushkas: Pattie and Babs a foot tall, and in four colors, like Dixie Dugan on Sundays. The mother of the two girls wept herself right into the arms of a local newspaper lady, who apparently set up her typewriter on the Grimes's front porch and turned out a column a day, telling us that these had been good girls, hardworking girls, average girls, churchgoing girls, et cetera. Late in the evening one could watch television interviews featuring schoolmates and friends of the Grimes sisters: the teen-age girls look around, dying to giggle; the boys stiffen in their leather jackets. "Yeah, I knew Babs, yeah she was all right, yeah, she was popular . . . ." On and on until at last comes a confession. A Skid Row bum of thirty-five or so, a dishwasher, a prowler, a no-good named Benny Bedwell, admits to killing both girls, after he and a pal had cohabited with them for several weeks in various flea-bitten hotels. Hearing the news, the mother weeps and cries and tells the newspaper lady that the man is a liar—her girls, she insists now, were murdered the night they went off to the movie. The coroner continues to maintain (with rumblings from the press) that the girls show no signs of having had sexual intercourse. Meanwhile, everybody in Chicago is buying four papers a day, and Benny Bedwell, having supplied the police with an hour-by-hour chronicle of his adventures, is tossed in jail. Two nuns, teachers of the girls at the school they attended, are sought out by the newspapermen. They are surrounded and questioned and finally one of the sisters explains all. "They were not exceptional girls," the sister says, "they had no hobbies." About this time, some good-natured soul digs up Mrs. Bedwell, Benny's mother, and a meeting is arranged between this old woman and the mother of the slain teen-agers. Their picture is taken together, two overweight, overworked American ladies, quite befuddled but sitting up straight for the photographers. Mrs. Bedwell apologizes for her Benny. She says, "I never thought any boy of mine would do a thing like that." Two weeks later, or maybe three, her boy is out on bail, sporting several lawyers and a new one-button roll suit. He is driven in a pink Cadillac to an out-of-town motel where he holds a press conference. Yes—he barely articulates—he is the victim of police brutality. No, he is not a murderer; a degenerate maybe, but even that is going out the window. He is changing his life—he is going to become a carpenter (a carpenter!) for the Salvation Army, his lawyers say. Immediately, Benny is asked to sing (he plays the guitar) in a Chicago night spot for two thousand dollars a week, or is it ten thousand? I forget. What I remember is that suddenly there is a thought that comes flashing into the mind of the spectator, or newspaper reader: is this all Public Relations? But of course not—two girls are dead. At any rate, a song begins to catch on in Chicago, "The Benny Bedwell Blues." Another newspaper launches a weekly contest: "How Do You Think the Grimes Girls Were Murdered?" and a prize is given for the best answer (in the opinion of the judges). And now the money begins; donations, hundreds of them, start pouring in to Mrs. Grimes from all over the city and the state. For what? From whom? Most contributions are anonymous. Just money, thousands and thousands of dollars—the *Sun-Times* keeps us informed of the grand total. Ten thousand, twelve thousand, fifteen thousand. Mrs. Grimes sets about refinishing and redecorating her house. A strange man steps forward, by the name of Shultz or Schwartz—I don't really remember, but he is in the appliance business and he presents Mrs. Grimes with a whole new kitchen. Mrs. Grimes, beside herself with appreciation and joy, turns to her surviving daughter and says, "Imagine me in that kitchen!" Finally the poor woman goes out and buys two parakeets (or maybe another Mr. Shultz presented them as a gift); one parakeet she calls "Babs," the other, "Pattie." At just about this point, Benny Bedwell, doubtless having barely learned to hammer a nail in straight, is extradited to Florida on the charge of having raped a twelve-year-old girl there. Shortly thereafter I left Chicago myself, and so far as I know, though Mrs. Grimes hasn't her two girls, she has a brand new dishwasher and two small birds.

And what is the moral of so long a story? Simply this: that the American writer in the middle of the 20th century has his hands full in trying to understand, and then describe, and then make *credible* much of the American reality. It stupefies, it sickens, it infuriates, and finally it is even a kind of embarrassment to one's own meager imagination. The actuality is continually outdoing our talents, and the culture tosses up figures almost daily that are the envy of any novelist. Who, for example, could have invented Charles Van Doren? Roy Cohn and David Schine? Sherman Adams and Bernard Goldfine? Dwight David Eisenhower? Several months back most of the country heard one of the candidates for the presidency of the United States, the office of Jefferson, Lincoln, and FDR, say something like, "Now if you feel that Senator Kennedy is right, then I sincerely believe you should vote for Senator Kennedy, and if you feel that I am right, I humbly submit that you vote for me. Now I feel, and this is certainly a personal opinion, that I am right . . . ." and so on. Though it did not appear quite this way to some thirty-four million voters, it still seems to me a little easy to pick on Mr. Nixon as someone to ridicule, and it is not for that reason that I have bothered to paraphrase his words here. If one was at first amused by him, one was ultimately astonished. As a literary creation, as some novelist's image of a certain kind of human being, he might have seemed believable, but I myself found that on the TV screen, as a real public image, a political fact, my mind balked at taking him in. Whatever else the television debates produced in me, I should like to point out, as a literary curiosity, that they also produced a type of professional envy. All the machinations over make-up, rebuttal time, all the business over whether Mr. Nixon should look at Mr. Kennedy when he replied, or should look away—all of it was so beside the point, so fantastic, so weird and astonishing, that I found myself beginning to wish I had invented it. That may not, of course, be a literary fact at all, but a simple psychological one—for finally I began to wish that *someone* had invented it, and that it was not real and with us.

The daily newspapers then fill one with wonder and awe: is it possible? is it happening? And of course with sickness and despair. The fixes, the scandals, the insanities, the treacheries, the idiocies, the lies, the pieties, the noise . . . . Recently, in COMMENTARY, Benjamin DeMott wrote that the "deeply lodged suspicion of the times [is] namely, that events and individuals are unreal, and that power to alter the course of the age, of my life and your life, is actually vested nowhere." There seems to be, said DeMott, a kind of "universal descent into unreality." The other night—to give a benign example of the descent—my wife turned on the radio and heard the announcer offering a series of cash prizes for the three best television plays of five minutes' duration written by children. At such moments it is difficult to find one's way around the kitchen; certainly few days go by when incidents far less benign fail to remind us of what DeMott is talking about. When Edmund Wilson says that after reading *Life* magazine he feels that he does not belong to the country depicted there, that he does not live in that country, I think I understand what he means.

However, for a writer of fiction to feel that he does not really live in the country in which he lives—as represented by *Life* or by what he experiences when he steps out his front door—must certainly seem a serious occupational impediment. For what will be his subject? His landscape? It is the tug of reality, its mystery and magnetism, that leads one into the writing of fiction—what then when one is not mystified, but stupefied? not drawn but repelled? It would seem that what we might get would be a high proportion of historical novels or contemporary satire—or perhaps just nothing. No books. Yet the fact is that almost weekly one finds on the best-seller list another novel which is set in Mamaroneck or New York City or Washington, with people moving through a world of dishwashers and TV sets and advertising agencies and Senatorial investigations. It all *looks* as though the writers are still turning out books about our world. There is *Cash McCall* and *The Man in the Gray Flannel Suit* and *Marjorie Morningstar* and *The Enemy Camp* and *Advise and Consent,* and so on. But what is crucial, of course, is that these books aren't very good. Not that these writers aren't sufficiently horrified with the landscape to suit me—quite the contrary. They are generally full of concern for the world about them; finally, however, they just don't seem able to imagine the corruptions and vulgarities and treacheries of American public life any more profoundly than they can imagine human character—that is, the country's private life. All issues are generally solvable, which indicates that they are not so much wonder-struck or horrorstruck or even plain struck by a state of civilization, as they are provoked by some topical controversy. "Controversial" is a common word in the critical language of this literature as it is, say, in the language of the TV producer. But it is clear that though one may refer to a "problem" as being controversial, one does not usually speak of a state of civilization as controversial, or a state of the soul.

It is hardly news that in best-sellerdom we frequently wind up with the hero coming to terms and settling down in Scarsdale, or wherever, knowing himself. And on Broadway, in the third act, someone says, "Look, why don't you just love each other?" and the protagonist, throwing his hand to his forehead, cries, "Oh God, why didn't *I* think of that!" and before the bulldozing action of love, all else collapses—verisimilitude, truth, and interest. It is like "Dover Beach" ending happily for Matthew Arnold, and for us, because the poet is standing at the window with a woman who understands him. If the investigation of our times and the impact of these times upon human personality were to become the sole property of Wouk, Weidman, Sloan Wilson, Cameron Hawley, and the theatrical *amor-vincit-omnia* boys it would indeed be unfortunate, for it would be somewhat like leaving sex to the pornographers, where again there is more to what is happening than first meets the eye.

And of course the times have not yet been left completely to lesser minds and talents. There is Norman Mailer. And he is an interesting example, I think, of one in whom our era has provoked such a magnificent disgust that dealing with it in fiction has almost come to seem, for him, beside the point. He has become an actor in the cultural drama, the difficulty of which, I should guess, is that it leaves one with considerably less time to be a writer. For instance, to defy the Civil Defense authorities and their H-bomb drills, you have to take off a morning from the typewriter and go down and stand outside of City Hall; then if you're lucky and they toss you in jail, you have to give up an evening at home and your next morning's work as well. To defy Mike Wallace, or challenge his principle-less aggression, or simply use him or straighten him out, you must first go on the program—there's one night shot. Then you may well spend the next two weeks (I am speaking from memory) disliking yourself for having gone, and then two more writing an article (or a confession to a gentle friend) in which you attempt to explain why you did it and what it was like. "It's the age of the slob," says a character in William Styron's new novel. "If we don't watch out they're going to drag us under. . . ." And the dragging under, as we see, takes numerous forms. We get, for instance, from Mailer a book like *Advertisements for Myself,* a chronicle for the most part of why I did it and what it was like— and who I have it in for: life as a substitute for fiction. An infuriating, self-indulgent, boisterous, mean book, not much worse than most advertising we have to put up with, I think—but also, taken as a whole, a curiously moving book, moving in its revelation of the connection between one writer and the times that have given rise to him, in the revelation of a despair so great that the man who bears it, or is borne by it, seems for the time being—out of either choice or necessity—to have given up on making an imaginative assault upon the American experience, and has become instead the champion of a kind of public revenge. Unfortunately, however, what one is champion of one day, one may wind up victim of the next; that is everybody's risk. Once having written *Advertisements for Myself,* I don't see that you can write it again. Mr. Mailer probably now finds himself in the unenviable position of having to put up or shut up. Who knows—maybe it's where he wanted to be. My own feeling is that times are tough for a writer when he takes to writing letters to his newspaper rather than those complicated, disguised letters to himself, which are stories.

The last is not meant to be a sententious, or a condescending remark, or even a generous one. However one suspects Mailer's style or his reasons, one sympathizes with the impulse that leads him to be—or to want to be—a critic, a reporter, a sociologist, a journalist, a figure, or even Mayor of New York. For what is particularly tough about the times is writing about them, as a serious novelist or storyteller. Much has been made, much of it by the writers themselves, of the fact that the American writer has no status and no respect and no audience: the news I wish to bear is of a loss more central to the task itself, a loss of subject; or if not a loss, if to say that is, romantically and inexactly and defensively, an attempt to place most of the responsibility outside the writer for what may finally be nothing more than the absence of genius in our times—then let me say a voluntary withdrawal of interest by the writer of fiction from some of the grander social and political phenomena of our times.

Of course there have been writers who have tried to meet these phenomena head-on. It seems to me I have read several books or stories in the past few years in which one character or another starts to talk about "The Bomb," and the conversation generally leaves me feeling half convinced, and in some extreme instances, even with a certain amount of sympathy for fall-out; it is like people in college novels having long talks about what kind of generation they are. But what then? What can the writer do with so much of the American reality as it is? Is the only other possibility to be Gregory Corso and thumb your nose at the whole thing? The attitude of the Beats (if such a phrase has meaning) is not in certain ways without appeal. The whole thing is a kind of joke. America, ha-ha. The only trouble is that such a position doesn't put very much distance between Beatdom and its sworn enemy, best-sellerdom—not much more, at any rate, than what it takes to get from one side of a nickel to the other: for what is America, ha-ha, but the simple reverse of America, hoo-ray?

It is possible that I have exaggerated both the serious writer's response to our cultural predicament, and his inability or unwillingness to deal with it imaginatively. There seems to me little, in the end, to be used as proof for an assertion having to do with the psychology of a nation's writers, outside, that is, of their books themselves. So, with this particular assertion, the argument may appear to be somewhat compromised in that the evidence to be submitted is not so much the books that have been written, but the ones that have been left unwritten and unfinished, and those that have not even been considered worthy of the attempt. Which is not to say that there have not been certain literary signs, certain obsessions and innovations and concerns, to be found in the novels of our best writers, supporting the notion that the world we have been given, the society and the community, has ceased to be as suitable or as manageable a subject for the novelist as it once may have been.

Let me begin with some words about the man who, by reputation at least, is *the* writer of the age. The response of college students to the works of J. D. Salinger should indicate to us that perhaps he, more than anyone else, has not turned his back on the times, but instead, has managed to put his finger on what is most significant in the struggle going on today between the self (all selves, not just the writer's) and the culture. *The Catcher in the Rye* and the recent stories in the *New Yorker* having to do with the Glass family surely take place in the social here and now. But what about the self, what about the hero? This question seems to me of particular interest here, for in Salinger more than in most of his contemporaries, there has been an increasing desire of late to place the figure of the writer himself directly in the reader's line of vision, so that there is an equation, finally, between the insights of the narrator as, say, brother to Seymour Glass, and as a man who is a writer by profession. And what of Salinger's heroes? Well, Holden Caulfield, we discover, winds up in an expensive sanitarium. And Seymour Glass commits suicide finally, but prior to that he is the apple of his brother's eye—and why? He has learned to live in this world—but how? By not living in it. By kissing the soles of little girls' feet and throwing rocks at the head of his sweetheart. He is a saint, clearly. But since madness is undesirable and sainthood, for most of us, out of the question, the problem of how to live in this world is by no means answered; unless the answer is that one cannot. The only advice we seem to get from Salinger is to be charming on the way to the loony bin. Of course, Salinger is under no burden to supply us, writers or readers, with advice, though I must admit that I find myself growing more and more curious about this professional writer, Buddy Glass, and how *he* manages to coast through this particular life in the arms of sanity.

It is not Buddy Glass, though, in whom I do not finally believe, but Seymour himself. Seymour is as unreal to me as his world, in all its endless and marvelous detail, is decidedly credible. I am touched by the lovingness that is attributed to him, as one is touched by so many of the gestures and attitudes in Salinger, but this lovingness, in its totality and otherworldliness, becomes for me in the end an attitude of the writer's, a cry of desperation, even a program, more than an expression of character. If we forgive this lapse, it is, I think, because we understand the depth of the despairing.

There is, too, in Salinger the suggestion that mysticism is a possible road to salvation; at least some of his characters respond well to an intensified, emotional religious belief. Now my own involvement with Zen is slight, but as I understand it in Salinger, the deeper we go into this world, the further we can get away from it. If you contemplate a potato long enough, it stops being a potato in the usual sense; unfortunately, though, it is the usual sense that we have to deal with from day to day. For all the loving handling of the world's objects, for all the reverence of life and feeling, there seems to me, in the Glass family stories as in *The Catcher,* a spurning of life as it is lived in this world, in this reality—this place and time is seen as unworthy of those few precious people who have been set down in it only to be maddened and destroyed.

A spurning of our world—though of a much different order—seems to occur in another of our most talented writers, Bernard Malamud. Even, one recalls, when Malamud writes a book about baseball, a book called *The Natural,* it is not baseball as it is played in Yankee Stadium, but a wild, wacky baseball, where a player who is instructed to knock the cover off the ball promptly steps up to the plate and knocks it off; the batter swings and the inner hard string core of the ball goes looping out to centerfield, where the confused fielder commences to tangle himself in the unwinding sphere; then the shortstop runs out, and with his teeth, bites the center-fielder and the ball free from one another. Though *The Natural* is not Malamud's most successful, nor his most significant book, it is at any rate our introduction to his world, which has a kind of historical relationship to our own, but is by no means a replica of it. By historical I mean that there are really things called baseball players and really things called Jews, but there much of the similarity ends. The Jews of *The Magic Barrel* and the Jews of *The Assistant,* I have reason to suspect, are not the Jews of New York City or Chicago. They are a kind of invention, a metaphor to stand for certain human possibilities and certain human promises, and I find myself further inclined to believe this when I read of a statement attributed to Malamud which goes, "All men are Jews." In fact we know this is not so; even the men who are Jews aren't sure they're Jews. But Malamud, as a writer of fiction, has not shown specific interest in the anxieties and dilemmas and corruptions of the modern American Jew, the Jew we think of as characteristic of our times; rather, his people live in a timeless depression and a placeless Lower East Side; their society is not affluent, their predicament not cultural. I am not saying—one cannot, of Malamud—that he has spurned life or an examination of the difficulties of being human. What it is to be human, to be humane, is his subject: connection, indebtedness, responsibility, these are his moral concerns. What I do mean to point out is that he does not—or has not yet—found the contemporary scene a proper or sufficient backdrop for his tales of heartlessness and heartache, of suffering and regeneration.

Now Malamud and Salinger do not speak, think, or feel for all writers, and yet their fictional response to the world about them—what they choose to mention, what they choose to avoid—is of interest to me on the simple grounds that they are two of our best. Surely there are other writers around, and capable ones too, who have not taken the particular roads that these two have; however, even with some of these others, I wonder if we may not be witnessing a response to the times, perhaps not so dramatic as in Salinger and Malamud, but a response nevertheless.

Let us take up the matter of prose style. Why is everybody so bouncy all of a sudden? Those who have been reading in the works of Saul Bellow, Herbert Gold, Arthur Granit, Thomas Berger, Grace Paley, and others will know to what I am referring. Writing recently in the *Hudson Review,* Harvey Swados said that he saw developing "a nervous muscular prose perfectly suited to the exigencies of an age which seems at once appalling and ridiculous. These are metropolitan writers, most of them are Jewish, and they are specialists in a kind of prose-poetry that often depends for its effectiveness as much on how it is ordered, or how it looks on the printed page, as it does on what it is expressing. This is risky writing, . . ." Swados added, and perhaps it is in its very riskiness that we can discover some kind of explanation for it. I should like to compare two short descriptive passages, one from Bellow's *The Adventures of Augie March,* the other from Gold's new novel, *Therefore Be Bold,* in the hope that the differences revealed will be educational.

As has been pointed out by numerous people before me, the language of *Augie March* is one that combines a literary complexity with a conversational ease, a language that joins the idiom of the academy with the idiom of the streets (not all streets—certain streets); the style is special, private, and energetic, and though occasionally unwieldly and indulgent, it generally, I believe, serves the narrative, and serves it brilliantly. Here for instance is a description of Grandma Lausch:

> With the [cigarette] holder in her dark little gums between which all her guile, malice, and command issued, she had her best inspirations of strategy. She was as wrinkled as an old paper bag, an autocrat, hard-shelled and jesuitical, a pouncy old hawk of a Bolshevik, her small ribboned gray feet immobile on the shoe-kit and stool Simon had made in the manual-training class, dingy old wool Winnie [the dog] whose bad smell filled the flat on the cushion beside her. If wit and discontent don't necessarily go together, it wasn't from the old woman that I learned it.

Herbert Gold's language has also been special, private, and energetic. One will notice in the following passage from *Therefore Be Bold* that here too the writer begins by recognizing a physical similarity between the character described and some unlikely object, and from there, as in Bellow's Grandma Lausch passage, attempts to move into a deeper, characterological description, to wind up, via the body, making a discovery about the soul. The character described is named Chuck Hastings.

> In some respects he resembled a mummy—the shriveled yellow skin, the hand and head too large for a wasted body, the bottomless eye sockets of thought beyond the Nile. But his agile Adam's apple and point-making finger made him less the Styx-swimmer dog-paddling toward Coptic limbos than a high school intellectual intimidating the navel-eyed little girl.

First I must say that the grammar itself has me baffled: ". . . bottomless eye sockets of thought beyond the Nile." Is the thought beyond the Nile, or are the eye sockets? What does it mean to be beyond the Nile anyway? The a-grammaticality of the sentence has little in common with the ironic inversion with which Bellow's description begins: "With the holder in her dark little gums between which all her guile, malice, and command issued. . . ." Bellow goes on to describe Grandma Lausch as "an autocrat," "hard-shelled," "jesuitical," "a pouncy old hawk of a Bolshevik"—imaginative terms certainly, but toughminded, exact, and not exhibitionistic. Of Gold's Chuck Hastings, however, we learn, "His agile Adam's-apple and point-making finger made him less the Styx-swimmer dog-paddling toward Coptic limbos etc. . . ." Is this language in the service of the narrative, or a kind of literary regression in the service of the ego? In a recent review of *Therefore Be Bold,* Granville Hicks quoted this very paragraph in praise of Gold's style. "This is high-pitched," Mr. Hicks admitted, "but the point is that Gold keeps it up and keeps it up." I take it that Mr. Hicks's sexual pun is not deliberate; nevertheless, it should remind us all that showmanship and passion are not, and never have been, one and the same. What we have here, it seems to me, is not so much stamina or good spirits, but reality taking a backseat to personality—and not the personality of the character described, but of the writer who is doing the describing. Bellow's description seems to arise out of a firm conviction on the part of the writer about the character: Grandma Lausch IS. Behind the description of Chuck Hastings there seems to me the conviction—or the desire for us to be convinced—of something else: Herbert Gold IS. I am! I am! In short: look at me, I'm writing.

Because Gold's work serves my purposes, let me say a word or two more about him. He is surely one of our most productive and most respected novelists, and yet he has begun to seem to me a writer in competition with his own fiction. Which is more interesting—my life or my work? His new book of stories, *Love and Like,* is not over when we have finished reading the last narrative. Instead we go on to read several more pages in which the author explains why and how he came to write each of the preceding stories. At the end of *Therefore Be Bold* we are given a long listing of the various cities in which Gold worked on this book, and the dates during which he was living or visiting in them. It is all very interesting if one is involved in tracing lost mail, but the point to be noted here is that how the fiction has come to be written is supposed to be nearly as interesting as what is written. Don't forget, ladies and gentlemen, that behind each and every story you have read here tonight is—me. For all Gold's delight with the things of this world—and I think that his prose, at its best, is the expression of that delight—there is also a good deal of delight in the work of his own hand. And, I think, with the hand itself.

Using a writer for one's own purposes is of course to be unfair to him (nearly as unfair as the gambit that admits to being unfair); I confess to this, however, and don't intend to hang a man for one crime. Nevertheless, Gold's extravagant prose, his confessional tone (the article about divorce; then the several prefaces and appendices about his own divorce—my ex-wife says this about me, etc.; then finally the story about divorce)—all of this seems to have meaning to me in terms of this separation I tried to describe earlier, the not-so-friendly relationship between the writer and the culture. In fact, it is paradoxical really, that the very prose style which, I take it, is supposed to jolt and surprise us, and thereby produce a new and sharper vision, turns back upon itself, and the real world is in fact veiled from us by this elaborate and self-conscious language-making. I suppose that in a way one can think of it as a sympathetic, or kinetic, response to the clamor and din of our mass culture, an attempt to beat the vulgar world at its own game. I am even willing to entertain this possibility. But it comes down finally to the same thing: not so much an attempt to understand the self, as to assert it.

I must say that I am not trying to sell selflessness. Rather, I am suggesting that this nervous muscular prose that Swados talks about may perhaps have to do with the unfriendliness between the self of the writer and the realities of the culture. The prose suits the age, Swados suggests, and I wonder if it does not suit it, in part, because it rejects it. The writer pushes before our eyes—it is in the very ordering of our sentences—personality, in all its separateness and specialness. Of course the mystery of personality is nothing less than the writer's ultimate concern; and certainly when the muscular prose is revelatory of character—as in *Augie March*—then it is to be appreciated; at its worst, however, as a form of literary onanism, it seriously curtails the fictional possibilities, and may perhaps be thought of, and sympathetically so, as a symptom of the writer's loss of the community as subject.

True, the bouncy style can be understood in other ways as well. It is not surprising that most of these writers Swados sees as its practitioners are Jewish. When writers who do not feel much of a connection to Lord Chesterfield begin to realize that they are under no real obligation to try and write like that distinguished old stylist, they are quite likely to go out and be bouncy. Also, there is the matter of the spoken language which these writers have heard, as our statesmen might put it, in the schools, in the homes, in the churches and the synagogues; I should even say that when the bouncy style is not an attempt to dazzle the reader, or one's self, but to incorporate into written prose the rhythms, the excitements, the nuances and emphases of urban speech, or immigrant speech, the result can sometimes be a language of new and rich emotional subtleties, with a kind of back-handed grace and irony all its own, as say the language of Mrs. Paley's book of stories, *The Little Disturbances of Man.*

But whether the practitioner is Gold or Bellow or Paley, there is one more point to be made about bounciness, and that is that it is an expression of pleasure. One cannot deny that there is that in it. However, a question arises: if the world is as crooked and unreal as I think it is becoming, day by day; if one feels less and less power in the face of this unreality, day by day; if the inevitable end is destruction, if not of all life, then of much that is valuable and civilized in life—then why in God's name is the writer pleased? Why don't all of our fictional heroes wind up in institutions like Holden Caulfield, or suicides like Seymour Glass? Why is it, in fact, that so many of our fictional heroes—not just the heroes of Wouk and Weidman, but of Bellow, Gold, Styron, and others—wind up affirming life? For surely the air is thick these days with affirmation, and though we shall doubtless get this year our annual editorial from *Life* calling for affirmative novels, the plain and simple fact is that more and more books by serious writers seem to end on a note of celebration. Not just the tone is bouncy, but the moral is bouncy too. In *The Optimist,* another novel of Gold's, the hero, having taken his lumps, cries out at the conclusion, "More. More. More! More! More!" This is the book's last line. Curtis Harnack's novel, *The World of an Ancient Hand,* ends with the hero filled with "rapture and hope" and saying aloud, "I believe in God." And Saul Bellow's *Henderson the Rain King* is a book which is given over to celebrating the regeneration of a man's heart, feelings, blood, and general health. Of course it is of crucial importance, I think, that the regeneration of Henderson takes place in a world that is thoroughly and wholly imagined, *but does not really exist;* that is, it is not a part of that reality which we all read about and worry over—this is not the tumultuous Africa of the newspapers and the United Nations discussions that Eugene Henderson visits. There is nothing here of nationalism or riots or *apartheid*. But then, why should there be? There is the world, but there is also the self. And the self, when the writer turns upon it all his attention and talent, is revealed to be a remarkable thing. First off, it exists, it's real. *I am,* the self cries, and then, taking a nice long look, it adds, *and I am beautiful.*

At the conclusion of Bellow's book, the hero, Eugene Henderson, a big, sloppy millionaire, is returning to America, coming home from a trip to Africa where he has been plague-fighter, lion-tamer, and rainmaker; he is bringing back with him a real lion. Aboard the plane he befriends a small Persian boy, whose language he cannot understand. Still, when the plane lands at Newfoundland, Henderson takes the child in his arms and goes out onto the field. And then:

> Laps and laps I galloped around the shining and riveted body of the plane, behind the fuel trucks. Dark faces were looking from within. The great, beautiful propellers were still, all four of them. I guess I felt it was my turn now to move, and so went running—leaping, leaping, pounding, and tingling over the pure white lining of the gray Arctic silence.

And so we leave Henderson, a very happy man. Where? In the Arctic. This picture has stayed with me since I read the book a year or so ago: of a man who finds energy and joy in an imagined Africa, and celebrates it on an unpeopled, icebound vastness.

Earlier I quoted from Styron's new novel, *Set This House on Fire.* Now Styron's book, like Bellow's, is also the story of the regeneration of a man, and too of an American who leaves his own country and goes abroad for a while to live. But where Henderson's world is removed from our own, not about riots or nationalism, Kinsolving, Styron's hero, inhabits a planet we immediately recognize. The book is drenched in details that twenty years from now will surely require footnotes to be thoroughly understood. The hero of the book is an American painter who has taken his family to live in a small town on the Amalfi coast. Cass Kinsolving detests America, and himself to boot. Throughout most of the book he is taunted and tempted and disgraced by Mason Flagg, a fellow countryman, rich, boyish, naive, licentious, indecent, and finally, cruel and stupid. Kinsolving, by way of his attachment to Flagg, spends most of the book choosing between living and dying, and at one point, in a language and tone that are characteristic, he says this, concerning his expatriation:

> . . . . the man I had come to Europe to escape [why he's] the man in all the car advertisements, you know, the young guy waving there—he looks so beautiful and educated and everything, and he's got it *made,* Penn State and a blonde there, and a smile as big as a billboard. And he's going places. I mean electronics. Politics. What they call communication. Advertising. Saleshood. Outer space. God only knows. And he's as ignorant as an Albanian peasant.

However, at the end of the book, for all his disgust with what the American public life does to a man's private life, Kinsolving, like Henderson, has come back to America, having opted for existence. But the America that we find him in seems to me to be the America of his childhood, and, if only in a metaphoric way, of all our childhoods: he tells his story while he fishes from a boat in a Carolina stream. The affirmation at the conclusion is not as go-getting as Gold's "More! More!" nor as sublime as Harnack's, "I believe in God," nor as joyous as Henderson's romp on the Newfoundland airfield. "I wish I could tell you that I had found some belief, some rock . . ." Kinsolving says, "but to be truthful, you see, I can only tell you this: that as for being and nothingness, the only thing I did know was that to choose between them was simply to choose being . . ." Being. Living. Not where one lives or with whom one lives—but that one lives.

And now, alas, what does all of this add up to? It would certainly be to oversimplify the art of fiction, and the complex relationship between a man and his times, to ignore the crucial matters of individual talent, history, and character, to say that Bellow's book, or Styron's, or even Herbert Gold's prose style, arise naturally out of our distressing cultural and political predicament. However, that our communal predicament is a distressing one, is a fact that weighs upon the writer no less, and perhaps even more, than his neighbor— for to the writer the community is, properly, both his subject and his audience. And it may be that when the predicament produces in the writer not only feelings of disgust, rage, and melancholy, but impotence, too, he is apt to lose heart and finally, like his neighbor, turn to other matters, or to other worlds; or to the self, which may, in a variety of ways, become his subject, or even the impulse for his technique. What I have tried to point out is that the sheer fact of self, the vision of self as inviolable, powerful, and nervy, self as the only real thing in an unreal environment, that that vision has given to some writers joy, solace, and muscle. Certainly to have come through a holocaust in one piece, to have survived, is nothing to be made light of, and it is for that reason, say, that Styron's hero manages to engage our sympathies right down to the end. However, when survival itself becomes one's *raison d'être,* when one cannot choose but be ascetic, when the self can only be celebrated as it is excluded from society, or as it is exercised and admired in a fantastic one, we then, I think, do not have much reason to be cheery. Finally there is for me something hollow and unconvincing about Henderson up there on top of the world dancing around that airplane. Consequently, it is not with this image that I should like to conclude, but instead with the image that Ralph Ellison gives to us of his hero at the end of *Invisible Man.* For here too the hero is left with the simple stark fact of himself. He is as alone as a man can be. Not that he hasn't gone out into the world; he has gone out into it, and out into it, and out into it—but at the end he chooses to go underground, to live there and to wait. And it does not seem to him a cause for celebration either.

Form as a Response to Doubt

Lydia Davis

Excerpts from a talk given by Lydia Davis, November 20, 1986, at New Langton Arts, San Francisco.

Doubt, uneasiness, dissatisfaction with writing or with existing forms may result in the formal integration of these doubts by the creation of new forms, forms that in one way or another exceed or surpass our expectations. Whereas repeating old forms implies a lack of desire or compulsion, or a refusal, to entertain doubt or feel dissatisfaction.

To work deliberately in the form of the fragment can be seen as stopping or appearing to stop a work closer, in the process, to what Blanchot would call the origin of writing, the center rather than the sphere. It may be seen as a formal integration, an integration into the form itself, of a question about the process of writing.

It can be seen as a response to the philosophical problem of seeing the written thing replace the subject of the writing. If we catch only a little of our subject, or only badly, clumsily, incoherently, perhaps we have not destroyed it. We have written about it, written it, and allowed it to live on at the same time, allowed it to live on in our ellipses, our silences.

Interruption

Doesn't the unfinished work tend to throw our attention onto the work as artifact, or the work as process, rather than the work as conveyer of meaning, of message? Does this add to the pleasure or the interest of the text?

Any interruption, either of our expectations or of the smooth surface of the work itself--either by breaking it off, confusing it, leaving it actually unfinished--foregrounds the work as artifact, as object, rather than as invisible purveyor of meaning, emotion, atmosphere. Constant interruption, fragmentation, also keeps returning the reader not only to the real world, but to a consciousness of his or her own mind at work.

". . . Without thinking of whole. . . "

Here is Maurice Blanchot on Joseph Joubert: ". . . What he was seeking--this source of writing, this space in which to write, this light to circumscribe in space--. . . made him unfit for all ordinary literary work. . . ."--or, as Joubert said of himself, "unsuited to continuous discourse"--"preferring the center to the sphere, sacrificing results to the discovery of their conditions, and writing not in order to add one book to another but to take command of the point from which it seemed to him all books issued. . . ."

We can't think of fragment without thinking of whole. The word fragment implies the word whole. A fragment would seem to be a part of a whole, a broken-off part of a whole. Does it also imply, as with other broken-off pieces, that enough of them would make a whole, or remake some original whole, some ideal whole? Fragment, as in ruin, may also imply something left behind from a past original whole. In the case of Hölderlin's fragments, the only parts showing of a madman's poems, the rest of which are hidden somewhere in his mind; or the only parts showing of a logical whole whose logic is unavailable to us, fragments that seem fragments only to us, and seem to him to make a whole--for there is only a thin line between what is so new to us that it changes our way of thinking and seeing and what is so new to us that we can't recognize it as a coherent thought or piece of writing, i.e., can't see the connections the author sees, or even sense that they are there. Or fragments that seem to him to make a whole and to us eventually, also, to make a whole, though from a different angle.

Or, as with Mallarmé's fragmentary poems for his dead son, Anatole, the fragment is something left from some projected whole, some future whole, i.e., fragments destined one day to be pieced together with other elements to make a whole; or the fragments of ideal poems shattered by grief; fragments comparable to the incoherent utterances of voiced grief; inarticulateness being in this case the most credible expression of grief: no more than a fragment could be uttered, so overwhelming was the unuttered whole. In the silences, the grief is alive.

Barthes justifies his own early choice of the fragment as form by saying that "incoherence is preferable to a distorting order." In the case of Mallarmé, inarticulateness might seem preferable to articulateness when it comes to expressing a grief that is unutterable. Mallarmé failed to transcend his grief; he remained inside it, and the "notes," too, remain inside it. They become the most immediate expression, the closest mirroring, of the writer's emotion at the inspiring subject, the writer's stutter, and the reader, witnessing the writer's stutter, is witness not only to his grief, but also to his process, to the workings of his mind, to his mind, closer to what we might think of as the origins of his writing.

How to Write About Africa

Binyavanga Wainaina

Always use the word 'Africa' or 'Darkness' or 'Safari' in your title. Subtitles may include the words 'Zanzibar', 'Masai', 'Zulu', 'Zambezi', 'Congo', 'Nile', 'Big', 'Sky', 'Shadow', 'Drum', 'Sun' or 'Bygone'. Also useful are words such as 'Guerrillas', 'Timeless', 'Primordial' and 'Tribal'. Note that 'People' means Africans who are not black, while 'The People' means black Africans.

Never have a picture of a well-adjusted African on the cover of your book, or in it, unless that African has won the Nobel Prize. An AK-47, prominent ribs, naked breasts: use these. If you must include an African, make sure you get one in Masai or Zulu or Dogon dress.

In your text, treat Africa as if it were one country. It is hot and dusty with rolling grasslands and huge herds of animals and tall, thin people who are starving. Or it is hot and steamy with very short people who eat primates. Don't get bogged down with precise descriptions. Africa is big: fifty-four countries, 900 million people who are too busy starving and dying and warring and emigrating to read your book. The continent is full of deserts, jungles, highlands, savannahs and many other things, but your reader doesn't care about all that, so keep your descriptions romantic and evocative and unparticular.

Make sure you show how Africans have music and rhythm deep in their souls, and eat things no other humans eat. Do not mention rice and beef and wheat; monkey-brain is an African's cuisine of choice, along with goat, snake, worms and grubs and all manner of game meat. Make sure you show that you are able to eat such food without flinching, and describe how you learn to enjoy it—because you care.

Taboo subjects: ordinary domestic scenes, love between Africans (unless a death is involved), references to African writers or intellectuals, mention of school-going children who are not suffering from yaws or Ebola fever or female genital mutilation.

Throughout the book, adopt a *sotto* voice, in conspiracy with the reader, and a sad *I-expected-so-much* tone. Establish early on that your liberalism is impeccable, and mention near the beginning how much you love Africa, how you fell in love with the place and can't live without her. Africa is the only continent you can love—take advantage of this. If you are a man, thrust yourself into her warm virgin forests. If you are a woman, treat Africa as a man who wears a bush jacket and disappears off into the sunset. Africa is to be pitied, worshipped or dominated. Whichever angle you take, be sure to leave the strong impression that without your intervention and your important book, Africa is doomed.

Your African characters may include naked warriors, loyal servants, diviners and seers, ancient wise men living in hermitic splendour. Or corrupt politicians, inept polygamous travel-guides, and prostitutes you have slept with. The Loyal Servant always behaves like a seven-year-old and needs a firm hand; he is scared of snakes, good with children, and always involving you in his complex domestic dramas. The Ancient Wise Man always comes from a noble tribe (not the money-grubbing tribes like the Gikuyu, the Igbo or the Shona). He has rheumy eyes and is close to the Earth. The Modern African is a fat man who steals and works in the visa office, refusing to give work permits to qualified Westerners who really care about Africa. He is an enemy of development, always using his government job to make it difficult for pragmatic and good-hearted expats to set up NGOs or Legal Conservation Areas. Or he is an Oxford-educated intellectual turned serial-killing politician in a Savile Row suit. He is a cannibal who likes Cristal champagne, and his mother is a rich witch-doctor who really runs the country.

Among your characters you must always include The Starving African, who wanders the refugee camp nearly naked, and waits for the benevolence of the West. Her children have flies on their eyelids and pot bellies, and her breasts are flat and empty. She must look utterly helpless. She can have no past, no history; such diversions ruin the dramatic moment. Moans are good. She must never say anything about herself in the dialogue except to speak of her (unspeakable) suffering. Also be sure to include a warm and motherly woman who has a rolling laugh and who is concerned for your well-being. Just call her Mama. Her children are all delinquent. These characters should buzz around your main hero, making him look good. Your hero can teach them, bathe them, feed them; he carries lots of babies and has seen Death. Your hero is you (if reportage), or a beautiful, tragic international celebrity/aristocrat who now cares for animals (if fiction).

Bad Western characters may include children of Tory cabinet ministers, Afrikaners, employees of the World Bank. When talking about exploitation by foreigners mention the Chinese and Indian traders. Blame the West for Africa's situation. But do not be too specific.

Broad brushstrokes throughout are good. Avoid having the African characters laugh, or struggle to educate their kids, or just make do in mundane circumstances. Have them illuminate something about Europe or America in Africa. African characters should be colourful, exotic, larger than life—but empty inside, with no dialogue, no conflicts or resolutions in their stories, no depth or quirks to confuse the cause.

Describe, in detail, naked breasts (young, old, conservative, recently raped, big, small) or mutilated genitals, or enhanced genitals. Or any kind of genitals. And dead bodies. Or, better, naked dead bodies. And especially rotting naked dead bodies. Remember, any work you submit in which people look filthy and miserable will be referred to as the 'real Africa', and you want that on your dust jacket. Do not feel queasy about this: you are trying to help them to get aid from the West. The biggest taboo in writing about Africa is to describe or show dead or suffering white people.

Animals, on the other hand, must be treated as well rounded, complex characters. They speak (or grunt while tossing their manes proudly) and have names, ambitions and desires. They also have family values: *see how lions teach their children?* Elephants are caring, and are good feminists or dignified patriarchs. So are gorillas. Never, ever say anything negative about an elephant or a gorilla. Elephants may attack people's property, destroy their crops, and even kill them. Always take the side of the elephant. Big cats have public-school accents. Hyenas are fair game and have vaguely Middle Eastern accents. Any short Africans who live in the jungle or desert may be portrayed with good humour (unless they are in conflict with an elephant or chimpanzee or gorilla, in which case they are pure evil).

After celebrity activists and aid workers, conservationists are Africa's most important people. Do not offend them. You need them to invite you to their 30,000-acre game ranch or 'conservation area', and this is the only way you will get to interview the celebrity activist. Often a book cover with a heroic-looking conservationist on it works magic for sales. Anybody white, tanned and wearing khaki who once had a pet antelope or a farm is a conservationist, one who is preserving Africa's rich heritage. When interviewing him or her, do not ask how much funding they have; do not ask how much money they make off their game. Never ask how much they pay their employees.

Readers will be put off if you don't mention the light in Africa. And sunsets, the African sunset is a must. It is always big and red. There is always a big sky. Wide empty spaces and game are critical—Africa is the Land of Wide Empty Spaces. When writing about the plight of flora and fauna, make sure you mention that Africa is overpopulated. When your main character is in a desert or jungle living with indigenous peoples (anybody short) it is okay to mention that Africa has been severely depopulated by Aids and War (use caps).

You'll also need a nightclub called Tropicana, where mercenaries, evil nouveau riche Africans and prostitutes and guerrillas and expats hang out.

Always end your book with Nelson Mandela saying something about rainbows or renaissances. Because you care.

Refer Madness: Writing in an Age of Allusion

Robert Cohen

Here in its entirety is a short story by Kafka, called "The Wish to be a Red Indian":

> If one were only an Indian, instantly alert, and on a racing horse, leaning against the wind, kept on quivering jerkily over the quivering ground, until one shed one's spurs, for there needed no spurs, threw away the reins, for there needed no reins, and hardly saw that the land before one was smoothly shorn heath when horse's neck and head would be already gone.

This sentence, a plaintive and mysterious journey into white space, both expresses and embodies a yearning as physical as it is metaphysical, a yearning typical of its writer and indeed all writers: the wish to be a more natural, less self-conscious being. Or to put it another way, to not be a writer at all. Let's face it, no one's better at writing about not wanting to be a writer than someone who actually *is* a writer, and among writers, no one's better than Kafka, for whom wanting and being are almost never in synch. "The impossibility of not writing, the impossibility of writing German, the impossibility of writing differently," he laments in one letter. "One might also add a fourth impossibility, the impossibility of writing." But then he's hardly alone in this. "Live, live all you can" – the Master himself says, or rather writes -- "it's a mistake not to." Who wouldn't trade in all that fretting irritability, all that envy and eye strain, for the life of an (okay, rather absurdly notional) "Indian", someone wild and natural and sure, plunging head-long through space with such velocity and purpose that no spurs or reins are necessary? Though maybe head-*short* would be more accurate in this case, for the head in Kafka's story, when it finally appears, is something of an afterthought; a head as attenuated from its body as a Giacometti, a head syntactically and existentially, almost Twilight Zone-ishly, "already gone."

We find this same itch for unfettered animal movement -- for existence reduced, or enhanced, to mere body-in-motion, shorn of mental entanglements and obligations and "quivering with the fever of life" -- everywhere in Kafka's work, to say nothing of his life. Take this entry in the Octavo Notebooks: "He leaves the house, he finds himself in the street, a horse is waiting, a servant is holding the stirrup, the ride takes him through an echoing wilderness." Or the narrator of "The Departure," who having ordered his servant to fetch his horse from the stables, is stopped at the gate and asked where he's going. "I don't know," he says, "just out of here, just out of here. Out of here, nothing else, it's the only way I can reach my goal." "So you know your goal?" the servant asks. "Yes," he replies, "I've just told you. Out of here—that's my goal."

But of course one can't *get* out of here in Kafka's world. There may be horses, but they are never ours; there may be Indians, but they are never us; there may be gates that lend access to the Law, but for us they're forever closed. For us there are always shackles, cages, constrictions. We are not pure beings, not whole selves; not animals, not gods. For all the purity of our aspirations we live, as Kafka did, in the middle of things, in a room between other rooms, a self among other selves, in what literary types call a liminal space. Trapped between two realms, the earthly and the heavenly, we're unable to fully inhabit, or escape, either one, but can only gesture longingly in both directions, flailing our useless limbs, like an upended beetle trying to get out of bed. "It's the old joke," Kafka writes. "We hold the world fast and complain that it is holding us."

Which brings me to my subject: our ways of holding the world fast, even in fiction -- e*specially* in fiction – and how, the faster the great world spins, and the smaller, more involuted, more densely thronged with interconnections it feels, the tighter we clutch onto its fabric. And I mean this literally: with the fingers, the very digital instruments, of our hands.

Speaking of digital instruments: it's been pretty well documented by now that this great web we're all caught in and borne up by is changing us every which way, not just how we interact (or don't) but how we read (ditto) and think (ditto). And how do I know this? The same way you do: by power-browsing websites, skimming articles by the likes of Nicholas Carr and Jaron Lanier – or rather skimming articles by *other* writers who have skimmed articles by the likes of Carr and Lanier -- memorizing a fact or two, a quote or two, and interweaving it with my own anecdotal experience and those of friends. This is what passes for "knowledge" now. There's no need to make a moral judgment about this (okay, maybe there *is* a need to make a judgment about this) but those of us who read and write for a living can't help but wonder about the implications -- even if those implications, like the technologies that give rise to them, present a moving target, a machine perpetually on Fast Forward.

Where reading is concerned we all know the liturgy by now, and can recite it by heart like our own gloomy Spenglerian Kol Nidre. *Our Father Our King, we have sinned before you: we've scanned, we've skimmed, we've skipped blithely from link to link and retained nothing; and for most of us the prospect of buying, let alone opening, let alone finishing, the sort of fat three-decker novel – Middlemarch, The Magic Mountain, The Man Who Loved Children – we used to devour almost routinely has become as lonely and remote, as haloed by a nimbus of virtuous nostalgia, as a trip to the moon.*

On the other hand, how could it be otherwise? "We are not only what we read, we are *how* we read," writes the developmental psychologist Maryanne Wolf. Reading is not instinctual; it's learned behavior, and like all learned behavior it effects and to some extent re-shapes the neural circuits in our brains. Studies show that readers of ideograms, for instance, like the Chinese, develop a radically different mental circuitry from those whose written language employs an alphabet. Given that the average American spends eight and a half hours a day in front of a screen, that's a lot of re-wiring going on. No wonder our heads feel so thronged -- like people who spend too much time in the gym, for all our furious running somehow at the end of the day it turns out we haven't quite *gone* anywhere. Meanwhile the screens keep blaring. "When things come at you very fast," Marshall McLuhan once said, "naturally you lose touch with yourself." And, we might add, with "things" too.

It stands to reason, then, that if our reading is changing our thinking too must be changing, and if our thinking is changing then so is both the stuff and the way we write. Or perhaps it's only the pace of change itself that's changing. A century ago Walter Benjamin warned of a menacing new form of communication that was "incompatible with the spirit of story-telling." Information, he said, was the "rustling in the leaves that drives away... the dream-bird that hatches the egg of experience." And if the very machine one writes -- and increasingly, reads -- one's dreamy stories upon is also a roaring, cyclonic leaf-blower? What then? According to Nietzsche, "our writing equipment takes part in the forming of our thoughts." And he should know: once he switched from the pen to the typewriter his own prose rhythms, never exactly temperate to begin with, turned jittery and declarative, full of aphorisms, puns, and staccato proclamations. You can see this on the page, or rather *feel* it on the page, the brutal, clattering force of a new technology seeking and finding expression in thought, rather than the other way around.

Writers of my generation, many of whom wrote their first books on hulking Selectrics, understand this all too well. The days when you'd have no words in your head and yet go on typing anyway, as if riding the wave of some vast, furiously thrumming current. But then came the giddy liberation of those first excursions into "word processing" -- to be relieved of all that laborious re-typing! that interminable cutting and pasting! -- and then, as the futzing and tinkering, the finding and replacing, the Control C's and Control V's grew more and more habitual, the dawning recognition that the great liberator might in fact be only another occupier, with its own ruthless and quietly insidious laws. That the bars of the cell are plastic rather than iron does not make them, in the end, any less confining. Whether it makes them *more* confining is a question well worth asking, or Googling, or typing into one's smart phone, provided of course one *has* a smart phone, which I personally do not.

No, my own phone I'm afraid is a dumb phone - a phone so remedial, so not-gifted and not-talented, so slablike and lethargic and inexpressive, it can barely get it up to ring. My phone has no idea what an app is. It sends no email, it can't read a blog, it plays no music, it has no GPS, and if I hold it up to one of those little squares of frozen static that sit like Rorschach blots beside virtually every material item in America, my phone just stares at it dumbly, breathing through whatever the equivalent of its mouth is. To be fair, at some point no doubt my phone was the very newest, smartest thing, sleek and powerful as a phaser. But I didn't buy it at that point. No, by the time I bought it, the heyday of your basic Samsung clamshell flip-style had long since passed into history, like the rotary dial, the telegraph, and the carrier pigeon before it, which was why I was able to get it so cheap (the primary, in fact *only* factor in my decision) and why the moment they saw it my children laughed and rolled their eyes, as if this was only the latest, most damning evidence of cluelessness in that losing trial, my life.

But never mind. I don't own a smart phone (yet) for a very simple reason: because I know I would abuse it. Because, like most people who cultivate an air of brooding intensity, I am in fact a rather shallow person with lousy concentration and dilettante-ish tendencies. Already I don't so much live my life as *refer* to it. Already each day for me is a Talmudic text, a dense, ever-evolving symbolic narrative that can only be comprehended, or for that matter endured, by a prodigious amount of inter-textual commentary. Nothing for me is ever simply itself, solo and unencumbered; there's always an entourage of references loitering around, emptying the mini-bar and stealing the robes. A raging old man is always a Lear; a big talker always straight out of Bellow; every unhappy family Tolstoyan in its own way. To be sleepy is Oblomovian; to be restless Chatwinian; to be hungry Hamsunian; and the sight of my enormous honker in the mirror, it goes without saying, is positively Gogolesque. In short, there is virtually no element of my conscious life (about my unconscious life it's harder to say; I am unconscious of my unconscious life) that is not contaminated by reference, and I don't even *own* a smart phone yet.

My wife finds all this objectionable not just on the obvious gender grounds (i.e. that it makes me tiresome, boring, and pedantic, like a clerk in a used record store, or a guy who writes into sports blogs) but on a deeper spiritual level as well, in the sense that if I am always comparing, always referring, I am never just *being*. And the person I am never just being, it goes without saying, is myself. No wonder I hate yoga, she thinks. No wonder I don't meditate, or go on Buddhist retreats, or write poetry. Everything that goes on outside my head has a set of corresponding and often much more pressing references inside it, and everything inside it has a set of corresponding and much more pressing references outside it, and so much of the time I am neither here nor there but rather, as Milan Kundera might say, elsewhere.

Case in point: in an ideal world I would not have made reference to Kundera just now, because it sounds so pretentious, especially as I'm only name-checking the *title* of his novel and not even delving into the substance. Then too in an ideal world I would not go on to compare this condition of feeling like one slim, heavily annotated volume in a vast universal library to something out of Borges or Jung, though in truth these do seem like fair comparisons, or in any case inevitable ones. But there you go: there's no way to diagnose this affliction that doesn't succumb to it that much further. The cure is indistinguishable from the disease. No matter how much one struggles to wriggle free, in life and on the page, from the headlock of reference, there's no way out, only further in, submitting to its grip even further, quoting Bellow for instance ("Perhaps, finding oneself lost, one should get loster"), and just generally ransacking the library for references to others who have grappled with this same problem of making reference to others, as if we are all condemned to flop and thrash forever in the same infinitely pliable and inclusive net.

Well, you're thinking, so what? It's the postmodern condition: our heads are full of secondhand data, viral videos, forwarded twitters and tweets. Nothing to be done. Anyway it's not such a terrible affliction in the scheme of things, to have a library vaster than Alexandria's bulging in the pockets of your pants. Access to knowledge, or information anyway, is no longer the preserve of the culturati, the expensively over-educated one percent. Occupy Positively Fourth Street! How can we not get down with that? And if the cost of all this access is that every bullshit remark one advances over dinner gets shot down by some wise guy Googling under the table; or that watching a movie with your teenage son means being peppered by factoids from the IMDB, not just the gross receipts but the AD, the filmography of the second lead, and the name of the catering company that supplied the bagels; or the unsettling suspicion, as you flit from link to link, that someone has a *financial* stake in the crumbs of data you leave behind, that what you assume to be voluntary behavior is in fact highly manipulated, that, as Carr puts it, "it's in their economic interest to drive us to distraction"…well, so be it. A small price to pay. And if it's maybe a little harder than it used to be to concentrate on, well, *any*thing -- to locate, amidst so much refracted noise, the timid sonar-beam of your own personal signal, your own original and essential truth -- so be that too. Every revolution has its winners and losers. Besides, notions like "personal" and "original", absent the usual ironic air quotes, haven't aged very well, have they? They're faded and baggy as old tee-shirts: you can hardly go out in them anymore. No, even irony is looking a bit shopworn these days. Irony after all is only a gloss on something, not the thing itself. Like Google, it blurs the line between knowingness and knowledge, feeds upon pre-existing sources that it vaguely cheapens and diminishes along the way.

And if nothing is just itself, but only a link that points us somewhere else, where does it end? Or *should* it end? After all, what's so great about originality anyway? The energies of evolution, in art as in life, are cyclical, interconnecting, co-dependent; we progress, if at all, not by leaps and bounds but tiny incremental variations. "Nothing goes away," Thomas Pynchon once wrote, "it only changes form."

Pynchon himself was never shy, early on, about name-checking his influences, be they Henry Adams, Dashiell Hammett, the Beats, or, in one jauntily anachronistic hat-tip midway through Gravity's Rainbow, Ishmael Reed. Like *V*'s Herbert Stencil, he'll strew discrete bits of referential data around like so many clues at a crime scene, then make us do the detective work of connecting the dots -- all the while hinting that the joke is on us, that no one stands behind the curtain, no one's working the levers; that confronted with the blank screen of the case that is the world, we are forever projecting onto it our own plots and conspiracies, our own constellated reference points, our own fiercely home-spun webs. Better an imagined coherence, even a paranoid one, than no coherence at all. Hence it's no surprise to discover the tracks of other writers all over V 's shifting sands, like that massive big-foot, William Gaddis' *The Recognitions* -- a novel all about the virtues, or necessities rather, of copying Old Masters. For all the farcical camouflage of its thousand pages, the book delivers its theme brazenly in a droll bit of shorthand: "*Orignlty not inventn bt snse of recall, recgntion, pattrns alrdy thr.*"

Half a century later, from the far side of the postmodern age, this view of originality as more discovery than invention, more systemic wave than idiosyncratic particle, seems so ubiquitous, so culturally assimilated -- so unoriginal in short – it's almost boring to talk about. "I wonder if this thing we call originality," David Mitchell posits in a recent interview, "isn't an electric motor powered by the two poles off the already done and the new twist, or the familiar and the far-out." If that sounds a bit mechanistic and dream-factoryish, Mitchell sees no need to apologize: like Pynchon, or his more obvious influence Murukami, he delights in conflating high and low cultural forms, as happy to plunder from Captain Jack Sparrow or The Matrix as from Nabokov, Borges, or Calvino. Indeed, reading *Cloud Atlas*, with its zigzagging narratives, its gorgeously over-stuffed set-pieces and its declamatory rhetorical flourishes, is like being locked in the wardrobe closet of some insanely well-funded provincial theater company. Let's see, here's a sea captain's hat, here's a tweedy English jacket, a pair of leather pants from San Francisco, a silken waistcoat in the Ottoman style, some sort of fusiony, futuristic kimono... The presence of so many florid costumes, so many disparate narrative forms in a single work (sea story, dystopian sci-fi, seventies political thriller, and others) creates its own dizzying centrifugal effect(s). It's as if Mitchell has set out to trump Samuel Goldwyn's maxim, cited approvingly in the same interview: "Let's have some new clichés."

Given the breadth of his historical reach; the acuity and supple facility of his prose; the boldness of his refusal to cover his own source-tracks – for *Cloud Atlas* is riddled with attention-seizing references to Melville, Defoe, Huxley, Orwell, Thornton Wilder, and many other novels, including other *David Mitchell* novels -- and the giddy relish with which he spins his genre-hopping, borderline-pulpy yarns, Mitchell may turn out to be the closest thing we have to a representative writer for this globalized age, in that he makes this vast unsettling interconnectivity of ours both subject and method, both engine and fuel. Or perhaps it's that he portrays this as a *good* thing. ("Separateness, that's what went wrong... Everything withholding itself from everything else... Everything vain, asserting itself": Gaddis again). Characters in Mitchell tend to move like clouds across spatial and temporal and personal lines, drifting along pre-existent songlines towards memory and myth, deeply inlaid species codes. For all the violence and melodrama he offers an affirmative vision, the bright side of the Pynchonian moon. Here too is a flickering projection of coherence. And hasn't it always been our lot, as writers, readers, and human selves, to warm our hands by the same fires, sharing the same source materials, passing along the same tribal myths and narrative codes, all of us living, for better and for worse, in the same tent city, the same farflung, shimmering web? If so, then artists are only embroidering a fabric that already exists.

As Emerson puts it: "Old and new make the warp and woof of every moment. There is no thread that is not a twist of these two strands. By necessity, by proclivity, and by delight, we all quote."

Upon examination, of course, every strand of the old turns out to be more of a thickened braid, a double or triple helix in its own right, as I have just demonstrated for example by quoting Emerson in a way that implies I have a volume of his essays open beside me, when in truth I have copied this quote not from Emerson but from Jonathan Lethem's ingenious *Harpers* piece, "The Ecstasy of Influence" -- an essay that at once documents, investigates, and, because it's comprised almost entirely of quotes from other writers, formally embodies an "open source" approach to art. And I'd be willing to bet that Lethem, as he wrote, didn't have Emerson open beside *him* either.

It's all fair use, in other words -- in fact in *those* words -- and that's fine. Same as it ever was. Plagiarism, as plagiarists are eager to remind us, is a fairly recent concept. The ancient poets copied freely, often verbatim and without citation, recasting existing works to suit the poet's purpose and taste. The Hebrews ripped off the Canaanites. Virgil ripped off Homer, Dante ripped off Virgil, Matthew and Luke ripped off Mark; Shakespeare ripped off Plutarch, Eliot ripped off Shakespeare, Dylan rips off everybody, and my sweet lord, George Harrison ripped off the Chiffons. And so it goes. It's an eternal, self-renewing process, the great daisy chain of literary influence. Or to phrase it less romantically, *Language is the common whore whom each writer tries to make his own bitch.*

That's a direct quote from Auden by the way, though it pains me to cite him in this context, as I haven't *read* Auden in years, and so consequently have no idea how and where I came by this quote, which is therefore come to think of it not direct at all. Maybe it's not even from Auden. It sounds more like Mickey Spillane. If only I owned a smart phone I could tell you for sure. Though surely by now you have long since gotten your own smart phones out and could just as easily tell *me*.

Still, whatever we want to call this tradition -- fair use, open source, public commons, digital sampling, everything up for grabs and equally viable -- how such referential sampling plays out over time for the working artist, let alone that beleaguered, almost comically antiquated species, the individual in society, whether it opens outward to a rich world of dizzying possibilities or flattens into a shallow, enervating plane of the already-done, remains, to me anyway, yet another open question.

When I talk about flattening I have in mind someone like John Leonard, the late book critic, whose gift for referentiality, for going culturally broad as a way of going artistically deep, for turning every review into a swinging cocktail party with himself in the role of maniacally chatty host, is both virtuosic and exhausting. Take for example his Times review of H*arry Potter and the Order of the Phoenix.* First he ushers in the distinguished early arrivals like Tolkien, Joseph Campbell, and C.S. Lewis; then he proceeds down the hall -- by way of Wonderland, Camelot, Brigadoon, Macondo, and Oz -- to the library, where William Blake, George Orwell, Jacques Lacan, Lewis Carroll, Cyrus of Herodotus, St. John of the Cross, St. Teresa of Avila, the Old Testament, the New Testament, the Hindu Krishna, the Epic of Gilgamesh, and the Song of Roland await. Along the way he stops to chat with some boisterous, colorfully-dressed old friends: Mary Poppins, the Brothers Grimm, Scheherazade, Hercules, Godzilla, Sinbad the Sailor, the Flying Dutchman, Luke Skywalker, T. H. White, *Snow* White, Peter Pan, Caliban, Superman, and Doctor Who. And wait, did we leave out Judith Krantz? Because you can be sure Leonard didn't. How could we leave out Judith freaking Krantz?

While it's easy, and probably advisable, to make fun of Leonard's promiscuous way with the Caps key, he's hardly unique. The entire oeuvre of George Steiner, as John Simon once said, "reads like a university library card catalogue hit by a tornado." This is more or less what critics do with books: they fling other books at the page like so much spaghetti and see what sticks. Never mind that half or more of such references, as any honest writer will concede, are unintentional; the reader gets the final say. "Inter-textuality, like all aspects of literary reception, is ultimately located in reading practice," writes the theorist Don Fowler. "Meaning is realized at the point of reception, and what counts as an intertext and what one does with it depends on the reader." The very form of such criticism as Leonard's reminds us that connectivity is the reader's province, that no work is ever truly singular, but demands to be read in the constellated lights of every other work, lights it both absorbs and then atomizes in myriad directions, towards works already written and those far off in the dark matter, waiting to emerge.

Borges, in his marvelous essay "Kafka and His Precursors", takes this idea, as he takes everything, one step further in the direction of the cosmic, unfurling a multi-dimensional map of literary influence where the streets are not one-way or two-way but rather an infinite series of forking paths. "The fact is that each writer creates his precursors. His work modifies our conception of the past, as it will modify the future. In this correlation, the identity or plurality of men doesn't matter." Like Gaddis and Mitchell, Borges, the blind librarian, seeks to undermine if not negate our conventional notions of originality -- even as he also seeks to rescue it through the even *more* original, *more* creative act of referential reading.

Let's pause here to concede the obvious: novels have *always* depended upon reference, both inter-textual, to the novels that precede them, and extra-, to the great, teeming world beyond their bindings. Think of Stendhal's Paris, Dickens' (or Zadie Smith's) London, Doestoevsky's Petersburg, Joyce's Dublin, Paley's New York, Bellow's Chicago...these are not strictly inventions, but rather *loosely* inventions, their atmospheres dense with soot-particles of the "real", references to the pre-existing, the unalterable and uninventable, towards which they are often deferential to the point of fetishistic. Illusion and allusion go hand in hand. Even a quaint old convention like the name dash (as in "He wrote to Madame G—" or "That day she made the long train journey to S---"), manages to conflate realism and artifice in such a way as to heighten and subvert any distinction, suggesting at once the inside authority of personal discretion (you and I both know who I'm really talking about here, so why spell it out) and the impersonal mystery of art (why *not* spell it out?). "I hate things all fiction," Byron wrote. "There should always be some foundation of fact for the most airy fabric - and pure invention is but the talent of a liar." Generally the line between what goes on inside the margins and what goes on outside is porous at best; at worst it's so thin as to barely register. To straddle this line is to generate either a peculiarly artful form of narrative tension (as in

George Perec's stunning Holocaust work W, or the Mystery of Childhood, with its alternating planes of poorly-remembered facts and allegorical invention), or a kind of narcissistic blur. Or, in the case of someone like Marguerite Duras -- whose narrators, even as they fumble in a memory-fog towards the window of public realities, keep bumping into the mirror of their own artifices -- both. "Yes, it's the big funereal car that's in my books…a Morris Leon Bollee. The black Lancia at French embassy in Calcutta hasn't yet made its entrance on the literary scene."

It seems unlikely that this was what Byron had in mind. Nor would he approve in all likelihood of fiction like Kafka's or Beckett's, which is almost mystically purged of fact, shorn of anything that resembles a foundation, other than the grave. And yet it's doubtful that writers on the other, more material end of the spectrum, who litter their work with the proper nouns of the day, would charm him much either. How much purity is too much, in short, and how much not enough? How much of our reading of Don Quixote, say, depends upon some acquaintance with the chivalric romances its lampooning? What about Madame Bovary? What about Virginia Woolf? If the moderns require us to revisit the very pre-moderns from which they're radically departing, and high-modernist strategies like parody and myth (think of Ulysses, of Lolita) draw their fullest power and extension from systematic reference to bodies of extra-textual material, and then postmodernism comes along and gleefully rides that horse into the sunset, or rather *towards* the sunset…for somehow we never quite make it to the terminal point, do we, the point beyond which one cannot turn back, but invariably wind up stranded in that noisy, brightly-lit cul-de-sac we call pastiche….how will we ever get free of the library, out into the muck and mess of the day?

Pastiche of course gets a bad rap these days – "parody without any of parody's ulterior motives," Frederic Jameson calls it, "amputated of the satiric impulse, devoid of laughter" -- as Las Vegas gets a bad rap, and yet both have their appeal, as well as a certain cultural inevitability. "Ironically," Kurt Anderson remarks,

> "new technology has reinforced the nostalgic cultural gaze: now that we have instant universal access to every old image and recorded sound, the future

has arrived and it's all about dreaming of the past. Our culture's primary M.O. now consists of promiscuously and sometimes compulsively reviving and rejiggering old forms. It's the rare "new" cultural artifact that doesn't seem a lot like a cover version of something we've seen or heard before. Which means the very idea of datedness has lost the power it possessed during most of our lifetimes."

Still, even as we decry the practice of cannibalizing the museum, it's hard to resist the opportunities it offers for serious play, for trying on masks and appropriating genres in a way that both transgresses and transforms them. "Writers signify upon each other's texts," says Henry Louis Gates, "by rewriting the received textual tradition." We have become so accustomed to this signifying in the arts -- in music, in painting and photography, in such cinematic pastiche-meisters as Todd Haynes, the Coen Brothers, and Quentin Tarantino -- we may no longer even be conscious of it as such; which may be why recent novels have had to work extra hard to call attention to it. I'm thinking of novels like Percival Everett's Erasure, which works off Ralph Ellison; in Mat Johnson's Pym, which riffs on Poe; in Arthur Phillips' The Tragedy of Arthur, with its gleefully extended non-parody of Shakespeare, and Benjamin Markovits' Byron-soaked Childish Loves, and many others. Sometimes it seems like *everything* is pastiche, that nothing in our culture is immune to infection by that corrosive germ. These are the moments that make us almost literally sick. When no equal-and-opposite force is deployed against it, referentiality, for all its aesthetic justifications, comes off as mere glorified cleverness, so much smart-alecky dick-swinging: a low-impact sport where the brainiacs and bookworms finally get picked first. Of course sometimes it's nice just to be on a team. The anxiety and loneliness of creation makes us long for sociability, for commonality, for historical continuity, some wider safety net for the self as it plunges towards the void of the page. Anyway Benjamin knew what he was talking about: there's no going back. Like it or not, the tide of information isn't likely to recede. One must find a way not to drown but to swim. Our Grand Allusions should be not destination but departure point, not discovery but "recogntn." What forms this will or should take is impossible to predict in anything but their multiplicity, their flexibility, their spirit of "impure invention". Not the lie of pure originality, but not the echo chamber of mere secondhand reference either. As Valery puts it: "Nothing more original, nothing more unique than to feed off others. But they must be digested -- the lion achieves his form by assimilating sheep."

All of which takes us a long way from Kafka's Red Indian, that pure, untrammeled being. Or does it? Maybe in the end Kafka is just too severe, too much the perfectionist, too willing to spurn the communal enterprise, with its contaminations and compromises, in art as in life. None of us, in the end, actually *are* Red Indians. We're more like the mouse folk who listen to Josephine, or the crowd that files by the Hunger Artist's cage -- transfixed, for a while anyway, by admiration for that very purity we can neither achieve nor maintain -- before we return to the stream of human traffic he calls the *Verkeh*. But then even Kafka's story is not entirely reference-free. It too directs us outward, first to whatever a "red Indian" might be, and then to whatever historical context might help us comprehend how and why a finicky neurotic German-writing Jew in the middle of the Austro-Hungarian empire might refer to such a figure. If ours is not an age of pure expression, neither was Kafka's. No age is conducive to purity, which is probably why we're always longing for it. (Didn't Minimalism flourish in the 1960s?). So even if it's true that accelerated access to data of every kind will continue to tip the balance even further from invention to fact, or to the kind of heavily-Googled works of social realist fiction that depend upon technology to provide the weapons they will use (feebly, for the most part) to attack it; and even if it's true that as a consequence we are now exploring the outer reaches or lower depths of referentiality, wondering how far the rubber band might stretch before it snaps; we are still impelled onward, I would argue, by the same old longings, the same old methods. Still using language like feelers, inching our way towards the edge beyond which language can't go, the happiness (as they say) that writes white.

The Nature of the Fun

David Foster Wallace

The best metaphor I know of for being a fiction writer is in Don DeLillo's "Mao II," where he describes a book-in-progress as a kind of hideously damaged infant that follows the writer around, forever crawling after the writer (dragging itself across the floor of restaurants where the writer's trying to eat, appearing at the foot of the bed first thing in the morning, etc.), hideously defective, hydrocephalic and noseless and flipper-armed and incontinent and retarded and dribbling cerebo-spinal fluid out of its mouth as it mewls and blurbles and cries out to the writer, wanting love, wanting the very thing its hideousness guarantees it'll get: the writer's complete attention.

The damaged-infant trope is perfect because it captures the mix of repulsion and love the fiction writer feels for something he's working on. The fiction always comes out so horrifically defective, so hideous a betrayal of all your hopes for it - a cruel and repellent caricature of the perfection of its conception - yes, understand: grotesque because imperfect. And yet it's yours, the infant is, it's you, and you love it and dandle it and wipe the cerebro-spinal fluid off its slack chin with the cuff of the only clean shirt you have left (you have only one clean shirt left because you haven't done laundry in like three weeks because finally this one chapter or character seems like it's finally trembling on the edge of coming together and working and you're terrified to spend any time on anything other than working on it because if you look away for a second you'll lose it, dooming the whole infant to continued hideousness). And but so you love the damaged infant and pity it and care for it; but also you hate it - hate it - because it's deformed, repellent, because something grotesque has happened to it in the parturition from head to page; hate it because its deformity is your deformity (since if you were a better fiction writer your infant would of course look like one of those babies in catalogue ads for infant wear, perfect and pink and cerebro-spinally continent) and its every hideous incontinent breath is a devastating indictment of you, on all levels...and so you want it dead, even as you dote and wipe it and dandle it and sometimes even apply CPR when it seems like its own grotesqueness has blocked its breath and it might die altogether.

The whole thing's all very messed up and sad, but simultaneously it's also tender and moving and noble and cool - it's a genuine relationship, of a sort - and even at the height of its hideousness the damaged infant somehow touches and awakens what you suspect are some of the very best parts of you: maternal parts, dark ones. You love your infant very much. And you want others to love it, too, when the time finally comes for the damaged infant to go out and face the world.

Foolish or fooling?

So you're in a bit of a dicey position: You love the infant and you want others to love it but that means that you hope others won't see it correctly. You want to sort of fool people; you want them to see as perfect what you in your heart know is a betrayal of all perfection.

Or else you don't want to fool these people; what you want is you want them to see and love a lovely, miraculous, perfect, ad-ready infant and to be right, correct, in what they see and feel. You want to be terribly wrong, you want the damaged infant's hideousness to turn out to have been nothing but your own weird delusion or hallucination. But that'd mean you were crazy; you have seen, been stalked by, and recoiled from hideous deformities that in fact (others persuade you) aren't there at all. Meaning you're at least a couple of fries short of a Happy Meal, surely. But worse: It'd also mean you see and despise hideousness in a thing you made (and love), in your spawn and in certain ways you.

And this last, best hope - this'd represent something way worse than just very bad parenting; it'd be a terrible kind of self-assault, almost self-torture. But that's still what you most want: to be completely, insanely, suicidally wrong.

Fun where you find it

But it's still a lot of fun. Don't get me wrong. As to the nature of that fun, I keep remembering this strange little story I heard in Sunday school when I was about the size of a fire hydrant. It takes place in China or Korea or someplace like that. It seems there was this old farmer outside a village in the hill country who worked his farm with only his son and his beloved horse. One day the horse, who was not only beloved but vital to the labor-intensive work on the farm, picked the lock on his corral or whatever and ran off into the hills. All the old farmer's friends came around to exclaim what bad luck this was. The farmer only shrugged and said, "Good luck, bad luck, who knows?" A couple days later the beloved horse returned from the hills in the company of a whole priceless herd of wild horses, and the farmer's friends all come around to congratulate him on what good luck the horse's escape turned out to be. "Good luck, bad luck, who knows?" is all the farmer says in reply, shrugging. The farmer now strikes me as a bit Yiddish-sounding for an old Chinese farmer, but this is how I remember it. But so the farmer and his son set about breaking the wild horses, and one of the horses bucks the son off his back with such wild force that the son breaks his leg. And here come the friends to commiserate with the farmer and curse the bad luck that had ever brought these accursed horses onto the farm. The old farmer just shrugs and says, "Good luck, bad luck, who knows?" A few days later the Imperial Sino-Korean Army or something like that comes marching through the village, conscripting every able-bodied male between like 10 and 60 for cannon-fodder for some hideously bloody conflict that's apparently brewing, but when they see the son's broken leg, they let him off on some sort of feudal 4F, and instead of getting shanghaied the son stays on the farm with the old farmer. Good luck? Bad luck?

This is the sort of parabolic straw you cling to as you struggle with the issue of fun, as a writer. In the beginning, when you first start out trying to write fiction, the whole endeavor's about fun. You don't expect anybody else to read it. You're writing almost wholly to get yourself off. To enable your own fantasies and deviant logics and to escape or transform parts of yourself you don't like. And it works - and it's terrific fun. Then, if you have good luck and people seem to like what you do, and you actually start to get paid for it, and get to see your stuff professionally typeset and bound and blurbed and reviewed and even (once) being read on the a.m. subway by a pretty girl you don't even know it seems to make it even more fun. For a while. Then things start to get complicated and confusing, not to mention scary. Now you feel like you're writing for other people, or at least you hope so. You're no longer writing just to get yourself off, which - since any kind of masturbation is lonely and hollow - is probably good. But what replaces the onanistic motive? You've found you very much enjoy having your writing liked by people, and you find you're extremely keen to have people like the new stuff you're doing. The motive of pure personal starts to get supplanted by the motive of being liked, of having pretty people you don't know like you and admire you and think you're a good writer. Onanism gives way to attempted seduction, as a motive. Now, attempted seduction is hard work, and its fun is offset by a terrible fear of rejection. Whatever "ego" means, your ego has now gotten into the game. Or maybe "vanity" is a better word. Because you notice that a good deal of your writing has now become basically showing off, trying to get people to think you're good. This is understandable. You have a great deal of yourself on the line, writing - your vanity is at stake. You discover a tricky thing about fiction writing; a certain amount of vanity is necessary to be able to do it all, but any vanity above that certain amount is lethal. At some point you find that 90% of the stuff you're writing is motivated and informed by an overwhelming need to be liked. This results in shitty fiction. And the shitty work must get fed to the wastebasket, less because of any sort of artistic integrity than simply because shitty work will cause you to be disliked. At this point in the evolution of writerly fun, the very thing that's always motivated you to write is now also what's motivating you to feed your writing to the wastebasket. This is a paradox and a kind of double-bind, and it can keep you stuck inside yourself for months or even years, during which period you wail and gnash and rue your bad luck and wonder bitterly where all the fun of the thing could have gone.

Try to remember

The smart thing to say, I think, is that the way out of this bind is to work your way somehow back to your original motivation - fun. And, if you can find your way back to fun, you will find that the hideously unfortunate double-bind of the late vain period turns out really to have been good luck for you. Because the fun you work back to has been transfigured by the extreme unpleasantness of vanity and fear, an unpleasantness you're now so anxious to avoid that the fun you rediscover is a way fuller and more large-hearted kind of fun. It has something to do with Work as Play. Or with the discovery that disciplined fun is more than impulsive or hedonistic fun. Or with figuring out that not all paradoxes have to be paralyzing. Under fun's new administration, writing fiction becomes a way to go deep inside yourself and illuminate precisely the stuff you don't want to see or let anyone else see, and this stuff usually turns out (paradoxically) to be precisely the stuff all writers and readers everywhere share and respond to, feel. Fiction becomes a weird way to countenance yourself and to tell the truth instead of being a way to escape yourself or present yourself in a way you figure you will be maximally likable. This process is complicated and confusing and scary, and also hard work, but it turns out to be the best fun there is.

The fact that you can now sustain the fun of writing only by confronting the very same unfun parts of yourself you'd first used writing to avoid or disguise is another paradox, but this one isn't any kind of bind at all. What it is is a gift, a kind of miracle, and compared to it the rewards of strangers' affection is as dust, lint.

Fail Better

Zadie Smith

1 The tale of Clive

I want you to think of a young man called Clive. Clive is on a familiar literary mission: he wants to write the perfect novel. Clive has a lot going for him: he's intelligent and well read; he's made a study of contemporary fiction and can see clearly where his peers have gone wrong; he has read a good deal of rigorous literary theory - those elegant blueprints for novels not yet built - and is now ready to build his own unparalleled house of words. Maybe Clive even teaches novels, takes them apart and puts them back together. If writing is a craft, he has all the skills, every tool. Clive is ready. He clears out the spare room in his flat, invests in an ergonomic chair, and sits down in front of the blank possibility of the Microsoft Word program. Hovering above his desktop he sees the perfect outline of his platonic novel - all he need do is drag it from the ether into the real. He's excited. He begins.

Fast-forward three years. Somehow, despite all Clive's best efforts, the novel he has pulled into existence is not the perfect novel that floated so tantalisingly above his computer. It is, rather, a poor simulacrum, a shadow of a shadow. In the transition from the dream to the real it has shed its aura of perfection; its shape is warped, unrecognisable. Something got in the way, something almost impossible to articulate. For example, when it came to fashioning the character of the corrupt Hispanic government economist, Maria Gomez, who is so vital to Clive's central theme of corruption within American identity politics, he found he needed something more than simply "the right words" or "knowledge about economists". Maria Gomez effectively proves his point about the deflated American dream, but in other, ineffable, ways she seems not quite to convince as he'd hoped. He found it hard to get into her silk blouse, her pencil skirt - even harder to get under her skin. And then, later, trying to describe her marriage, he discovered that he wanted to write cleverly and aphoristically about "Marriage" with a capital M far more than he wanted to describe Maria's particular marriage, which, thinking of his own marriage, seemed suddenly a monumentally complex task, particularly if his own wife, Karina, was going to read it. And there are a million other little examples ... flaws that are not simply flaws of language or design, but rather flaws of ... what? Him? This thought bothers him for a moment. And then another, far darker thought comes. Is it possible that if he were only the reader, and not the writer, of this novel, he would think it a failure?

Clive doesn't wallow in such thoughts for long. His book gets an agent, his agent gets a publisher, his novel goes out into the world. It is well received. It turns out that Clive's book smells like literature and looks like literature and maybe even, intermittently, feels like literature, and after a while Clive himself has almost forgotten that strange feeling of untruth, of self-betrayal, that his novel first roused in him. He becomes not only a fan of his own novel, but its great defender. If a critic points out an overindulgence here, a purple passage there, well, then Clive explains this is simply what he intended. It was all to achieve a certain effect. In fact, Clive doesn't mind such criticism: nit-picking of this kind feels superficial compared to the bleak sense he first had that his novel was not only not good, but not true. No one is accusing him of so large a crime. The critics, when they criticise, speak of the paintwork and brickwork of the novel, a bad metaphor, a tedious denouement, and are confident he will fix these little mistakes next time round. As for Maria Gomez, everybody agrees that she is just as you'd imagine a corrupt Hispanic government economist in a pencil skirt to be. Clive is satisfied and vindicated. He begins work on a sequel.

2 The craft that defies craftsmanship

That is the end of the tale of Clive. Its purpose was to suggest that somewhere between a critic's necessary superficiality and a writer's natural dishonesty, the truth of how we judge literary success or failure is lost. It is very hard to get writers to speak frankly about their own work, particularly in a literary market where they are required to be not only writers, but also hucksters selling product. It is always easier to depersonalise the question. In preparation for this essay I emailed many writers (under the promise of anonymity) to ask how they judge their own work. One writer, of a naturally analytical and philosophical bent, replied by refining my simple question into a series of more interesting ones:

I've often thought it would be fascinating to ask living writers: "Never mind critics, what do you yourself think is wrong with your writing? How did you dream of your book before it was created? What were your best hopes? How have you let yourself down?" A map of disappointments - that would be a revelation.

Map of disappointments - Nabokov would call that a good title for a bad novel. It strikes me as a suitable guide to the land where writers live, a country I imagine as mostly beach, with hopeful writers standing on the shoreline while their perfect novels pile up, over on the opposite coast, out of reach. Thrusting out of the shoreline are hundreds of piers, or "disappointed bridges", as Joyce called them. Most writers, most of the time, get wet. Why they get wet is of little interest to critics or readers, who can only judge the soggy novel in front of them. But for the people who write novels, what it takes to walk the pier and get to the other side is, to say the least, a matter of some importance. To writers, writing well is not simply a matter of skill, but a question of character. What does it take, after all, to write well? What personal qualities does it require? What personal resources does a bad writer lack? In most areas of human endeavour we are not shy of making these connections between personality and capacity. Why do we never talk about these things when we talk about books?

It's my experience that when a writer meets other writers and the conversation turns to the fault lines of their various prose styles, then you hear a slightly different language than the critic's language. Writers do not say, "My research wasn't sufficiently thorough" or "I thought Casablanca was in Tunisia" or "I seem to reify the idea of femininity" - at least, they don't consider problems like these to be central. They are concerned with the ways in which what they have written reveals or betrays their best or worst selves. Writers feel, for example, that what appear to be bad aesthetic choices very often have an ethical dimension. Writers know that between the platonic ideal of the novel and the actual novel there is always the pesky self - vain, deluded, myopic, cowardly, compromised. That's why writing is the craft that defies craftsmanship: craftsmanship alone will not make a novel great. This is hard for young writers, like Clive, to grasp at first. A skilled cabinet-maker will make good cabinets, and a skilled cobbler will mend your shoes, but skilled writers very rarely write good books and almost never write great ones. There is a rogue element somewhere - for convenience's sake we'll call it the self, although, in less metaphysically challenged times, the "soul" would have done just as well. In our public literary conversations we are squeamish about the connection between selves and novels. We are repelled by the idea that writing fiction might be, among other things, a question of character. We like to think of fiction as the playground of language, independent of its originator. That's why, in the public imagination, the confession "I did not tell the truth" signifies failure when James Frey says it, and means nothing at all if John Updike says it. I think that fiction writers know different. Though we rarely say it publicly, we know that our fictions are not as disconnected from our selves as you like to imagine and we like to pretend. It is this intimate side of literary failure that is so interesting; the ways in which writers fail on their own terms: private, difficult to express, easy to ridicule, completely unsuited for either the regulatory atmosphere of reviews or the objective interrogation of seminars, and yet, despite all this, true.

3 What writers know

First things first: writers do not have perfect or even superior knowledge about the quality or otherwise of their own work - God knows, most writers are quite deluded about the nature of their own talent. But writers do have a different kind of knowledge than either professors or critics. Occasionally it's worth listening to. The insight of the practitioner is, for better or worse, unique. It's what you find in the criticism of Virginia Woolf, of Iris Murdoch, of Roland

Barthes. What unites those very different critics is the confidence with which they made the connection between personality and prose. To be clear: theirs was neither strictly biographical criticism nor prescriptively moral criticism, and nothing they wrote was reducible to the childish formulations "only good men write good books" or "one must know a man's life to understand his work". But neither did they think of a writer's personality as an irrelevance. They understood style precisely as an expression of personality, in its widest sense. A writer's personality is his manner of being in the world: his writing style is the unavoidable trace of that manner. When you understand style in these terms, you don't think of it as merely a matter of fanciful syntax, or as the flamboyant icing atop a plain literary cake, nor as the uncontrollable result of some mysterious velocity coiled within language itself. Rather, you see style as a personal necessity, as the only possible expression of a particular human consciousness. Style is a writer's way of telling the truth. Literary success or failure, by this measure, depends not only on the refinement of words on a page, but in the refinement of a consciousness, what Aristotle called the education of the emotions.

4 Tradition versus the individual talent

But before we go any further along that track we find TS Eliot, that most distinguished of critic-practitioners, standing in our way. In his famous essay of 1919, "Tradition and the Individual Talent", Eliot decimated the very idea of individual consciousness, of personality, in writing. There was hardly any such thing, he claimed, and what there was, was not interesting. For Eliot the most individual and successful aspects of a writer's work were precisely those places where his literary ancestors asserted their immortality most vigorously. The poet and his personality were irrelevant, the poetry was everything; and the poetry could only be understood through the glass of literary history. That essay is written in so high church a style, with such imperious authority, that even if all your affective experience as a writer is to the contrary, you are intimidated into believing it. "Poetry," says Eliot, "is not a turning loose of emotion, but an escape from emotion; it is not the expression of personality, but an escape from personality." "The progress of an artist," says Eliot, "is a continual self-sacrifice, a continual extinction of personality." These credos seem so impersonal themselves, so disinterested, that it is easy to forget that young critic-practitioners make the beds they wish to lie in, and it was in Eliot's interest - given the complexity and scandals of his private life and his distaste for intrusion - ruthlessly to separate the personal from the poetry. He was so concerned with privacy that it influences his terminology: everywhere in that essay there is the assumption that personality amounts to simply the biographical facts of one's life - but that is a narrow vision. Personality is much more than autobiographical detail, it's our way of processing the world, our way of being, and it cannot be artificially removed from our activities; it is our way of being active.

Eliot may have been ruthlessly impersonal in his writing in the superficial sense (if by that we mean he did not reveal personal details, such as the tricky fact that he had committed his wife to an asylum), but never was a man's work more inflected with his character, with his beliefs about the nature of the world. As for that element of his work that he puts forward as a model of his impersonality - a devotion to tradition - such devotion is the very definition of personality in writing. The choices a writer makes within a tradition - preferring Milton to Moliere, caring for Barth over Barthelme - constitute some of the most personal information we can have about him.

There is no doubt that Eliot's essay, with its promise to "halt at the frontiers of metaphysics or mysticism", is a brilliant demarcation of what is properly within the remit of, as he puts it, "the responsible person interested in poetry". It lays out an entirely reasonable boundary between what we can and cannot say about a piece of writing without embarrassing ourselves. Eliot was honest about wanting both writing and criticism to approach the condition of a science; he famously compared a writer to a piece of finely filiated platinum introduced into a chamber containing oxygen and sulphur dioxide. This analogy has proved a useful aspiration for critics. It has allowed them to believe in the writer as catalyst, entering into a tradition, performing an act of meaningful recombination, and yet leaving no trace of himself, or at least none the critic need worry himself with. Eliot's analogy freed critics to do the independent, radically creative, non- biographical criticism of which they had long dreamt, and to which they have every right. For writers, however, Eliot's analogy just won't do. Fiction writing is not an objective science and writers have selves as well as traditions to understand and assimilate. It is certainly very important, as Eliot argues, that writers should foster an understanding of the cultures and the books of the past, but they also unavoidably exist within the garden of the self and this, too, requires nurture and development. The self is not like platinum - it leaves traces all over the place. Just because Eliot didn't want to talk about it, doesn't mean it isn't there.

5 Writing as self-betrayal

Back to my simple point, which is that writers are in possession of "selfhood", and that the development or otherwise of self has some part to play in literary success or failure. This shameful fact needn't trouble the professor or the critic, but it is naturally of no little significance to writers themselves. Here is the poet Adam Zagajewski, speaking of The Self, in a poem of the same title:

> It is small and no more visible than a cricket
> in August. It likes to dress up, to masquerade,
> as all dwarves do. It lodges between
> granite blocks, between serviceable
> truths. It even fits under
> a bandage, under adhesive. Neither custom officers
> nor their beautiful dogs will find it. Between
> hymns, between alliances, it hides itself.

To me, writing is always the attempted revelation of this elusive, multifaceted self, and yet its total revelation - as Zagajewski suggests - is a chimerical impossibility. It is impossible to convey all of the truth of all our experience. Actually, it's impossible to even know what that would mean, although we stubbornly continue to have an idea of it, just as Plato had an idea of the forms. When we write, similarly, we have the idea of a total revelation of truth, but cannot realise it. And so, instead, each writer asks himself which serviceable truths he can live with, which alliances are strong enough to hold. The answers to those questions separate experimentalists from so-called "realists", comics from tragedians, even poets from novelists. In what form, asks the writer, can I most truthfully describe the world as it is experienced by this particular self? And it is from that starting point that each writer goes on to make their individual compromise with the self, which is always a compromise with truth as far as the self can know it. That is why the most common feeling, upon re-reading one's own work, is Prufrock's: "That is not it at all ... that is not what I meant, at all ..." Writing feels like self-betrayal, like failure.

6 Writing as inauthenticity

Here is another novelist, in another email, answering the question: "How would you define literary failure?"

I was once asked by a high-school student in an audience in Chennai: "Why, sir, are you so eager to please?" That's how I tend to define failure - work done for what Heidegger called "Das Mann", the indeterminate "They" who hang over your shoulder, warping your sense of judgment; what he (not me) would call your authenticity.

That novelist, like me, I suppose like all of us who came of age under postmodernity, is naturally sceptical of the concept of authenticity, especially what is called "cultural authenticity" - after all, how can any of us be more or less authentic than we are? We were taught that authenticity was meaningless. How, then, to deal with the fact that when we account for our failings, as writers, the feeling that is strongest is a betrayal of one's deepest, authentic self?

That sounds very grand: maybe it's better to start at the simplest denomination of literary betrayal, the critic's favourite, the cliche. What is a cliche except language passed down by Das Mann, used and shop-soiled by so many before you, and in no way the correct jumble of language for the intimate part of your vision you meant to express? With a cliche you have pandered to a shared understanding, you have taken a short-cut, you have re-presented what was pleasing and familiar rather than risked what was true and strange. It is an aesthetic and an ethical failure: to put it very simply, you have not told the truth. When writers admit to failures they like to admit to the smallest ones - for example, in each of my novels somebody "rummages in their purse" for something because I was too lazy and thoughtless and unawake to separate "purse" from its old, persistent friend "rummage". To rummage through a purse is to sleepwalk through a sentence - a small enough betrayal of self, but a betrayal all the same. To speak personally, the very reason I write is so that I might not sleepwalk through my entire life. But it is easy to admit that a sentence makes you wince; less easy to confront the fact that for many writers there will be paragraphs, whole characters, whole books through which one sleepwalks and for which "inauthentic" is truly the correct term.

7 Do writers have duties?

All this talk of authenticity, of betrayal, presupposes a duty - an obligation that the writers and readers of literature are under. It is deeply unfashionable to conceive of such a thing as a literary duty; what that might be, how we might fail to fulfil it. Duty is not a very literary term. These days, when we do speak of literary duties, we mean it from the reader's perspective, as a consumer of literature. We are really speaking of consumer rights. By this measure the duty of writers is to please readers and to be eager to do so, and this duty has various subsets: the duty to be clear; to be interesting and intelligent but never wilfully obscure; to write with the average reader in mind; to be in good taste. Above all, the modern writer has a duty to entertain. Writers who stray from these obligations risk tiny readerships and critical ridicule. Novels that submit to a shared vision of entertainment, with characters that speak the recognisable dialogue of the sitcom, with plots that take us down familiar roads and back home again, will always be welcomed. This is not a good time, in literature, to be a curio. Readers seem to wish to be "represented", as they are at the ballot box, and to do this, fiction needs to be general, not particular. In the contemporary fiction market a writer must entertain and be recognisable - anything less is seen as a failure and a rejection of readers.

Personally, I have no objection to books that entertain and please, that are clear and interesting and intelligent, that are in good taste and are not wilfully obscure - but neither do these qualities seem to me in any way essential to the central experience of fiction, and if they should be missing, this in no way rules out the possibility that the novel I am reading will yet fulfil the only literary duty I care about. For writers have only one duty, as I see it: the duty to express accurately their way of being in the world. If that sounds woolly and imprecise, I apologise. Writing is not a science, and I am speaking to you in the only terms I have to describe what it is I persistently aim for (yet fail to achieve) when I sit in front of my computer.

When I write I am trying to express my way of being in the world. This is primarily a process of elimination: once you have removed all the dead language, the second-hand dogma, the truths that are not your own but other people's, the mottos, the slogans, the out-and-out lies of your nation, the myths of your historical moment - once you have removed all that warps experience into a shape you do not recognise and do not believe in - what you are left with is something approximating the truth of your own conception. That is what I am looking for when I read a novel; one person's truth as far as it can be rendered through language. This single duty, properly pursued, produces complicated, various results. It's certainly not a call to arms for the autobiographer, although some writers will always mistake the readerly desire for personal truth as their cue to write a treatise or a speech or a thinly disguised memoir in which they themselves are the hero. Fictional truth is a question of perspective, not autobiography. It is what you can't help tell if you write well; it is the watermark of self that runs through everything you do. It is language as the revelation of a consciousness.

8 We refuse to be each other

A great novel is the intimation of a metaphysical event you can never know, no matter how long you live, no matter how many people you love: the experience of the world through a consciousness other than your own. And I don't care if that consciousness chooses to spend its time in drawing rooms or in internet networks; I don't care if it uses a corner of a Dorito as its hero, or the charming eldest daughter of a bourgeois family; I don't care if it refuses to use the letter e or crosses five continents and two thousand pages. What unites great novels is the individual manner in which they articulate experience and force us to be attentive, waking us from the sleepwalk of our lives. And the great joy of fiction is the variety of this process: Austen's prose will make you attentive in a different way and to different things than Wharton's; the dream Philip Roth wishes to wake us from still counts as sleep if Pynchon is the dream-catcher.

A great piece of fiction can demand that you acknowledge the reality of its wildest proposition, no matter how alien it may be to you. It can also force you to concede the radical otherness lurking within things that appear most familiar. This is why the talented reader understands George Saunders to be as much a realist as Tolstoy, Henry James as much an experimentalist as George Perec. Great styles represent the interface of "world" and "I", and the very notion of such an interface being different in kind and quality from your own is where the power of fiction resides. Writers fail us when that interface is tailored to our needs, when it panders to the generalities of its day, when it offers us a world it knows we will accept having already seen it on the television. Bad writing does nothing, changes nothing, educates no emotions, rewires no inner circuitry - we close its covers with the same metaphysical confidence in the universality of our own interface as we did when we opened it. But great writing - great writing forces you to submit to its vision. You spend the morning reading Chekhov and in the afternoon, walking through your neighbourhood, the world has turned Chekhovian; the waitress in the cafe offers a non- sequitur, a dog dances in the street.

9 The dream of a perfect novel drives writers crazy

There is a dream that haunts writers: the dream of the perfect novel. It is a dream that causes only chaos and misery. The dream of this perfect novel is really the dream of a perfect revelation of the self. In America, where the self is so neatly wedded to the social, their dream of the perfect novel is called "The Great American Novel" and requires the revelation of the soul of a nation, not just of a man … Still I think the principle is the same: on both sides of the Atlantic we dream of a novel that tells the truth of experience perfectly. Such a revelation is impossible - it will always be a partial vision, and even a partial vision is incredibly hard to achieve. The reason it is so hard to think of more than a handful of great novels is because the duty I've been talking about - the duty to convey accurately the truth of one's own conception - is a duty of the most demanding kind. If, every 30 years, people complain that there were only a few first-rate novels published, that's because there were only a few. Genius in fiction has always been and always will be extremely rare. Fact is, to tell the truth of your own conception - given the nature of our mediated world, given the shared and ambivalent nature of language, given the elusive, deceitful, deluded nature of the self - truly takes a genius, truly demands of its creator a breed of aesthetic and ethical integrity that makes one's eyes water just thinking about it.

But there's no reason to cry. If it's true that first-rate novels are rare, it's also true that what we call the literary canon is really the history of the second-rate, the legacy of honourable failures. Any writer should be proud to join that list just as any reader should count themselves lucky to read them. The literature we love amounts to the fractured shards of an attempt, not the monument of fulfilment. The art is in the attempt, and this matter of understanding-that-which-is-outside-of-ourselves using only what we have inside ourselves amounts to some of the hardest intellectual and emotional work you'll ever do. It is a writer's duty. It is also a reader's duty. Did I mention that yet?

10 Note to readers: A novel is a two-way street

A novel is a two-way street, in which the labour required on either side is, in the end, equal. Reading, done properly, is every bit as tough as writing - I really believe that. As for those people who align reading with the essentially passive experience of watching television, they only wish to debase reading and readers. The more accurate analogy is that of the amateur musician placing her sheet music on the stand and preparing to play. She must use her own, hard-won, skills to play this piece of music. The greater the skill, the greater the gift she gives the composer and the composer gives her.

This is a conception of "reading" we rarely hear now. And yet, when you practise reading, when you spend time with a book, the old moral of effort and reward is undeniable. Reading is a skill and an art and readers should take pride in their abilities and have no shame in cultivating them if for no other reason than the fact that writers need you. To respond to the ideal writer takes an ideal reader, the type of reader who is open enough to allow into their own mind a picture of human consciousness so radically different from their own as to be almost offensive to reason. The ideal reader steps up to the plate of the writer's style so that together writer and reader might hit the ball out of the park.

What I'm saying is, a reader must have talent. Quite a lot of talent, actually, because even the most talented reader will find much of the land of literature tricky terrain. For how many of us feel the world to be as Kafka felt it, too impossibly foreshortened to ride from one village to the next? Or can imagine a world without nouns, as Borges did? How many are willing to be as emotionally generous as Dickens, or to take religious faith as seriously as did Graham Greene? Who among us have Zora Neale Hurston's capacity for joy or Douglas Coupland's strong stomach for the future? Who has the delicacy to tease out Flaubert's faintest nuance, or the patience and the will to follow David Foster Wallace down his intricate recursive spirals of thought? The skills that it takes to write it are required to read it. Readers fail writers just as often as writers fail readers. Readers fail when they allow themselves to believe the old mantra that fiction is the thing you relate to and writers the amenable people you seek out when you want to have your own version of the world confirmed and reinforced. That is certainly one of the many things fiction can do, but it's a conjurer's trick within a far deeper magic. To become better readers and writers we have to ask of each other a little bit more.

Credits

with permission of Princeton University Press; permission conveyed through Copyright Clearance Center, Inc.

Davis, Lydia. "Form as a Response to Doubt." Originally published in *HOW(ever)*. Copyright © 1987 by Lydia Davis. Reprinted with permission of the Denise Shannon Literary Agency, Inc. All rights reserved.

Ginzburg, Natalia. "My Vocation" from *The Little Virtues*. Translated by Dick Davis. Published by Arcade Publishing/Carcanet Press Limited, 2013. Reprinted by permission of Arcade Publishing, an imprint of Skyhorse Publishing, Inc., and by permission of Carcanet Press Limited.

James, Henry. "The Art of Fiction." Originally published in *Longman's Magazine*, September 1884.

Jin, Ha. "Deciding to Write in English" from *The Art of the Short Story: 52 Great Authors, Their Best Short Fiction, and Their Insights on Writing*, edited by Dana Gioia and R. S. Gwynn. Published by Pearson Longman, 2006. Reproduced by permission of Ha Jin.

Kiš, Danilo. "Advice to a Young Writer," from *Homo Poeticus: Essays and Interviews*. Translated by Ralph Manheim, Francis Jones, and Michale Henry. Translation copyright © 1995 by Farrar, Straus and Giroux, LLC. Reprinted by permission of Farrar, Straus and Giroux, LLC.

Michaels, Leonard. "Writing About Myself" from *The Essays of Leonard Michaels*. Copyright © 2009 by Katherine Ogden Michaels. Reprinted by permission of Farrar, Straus and Giroux. Originally published in *The Partisan Review* as "The Personal and the Individual." Copyright © 2001 by Leonard Michaels. Reprinted by permission of the author.

Miller, Henry. "Reading in the Toilet" from *The Books in My Life*, copyright © 1969 by New Directions Publishing Corp. Reprinted by permission of New Directions Publishing Corp.

Montaigne, Michel de. "Of Books," from *The Essays of Michel De Montaigne*. Translated by Charles Cotton, edited by William Carew Hazlitt. Published by Reeves and Turner, 1877.

O'Connor, Flannery. "The Nature and Aim of Fiction" from *Mystery and Manners* by Flannery O'Connor, edited by Sally and Robert Fitzgerald. Copyright © 1969 by the Estate of Mary Flannery O'Connor. Reprinted by permission of Farrar, Straus and Giroux, LLC.

Olsen, Tillie. "Silences: When Writers Don't Write," from *Silences* (New York: Delacorte/Seymour Lawrence, 1978), pp. 6-21. Originally published in *Harpers*, October 1965. Reprinted by permission of The Feminist Press.

Ozick, Cynthia. "The Lesson of the Master," copyright © 1982 by Cynthia Ozick. Originally published in *The New York Review of Books*, August 1982. Reprinted by permission of Melanie Jackson Agency, LLC.

Parini, Jay. "Mentors" from *Some Necessary Angels: Essays on Writing and Politics*. Published by Columbia University Press, 1997. Reprinted by permission of Columbia University Press.

Perec, Georges. "Approaches to What?" from *Species of Spaces and Other Pieces*. Translated by John Sturrock (Penguin Classics, 1997, 1999). Translation and notes copyright © John Sturrock, 1997, 1999. Especes d'Espaces copyright © Editions Galilee, 1994. Je suis ne copyright (c) Editions du Seuil, 1994. Penser/Classer copyright (c) Hachette, 1985. La Infra-ordinaire copyright (c) Editions du Sueil, 1989. I.G. copyright (c) Editions du seuil, 1992. Cantarix Sopranica I copryight (c) Editions du Seuil, 1991. Le Voyage d'Hiver copyright (c) Editions du Seuil, 1993.

Porter, Katherine Anne. "My First Speech" from *The Collected Essays and Occasional Writings of Katherine Anne Porter*. Published by Delacorte Press, 1970. Reprinted by permission of the Literary Trust of Katherine Anne Porter.

Notes on Contributors

Julia Alvarez (1950–) is an American poet, novelist, story writer, essayist, and author of books for children, who was born in the Dominican Republic, where she spent her first ten years (before her family fled from Trujullo's dictatorship). Her novels include *How the García Girls Lost Their Accents, In the Time of the Butterflies, In the Name of Salomé* and *Saving the World*. She has been a major voice among Latina writers in the United States over many decades, and won many prizes for her work. She is writer-in-residence at Middlebury College and lives in Vermont.

Donald Barthelme (1931–89) was one of the most beloved and inimitable (if widely imitated) short story writers of the last half century. His experimentalist, often surreal fictions, with their deadpan absurdities, their intuitive, collage-like structures, and their threads of gentle melancholy, remain founding documents of American postmodernism. His books include *Come Back Dr Caligari, City Life, The Dead Father,* and *Overnight to Many Distant Cities,* among many others.

Charles Baxter (1947–) is an American short story writer and novelist. His books include *The Feast of Love, Believers, Saul and Patsy, There's Something I Want You to Do,* and many other works of fiction, as well as *Burning Down the House,* a collection of literary essays. He lives in Minneapolis.

Walter Benjamin (1892–1940) was a major German-Jewish writer known for his contributions to aesthetic and cultural theory. His essays on Goethe, Kafka, Proust, and Baudelaire have been key documents in modern literary criticism.

The Work of Art in the Age of Mechanical Reproduction remains among the most influential essays of the modern era. A Marxist who ventured into Jewish mysticism at times, he died on the Franco-Spanish border while in flight from Nazi persecution.

John Berger (1926–) is an English novelist, essayist, screenwriter, art critic, painter, and poet. He is the author of the Booker Prize-winning novel *G.*, *Corker's Freedom*, the *Into Their Labors* trilogy, and many other works that reflect a wide range of erudition and interest. *Ways of Seeing*, his book of art criticism, written as an accompaniment to a BBC series, is widely used as a university text.

Roberto Bolaño (1953–2003) was a Chilean poet, novelist, and short story writer, widely considered the most significant and influential Latin-American literary figure of his generation. His prolific, often dizzying novels include *The Savage Detectives, By Night in Chile*, and his posthumously published *2666*. For all their extraordinary range they share certain elements in common: an ardor for poetry and poets, a dark, acidic humor, and an extraordinary relish for "the fabric of the particular"—a restless weave of literature and life and politics and aesthetics, a culture not so much of place as of a teeming, multivalent state of mind.

Jorge Luis Borges (1899–1986) was an Argentine poet, essayist, and the author of some of the most influential short stories of the twentieth century, many of them published in *Ficciones* and *The Aleph*. His eccentric, brilliant stories had the flavor of essays, and his essays had the flavor of fiction. He was one of the writers associated with the so-called Boom in Latin-American literature, which brought to the fore a number of major authors, including Gabriel García Márquez, Mario Vargos Llosa, and Pablo Neruda.

Italo Calvino (1923–85) was a major Italian author, the inventive writer of speculative fiction that included stories and fiction. His essays, too, were widely admired for their originality. Among his best-known novels are *Invisible Cities* and *If on a winter's night a traveller*. He began writing stories after the war, beginning with *The Path to the Nest of Spiders*, a fairly conventional collection unlike his later stories, such as those found in *Cosmicomics*. He edited an important collection of Italian folktales, and he remains a key figure in European postwar fiction.

Willa Cather (1873–1947) was an American author known for her strong novels of frontier life in the West, including *O Pioneers!*, *My Ántonia* and *Death Comes to the Archbishop*. She won a Pulitzer Prize in 1922 for her novel of First World War, *One of Ours*. A prolific journalist and essayist, she spent much of her life in New York City, although she remains identified with Nebraska, where she spent part of her childhood. She lived from 1908 until her death with the editor Edith Lewis.

Robert Cohen (1957–) is an American novelist, short story writer, and essayist. His novels include *Inspired Sleep, Amateur Barbarians, The Here and Now* and *The Organ Builder*. Among his awards are a Whiting Writers Award, a Guggenheim Fellowship, and a Lila Wallace Writers Prize. He teaches at Middlebury College.

Edwidge Danticat (1969–) was born in Haiti and immigrated to New York when she was two. Her books include novels such as *Breath, Eyes, Memory*, *Krik? Krak!* and *The Dew Breaker*, and a collection of essays, *Create Dangerously*. Among her many awards, she has received a National Book Critics Circle Award and a MacArthur Fellowship.

Lydia Davis (1947–) is an American writer, known both for her witty, coiled, often elliptical short stories, as well as her translations of Proust, Foucault, and other French authors. Her collections of stories (among them *Break It Down, Varieties of Disturbance, Can't and Won't*) have earned her a number of important awards, including a MacArthur Fellowship, a Man Booker International Prize, and many others.

Natalia Ginzburg (1916–91), an Italian novelist and writer of stories and essays, was born in Sicily and was an active anti-Fascist writer during the thirties and forties. After the war, she came into her own as one of the most original Italian voices of her generation. She was active in politics for many decades, as a Communist for a period, then as an independent, as a member of the Italian parliament in the eighties. Her widely translated works include *Never Must You Ask Me, The Little Virtues*, and *The City and the House.*

Henry James (1843–1916) was an American novelist and writer of short stories who spent much of his adult life in England. He was a major figure of modern fiction, a pioneer in the "international theme," writing about the clash of American and European values. He is the author of classic works such as *Daisy Miller, The Portrait of a Lady, What Maisie Knew, The Ambassadors, The Golden Bowl*, and *The Wings of the Dove.* James was a major critic as well as a writer of fiction, and his prefaces to the collected edition of his novels have been hugely influential in the twentieth century and beyond.

Ha Jin (1956–) is the pen name of Zuefei Jin, born in mainland China shortly before the start of the Cultural Revolution. He taught himself English from a radio course while in the army. In 1985 Jin began his long exile in America, writing poetry and fiction in English at Brandeis, where he completed his doctorate. His first story collection, *Ocean of Words*, won the PEN/Hemingway Award; his novel *Waiting* won both the National Book Award and the PEN/Faulkner. In 2008, he published *The Writer as Migrant*, a collection of essays.

Danilo Kiš (1935–89) was a leading Serbo-Croation novelist, short story writer, and poet who divided his time between Belgrade and Paris. His most well-known books were *A Tomb for Boris Davidovich* and *The Encyclopedia of the Dead.* A prolific writer, his work was deeply influenced by Jorge Luis Borges and Bruno Schultz, whose myth-making and multilayered works were touchstones for his own.

Leonard Michaels (1933–2003) was a New York—born short story writer and essayist. His first two collections, *Going Places* and *I Would Have Saved Them*

If I Could, established him as one of his era's most brilliant and idiosyncratic talents. His edgy, urbane stories with their sharp musical turns and distinctive, Isaac Babel—like diction have been widely anthologized.

Henry Miller (1891–1980) was raised in Brooklyn, moved as a young man to Paris and Greece, and spent his later years in Big Sur, California. He is best known for his experimental, "first person, uncensored, formless—fuck everything!" novel, *Tropic of Cancer.* His many subsequent works include *Black Spring, Sexus, Tropic of Capricorn,* and *The Colossus of Maroussi.* His books were widely banned in his own country for many years; despite and because of this they eventually became, in the 1960s, enormously popular.

Michel de Montaigne (1533–92) was a French essayist, philosopher, and statesman who is considered a pioneer in the genre of the essay. He blended autobiographical asides with keen philosophical speculation and immense erudition and wit. His skepticism, his candor, his freedom from conventional thinking, and his curiosity about what it means to be human combine to make his massive volume of *Essais* no less relevant and surprising and instructive today than they were in his own time.

Flannery O'Connor (1925–64) was an important voice from the American South, known for her essays and, more importantly, two novels and thirty-two stories that at times seemed both grotesque and wildly funny. A devout Roman Catholic, her work had a moral, occasionally even apocalyptic dimension. Among her well-known books of stories were *A Good Man Is Hard to Find* and *Everything that Rises Must Converge.* She won a National Book Award for her fiction in 1972 for *The Complete Stories,* which remains a landmark volume in American literature.

Tillie Olsen (1912–2007) was born in Nebraska and spent most of her life in San Francisco. She was fiercely political, active in the Communist Party in the 1930s, married to a union organizer, and the mother of four children. Her books include *Tell Me a Riddle, Yononndio: From the Thirties,* and the essay collection *Silences,* a meditation upon, among other things, the challenges faced by working class and women writers. She was awarded the Rea Award for the Short Story for a lifetime of outstanding achievement.

Cynthia Ozick (1928–) is an American-Jewish novelist and essayist, and one of the most accomplished, graceful stylists of her time. Her works of fiction include *The Pagan Rabbi and Other Stories, Levitation, The Cannibal Galaxy*, and *The Messiah of Stockholm*; her much-acclaimed essay collections include *Art and Ardor, Metaphor and Memory*, and *Fame and Folly*. Among her awards are the Rea Prize for the Short Story, the PEN/Malamud Award, and three O. Henry prizes.

Jay Parini (1948–) is an American poet, novelist, and biographer. His novels include *The Last Station, Benjamin' Crossing, The Apprentice Lover*, and *The Passages of H.M.* He has written biographies of Steinbeck, Frost, Faulkner, Jesus and Gore Vidal. His poetry includes *New and Collected Poems, 1975-2015*. He has also written various works of nonfiction, such as *Promised Land: Thirteen Books that Changed America* and *Why Poetry Matters*.

Georges Perec (1936–82) was a French novelist and essayist, and a member of the Oulipo group, a loose gathering of European writers using techniques of "constrained writing" in the creation of their works. His novels—all structurally demanding, linguistically playful, and strangely moving—include *Life: A User's Manual, A Void* and *W, or the Memory of Childhood*.

Katherine Anne Porter (1890–1980) achieved fame with her first collection of stories, *Flowering Judas* and *Noon Wine*, a novel. She traveled and lectured widely and had, in her own words, "always restless, always a roving spirit." Her *Collected Stories* (1965) won both the Pulitzer Prize and the National Book Award.

Philip Roth (1933–) is, by a considerable margin, the most highly decorated writer in English of the past several decades. In a career spanning fifty years and forty-some novels—*Goodbye Columbus, Portnoy's Complaint, The Ghost Writer, American Pastoral* and *Sabbath's Theater* among them—his nervy intensity, his intelligence, his thematic and stylistic boldness, and his acutely sensitive ear for the postures and depravities of American life have never flagged.

Zadie Smith (1975–) is an English novelist and essayist. Her precocious, critically acclaimed debut, *White Teeth*, written at university, established her as a major new voice in world literature. Her subsequent works include *The Autograph Man, On Beauty, NW*, and *Changing My Mind*, a collection of essays. She teaches at New York University and divides her time between New York and London.

Ted Solotaroff (1928–2008) was an American writer, editor, and literary critic, and the founder of the *New American Review*, one of the most influential literary magazines of the past half century. His books of essays and memoir include *Truth Comes in Blows, The Red Hot Vacuum*, and *A Few Good Voices in My Head*.

Robert Louis Stevenson (1850–94) was a Scottish novelist, essayist, travel writer, and poet. His work was immensely popular during his lifetime and after, and was perhaps best known for *Treasure Island, Kidnapped*, and *The Strange Case of Dr. Jekyll and Mr. Hyde*. He spent his last years on the Pacific island of Samoa, where he died at the age of forty-four, leaving behind a vast shelf of books.

Colm Tóibín (1955–) is a versatile Irish writer who has written novels, short stories, essays, criticism, plays, and poetry. Educated at University College, Dublin, he was a journalist for many years. His many novels include *The Master* (nominated for the Booker Prize) and *Brooklyn*. *The Testament of Mary* was popular as both a novel and a play. He lives in New York and Dublin and teaches at Columbia University.

Binyavanga Wainaina (1971–) is a Kenyan novelist, editor, and journalist, and the director of the Chinua Achebe Center for African Literature and Languages at Bard College. He is the founding editor of *Kwani?*, an important source of new writing from Africa. His debut, the memoir *One Day I Will Write About This Place*, was published in 2011.

David Foster Wallace (1962–2008) was arguably the most innovative and influential American writer of the past two decades. His supple and distinctive high-low voice—with its hyper-verbal intelligence, its intensity, its sensitivity to idiom and jargon and the fragmentation of thought—is as finely tuned to the excesses of our culture, and the longing for authentic, un-ironic experience inside it, as it is addictive and contagious for a generation of readers. His novels and nonfiction works include *Infinite Jest*, *Oblivion*, *The Pale King*, and *A Supposedly Fun Thing I'll Never Do Again*. At the time of his premature death, he was a beloved teacher of writing and literature at Pomona College.

Virginia Woolf (1882–1941) was a founding figure of literary modernism in England. Her novels, such as *Mrs. Dalloway*, *To the Lighthouse* and *Orlando*, helped to reinvent the novel for the twentieth century. She was a highly influential member of the Bloomsbury group of writers (which included E. M. Forster) in the years between the two wars. She was a prolific essayist and book critic from the outset, and became a pioneering feminist thinker with *A Room of One's Own*, an extended essay that began as a series of lectures at Cambridge.